THE PURITAN GENTRY

The Great Puritan Families of
Early Stuart England

J. T. Cliffe

ROUTLEDGE & KEGAN PAUL
LONDON, BOSTON, MELBOURNE AND HENLEY

First published in 1984
by Routledge & Kegan Paul plc
39 Store Street, London WC1E 7DD, England
9 Park Street, Boston, Mass. 02108, USA
464 St Kilda Road, Melbourne, Victoria 3004, Australia
Broadway House, Newtown Road,
Henley-on-Thames, Oxon RG9 1EN, England

Phototypeset in Linotron Baskerville by Input Typesetting Ltd, London
and printed in Great Britain by
Billings Ltd, Worcester

© J. T. Cliffe 1984

Library of Congress Cataloging in Publication Data

Cliffe, J. T. (John Trevor), 1931–
The Puritan gentry.
Bibliography: p.
Includes index.
1. Puritans—England. 2. England—Religious life
and customs. 3. England—Gentry. I. Title.
BX9333.C58 1983   941.06'1'088258   83–15969

British Library CIP available

ISBN 0-7102-0007-2

CONTENTS

ACKNOWLEDGMENTS

I should like to record my grateful thanks to the following owners and trustees for permission to make use of material in manuscript collections which have been deposited on loan: the Earl of Onslow (Onslow MSS in the Guildford Muniment Room); Lady Anne Bentinck (Portland MSS in the British Library); Mr J. L. Jervoise (Jervoise of Herriard Park MSS in the Hampshire Record Office); Mr J. R. More-Molyneux (Loseley MSS in the Guildford Muniment Room); trustees of the late Mrs C. Dryden (Dryden MSS in the Northamptonshire Record Office); trustees of the late Sir Gyles Isham, Bart. (Isham Correspondence in the Northamptonshire Record Office).

I am also grateful to the librarians and custodians of archives for allowing me access to manuscripts in the libraries and record offices listed in the Bibliography.

ABBREVIATIONS

Al.Cant.	*Alumni Cantabrigienses. A Biographical List of all Known Students, Graduates and Holders of Office at the University of Cambridge, from the Earliest Times to 1751*, ed. J. and J. A. Venn, 4 vols, 1922–7.
Al. Oxon.	*Alumni Oxonienses: the Members of the University of Oxford, 1500–1714*, ed. J. Foster, 4 vols, 1892.
BL	British Library.
C.	Calendar.
C.J.	*Commons Journals.*
Calamy, Account	Edmund Calamy, *An Account of the Ministers, Lecturers, Masters and Fellows of Colleges and Schoolmasters who were Ejected or Silenced after the Restoration in 1660* (vol. 2 of a two-volume work), 1713.
Calamy, Continuation	Edmund Calamy, *A Continuation of the Account of the Ministers, Lecturers, Masters and Fellows of Colleges and Schoolmasters who were Ejected and Silenced after the Restoration in 1660*, 2 vols, 1727.
Clarendon	*The History of the Rebellion and Civil Wars in England . . . by Edward, Earl of Clarendon*, ed. W. D. Macray, 6 vols, 1888.
DNB	*Dictionary of National Biography.*
HMC	*Historical Manuscripts Commission Reports.*
Hutchinson Memoirs	Lucy Hutchinson, *Memoirs of the Life of Colonel Hutchinson*, ed. James Sutherland, 1973.
PRO	Public Record Office.
Rushworth	John Rushworth, *Historical Collections of Private Passages of State, Weighty Matters in Law, Remarkable Proceedings in Five Parliaments*, 8 vols, 1721.
S.P.Dom.	State Papers Domestic, Public Record Office.
V.C.H.	*Victoria County History.*

INTRODUCTION

This study is an account of the Puritan country gentry, and more particularly the kind of families which governed the counties, in the period between the accession of James I and the outbreak of the Civil War. A list of the families which make their appearance is given in the appendix; it includes some well-known names such as Hampden, D'Ewes and Harley and others which are less familiar. As will be seen, most of the families covered had estates worth £1000 a year or more which in the early seventeenth century meant that in financial terms at least they were in the forefront of their class; and indeed some of them were wealthier than the less substantial families among the nobility.

There is a tendency among present-day historians, whether Marxist or otherwise, to portray the religious loyalties of Puritan gentlemen as little more than a reflection of their economic or political aspirations. Religion, however, was a potent force in seventeenth-century England and the validity of this type of judgment is far from self-evident. In the course of this study an attempt has been made to answer a number of important questions concerning the Puritan gentry. Why did persons of wealth and position profess what the Puritans termed 'true religion'? What were the major influences at work? What part did religion play in the lives of these families? Did it have any real impact on their social and economic outlook?; or, to put it another way, what was the outcome of the inherent conflict between the demands of their religion and the general attitudes of their class? Is it possible to detect the 'spirit of capitalism' among these landed families? How did the Puritan gentry respond to Laud's ecclesiastical policy and the growth of Arminianism? What contribution did they make to the Puritan cause? And how radical was their thinking on the issue of church reform?

A recurring theme throughout the study is the character of the relationship which existed between the Puritan gentry and the godly divines. The latter appear in various roles: as authors, schoolmasters, university dons, chaplains, parish clergy and lecturers. The Puritan squire, for his part, had the key role of patron.

The idea that a great gulf separated the Puritans from their fellow Protestants can no longer be seriously entertained: in particular, there were no significant doctrinal differences until Arminianism began to assume importance during the 1620s. On the other hand, those who suggest that the term 'Puritan' had little meaning in the half-century which preceded the calling of the Long Parliament pay too little regard to the fact that it was in common use during this period and not only as a propaganda weapon.[1] It would not be appropriate at this stage to discuss the problem of definition in detail since the basic features of Puritan thought and conduct are considered at length during the course of this work; but if a working definition is needed, the true Puritan of the early seventeenth century may be described, in broad terms, as 'a zealous Calvinist who placed a very high value on piety and holiness (to the extent that he might be considered "precise") and who preferred a plain form of religious worship with the emphasis on godly preaching'.[2]

In this study much use has been made of both the private papers and the published writings of Puritan gentlemen. Among those whose religious views found expression on paper were Sir Edward Peyton, Sir Thomas Wroth, Sir James Harrington, Sir Robert Harley and his wife Lady Brilliana, Sir William Waller, Sir Simonds D'Ewes, Sir Thomas Wodehouse, Sir Thomas Barrington, Sir Henry Vane the younger, Lady Elizabeth Brooke, Harbottle Grimston, William Martyn, Walter Yonge and Lucy Hutchinson. In addition, a good deal of material has been drawn from published funeral sermons and the often lengthy dedications which Puritan divines were in the habit of inserting in their printed works. The kind of criticism which the use of such sources is liable to attract was anticipated by Samuel Fairclough when he delivered the sermon at the funeral of his patron Sir Nathaniel Barnardiston in 1653:

rather then I would speak one syllable in this place which I did not either know to be true, on mine own knowledge, or believe it to be so from the testimony of unquestionable witnesses of the same, I would have totally stopped my mouth and imposed an absolute silence thereon.[3]

In fact the funeral sermon and the epistle dedicatory can be of great value to the discriminating historian. At the very least they provide evidence of the close ties between members of the Puritan gentry and the brotherhood of godly divines but much more than this there is often a significant amount of solid factual information to be extracted once the general stereotyped praise has been stripped away.

CHAPTER ONE

GOD'S ELECT

Looking back on the reign of Charles I, a nonconformist divine wrote that the country was 'then mostly divided into but Two Parties, Puritan and Prophane'.[1] There is a common belief among historians that in the time of Elizabeth and her early Stuart successors the name 'Puritan' was used only as a term of abuse. This, however, is not strictly true. Often it was employed in a neutral sense, without any polemical overtones, as when James I gave direction, in August 1622, that no preacher should inveigh against the persons of either papists or Puritans without just cause or 'invitation from the text', or when Sir James Oxinden asked one of his nephews, in December 1641, to make approaches to as many Puritan divines as possible.[2] What is true is that, in the main, those who were accounted Puritans by their contemporaries indignantly rejected the title as a 'false and adulterate nickname'.[3]

Persons of quality who objected to being termed Puritans did so because the name had associations for many Englishmen with narrow-mindedness, hypocrisy and opposition to the established order in the Church and Commonwealth. The ruling classes had a horror of factions but in any event the Puritans considered themselves to be the guardians of orthodoxy in doctrine and, at least in the Laudian era, in matters of worship; if there were divisions within the Church these, they maintained, were primarily due to the 'Arminians'. If, however, they resented any suggestion that they were a faction they undoubtedly saw themselves as a spiritual elite. The wife of Sir William Springett, a man who was highly critical of the Church, related how he had joined with the Puritans, 'a

4

nickname which those who feared the Lord in that day went under'. Sir Simonds D'Ewes condemned the practice of deriding 'those whose lives in respect of outward testimonie doe onlie witnes our religion to bee true and branding them by those foolish and senceles titles of Puritans, Prescitians'. In doing so he drew support from certain passages in Isaiah and the Book of Proverbs:

> Woe unto them that call evil good, and good evil. . . .
> Which justify the wicked for reward, and take away the righteousness of the righteous. . . . He that justifieth the wicked, and he that condemneth the just, even they both are abomination to the Lord.[4]

Bulstrode Whitelocke records in his autobiography that his mother was extremely zealous and devout,

> being of that persuasion and practise which was then in scorne termed Puritanisme, which how ever derided by men of the world will be found acceptable with God . . . certainly she feared God truely and if that be to be a Puritan she was so and happy in being so.

Recalling a visit he had made to Banbury, that citadel of Oxfordshire Puritanism, he told his children

> Heer (as in other places) were two sorts of Puritans, a knave Puritan or an Hippocrite and a knave's Puritan, one that is religious in heart as well as in profession butt knaves reproach him with the name of Puritan because he will not doe ill as they doe; may you all be such Puritans.[5]

In describing the spiritual brotherhood to which they belonged the Puritans tended to use such words as 'the godly', 'the saints', 'the professors of religion', 'the truly religious' and even simply 'the religious'. Generally they thought of themselves as a small minority among a large mass of merely nominal Christians, despised and scoffed at by the worldly because of their zeal for religion and their strict code of morality; and indeed this accorded well with their belief that the elect were relatively few in number in comparison with the legions of the damned.

In 1623 Sir Martin Stuteville sent his friend Joseph Mede of Christ's College, Cambridge some verse which he had composed on the subject of Puritanism. In acknowledging receipt of this verse

Mede wrote that he had found in it three types of Puritan: first, there was the 'Puritan in Politicks or the Politicall Puritan' whose concern was with such matters as the liberties of the people and the prerogatives of sovereigns; second, the 'Ecclesiasticall Puritan for the Church Hierarchie and ceremonies who was at first the onely Puritan'; and finally the 'Puritan in Ethicks or morall Puritan sayd to consist in singularity of living and hypocrisie both civill and religious which may be called the vulgar Puritan and was the second in birth and hath made too many ashamed to be honest.'[6] As Mede clearly recognised, the character of Puritanism as a religious force had not remained static since the word 'Puritan' had first made its appearance during the early years of Elizabeth's reign; on the other hand, it is also true that there was no fundamental break in continuity between Elizabethan Puritanism and the Puritanism of Charles I's reign. Under governmental pressure the Presbyterian movement had petered out before the end of the sixteenth century and there would be no further attempt to secure a major alteration in the system of church government until the time of the Long Parliament. The fact remains, however, that Presbyterian ideas had never been embraced by more than a small minority of the Puritan clergy and laity.[7] At the Hampton Court Conference in 1604 the debate was primarily concerned neither with church government nor with doctrine but with matters of worship. Soon afterwards the public agitation over the Church's ceremonial requirements completely subsided and it was not until the advent of the Laudian innovations that there was a reawakening of controversy. Yet this apparent acquiescence does not mean that the Puritans had suddenly changed their convictions. Two main factors were responsible: in the first place, the campaign which Archbishop Bancroft waged against the dissenting clergy induced many of them to conform sufficiently to ensure that their congregations continued to enjoy the benefits of godly preaching; second, a great deal of nonconformity went unpunished under the liberal rule of Archbishop Abbot. Although there is some substance in Mede's opinion that the moral Puritan emerged after the ecclesiastical Puritan it cannot be accepted without qualification. The exacting standards of human behaviour to which the Puritans subscribed were basically a product of Calvinist doctrine which the Marian exiles, men such as Laurence Humphrey and William Cole, did much to propagate following their return to England after the accession of Elizabeth.

Humphrey, who was for many years President of Magdalen College, Oxford, wrote a treatise on education in which he stressed the importance of such qualities as humility, temperance, continence and thrift: this was published in 1563, eight years before the commencement of the parliamentary campaign for ecclesiastical reform.[8] Nevertheless Mede was right in the sense that matters of private morality and conduct received much greater attention in Puritan circles during the early seventeenth century. From the beginning of James I's reign there was an unprecedented flow of Puritan manuals offering detailed guidance for those who aspired to walk in holiness while the Puritan group in the House of Commons made persistent efforts to secure the passage of legislation aimed at punishing such evils as swearing, drunkenness and adultery.[9]

Aside from their dislike of ceremonial in public worship which predated the Laudian innovations the general attitude of the Puritans on religious matters did not differ fundamentally from that of large numbers of their fellow Protestants. Neither the belief in the necessity of keeping holy the Sabbath nor the practice of regular Bible reading was an exclusively Puritan characteristic. Many who accepted the validity of Calvinist doctrine were to be found outside the ranks of the Puritans and indeed were sometimes sharply critical of them: in November 1628, for example, Bishop Davenant of Salisbury complained in a letter to another Calvinist divine that he could not understand why the doctrine of predestination was now regarded as a Puritan doctrine when it was embraced by those 'who have done our Church the greatest service in beating down Puritanisme'.[10] To a large extent the Puritans were distinguished from other Protestants by differences of degree rather than of kind. The conviction that the Bible was the supreme authority on issues of religion was part of the mainstream Protestant tradition; the Puritans, however, were fundamentalists *par excellence*. In a treatise published in 1605 William Bradshaw, a nonconformist divine, described the principal opinions of 'the rigidest sort of those that are called Puritans' and assigned pride of place to the belief that

the word of God contained in the writings of the Prophets and Apostles is of absolute perfection, given by Christ the head of the Church to bee unto the same the sole Canon and rule of all matters of Religion and the worship and service of God

7

whatsoever. And that whatsoever done in the same service and worship cannot be iustified by the said word is unlawfull.[11]

The Puritans did not merely accept that Calvinist doctrine was scripturally well founded: they were convinced that it was necessary to do more than pay lip-service to the stringent requirements which it laid on the individual. As their ministers never tired of reiterating, true religion demanded total commitment and the subordination of all worldly interests. When publishing the sermon which he had delivered at the funeral of Lady Judith Barrington an Essex clergyman wrote in the epistle dedicatory

> Looke first with all Possible care to your foundation, that it be well laid in Regeneration and heart-renovation; then build upwards, as high as you can in a holy life and heavenly Conversation. Make Religion your Businesse and let the Exercises of it in Publick, Private and Secret have the Preheminence of all your Employments.[12]

Puritan worship tended to be frequent and prolonged and it required a rare kind of diligence. According to a contemporary account Sir Thomas Scott was religious without pretending to any extraordinary piety and for this reason he neither loved nor was commended by the Puritans. Writing to Viscount Cranborne in 1604, Archbishop Hutton of York assured him that the Puritans, though fantastically zealous, were substantially the same in religion as the Reformed Church.[13] At the same time they recognised that it was incumbent on them to live their daily lives in accordance with their religious beliefs. Lucy Hutchinson tells us much about the character of Puritanism when describing how the godly had been maligned:

> whoever was zealous for God's glory or worship, could not endure blasphemous oathes, ribald conversation, prophane scoffes, sabbath breach, derision of the word of God, and the like; whoever could endure a sermon, modest habitt or conversation, or aniething that was good, all these were Puritanes.[14]

As the Puritan divines were not slow to recognise, the wealthy squires who ruled the counties and often had considerable resources of ecclesiastical patronage at their disposal would have much to contribute if they could be won over to the cause of true religion. Thomas Gataker, who as a lecturer at Lincoln's Inn had made the acquaintance of many young heirs, acknowledged the point when dedicating one of his published works to John Hobart, the son of Sir Henry Hobart, the Lord Chief Justice of the Common Pleas and the owner of the Blickling estate in Norfolk. By setting a good example, he told him, those who were 'more eminent than ordinary, either for place or parentage' could draw many others on. 'In this ranke it hath pleased God to range your Worship whose religious cariage therefore shall not onely benefit your selfe but may pricke on and encourage others, both at home and abroad.'[15] Another Puritan author, Richard Baxter, put the matter more bluntly:

> O what a world of good might Gentlemen and Knights and Lords do that have a good many of Tenants and that are the leaders of the Country if they had but hearts to improve their interest and advantage! . . . You have the greatest opportunities to do good of most men in the world. Your Tenants dare not contradict you lest you dispossesse them or their children of their habitations. They fear you more than they do God himself.[16]

In practice it was not easy for a man of social position to embrace the ideals of the Puritans. In making open profession he ran the risk of being held up to ridicule. During the reign of James I, writes Lucy Hutchinson, the enemies of the Puritans

> made them not only the sport of the pulpitt, which was become but a more solemne stage, but every stage and every table and every puppett-play belcht forth prophane scoffes upon them; all the drunkards made them their songs, all fidlers and mimicks learnt to abuse them, as finding it the most gainefull way of fooling.[17]

Perhaps even more important, there was the consideration that such a radical step involved a much greater degree of self-sacrifice for a wealthy landed family than for the majority of those who sought to live godly lives. On the face of it, the austere philosophy of the Puritans was unlikely to have much appeal for the more substantial gentry: there is after all no lack of contemporary evidence testifying to their pride and arrogance, their liking for conspicuous consumption and their pursuit of worldly pleasures. Richard Baxter was under no illusion in this respect. In an epistle dedicatory he entreated his friend Sir Thomas Rous to be 'the more diligent and unwearied' in the practice of religion

> because as you may take more time for it then the poor can do, so have you far stronger temptations to divert you; it being extremely difficult for those that have fulness of all things here to place their happiness really in another life and to set their hearts there, as the place of their Rest; which yet must be done by all that will be saved.

Later on in the body of the work Baxter elaborated on this theme in the most forthright terms. Exhorting the gentry not to despise their tenants because they were poor and simple men he reminded them that death was a great leveller and told them plainly that in his estimation few persons of wealth were likely to experience the delights of eternal life:

> Remember, God is no respecter of persons. Your flesh is of no better mettal then theirs; nor will the worms spare your faces or hearts any more than theirs; nor will your bones or dust bear the badge of your Gentility. You must all be equals when you stand in Judgement . . . let men see that you excel others as much in piety, heavenliness, compassion and diligence in God's work as you do in riches and honour in the world. I confess you are like to be singular if you take this course, but then remember you shall be singular in glory, for few great and mighty and noble are called.[18]

Baxter was not the only Puritan minister who was openly critical of the upper classes. Many of the wealthy and great, declared John Dod and Robert Cleaver in a collaborative work, were puffed up with pride, and practised cruelty, and professed adultery, and breathed out blasphemies, and lived in voluptuousness and hardly forbore any kind of iniquity. Preaching at the Northampton assizes in 1630 Robert Bolton told the assembled landowners and burgesses that men of their position could not bear to be called Puritans, 'much lesse to become such; and yet without purity none shall ever see the face of GOD with comfort'.[19] Even within the ranks of the gentry there were some who condemned the indifference shown towards religion and the moral laxity to be found in the upper levels of society. Great houses, claimed Sir William Waller, were often theatres of debauchery and viciousness. For the wealthy were inclined to have 'a strange perverseness in them; they covet to have good houses, good stuff, good fare and to have every good to their very horses and dogs but themselves and their Houshold'.[20] Similarly, Lucy Hutchinson tells us that from childhood God had preserved her husband

> from wallowing in the mire of sinne and wickednesse wherein most of the gentry . . . were miserably plunged, except a few that were therefore the scorne of mankind; and but few of those few that had not naturall and superstitious follies that were in some kind justly ridiculous and contemptible.[21]

Inherited wealth and godliness were not the most natural bedfellows yet they could sometimes be found cohabiting. When John Wing, the minister of the English church at Flushing, published a theological treatise in 1624 he dedicated it to Sir Francis Barrington, his son Sir Thomas and his son-in-law Sir William Masham, acknowledging the help they had given him and rejoicing in the fact that God had enriched them 'with that glorious Advantage and Prerogative, to be called his Saints'. The same year Sir Francis had another work dedicated to him. Jeremiah Dyke, a Puritan minister at Epping in Essex, told him that there was no one so well qualified to be the patron of a treatise on the subject of a good conscience as 'he that hath beene a religious both professor and protector of the practise thereof'.[22] Sir Robert Harley earned many plaudits from the godly divines with whom he was acquainted. Robert Bolton, who clearly exempted him from his general indictment of the upper classes, once commented in a letter to him: 'Happy are you that preferre the prerogatives of Christianity before the transitorines of earthly Glory; your peace, comfort and reward shall bee without end.' Sir Robert's 'aim and end', wrote Timothy Woodroffe, 'was to live in Jesus and to dye in Jesus.' He did 'most religiously and sincerely bless God (in my hearing) that for forty years or thereabouts before his death his soul was fixedly resolved to live to God'.[23] Sir John Bourchier was 'a serious person, an open professor of Religion, and gave Encouragement and Protection to those that did so', while Sir Nathaniel Barnardiston was 'a man very famous for the profession and practice of Religion and the open Countenance he gave to it, of great integrety and reputation'.[24] Wealthy gentlemen of this type were to be found in most parts of the kingdom, though it was only in such counties as Devon, Essex, Northamptonshire and Suffolk that they were concentrated in any numbers. A few of them were even prepared to acknowledge that they were Puritans in name as well as in profession. Sir Henry Yelverton, a judge of the Court of Common Pleas, was reported to have said at the Durham assizes that he had always been accounted a Puritan and he thanked God for it, and that so he would die; Sir Arthur Hesilrige told his parliamentary colleagues in 1659 that he had been bred a Puritan; while Sir Robert Harley once described himself, half-jokingly, as a plain Puritan.[25]

While the character of Puritanism did not remain completely static between the reigns of Elizabeth and Charles I it is noteworthy that many of the great parliamentarian families had a long history of 'forwardness in religion'. Often the heads of these families were the descendants of Marian exiles who had drunk deep at the fountains of Continental Protestantism or of men who had been actively engaged in the campaign for ecclesiastical reform which had been mounted in the Elizabethan House of Commons. Sir William Strickland, 'a publick Professor of Religion',[26] was the grandson of two of the most prominent members of the Elizabethan reform party, William Strickland and Peter Wentworth. Sir Christopher Yelverton was another third-generation Puritan. His grandfather and namesake had supported the Puritan cause both as a member of the Commons and in Northamptonshire where he had his estates and on one occasion had exhorted his colleagues at Gray's Inn 'to be more forward in the hearing of the word, more earnest in the Profession of the ghospell, and more zealous in the furtherance of religion'.[27] Sir Nathaniel Barnardiston's grandfather had actually studied under Calvin at Geneva, though it would appear that in some respects the experience was not so fruitful as it might have been. After referring to this episode Sir Nathaniel's biographer adds the cryptic comment that 'if the Grandfather failed to live according to that Education in some part of his life yet his Grandson endeavoured to live it for him.' In contrast, Sir Nathaniel considered his father to be a very godly man.[28]

Sir Robert Cooke was descended from Sir Anthony Cooke, Edward VI's tutor, who was not only a distinguished scholar but a man who, for his time, had advanced views in matters of religion. After spending four years in voluntary exile during the Catholic repression of Mary's reign he had returned to England on the accession of Elizabeth and had become one of the principal advocates of church reform in the Commons.[29] Sir Robert's parents were a well-matched pair in terms of religious outlook and background: his father, Sir William, was a patron of Puritan ministers, among them Thomas Gataker who served for some time as his chaplain, while his mother was a daughter of Sir Thomas Lucy who was 'very forward . . . for the promoting of a further Reformation in the Church and opening the Way for the Non-Conformists to enter into it'. When Gataker published *The Spirituall Watch* in 1619 he dedicated it to Robert Cooke, explaining that the work had originally been intended for his late father. In addressing the new head of the family, who had just come of age, he referred to 'those pregnant points as well of piety as other good parts evidently discovering themselves in your owne person, observed by others as well as my selfe, and the rather observed because so rare ordinarily in others of your yeares and of your ranck'. He went on to express the hope that he would follow the example set by his worthy parents, 'so exactly resembling them in their vertuous parts, and treading so precisely in their religious steps, that both they may seeme to survive in you and you be knowne thereby to have come of them'. Indeed he had some grounds for believing that the young man might surpass his father in these respects since God had called him sooner 'and you have the more day before you. Your worthy Father hath broken the ice to you, he hath laid you to your hand a good foundation of religious courses'.[30]

In the case of such families it can be argued that their Civil War loyalties were predetermined during the reign of Elizabeth, though religion was not necessarily the only factor which impelled them to take the side of Parliament. At the same time there were other wealthy parliamentarian families whose Puritan sympathies were of much more recent origin. Sir Robert Harley was the grandson of 'a very Zealous Romanist' who, it was said, had given shelter to the 'notorious Jesuits' Robert Persons and Edmund Campion. His father found it difficult to stomach the nonconformity of a Puritan minister whom Sir Robert had recruited and frequently complained about him to the diocesan authorities, though eventually he was persuaded to look more favourably on him. His mother came from a family of Shropshire Puritans, the Corbets of Moreton Corbet, but she died while he was still an infant and it was probably through the influence of such men as Cadwallader Owen, his tutor at Oriel

College, Oxford, and Thomas Pierson, the minister who had offended his father, that he was set firmly on the path of godliness.[31] In Somerset the Harrington family of Kelston underwent a religious transformation which in its own way was no less striking. Sir John Harrington was a celebrated court wit who lived extravagantly, wrote bawdy verse and hated Puritans: in one of his writings he quotes with obvious relish a saying that Puritans were Protestants who had been scared out of their wits. In contrast, his son John was a strict professor of religion whose austere temperament is well illustrated in the following prayer which he composed:

> work in mee a thorough humiliation in the sight and sence of that boundles and bottomles sea of corruption and wretchednes wherein I am overwhelmed that I may rightly value and prize and long after the salvation purchased for me by the deth and passion of Jesus Christ.

In 1604 Sir John sent his son to Trinity College, Oxford, and according to a traditional story placed him in the care of a tutor who was a rigid Puritan because he believed that the experience would be bound to instil in him a lifelong abhorrence of the philosophy which he himself regarded with complete disdain; but in the event this ingenious plan had precisely the opposite effect from what was intended.[32]

Theories which portray the religious loyalties of the Puritan gentry as primarily, if not wholly, attributable to socio-economic or political motives do scant justice to the genuine spiritual convictions with which they were often imbued. Although their ministers might assure them that those who were true followers of Christ were likely to prosper in this world[33] the factor which seems to have weighed most heavily was a desire to live eternally in the heavenly kingdom which God had reserved for his elect. In the seventeenth century the prevalence of disease, poor living conditions and an inadequate knowledge of medical and dietary matters combined to create a situation in which death was never very far away. A rich landowner could order his gates to be locked when he heard that the plague was in the neighbourhood and could afford to employ the services of the best physicians and take his family to a spa town such as Bath or Buxton; the fact remains, however, that even among the gentry there were many who died either in infancy or before reaching middle age. As Edmund Dunch, one of the leading Puritan

14

squires in Berkshire, observed in the preamble to his will, life on earth was beclouded with uncertainty; it 'passeth away as a shaddow and consumeth as the grasse of the feild'.[34] The brevity of human life was a favourite theme of the Puritan divines who emphasised that it was as nothing when compared with the joys of everlasting life. At the funeral of Lady Mary Strode in 1618 John Barlow, who was then a lecturer at Plymouth, turned to her husband during the course of his sermon to offer him some powerful words of exhortation:

> And you (Right Worshipfull) whom God hath made great in the Countrey and Common-weale; take heed what ye doe . . . what will your callings or riches profit you one day if you should loose your own soules? Is it or wil it be any benefit to have large possessions on earth and not a foot in heaven? . . . Therefore be friends to the word, procure its liberty to runne and doe you and yours runne after it too; for this shall one day be your best portion and great reward.[35]

William Chantrell wrote in a letter to Lady Joan Barrington that the sacrifices which were required of the godly during their earthly sojourn were a small price to pay for the benefits which were to follow: 'what if yow loose a few vayne pleasures and deceiptfull profittes and gaine stable and everlastinge promises?'; our loss is small, nay none, our gaine great; earth for heaven that our loss, paradise for dross that is our gaine.'[36] In a profoundly religious age such arguments could prove seductive.

For a man to have any hope of salvation it was necessary for him, according to Calvinist doctrine, to experience a spiritual conversion, for Jesus Christ had said, 'Except a man be born again he cannot see the kingdom of God.'[37] Whether he came of Puritan stock was immaterial: there was no right of heredity where the gift of eternal life was concerned. All men who had this gift bestowed upon them received a call from God which led to their conversion, though not all those who were called would taste the joys of immortality. In another of his published sermons John Barlow explained that a call could be 'effectuall or not effectuall. Many are called but not truly, savingly'. Those who were effectually called were 'made coheires with Christ and shall assuredly bee saved'.[38]

In one of his commonplace books Sir Simonds D'Ewes wrote that God usually converted the poor and meaner sort but went on:

Not but that God hath in all ages called some persons of Honour, noblenes, power, learning and eminent parts and when God doth give beleeving, holie and humble hearts to such they have the greater cause to blesse God for it and to walke moore warilie then the meaner sorte, being subiect to greater temptations.[39]

Although D'Ewes has left us an autobiography it contains no specific reference to his conversion but there are nevertheless a number of recorded cases relating to members of the Puritan gentry. According to the minister who preached her funeral sermon Lady Elizabeth Alston, the wife of Sir Thomas Alston, had been born again: 'God did even in her tender years season her heart with Grace and thereby take possession of her.'[40] Describing a visit which he had made to London during his adolescence Sir James Harrington recalled that Satan had revealed to him a variety of temptations following his 'first Conversion' but this had merely helped him to recognise 'the Vanities of all the World and the empty glory thereof'.[41] Sir Nathaniel Barnardiston is said to have been converted during his schooldays: in the words of one of his ministers, Samuel Fairclough, 'the Lord began to cast in the seed of regeneration when he was at school, the very time when others of his ranck and quality give up themselves to the greatest degrees of licentious wantonnesse.' The particular incident which made most impression on him was the reading of a biblical passage, 'Behold I am shapen in wickedness: in sin hath my mother conceived me.' By his second birth, comments Fairclough, he received 'soul-nobilitie and became heir to the second Adam'.[42] A contemporary biographer of Sir Henry Vane the younger relates that he was not actually called until the age of fourteen or fifteen, having previously consorted with those who were commonly known as 'good fellows'. The account continues:

Then God did by some signal impressions and awakening dispensations startle him into a view of the danger of his condition. On this, he and his former jolly Company came presently to a parting blow. Yea this change and new steering of his course contracted enmity to him in his father's house.

The conversion occurred while he was a scholar at Westminster

16

School where the headmaster, Lambert Osbaldeston, was a man of Puritan sympathies.[43]

In 1653 a Herefordshire minister, Timothy Woodroffe, described the spiritual conversion of Edward Harley, the eldest son of Sir Robert Harley, in a letter couched in the most condescending terms which was addressed to the young man himself. His soul, he told him, had been

> miraculously saved by the Lord and pulled out of the suburbs of hell soe unexpectedlie, soe undeservedly, soe freely . . . you then heard with other eares, understood with another intellect, spake with another spirit, yea and acted by other principles then before; old things then vanished away and all things became new.

Before his effectual calling, he went on, Harley had gone from flower to flower like a wandering bee.[44]

In some cases a spiritual conversion might be as dramatic as the sudden flash of light on the road to Damascus, in others it might be a more gradual process. Sir John Hobart had been brought up in a strongly Protestant household where his father had employed a succession of chaplains with decided Calvinist views; he was said, however, to have been a wild youth who had been unacquainted with 'the good ways of God'. In dedicating to him a sermon published in 1623 Thomas Gataker exhorted him to follow the example of his father, Sir Henry, whose life and deeds

> may be a lively Precedent for your direction and imitation herein. . . . Goe on therefore, Worthy Sir, I beseech you, having so rare a Paterne before you, to imitate him that goeth in and out before you, as you doe before others . . . in fashioning your life and courses to the Rules of God's will and word and in helping to support the practise and profession of pietie.

At the same time he recognised that it was not easy for a person of his social standing to become openly committed in this way: 'I am not ignorant what privie nips, yea and open pointings at . . . men of your ranke especially must make account to expose themselves unto if they will shew themselves religious and favourers of that which we all generally professe.'[45] In the course of time Sir John was persuaded to abandon his pursuit of worldly pleasure and to live a more godly life, mainly through the encouragement and coaxing of his second wife, Frances Egerton, one of the daughters of John Earl of Bridgwater, whom he had married in 1621. A woman of considerable personality, she was in the habit of describing herself as a Calvinist in point of doctrine and a Presbyterian in matters of discipline. 'By her prudent monitions and passionate intreaties', writes her biographer, Sir John 'was won from what had been the vanities of his youth.' As his faith grew stronger under her influence he began 'unweariedly to desire and to be present at private Fasts and other Religious duties, severely to reprove others (especially his servants) and admonish his friends of those errors which had formerly been too much his own pleasure and delight'. During the reign of Charles I Sir John's change of outlook earned him a warm tribute from Samuel Otes, the Puritan rector of Marsham, whose living was in his gift. In 1633 Otes published some sermons which had been delivered by his father (once Sir Henry's chaplain) and in dedicating the volume to his patron told him that he was 'a true lover of God and of his Word, so right honestly affected to Doctrine and Religion that your Comportment in God's Church and in all your courses and in all good causes perswades the Countrey your Pietie and Devotion to bee unfained'.[46]

In 1630 Samuel Brooke, the Master of Trinity College, Cambridge, wrote in a letter to his patron Bishop Laud that in his opinion the doctrine of predestination was 'the roote of Puritanisme'.[47] The Calvinist doctrine of predestination was indeed one of the great themes of Puritan literature and Puritan preaching. 'God', declared William Perkins, 'hath ordained certaine men to his glorious grace in the obtaining of their salvation and heavenly life by Christ'; the elect were many but 'if these same elect be compared with them that are iustly damned wee say according to the Scriptures that they are few.'[48] Before the time of the Civil War there was one minister of note who was accounted a Puritan yet held doctrinal views which were basically Arminian in character. John Goodwin, who in 1633 became vicar of St Stephen's, Coleman Street, had been propagating these views as a tutor at Queens' College, Cambridge during the years 1617 to 1627. Thomas Cawton, a nonconformist divine, had been entrusted to his care but, his son tells us, 'he sucked in none of his evil Principles which even then he endeavoured to infuse into his Pupils, though it were afterwards that he discovered himself more fully in setting his heretical Doctrines more openly to sale.'[49] Whether or not Goodwin can be regarded as a Puritan the fact remains that mainstream Puritanism owed much of its character to the doctrine of predestination and all that flowed from it. To a man like Sir Robert Harley it was inconceivable that a true professor of religion could have any other doctrinal background. In 1631 he told one of his clerical correspondents that Lord Herbert of Cherbury, who was seeking a new incumbent for the parish church of Montgomery, had said that he loved a Puritan but not a predestinator; obviously savouring the absurdity, as he saw it, of such a distinction, he added that 'I doubt not but God will give you wisdome to lett his Lordship know that That Mistery of Godliness is not to give liberty to presume to him but a restrainte from him'.[50]

Before the growth of Arminianism most of the clergy and laymen who took any serious interest in doctrinal matters would probably have subscribed to the view that salvation was reserved only for a privileged minority. There was, however, less unanimity over the question of whether it was possible for God's chosen ones to obtain assurance during their earthly lives that they were numbered among the elect. According to the Thirty Nine Articles God had decreed that some men should enjoy eternal life 'by his counsel secret to us' while the Lambeth Articles of 1595 contained the statement that 'The truly faithful man . . . is sure by full assurance of faith of the remission of sins and his eternal salvation through Christ.'[51] Calvinist theologians, for their part, maintained that with perseverance the elect could eventually secure confirmation that they would inherit eternal life. The surest indications that a man was saved were a deep-rooted faith in Jesus Christ and his redeeming power and a holy life which was the outward manifestation of a state of grace. 'There is the act of faith and the fruit of faith,' explained Richard Sibbes; 'the act of faith is to cast our selves upon God's mercy in Christ, the fruit of faith is in believing to be assured of this.'[52]

In his autobiography Sir Simonds D'Ewes records that in 1625 he was involved in an argument with a Norfolk parson, Edmund Cartwright, over the question of the Church of England's attitude to the doctrine of assurance. Sir Simonds contended that it was part of the Church's teaching that 'God's children in this life might attaine to a certaine knowledge of their own future salvacion by a true and livelie faith such as God ordinarilie wrought in his elect.' A few days later Cartwright wrote to his father, Paul D'Ewes, to say that he had consulted the works of William Perkins (whom Sir Simonds had quoted as an authority on the subject) and now accepted that he had been misguided in his opinion. The elder

D'Ewes had also disagreed with his son's thesis but in 1630, after reading the sermons of John Preston on the theme of God's all-sufficiency, he came round to the view that 'our faith ought to bee certaine and stable, and that God's children may by the same faith producing an holy life ordinarilie in this life attaine the Assurance of ther own Salvacion, and therefore are bound by all meanes to labour to attaine unto it'.[53]

As contemporary evidence abundantly testifies, Puritan squires and their wives were well acquainted with the doctrine of assurance and generally regarded it as not only valid but of direct personal relevance. In some scripture notes which have survived among the papers of Sir John Gell the point is made that in the First Epistle General of John 'multitude of markes, signes or discoveryes of a beleever's spirituall estate are plainely layd downe . . . more then in any other so short a piece of Scripture in the whole bible'. One passage in particular is singled out as providing substantiation for the doctrine of assurance: 'These things have I written unto you that believe on the name of the Son of God; that ye may know that ye have eternal life, and that ye may believe on the name of the Son of God.'[54] In one of his poems Sir Benjamin Rudyerd acknowledged his debt to God for the worldly benefits which he enjoyed but went on to say that he valued above all things the assurance of salvation which he had received:

> O God! My God! what shall I give
> To thee in thanks? I am and live
> In thee; and thou dost safe preserve
> My health, my fame, my goods, my rent;
> Thou mak'st me eat whilst others starve,
> And sing whilst others do lament,
> Such unto me thy blessings are,
> As though I were thine only care.
>
> But oh my God, thou art more kind
> When I look inward on my mind,
> Thou fill'st my heart with humble joy,
> With patience, meek and fervent love,
> (All other loves which doth destroy)
> With Faith which nothing can remove
> And hope assur'd of Heaven's bliss;
> This is my state, thy Grace is this.[55]

Even though a man might believe himself to have been called it was necessary for him to labour with all his strength to obtain assurance that he was truly saved: the house of Christ, Bulstrode Whitelocke told his family, consisted of 'those who give diligence to make their calling and election sure'.[56] Lady Elizabeth Masham confided to her mother that she was daily more convinced that there was no happiness in anything 'but in getting assurance of god's love'; for many of the godly, however, it could be a hard journey, particularly if their spiritual counsellors applied exceptionally stringent criteria when judging their candidature. Thomas Pierson, one of Sir Robert Harley's ministers, would often quote the comment of his friend William Perkins that 'Some Men hang salvation on so high a Pinne that many Poore Soules can never Reach it'; Pierson himself did not wish to load the righteous with too many burdens.[57]

In Puritan circles the term 'elect lady' represented an acknowledgement that there was sufficient evidence to show that everlasting life was assured. When John Ley, a Cheshire minister, published *A Patterne of Pietie* in 1640 he dedicated it to Lady Brilliana Harley and Lady Alice Lucy, commenting that 'I doubt not but (as Elect Ladies) your names are registred together in the booke of life. . . . It is a rare thing in your ranke to be so really religious, whereby your second birth shineth the more by reflexe from the first, and as rare.' At the funeral of Lady Anne Waller, who had written in her journal that she was anxious to make her calling and election sure, Edmund Calamy declared in his sermon that she was an elect lady, 'whether you take Elect for a choice and pretious Lady, or for one who was elected by God from all eternity unto life everlasting. She was one who made Religion her business, not (as some Ladies do) her Idle hour but her daily labour.'[58] Lady Joan Barrington was addressed by one of her relatives as 'a chosen and elect Lady' while William Chantrell once wrote to her that he had no doubt that she esteemed it the most precious pearl in her diadem that God 'hath enrowled your name in the booke of life and inwombed Christ the lord of life in your soule'. Even so, she had grave doubts about her election. In 1630 Ezekiel Rogers, who had formerly served as chaplain to the Barrington family, wrote to her from his Yorkshire parsonage

I have bene long a wittnesse how much the Lord hath shewed

his well-wishing to your soule, besides those actual workings
of his Spirit which hath bene a comfort to many. Though it
seemes that for the matter of Assurance he hath not dealt so
largely with you as with many of his saints whereby as yo
are hindred of much comfort which others doe inioy more
constantly.

His brother Daniel touched on the same point in the dedication
accompanying a work which was first published in 1633. In it he
told Lady Barrington that in conversing with her he had often
noticed 'some carefulnesse in you to be setled upon some good
evidences which might secure you of pardon and favour with God'.
In view of this he advised her, when reading his book, to pay
particular attention to those grounds of humiliation, self-denial and
faith which most concerned the main point of assurance. By the
time she drew up her will in October 1641 she may have resolved
her doubts: at all events she considered it appropriate to commend
her soul to God in 'assured persuasion' that through the intercession
of Jesus Christ and her faith in him she would enjoy 'a glorious
Immortalitie in the heavens.'[59]
    An assured belief that salvation had been granted did not necess-
arily give rise to complacency or moral laxity. On the contrary, it
was a basic tenet of Calvinist doctrine that those who had received
foreknowledge of their election would continue to live the kind of
life which reflected the workings of God's grace; their duty to God
required it and their appreciation of the favour he had shown them
helped to strengthen their determination to walk in holiness. 'It
hath been an old cavill', observed Richard Sibbes, 'that certainty
of salvation breeds security and loosenesse of life'; in fact, 'there is
nothing quickens a soule more to cheereful obedience than assurance of God's love and that our labour should not be in vain in the
Lord'.[60] According to his wife, John Hutchinson regarded the
doctrine of predestination as the most important of God's absolute
decrees but this was 'farre from producing a carelessnesse of life in
him': indeed 'it excited him to a more strict and holy walking in
thankfulnesse to God who had bene pleas'd to chuse him out of the
corrupted masse of lost mankind.'[61]
    Although the elect had been vouchsafed the supreme gift of
eternal life it did not follow that they would remain happily insu-
lated from all earthly tribulations. Nevertheless it was held that

under the terms of the covenant which he had with his chosen ones God had promised not only to make them partakers of his heavenly kingdom but to protect them and even to advance their material interests while they lived on earth. The covenant, John Preston maintained,

> enforceth sincerity: on God's part, he will be our God, our shield to preserve from evil, our sun to fill us with good, our exceeding great reward, our All-sufficient God every way. . . . Though holiness be reward enough in it self, yet even in this life a man shall not fare the worse in outward things for his holiness but, according to the evenness of his walking with God, he shall be more or less blessed in wife, children, wealth, credit, chearfulness of spirit, every thing.[62]

Among the Puritan gentry it was a firmly held conviction that God took particular care of the elect during their earthly sojourn. God, wrote William Martyn, the father of Sir Nicholas Martyn, the Devonshire parliamentarian, 'gratiously protecteth and defendeth his elected that not one of them can perish or come to an untimely end'; since he himself was in no doubt that he was a member of that privileged minority this belief must have been of great comfort to him.[63] With a religious faith of this kind a man could be resolute and steadfast, self-righteous and intolerant; and it might even embolden him to defy the power of the Church or State.

CHAPTER TWO

A LIFE OF PIETY

The craving for eternal life which was so much in evidence among the Puritans caused them to put an exceptionally high value on godly preaching. The Bible, they believed, contained all things necessary to salvation but the scriptual text had to be interpreted and explained to the laity and for this purpose there was no adequate substitute for the learned preaching minister. 'Pulpits', declared Sir James Harrington, 'are Heavenly Conduits from whence by Earthy Vessels, the Ministers' Voices . . . the Waters of Grace are conveyed into every open Ear.'[1] To the Puritans the task of expounding the scriptures was the most vital function of the parish clergy; they consider, wrote William Bradshaw, that 'the highest and supreame office and authoritie of the Pastor is to preach the gospell solemnly and publickly to the Congregation by interpreting the written word of God and applying the same by exhortation and reproofe unto them.'[2]

The Puritan appetite for preaching was almost insatiable. Two sermons every Sunday were generally regarded as the minimum requirement: indeed a Northamptonshire mercer told the High Commission in 1634 that it was necessary for salvation (though not of absolute necessity) to have two sermons on the Lord's Day.[3] There might also be opportunities to hear weekday sermons or lectures,[4] particularly in London and in market towns where Puritan influences were strong. Members of the Puritan gentry were often present at such lectures and sometimes helped to support them financially. Sir Francis Drake, a nephew of the circumnavigator, regularly attended the lectures delivered by John Barlow at

Plymouth and persuaded him to publish a sermon which had particularly impressed him. In the dedication Barlow thanked Drake for all the love he had shown him and went on: 'You are well acquainted with my familiar phrase [and] rude manner of speaking. . . . Hee . . . that will benefit the rude people must speake plainely, carry a low sayle and descend to their capacities.'[5] There was also a considerable demand for sermons on such special occasions as weddings, christenings and funerals. Some Puritans refused to have their children baptised by, or to receive communion from, a minister who was no preacher. Walter Yonge records in his diary that in 1614 the parish clergy of the Diocese of Exeter were instructed to make it clear to the laity that it was unnecessary to have the Word preached at the sacraments: despite such official disapproval, however, William Gouge was at pains to emphasise in a treatise published in 1622 that children should be baptised by a minister of the Word.[6] The Puritan funeral sermon was not simply a recital of the deceased's qualities: it was primarily regarded as an opportunity to remind the mourners that all flesh was mortal and to exhort them to put aside worldly thoughts and live in righteousness. When Sir John Davie made his will in 1639 he expressed the wish that a godly preacher should deliver the sermon at his funeral for the purpose of putting 'those that survive in minde of their mortallitye and the better preparinge and fittinge of them for the kingdome of heaven'.[7] Now and again a celebrated Puritan divine would accept an invitation to preach at some important family occasion or at a public gathering where such an address was considered appropriate. Thomas Gataker preached at the wedding of Sir Robert Harley and Brilliana Conway; Richard Sibbes praised the virtues of Sir Thomas Crewe when he was laid to rest in his new chapel at Steane in Northamptonshire; while Robert Bolton gave the sermon at the Lent assizes held at Northampton in 1631, no doubt at the request of the high sheriff, Francis Nichols, who was his friend and patron.[8]

Wealthy Puritan landowners often owned the patronage rights in parishes where they lived and were therefore able to put in ministers whose type of preaching best suited their requirements. In many cases there was a domestic chaplain who was expected to preach regularly to the household and sometimes the family might hear a sermon from a visiting minister. Lady Judith Barrington, the wife of Sir Thomas Barrington, wrote in a letter to the family steward that 'I had ill Luck in my absence at Christmas from London that thereby I missed Honest Mr King's kindnes who I hear came up a purpose to have given me a Sermon and so I perseve Mr Duport intended us a Sermon if [we] had been in Towne.' These men who were so anxious to please can be identified as Benjamin King, a Hertfordshire minister who is said to have been a veritable Boanerges in the pulpit, and James Duport who acted as tutor to at least one of Sir Thomas's sons at Trinity College, Cambridge.[9]

Anxious to extract the maximum value from godly preaching, many of the Puritan gentry diligently employed themselves in making notes and on returning home would often repeat and discuss what they had heard. Books of sermon notes are to be found among the papers of both Sir Henry Yelverton, who would have used the same technique on the judicial bench, and Sir Thomas Barrington who was a regular attender at the Saturday lectures delivered by James Harrison at Hatfield Broad Oak, the Essex parish where the Barringtons were seated. In 1605 Sir Henry published a collection of sermons by Edward Phillips, a Puritan preacher at St Saviour's, Southwark, which he had himself recorded.[10] Sir Simonds D'Ewes tells us that he began to make notes of sermons 'and soe to become a rationall hearer' when he was at school in London and that he continued this practice for the rest of his life. In December 1615 he sent his mother what may well have been his first summary of a sermon. This was based on a passage relating to the Gadarene swine and it is perhaps significant that one of the points which caught his attention was the proposition that 'if great men use ther greatnesse well they are lightly blessed, besides that great men being good will draw the common people to be good.' A considerable number of D'Ewes's sermon notes have survived and among the divines represented are Richard Holdsworth, who was his tutor at Cambridge, and Richard Chamberlain, a nonconformist minister with whom he was on close terms.[11]

Often it was the womenfolk who were the most zealous in recording sermons and studying their contents. Lady Mary Strode 'was a Notary and tooke the Sermons which she heard by her owne penne' while Lady Anne Waller was a 'constant Writer of Sermons and wrote them in her Heart as well as in her Book' so that her life was an exact commentary on the sermons which she heard.[12] Lady Elizabeth Brooke had such a great love of sermons that she had them repeated in her house and would then discourse on them at length. In addition, she 'wrote the substance of them and digested many of them into Questions and Answers, or under Heads of common Places, and then they became to her Matter for repeated Meditation.'[13]

The profitable sermon was what the Puritan gentry wanted above everything else when they attended their parish churches. At the same time they preferred a relatively plain form of worship conducted in surroundings which were devoid of any features associated with the sin of idolatry. This austere attitude might have been shaped by their experience at university, by the reading of Puritan literature or by the teaching and practice of Puritan ministers at the parish level. Inventions of men, noted Sir Henry Yelverton during the course of a sermon, provoked the wrath of God; no discipline or ceremony should be admitted if it was not allowed by the Word of God.[14] Among the Puritan gentry, however, there was a considerable range of opinion over the question of what was permissible and what was unlawful in matters of worship. At one extreme there was Sir William Springett who according to his wife had begun 'very early to see the superstitious follies and fruitless devotion both in the ministry and whole worship of the Church of England'. Sir William detested the Book of Common Prayer, the wearing of a surplice and the rites associated with such sacraments as baptism and holy communion. At their marriage in 1641 he dispensed with the use of a ring and rejected many of the 'dark, formal words' prescribed in the order of service. Both he and his wife objected to singing the metrical psalms (though in fact these were highly popular in Puritan circles) and even went so far as to tear them out of their Bibles.[15] At the other extreme Sir William Waller took a much less rigorous view of external ceremonies. 'No Christian church in the world,' he maintained, 'is, or can be, without the use of some ceremonies. . . . For my part I am not, nor ever was, against a modest dress of religion but I like not affected devotions.' At the same time (and here he was drawing on the teachings of St Paul) he was wholeheartedly in favour of having music in churches: 'there is nothing of greater use for the raising and sweetning of our affections towards God then the singing of his high praises in Psalmes and Hymns and Spiritual Songs.'[16]

The extremism of Sir William Springett was hardly typical of the Puritan gentry: indeed his wife testifies that he 'had cast off those dead superstitions which were manifest to him in that day beyond any I then knew of his rank and years'.[17] Few were in favour of the total abolition or fundamental revision of the Book of Common Prayer. Even Sir Robert Harley and his wife Lady Brilliana, who believed that it had serious defects, were unwilling to condemn it out of hand. In 1639 Lady Harley told her eldest son, who was then at Oxford, that under the influence of their schoolmaster his brothers were becoming more and more radical in religion and added that she feared that 'we shall be so ernest in beateing downe theare to much villifyeing of the Common Prayer Book that we shall say more for it than ever we intended.' In practice Sir Robert and his wife were able, even in the Laudian era, to participate in a form of worship which had been purged of at least some of the features which they found most objectionable. At their parish church of Brampton Bryan which was situated in a secluded corner of Herefordshire it seems to have been customary for the minister, whose living was in the gift of the Harley family, to leave out sections of the Prayer Book services and by this means to make more time available for the sermon. Besides his dislike of certain aspects of the liturgy Sir Robert had a marked aversion to many of the material accessories of religion and it was not without reason that in 1643 he was entrusted with the task of preparing an order for the banning of the surplice and was also appointed to a parliamentary committee which was empowered to destroy monuments of idolatry.[18]

The most common forms of clerical nonconformity, at least before the Laudian era, were a refusal to wear the surplice and the omission of the sign of the cross in baptism and it was no coincidence that such conduct often occurred in churches which were under the control of Puritan squires. Yet the Puritan patron was faced with a dilemma since, as Sir Benjamin Rudyerd emphasised, it was the diligent preachers who tended to be most troubled in their conscience by the Church's ceremonial requirements.[19] Given that regular access to godly preaching was a matter of crucial importance to him he might possibly encourage his minister to conform sufficiently to avoid suspension or deprivation. So far as the laity were concerned the most conspicuous form of dissent, if we exclude the practice of journeying to other parishes,[20] was a disinclination to receive communion in a kneeling position. This issue aroused considerable interest and even generated its own specialised literature. In 1629 Thomas Paybody published a large volume with the self-descriptive title *A Just Apologie for the Gesture of Kneeling in the Act of Receiving the Lord's Supper* and dedicated it to two Puritan knights, Sir Thomas Grantham and Sir Thomas Hutchinson, expressing the hope that they would grow 'in the exemplary practise of a godly life'. Both Grantham and Hutchinson appear to have accepted his basic thesis as he explains in the dedication that he had need of such patrons for his work as 'are able to iudge of the cause which I handle and themselves plentifully defend it'.[21] On the other hand, there were some Puritan gentlemen who preferred to receive communion while seated or standing. Sir Edward Peyton was the author of a tract published in 1642 with the formidable title *A Discourse Concerning the Fitnesse of the Posture Necessary to be Used in Taking the Bread and Wine at the Sacrament*. Addressing an unnamed minister of religion, be began by referring to an incident in which he had been personally involved:

> Though there hath elapsed a long time since your denying me the Sacrament, standing at the time of administring it, affirming that you had taken an Oath not to administer to any but did kneel, though I did kneel before and after: yet all this time you should (to a man of my fashion) have had the manners, by letter, to have given me satisfaction, being Curate and your duty.

The Book of Common Prayer, he argued, required the communicant to kneel during the confession of sins but not while he was receiving the bread and wine. There was no authority in the Bible for kneeling at the administration of the sacrament: on the contrary, Christ and his disciples had been seated when partaking of the Last Supper. Communicants, Calvin had emphasised, 'ought not . . . to kneel to adore the Sacrament, who securely may receive the Sacrament without adoration, not kneeling'. Similarly, William Perkins had written that 'Ceremonies and bending the knee at the Sacrament is to worship God otherwise than hee hath commanded and therefore it is Idolatry.'[22]

Whatever the degree of their antipathy towards ceremonial requirements in general the Puritan gentry were at one in their detestation of the Laudian innovations, though equally they were not the only Protestant critics of a programme which involved much greater emphasis on the externals of religious observance. To Sir William Armyne the concept of 'the beauty of holiness' was altogether repugnant: 'when all the world almost had swallowed downe those pretty bawbling fooleries wherewith the Bishops had baited Religion he counted them too poore a baite to nible at; he ever thought a Cappe and a Congy a sorry thing to please Almighty God with.'[23] Looking back on the reign of Charles I, Sir Edward Peyton castigated the Laudian clergy for their 'idolatrous cringing to the altar, bowing at the name of Jesus and making churches idolatrous'. Sir Simonds D'Ewes comments in his autobiography that since 1630 the Arminian bishops had endeavoured to increase the multitude and burden of ceremonies with a view to oppressing the conciences or ruin the estates of many godly Christians whom they falsely nicknamed Puritans, though they were 'free from all schismaticall and idle opinions'.[24] At the funeral of Dorothy Hanbury in 1642 the minister recalled with obvious admiration that she had been an implacable nonconformist during the Laudian era. She was, he declared, 'most resolute . . . against superstition; her spirit would rise against those cursed innovations which of late were introduced and obtruded upon men, neither would she (though sollicited) be brought into the practice of them.'[25]

If the Puritan gentry took exception to some of the Church's ceremonial requirements, both before and after the inauguration of the Laudian reform programme, there was at least the consolation that they mainly practised their religion in a domestic setting which was very largely free from the control or interference of the ecclesiastical authorities.[26] William Perkins stressed that the primary duty which was laid on the master of a household was

> to be the principall agent, directer and furtherer of the worship of God within his familie. . . . And this he doth partly by prayer for and with his household and partly by instructing them in the holy Scriptures and in the grounds of religion that they may grow in knowledge and reape benefit by the publike Ministerie.[27]

Richard Bernard published a treatise on this subject under the title *Iosuah's Resolution for the Well Ordering of his Household*. In this work, which appeared in 1629, he told his readers that it was incumbent on the governor of the household not only to ensure that all those who were under his care heard the public preaching of the Word but also to see to the performance of religious exercises in his house; and that these exercises were to include the reading of holy scripture, catechising, the singing of psalms and the repetition of sermons. Bernard dedicated the volume to two Devonshire squires, Sir Henry Rosewell and Sir John Drake, together with their wives, and in doing so explained why he had felt it appropriate to enlist their patronage: 'I have since my first knowledge of you much honoured you in my heart for your true love to Religion, your good respect to God's Ministers, and your care to advance your holy profession by words and workes.' A few years later Sir Henry was accused in the Court of High Commission of allowing conventicles to be held in his chapel at Forde Abbey.[28]

Over and above the normal routine of family worship and instruction it was the practice in many Puritan households to observe special fast days or days of humiliation when the participants made a lengthy confession of their sins, humbled themselves in a spirit of contrition and besought their maker to forgive them. Such exercises played an important part in fostering the conviction that salvation was assured since it was believed that only the elect experienced feelings of genuine repentance for the sins which they had committed. In a treatise relating to the duties of a Christian, Harbottle Grimston advised those anxious to show that they were truly sorry for their misdeeds to 'chastise and mortifie thy flesh by abating thy flesh of all pleasant food, by sobrietie and temperance in thy diet, by prayers, labours and fastings'.[29] Such wealthy Puritans as Sir Robert Harley, Sir Nathaniel Barnardiston and Sir Simonds D'Ewes had their days of humiliation, as did Lady Hester Honywood, the wife of Sir Thomas Honywood.[30] Among the papers of Sir Robert Harley there is a note entitled 'Scriptures to be read to further our Humiliation and to help our Confession'. Deuteronomy ch. 28 and Leviticus ch. 26 both provided a detailed account of the terrible punishments which the harsh God of the Old Testament had threatened to mete out to those who refused to obey his commandments while another of the biblical texts recorded Daniel's confession of sin:

And I set my face unto the Lord God, to seek by prayer and supplications, with fasting and sackcloth and ashes.

And I prayed unto the Lord my God, and made my confession, and said, O Lord, the great and dreadful God, keeping the covenant and mercy to them that love him, and to them that keep his commandments. We have sinned, and have committed iniquity, and have done wickedly and have rebelled, even by departing from thy precepts and from thy judgments.[31]

Sir Simonds D'Ewes writes that in 1627 he read a discourse by Henry Mason, a London minister, which 'stronglie prooveth that Christians ought to sett some times aparte for ther ordinarie humili-acion and fasting'. From then onwards he devoted one day virtually every month to this kind of religious exercise, abstaining from all food until six o'clock in the evening and spending eight or nine hours in confessing his sins and performing other spiritual duties. 'In the confession of our sinns', he observes, 'wee must doe it with a sincere heart and resolution to leave them, not make a reservation of anie as Naaman did to bow in the House of Rimmon.' When contemplating the possibility of involving others in his fast days he thought it prudent to seek the advice of a Puritan minister, Richard Chamberlain, on the legality of such proceedings. In reply Chamberlain told him that it was lawful 'for christians familiarly acquainted and bordering neighbors to meet togither after a spirituall maner, to conferr togither, mutually to exhort, comfort and admonish one another, to pray togither, and if need be to forebeare meat and drink till they have finished'. On 27 February 1630, relates D'Ewes, he spent most of the day in a private religious fast and humiliation with his whole company, 'it being the first familie fast that ever I observed my selfe, after which others followed which I performed with the moore comforte and securitie because it was neither repugnant to the Lawes of the Commonwealth nor of the Church'. Cautious by nature, Sir Simonds had no wish to be accused of holding conventicles.[32]

It was argued by Puritan authors that persons of substance should not only be careful to choose servants who were God-fearing but should also ensure that they were properly instructed in the principles of religion. John Dod thought it worth pointing out that apart from the spiritual benefits which would be conferred on the servants such a grounding would also produce valuable dividends for their employer:

godly men doe well consider that those that are most faithfull unto God will also shew themselves most faithfull unto them; they will not infect their children nor corrupt one another nor bee prodigall and wastfull nor blemish them and their families by raising up slanders and spreading abroad false reports and

tales, to their reproach and disgrace. They will also bee trusty
and painfull in their places and callings, even when their gover-
nours are absent . . . as knowing that though they bee not by
yet God is alwayes by, who will call them to an account for all
their workes.[33]

Such advice seems to have met with a ready response among the
Puritan gentry. We are told that Lady Frances Hobart took great
care 'to procure persons fearing God to be nigh unto her' and that
Lady Mary Armyne chose her servants for their holiness.[34] Sir
Robert Harley was no less insistent in this respect. The minister
who preached at his funeral testified that he 'was spirited with a
keen hatred of sin and prophanenesse. He would not, I may say,
he could not brook it in any under his Roof; he would often say He
cared not for the service of one that feared not God.' In 1612
Thomas Pierson, whom he had recently presented to the living of
Brampton Bryan, offered him the name of a cook who was 'a verie
proper man . . . relligious and sufficiently qualified for his place'.
Some years later Julines Herring, a Puritan lecturer at Shrewsbury,
wrote in a letter to Pierson that he had heard that his patron needed
a groom and was desirous 'to entertaine our relligion, if sett for that
course'; accordingly he wished to recommend the bearer of his
letter, having received very good testimony for his Christian
walking.[35]

Once they had taken up their employment the servants in Puritan
households were expected to participate in all the corporate religious
activities and were often given regular instruction in divinity.
Dorothy Hanbury is said to have been a religious governor of her
servants who sought to match them to Christ. Anxious to set them
a good example, she rose early on cold winter mornings in order to
attend household prayers. Lady Anne Waller, the wife of Sir
William Waller, catechised the children and servants once a week.
After returning from church she called her maidservants and any
boys who might be serving in the house to her chamber where she
asked them to give an account of the sermon which they had heard,
'helping their memories wherein they failed, clearing up the sense
of what was delivered, exhorting and pressing them to be doers of
the Word and not hearers only, concluding all in Prayer with them'.
As was customary Sir William left the instruction of the servants
to his wife but he writes that he 'would constantly observe to have

prayers at noon with my family and to be present my self at the duty; and that both for mine own comfort and for example to my Servants'.[36]

Now and again we are presented with a particularly detailed picture of the religious life of a Puritan manor-house. When the nonconformist Richard Sedgwick served as chaplain to Sir Edward Onslow, a pious gentleman who was 'eminent for the virtue and sanctity of his life', he spared no effort in ministering to the spiritual needs of the household.

> Every day his usuall course was to pray in the morning at six a clock with the Husbandmen, and at ten to pray with the rest of the Family and expound a Chapter. . . . His course at night was after Prayer to catechize the Family by turne, wherein he used no respect of persons, the meanest not being left out and the chiefest not forborn.

It was usual for the family to spend the winter in London and the summer at Sir Edward's country seat, Knowle, in the Surrey parish of Cranleigh. When they were living at Cranleigh, where there was no preaching minister, he delivered two sermons every Sunday and after public exercises called the whole family together to give an account of what they had heard. It was in this kind of environment that the parliamentarian Sir Richard Onslow, a man noted for his gravity and sobriety, spent the formative years of his childhood.[37] At Kedington Hall in Suffolk Sir Nathaniel Barnardiston was 'an excellent Master to his Servants', not only setting them a good example but giving them personal instruction for the benefit of their souls and bodies. Someone who knew the family well recalled that at one time he had ten or more servants whose piety was so impressive that he had seen nothing comparable in any other family in the land. In Sir Nathaniel's time Kedington Hall was 'a spirituall church and temple wherein were dayly offered up the spirituall sacrifices of reading the Word and prayer, morning and evening, of singing Psalmes constantly after every meal before any servant did rise from the table'. In addition to the days of extraordinary humiliation which were regularly observed it was the custom to commemorate two events of great significance for English Protestants, the accession of Queen Elizabeth and the discovery of the Gunpowder Plot.[38]

While the Puritan divines considered it essential that the whole

household should join together in daily worship they were adamant
that this was not to be regarded as a substitute for individual prayer
and meditation. John Dod emphasised that it was 'not sufficient to
come to publicke religious exercises in the family but every one
must performe the same in private and apart'. There were some
professors of religion, he declared, who had 'prayer and reading of
the Scriptures twice a day publicke with their whole family' but
never prayed in secret, meditated on the Word of God or confessed
their hidden corruptions.[39] Such activities, however, were common
among the Puritan gentry. Sir Thomas Wodehouse, who was
described as a severe man, kept a commonplace book in which he
entered religious observations and prayers and biblical quotations.
'Meditation', he wrote, 'is an intention and application of spirit to
devine things, a searching out all instruments to a holy life and a
devout consideration and production of those affections which are
in a direct order to the love of God and a pious conversation.'[40]
When her health permitted it Lady Mary Strode spent three or four
hours in her private closet every day in reading, meditating, praying
and writing; and there were other Puritan wives who were credited
with a similar diligence in the performance of private duties, among
them Lady Elizabeth Alston, Lady Mary Armyne, Lady Elizabeth
Brooke, Lady Lucy Jervoise and Lady Margaret Wroth.[41] In one
of his commonplace books John Harrington confided to himself his
fear that he had been negligent in such matters though there are
many other entries which suggest that he was being unduly self-
critical.[42] On the other hand, some Puritan ministers were afraid
that this kind of prolonged and intensive concentration on spiritual
things might prove injurious to health. Francis Tallents expressed
concern about the many weak and melancholy Christians who tired
themselves out in exercises of devotion and would advise them to
keep their minds as calm and sedate as possible and not seek to
put them always 'upon the stretch'. Even Sir Simonds D'Ewes
began to feel the strain in his private exercises of humiliation and
in 1638 found it necessary to reduce his ordinary fastings to one
every quarter.[43]

In devout Protestant households much time was spent in reading
the scriptures, a practice which St Paul had stressed could make a
man 'wise unto salvation'.[44] As may be judged from the libraries of
such families as D'Ewes, Harley and Yelverton[45] the Puritan gentry
often had large collections of religious literature. These would

usually contain John Foxe's *Book of Martyrs*, Calvin's *Institutes* and works by men whom Richard Baxter described in 1650 as 'our old solid Divines', William Perkins, Robert Bolton, John Dod, Richard Sibbes and John Preston.[46] At the same time there were many other authors who might be represented, among them Nicholas Byfield, Richard Capel, Thomas Gataker, William Gouge, Richard Greenham, Samuel Hieron, John Mayer, William Pemble and Henry Scudder. Much of this Puritan literature was of a kind known as practical divinity; in other words, it was primarily concerned with the application of scriptural precepts to everyday life.[47]

The collected works of William Perkins, which went through a number of editions between 1603 and 1635, enjoyed great popularity in Puritan circles. One of the editors of the three-volume version which was published in the years 1608 and 1609 was Thomas Pierson who had been a close friend of the author at Cambridge; in his will he bequeathed to his wife the works of William Perkins, Robert Bolton and John Preston.[48] His patron, Sir Robert Harley, had his own set of Perkins's works and copies were also to be found in the libraries of the D'Ewes, Knightley, Moundeford and Yelverton families. Sir William Gee, we are told, had a 'revered opinion' of him and always took great delight in reading his books. Among Perkins's works was a treatise which he personally dedicated to Valentine Knightley, the heir to Sir Richard Knightley, 'both for the profession of the faith which you make, as also for that Christian friendship you have shewed to me'. Another treatise was dedicated by Thomas Tuke, who had translated it from the Latin, to Sir William Armyne who was the patron of his father, a nonconformist minister in Lincolnshire. He had done so, Tuke explained, 'partly because it is a Thesaurus and store-house of excellent precepts . . . and partly to demonstrate my gratitude and devoted affection to you, who have alwaies beene a constant patron to my nearest and dearest friends'.[49]

Sir Thomas Crewe was the dedicatee of a work by Henry Scudder about the Lord's Prayer which was published in 1620. In the epistle dedicatory the author commented that

> though you be alreadie furnished and fully established in the truths therein delivered, yet it shall be profitable unto you, that with some varietie you be put to remembrance of the same things. Your children likewise (who may reape some good

hereby) will be induced to reade and make use of this booke,
the rather because it commeth through the hands and under
the patronage of their so loving and beloved father.[50]

Following the death of his friend Robert Bolton in 1631 Sir Thomas
took on responsibility for the publication of certain works of his
which eventually appeared in 1634 under the title *A Three-fold Treatise*. By then, however, Sir Thomas was also dead and the editor
therefore dedicated the volume to his son John. In his opinion it
was entirely fitting that the association with the Crewe family should
be maintained through the son who was admired and respected by
many God-fearing people for his 'care and endevour to advance the
glory of God, and to further the welfare and edification of his
Church, and for the love to godly and painefull Ministers and the
godlinesse professed, preached and practised by them'. When *Mr
Bolton's Last and Learned Worke of The Foure Last Things* was published
in 1632 the editor dedicated it to another Northamptonshire squire,
Francis Nichols, who had heard both the sermons which it
contained. It had been Bolton's express wish, he related, that the
work should bear this dedication as a token of his gratitude for the
many favours he had received from Sir Augustine Nichols, his
deceased patron, 'and from your selfe, his immediate heir and
successour'. In it, he went on, the author encouraged him still 'to
hold on to those good wayes of piety which you have ever loved'.[51]

John Dod had two great benefactors in Northamptonshire, Sir
Erasmus Dryden and Richard Knightley. In the epistle dedicatory
which prefaced a collaborative work published in 1609 he and
Robert Cleaver told Dryden that they had long been acquainted
with 'your willingness to read our bookes and your godly wisdome
to iudge and discerne of all that you read. . . . Our former writings
comming as strangers yet alwaies found all good and kinde enter-
tainment at your hands'.[52] Richard Knightley had several Puritan
works dedicated to him, among them John Dod's *A Plaine and
Familiar Exposition on the Lord's Prayer* which appeared in 1635 and
John Preston's *The Golden Scepter* which was published posthumously
in 1638. The editors of the latter volume, Thomas Goodwin and
Thomas Ball, explained that it was their practice when publishing
works by Preston to dedicate them to his special friends and recalled
that the author had died at Knightley's house.

During the years 1626 to 1635 when he was Master of St

Catharine Hall, Cambridge, Richard Sibbes sometimes went on a summer journey visiting the houses of his wealthy friends, 'where he was an instrument of much good'. Among them were Sir Robert Brooke and his wife Lady Elizabeth who were then living at Abbots Langley in Hertfordshire. When *A Fountaine Sealed* was published in 1637, two years after the author's death, the joint editors, Thomas Goodwin and Philip Nye, dedicated it to Lady Brooke, noting that 'your Ladyship's hand and Pen was in this his scribe and Amanuensis whilest hee dictated a first draught of it in private, with intention for the publique.' Her own life, they were at pains to stress, 'hath beene long exactly framed to the rules herein prescribed'.[53]

Nicholas Byfield, who was vicar of Isleworth in Middlesex, delivered two sermons every Sunday and two weekday lectures. Among his most appreciative listeners were Sir Thomas Hoby and his wife who when not residing in Yorkshire lived in a rented house in the neighbouring parish of Twickenham. In 1626, four years after Byfield's death, his son Adoniram published an unfinished work of his about the Apostle's Creed and dedicated it to the Hobys, referring to 'that love and respect which you were pleased . . . to expresse unto the Author of this Treatise' and also to

that good esteeme which you have ever had of this work, manifested, both, when you were pleased to bee diligent hearers of it when it was preached, so long as you were both resident in these parts, as also by your earnest desire of the publishing of it for the benefit of God's Church.[54]

Samuel Hieron, who was vicar of Modbury in Devon, enjoyed a great reputation as a preacher and his published sermons, which were strongly Calvinistic in character, must have been assured of a ready market in the West Country. One of his works was dedicated to Sir Francis Barrington, who had helped to support him at university, but in the main it was his friends among the Devonshire gentry who were singled out in this way. Sampson Hele, one of the richest Puritan squires in Devon, was described as a special friend from whom Hieron had received countenance and encouragement while Sir William Strode was commended for his 'affection to God's holy truth'. Sir William's wife, Lady Mary, received her share of praise in 1608 when a small volume entitled *A Helpe unto Devotion* made its appearance. This was a collection of prayers for special occasions which was primarily intended for the use of those who found it difficult to express themselves in their private devotions; the author hastened to add, however, that it was unlikely that she had any need of such guidance.[55]

Some men, observes Sir William Waller, 'covet to have Libraries in their houses as Ladies desire to have Cupboards of plate in their chambers, only for shew; as if they were only to furnish their roomes and not their mindes'.[56] The Puritans, however were inclined to be diligent and painstaking readers of spiritual works, often copying out extracts which could be used with profit in the course of private prayer and meditation. Sir Henry Vane the younger is said to have been assiduous in his 'continual searching' of the scriptures while Sir Nathaniel Barnardiston was drawing on his own experience when he advised his children to be 'constant in reading the Scriptures'. Bulstrode Whitelocke tells us that it was his practice after attending public worship to spend his hours of retirement in reading the Bible and the works of some of the biblical commentators and that he also studied Hebrew in order to improve his understanding of the text. In 1613 Sir Thomas Cheke was complimented by a Puritan minister for his love of divine knowledge, his proficiency in it and his willingness to give over much of his time to study 'towards the perfection of it'.[57] In common with many of the womenfolk Lady Lucy Jervoise, the wife of Sir Thomas Jervoise, showed no less zeal in her Bible reading: so familiar did the Word of God become to her that 'much of her ordinary language was in Scripture Phrase'.[58]

A considerable number of Puritan gentlemen were moved to write down their own reflections on matters of religion, either for their personal benefit or for the edification of their families. Sir James Harrington, who was the author of several published works, began to engage in this activity when he was still a young man. In 1627, at the age of twenty-one, he presented his parents with a discourse which he entitled 'Meditations Upon the Creation, Man's Fall and redemption by Christ'. As explained in the epistle dedicatory this represented 'the Fruits of some few hours destinated for the Lord's dayes Preparation'.[59]

An issue which did much to swell the volume of religious literature in the early seventeenth century was the Sabbatarian controversy.[60] The general attitude of the Sabbatarians was conveniently summarised by Robert Bolton in a funeral sermon delivered in 1616 when he exhorted his listeners to spend the Sabbath in a more holy and heavenly way, not only in

forebearing sin, the workes of your calling, idlenesse, vaine
sports (this is but only flying evill and privative good) but also
to ply with conscience and reverence all GOD's holy Ordinances; prayer, reading, singing of Psalmes publikely and privately; the Word preached specially, conference and the like.[61]

This extreme form of Sabbatarianism owed very little to Calvin,
who took a much less austere view: in the words of Lady Brilliana
Harley he was so earnest in opposing the popish holy days that he
entrenched upon the holy Sabbath.[62] As a practice Sabbatarianism
had a long history, at least in some parts of the country, but it was
not until the 1590s, with the publication of works by Nicholas
Bownd and Richard Greenham, that it acquired the status of a
doctrinal concept. In the early seventeenth century the doctrine was
adopted by the Puritans as a major article of their creed, though
they were not the only Englishmen who attached importance to
maintaining the sanctity of the Lord's Day: as Bulstrode Whitelocke
noted, the Declaration of Sports which was issued in 1633 'gave
great distaste to many, both others as well as those who were usually
termed Puritans'.[63]

Paul Micklethwaite, who was lecturer at the Temple church in
the years 1628 to 1639, argued in his sermons that while labouring
people were entitled to some recreation on Sundays it was necessary
for persons of quality, who as members of a leisured class might be
said to keep the Sabbath all week long, to observe the Lord's Day
more strictly and in particular to abstain from their own forms of
recreation.[64] Contemporary accounts of Puritan squires and their
wives often record that they looked forward with keen anticipation
to the Lord's Day, heard the preaching of the Word both in the
morning and the afternoon and spent the remainder of the day
performing religious exercises. Sir Robert Harley's library contained
copies of Nicholas Bownd's treatise, John Sprint's *Propositions
Tending to Proove the Necessarie Use of the Christian Sabbath* and an
abstract of the doctrine of the Sabbath by Henry Burton. Although
there were also some anti-Sabbatarian works in his library Sir
Robert was in no doubt about the truth of the doctrine: at his
funeral the minister testified that he 'paid a dear devotion of love
to the Lord's Day', adding that he had frequently 'heard him plead
it up with Excellency of Arguments.'[65] When Sir Thomas Crewe,
the Northamptonshire lawyer, was buried in 1634 Richard Sibbes

recalled that 'For the Lord's day . . . Hee had a wonderfull care to keep it holy. Hee was as eminent as any in his Profession for that. He would not entermeddle with the businesses of his calling on that day.' His son John also subscribed to the Sabbatarian doctrine. When Robert Cleaver published *A Declaration of the Christian Sabbath* he dedicated it to John Crewe and his Puritan relatives Edward Stephens and John Curzon, together with their wives. 'I am incouraged to make choyse of you for my speciall and selected Readers,' he told them, 'and ioyntly to salute you in publike as professed friends to the cause wherein I deale and Religious observers of that sacred Ordinance of God for which I contend.'[66] Walter Yonge noted in his diary that on Sunday 19 April 1635 while a number of men were playing at dice in the churchyard at Tiverton in Devon 'there fell downe a stone from the Churche and killed one of the players and dashed out his braynes'. He then proceeded to list various cases recorded in the Bible where Sabbath-breakers had come to an untimely end.[67]

When James I issued his Declaration of Sports in 1618 it met with a predictable reception in Puritan circles. Lady Abigail Moundeford wrote from London that the decree 'for the allowing of dancings and folleys upon the saboth day is exsedingly distated and I think the Carefull keping of it more earnestly called upon by the godly prechers then it was before'. King James, declared Sir Edward Peyton in an account of his reign, permitted dancing around Maypoles 'and so winked at breaking the Sabbath, a vice God curseth everywhere in Scripture'.[68] When Parliament met in 1621 Sir Walter Erle delivered in a bill on the Sabbath which had passed through the Commons in 1614. Since its object was to ban dancing, church ales and May games it had all the appearance of a deliberate challenge to the Declaration of Sports. At its second reading an opponent of the bill, Thomas Shepherd, made a bitter attack on its sponsors:

> The Kinge by his edict hath given leave to his subiects to daunce. . . . The occasion of the Bill growes from a kind of Cattle that will not submitt themselves to the Ceremonyes of the Church. It savours of the spirrit of a Puritan. I call not those Puritans that speake against Drunckennes. . . . But such as are refractorie to good order.

Sir George More spoke in defence of the bill, emphasising that such legislation had been a feature of every parliament which he had attended since first becoming an MP in 1584. In the end it was agreed that the bill should be referred to a committee which included Sir Walter Erle, whom Shepherd had described as a sectary and a disturber of the peace, Sir Francis Barrington, Sir George More and Thomas Crewe. As for Shepherd, the Puritans were so incensed that they would accept nothing less than his expulsion.[69]

In the event the bill did not reach the statute book nor did a similar bill which was introduced in the Parliament of 1624. 'In this parliament', wrote Walter Yonge, who was familiar with the works of Richard Greenham, 'there was a good bill past both houses against revels and for the sanctifying of the Sabbath but the king would not pass it.'[70] In the early years of Charles I's reign the efforts of the Puritan party in the Commons to promote the cause of Sabbatarianism did not go completely unrewarded. In 1625 an act was passed which prohibited bear-baiting, bull-baiting, inter-ludes, common plays and other 'unlawful' forms of recreation on the Lord's Day.[71] From the Puritan standpoint it was a useful piece of legislation but in effect it did no more than provide statutory cover for some of the more restrictive provisions of the Declaration of Sports. In the Parliament of 1628 Sir Robert Harley and Sir Nathaniel Barnardiston were both involved in the preparation of a bill which was directed against carriers, cattle-drovers and others who broke the fourth commandment by working on the Sabbath. This bill also received the royal assent but on the whole the parlia-mentary campaign for the vindication of the Sabbath met with only limited success and the Puritans were left to bemoan the Crown's indulgent attitude towards dancing and revels on the Lord's Day.[72]

CHAPTER THREE

HOLINESS AND SOBRIETY

When Sir Thomas Crewe, the Northamptonshire lawyer, built a new chapel at Steane, close to his house there, in 1620 he had an inscription placed over the west door: 'Holiness Becometh Thine Howse O Lord for Ever.' According to Calvinist doctrine those who were effectually called were immediately seized with an overwhelming desire to live in holiness. Through the grace of God working within them they were progressively sanctified though they could never achieve complete moral perfection during the course of their earthly lives. Sir Simonds D'Ewes wrote in a book of religious observations that 'We must labour for true holines ... because without holiness the image of God which was defaced by Adam's fall cannot be restored in us; which makes the godlie moore excellent then ther neighbours.' In the case of a truly sanctified man, he went on, his holiness was 'still Growing and encreasing and cannot stand at a stay'.[1] For the godly the life which they lived on earth was in the nature of a spiritual pilgrimage which had as its goal the celestial paradise reserved for the elect. It was a concept which was very familiar to such Puritan squires as Sir Edward Hungerford, who in his will recorded his thankfulness to God for providing him with a wife who had been 'both a Comfort and an ornament unto me in the dayes of my labour and pilgrimage here'.[2]

During the early seventeenth century there was a spate of Puritan manuals which had been written with the express intention of guiding the pilgrim on his journey through a world which was full of temptations. In 1603 Richard Rogers, an Essex minister, published his *Seven Treatises* which he described, with some justification,

43

as the first work which was specifically concerned with directing
the Christian in his daily living.[3] A copy of this book was acquired
by Sir Robert Harley whose library also contained copies of two
other works of the same kind, John Downame's *Guide to Godliness*
and Thomas Taylor's *The Progresse of Saints to Full Holinesse*. While
staying in London Sir Robert lived in the parish of St Mary Aldermanbury and attended the church where Taylor served as minister.
In December 1630 Taylor sent him a copy of his work, calling it 'a
poore token and testimony of my love . . . which will ever professe
my loving respect of yow and yours'. In addressing Sir Robert,
among others, in the epistle dedicatory he explained that

> These lines will call upon you for 3 duties especially. First,
> every day to strive in subduing in your selves your personall
> corruptions till you have brought downe every high thing and
> thought into holy subiection. Secondly, most inwardly to affect
> holinesse in your selves and most entirely to love such as walke
> most holily as being the likest, nearest and dearest unto God.
> Thirdly, to see that every part of your lives aime at progresse
> to full holinesse.[4]

Another popular manual of this type was Henry Scudder's *The
Christian's Daily Walk in Holy Securitie and Peace* which was first published in 1627 and reached its sixth edition in 1635; among the many
who read it was John Harrington who copied an extract from the
1633 version into his commonplace book.[5]

For those who were anxious to live in holiness it was necessary
to be very fastidious about the company they kept in order to
avoid the risk of contamination. Ezekiel Rogers, who had once been
chaplain to the Barrington family, felt obliged to tell Lady Joan
Barrington that he feared that she was too undiscriminating in her
choice of friends and advised her to discard those who would never
be profitable to her either by precept or example.[6] In practice it
was difficult for the Puritan gentry to avoid all social intercourse
with others of their class who had no pretensions to godliness, not
least because of the pressures on them to conform to the tradition
of good neighbourhood. Dorothy Hanbury, we are told, wished to
walk in the strictest and precisest way: consequently she grew
'weary of complementall visits . . . the vanity and frothinesse which
she saw and heard at some places whither she was invited was a
great vexation'.[7] At the same time there was a natural tendency to

prefer the company of the godly to that of the unregenerate. God had made it known, observed Sir Simonds D'Ewes, that 'wee should not make notorious sinners the neare companions of our lives'; and he also emphasised that 'wee must love all the Godlie, and that with a pure heart.'[8] That he took these precepts to heart may be judged by the fact that his closest friends among the Suffolk gentry were mainly Puritan squires, men such as Sir Nathaniel Barnardiston, Sir William Spring and Brampton Gurdon. Since there was also frequent intermarriage in the ranks of the Puritan gentry[9] they were almost as much a class within a class as the recusant gentry at the other end of the religious spectrum.

In a sermon preached in the summer of 1611 John Frewen described the moral transformation which took place in those who experienced a spiritual conversion:

> If before they were vain swearers, now they have regarde to use the Name of god with high reverence. . . . If before they have bin unchast and dissolute, nowe they have a care to keepe their bodies and souls chast and pure, as becom the temples of the holy ghost. If before they were given to quarrelling, contention and strife, now they are peace-makers. . . . If before they have bin scoffers, raylers, filthy talkers or slanderers, now their care wil be to speake the wordes of truth and sobernes.[10]

Among the Puritan gentry there were many who strove to subject themselves to the strict moral code which was supposed to govern the lives of those in whom the process of sanctification was at work. According to one of his ministers Sir William Armyne kept his body 'as became a Temple of the Holy Ghost . . . he could not endure any vice should be master over him. . . . I have heard him rebuke Vice with great gravitie and severitie.'[11] Sir Robert Harley was a man imbued with 'a keen hatred of sin and prophanesse' who had been heard to say that 'God . . . had kept him unstained from grosse sins'. Although Sir Simonds D'Ewes was meticulous in confessing his sins he was at pains to emphasise in his autobiography that these were all sins of omission since he had been careful to avoid doing anything which he considered to be unlawful in the sight of God. In his view it was impossible for a godly man 'to walke on in whooring, swearing, drunkenes and the like', though it was not inconceivable that as the result of some infirmity or some strong and sudden temptation he might fall into a great sin as Noah,

David and others had done. D'Ewes regarded the sin of lust with a particular revulsion: it was 'one of the most horrible and most emasculating sinns which drawe downe God's iudgment; soe as Adoration it selfe is called spirituall whoredome'.[12] Sir Nathaniel Barnardiston was warmly praised for the holiness of his life by Samuel Fairclough who had been his parish minister for many years: 'so free and pure was his life from any scandalous sinne, or any other actuall evil course, that for thirty yeares together I remember not he was soiled with any spot which might give occasion to any to suspect his eminent integrity and sincerity.' Following his death a number of his friends took the unusual step of publishing a collection of elegies which they had composed in his memory. One of the contributors to this work was Christopher Burrell, the Puritan rector of Great Wratting, whose lament was typical of the sentiments expressed:

> Shall I not once again on earth behold
> That countenance so grave, so brave, so bold
> Which with a look could daunt the face of sin
> And make offence to hide it selfe with in?[13]

If Puritan gentlemen were often depicted as paragons of virtue the same is no less true of their womenfolk. Henry Scudder, the author of *The Christian's Daily Walk*, wrote of Temperance Crewe, the wife of Sir Thomas Crewe and the mother of John Crewe, that

> amongst the many gracious women that I have knowne a more compleate Christian, to whom the Lord had bestowed such a sweet concurrence of gifts of grace and nature, have I not knowne. And though birth, beautie, wit, a large heart and good elocution (all which were eminent in her) without grace are vanitie, yet when these are accompanied with love out of a pure heart and of a good conscience and of faith unfained (all which abounded in her) each doth make other admirable.

In the epitaph on her tomb some play is made, perhaps inevitably, with her unusual Christian name:

> A true Temperans in deed and name,
> Now gone to Heaven from whence she came.[14]

Following the death of his wife in 1635 Sir Thomas Wroth composed a eulogistic account of her in both verse and prose but stressed that

An angel's tongue more fitter than my pen
To blaze abroad her worth and virtues rare,
She daily walked with God more than with men.

Similarly, John Hampden described his first wife Elizabeth as 'truely virtuous and pious' and 'an eternall paterne of goodnes'.[15]

One of the most characteristic features of the godly was the care they took to keep their speech free from all blasphemy and impurity. Swearing was regarded as a deadly sin: indeed Thomas Hobbes brackets 'vain swearing' with carnal lust as the two vices which the Puritan divines most frequently condemned.[16] That it received so much attention may have been partly due to the fact that at this time it was a common habit, not least at the upper levels of society; under the early Stuart kings, wrote Sir Edward Peyton, swearing was in great esteem, mainly because of the example set by King James; the great courtiers 'garnished their mouthes with Goddammees, as if they desired Damnation rather then Salvation'.[17] The Puritan gentry, on the other hand, had a very different attitude. 'O my Soul', declared Sir James Harrington in rhetorical vein, 'is cursing, swearing, vain, wanton and evil speaking the Root and Garb of the wicked; yea, the Language of Hell? And is holy and a religious discourse and communication the Character and Dialect of Saints upon Earth?' According to the inscription on his monument Sir John Franklin was a pious, humble and sober man who had never been heard to swear an oath, nor for that matter to speak ill of anyone. If this was literally true he was able to exercise much greater self-restraint than Sir John Hobart of whom it could be said that the spirit was willing but the flesh was weak. In the words of his chaplain he 'was naturally inclined to some excess in passion and in the vanity of his youth had contracted a habit of swearing, of the evil of which being convinced he found it yet difficult wholly to leave it'.[18]

While the godly believed themselves to be morally superior to other men they recognised that despite all their striving they would continue to sin throughout their mortal lives but drew much comfort from the conviction that since the elect were truly repentant God was willing to forgive them for their transgressions. In some reflections which he committed to paper Edward Harley, the eldest son of Sir Robert Harley, recalled that on 26 December 1649

I solemnly humbled my self for my Base Sin Into which after-

ward I did most vilely and wretchedly fall many Times. Farr
be it from mee to lessen my Guilt by calling it a sin of Infirmitie.
Alas tis no otherwise my Infirmitie Then it is the Infirmitie of
a Dunghil, of a Jackes to stink loathsomly, Of a Plague-struck
Carkass to be deadly noysome, of a serpent to spit out poyson
and venome . . . the desperat wickednes of my Heart searches
out how my Constitution is most able to break the Holy and
just and Good Comands of God.

Unfortunately the nature of this sin is not revealed to us.[19] When
drawing up their wills the Puritan gentry often seemed desperately
anxious to depict themselves as great sinners, though at the same
time they were in no doubt that their salvation was assured. Sir
Francis Barrington declared that his sins were 'for multitude . . . as
the Sands of the Sea and haires on my head' while Sir Christopher
Yelverton referred in a spirit of contrition to the millions of sins 'of
my youth and of my riper age'.[20] Such extravagant self-criticism
cannot, however, be taken too seriously, not least since the Puritan
definition of sin was a very comprehensive one which took in such
forms of negligence as the performance of spiritual duties with a
carnal heart.

In theory the Puritan family should have been a model of Christian harmony; in practice this was not always the case. Sir Edward
Peyton strongly condemned the evils of swearing, drunkenness,
fornication and adultery and his own conduct may well have been
entirely blameless in these respects; on the other hand, his relations
with his son and heir were severely strained by a financial dispute
which was fought out in the law courts. According to his son Sir
Edward had dishonoured an undertaking given at the time of his
marriage that he would allow him and his wife £300 a year for their
maintenance; as a result John Peyton had found himself in prison
for debt.[21] Sir Simonds D'Ewes quarrelled with his stepmother over
the jointure which had been settled on her. In correspondence she
urged him to consider the cause of the widow and deal justly with
her: if he was not disposed to do so he should see what was said in
ch. 22, vv. 22 to 24, of the Book of Exodus about the punishment
which awaited those who afflicted the widow and the fatherless. If
D'Ewes turned up this reference he would have read that God had
warned such wrongdoers that 'my wrath shall wax hot, and I will
kill you with the sword; and your wives shall be widows and your

children fatherless'.[22] Another Puritan squire, Sir John Rivers, was described in his father's will as 'my unkind son' and subsequently fell out with his wife, Lady Dulcibella, who was living apart from him at the time of his death.[23]

Occasionally the head of a Puritan family can be found behaving like the worst kind of domestic tyrant. Sir Richard Strode had a quarrelsome disposition which frequently landed him in trouble and no doubt provided a popular topic of conversation at West Country dinner tables. In 1638 his son William related in a petition to the king that following his marriage to Anne Button Sir Richard had been involved in a dispute with William's wife's mother over the financial settlement which had been made. As a result he was now without income and likely to be deprived of the lands of inheritance which had been settled on him. In a letter to her mother Anne Strode expressed the fear that Sir Richard would be an unkind father to his son: he was telling all the county that her husband had married against his wishes (which was untrue) and that he would therefore 'sell all hee cann away from him'. In the event the approach to the king seems to have done no more than exacerbate the situation. In October 1639 William Strode was writing to one of his sisters that he and his wife had been warned to leave his father's house. Despite this ultimatum the young couple went on living at Newnham Hall and found themselves under continuing harassment from the master of the house who often threatened to beat them and put them in prison: 'we live here in such a manner', William told his mother-in-law, 'that I wish you saw it besides the great quantities of money I am indebted.' On 31 March 1640, when Anne was great with child, Sir Richard burst into their chamber with two of his servants, smashed all the windows and carried away their bedding and a cot which was awaiting the arrival of their firstborn. Such was the domestic life of one of the major Puritan families in the west of England.[24]

One of the sayings of St Paul which was a particular favourite with the Puritans was his pronouncement that 'the grace of God that bringeth salvation' clearly indicated that 'denying ungodliness and worldly lusts, we should live soberly, righteously and godly in this present world'.[25] The words 'sober' and 'sobriety' figured prominently in the Puritan vocabulary. In the chapel at Noseley Hall in Leicestershire Sir Thomas Hesilrige is described on his tomb as a man of 'great temperance and sobriety' while his son Sir Arthur is said to have taken delight in sober company.[26] As explained in a funeral sermon which was published in 1640 the word 'sobriety', when used in its widest sense, embraced a whole philosophy of life:

> I speake not of sobrietie as it is opposed to drunkennesse, though that be one thing. . . . But I meane a further sobriety, that is, as it is opposed to worldly-mindednesse. Take heed that you plunge not your selves too much in the world, and worldly pleasures and cares: for these are against the rule of sobriety. Be sober in your diet, in your apparell, in your gaining, in your spending, in your mirth, in your company, in everything: that is, moderate your selves, and your affections in these things.[27]

Self-denial as an aid to spiritual betterment was not a new concept in religion but in the hands of the Puritan scholars, following on from Calvin, it took on the form of a general code of conduct which all who hoped for salvation were obliged to adhere to in their daily lives. If a man wished to follow Christ, declared John Preston, he must deny himself and his own flesh. It was not easy for him to part with worldly things which gave him pleasure but if he saw them as vanity he would despise them and unless he did so it was impossible for him to be saved. Richard Sibbes observed that there were wretches in the world who would deny their sinful nature nothing: 'if they have a disposition to pride they will be proud; if they have a lust to be rich, to live in pleasures, to follow the vanities of the times, they will do so; they will not say nay to corrupt nature in any thing.' On the other hand, those who practised self-denial could expect to be more than amply compensated: if this sprang from a genuine desire for closer communion with God the Almighty would not fail them in what they desired.[28]

Through their reading and the sermons which they heard the Puritan gentry were well acquainted with this philosophy. Sir Thomas Wodehouse thought it worth noting down a quotation from the First Epistle of John which was much to the taste of godly preachers: 'All that is in the world is the lust of the flesh, the lust of the eyes and the pride of life.' Lady Elizabeth Brooke, who was a close friend of Richard Sibbes, revealed how much she was in sympathy with his views when she wrote that 'the great property of true Religion is that it teaches Self-denial, which Self-denial is indeed the Foundation of Religion and the sum of all the Precepts of the Gospel.' In one of his commonplace books John Harrington recorded an exhortation which may have been derived from a sermon: 'Be sober . . . in the use of meat, drink, apparel, recreation, sleep . . . we must be holy and carry ourselves as becomes the people and children of God in every one of these.' Similarly, Harbottle Grimston urged his readers in a work entitled *A Christian New-Year's Gift* to

> Flie riot in clothes and feasting and all vain pomp and gaudi-
> nesse in familie or housholdstuff. . . . Let thy garments be
> neither too gay nor yet beggarly. . . . Pamper not thy flesh; soft
> raiment, drinking and daintie meat effeminate both mind and
> bodie . . . flie drunkennesse with all thy power and God's
> help.[29]

For men of wealth and position it was easier to talk of self-denial than to practise it, especially in an age when the well-to-do were expected to maintain a style of living appropriate to their status in society. Undoubtedly there were some who warmly commended the virtues of sobriety but felt under no compulsion to deprive them-selves of worldly pleasures and comfort. Sir Thomas Wroth, who was himself a Puritan, wrote of this type of individual

> Honest Sir John doth to his neighbours cry,
> Forsake the world and learne the way to dye;
> If this be wholesome counsell he doth give,
> Why then makes he himselfe such shift to live.[30]

Materialistic traits might arouse feelings of guilt but these were not always a sufficient deterrent. Sir William Waller admitted as much when he referred to his 'vanity in furniture', adding that he had been 'justly punished in the loss of a great part of itt'.[31] Nevertheless there is evidence to show that many of the Puritan gentry deliber-ately sought to follow a regime of austerity, at least in some aspects of their daily life. One man who appears to have taken this philos-ophy particularly seriously was John Hutchinson. His wife tells us that his 'whole life was the rule of temperance in meate, drinke, apparell, pleasure and all those things that may be lawfully enjoy'd'. Nor was this simply a reflection of his natural inclinations; it was 'a true, wise and religious government of the desire and delight he tooke in the things he enjoy'd'.[32]

In the manor-houses of England there was a long tradition of hearty self-indulgence at the dinner table and in the early seventeenth century this tradition acquired a new dimension through the growing taste for more elaborate dishes which were richly seasoned with tropical spices.[33] To Puritans like Sir William Waller this new fashion had nothing to commend it:

> people affect an ingenuity in luxury as if their wits lay in their bellies and not in their braines. It is not enough to have good meat if it have not a rellish of the East-Indies; it must be so spiced that an Aegyptian would think it were rather imbalmed to be buried and kept for Mummy then seasoned to be eaten; it must be so diversified and so disguised in the dressing that every dish must be a riddle.

In his view excessive feasting clouded the intellect, encouraged lust and bred ill humours. It was also a deplorable waste of money which could have been better spent on feeding the poor: 'How many empty stomachs might this superfluity have filled? Possibly less at the table and more at the door might have done better.' On the other hand, he was contemptuous of those who carried frugality to such extreme lengths that they endangered their health. His own preference was for the rule of moderation or, more graphically, for observing a mean between eating by the ounce and eating by the pound and he summed up his attitude in the dictum 'a sober competent enough is the best diet'.[34]

At a time when tea and coffee were virtually unknown in England it would have been difficult for even the most fanatical advocate of self-denial to have demanded total abstinence from strong drink except on special fast days. Although it was said of Kingsmill Lucy, a nephew of Sir Richard Lucy, the Hertfordshire parliamentarian, that for many years he had drunk nothing but water[35] this was by no means a typical case. In common with his fellow gentry the Puritan squire would usually take wine or beer with his meals: indeed, the beer would often have been produced in his own brewhouse from barley grown on his own demesnes. What the Puritans were really objecting to was excessive drinking which they were convinced could open the door to all manner of evil. Here again Sir William Waller was faithfully reflecting the general attitude of godly Englishmen when he wrote that he regarded it as necessary to avoid drinking further then for the satisfaction of nature, for of all sins that is the most bestial . . . it is a difficult matter to be drunk and no more. . . Let the jolly good fellowes of the World deride this as a morose and (it may be) a nice precise humour, I would have them know that I scorn to make my self a beast in a civility for any man's pleasure.[36]

Sir Simonds D'Ewes was of the opinion that those 'that accustome themselves to drinking are never able to leave it'. He was not best pleased when he heard that some of his brother's former schoolfellows had not only encouraged but forced his coachman to drink more than was good for him. This led him to warn his brother, who was then at Cambridge, that it was better that such young men 'whose praise is noe better than the brewer's horse (that they cann carrie much drinke) should account yow proud, precise or whatsoever else ther belching stomacks cann disgorge then they trample upon the innocencie of your youth and enrich themselves with the spoiles of your good beginnings'.[37]

As a general rule the Puritan gentry seem to have felt it necessary to follow the well-established custom of dispensing large quantities of beer or wine as a means of enlisting support at parliamentary elections or, when executing the office of sheriff, for the purpose of entertaining their guests during the assize week. On the other hand, they strongly disapproved of common drinking-houses which appeared to them to be 'the Nurses of all Drunkenness'[38] and indeed a source of every kind of iniquity. Sir James Harrington expressed his disgust in some verse which he composed about the first visit he had made to London:

> Then to Taverns I went in
> Which I found the sinks of sin
> There the Devil's Revels be
> Lust and Drinking, Gluttonie
> Swearing, Dancing, Carding, Dice,
> Cheating and all other Vice.[39]

While the Puritan divines exhorted the godly to eat and drink in moderation they were also anxious to make it clear that the wealthy had an obligation to dispense hospitality and in practice it was by no means unknown for self-restraint to go hand in hand with a reputation for liberality. In accordance with his own precepts[40] Sir

George More was inclined to eat very sparingly: indeed his son-in-law Sir John Oglander writes of him that in his diet he was the most temperate and 'the greatest paynetaker that ever I knewe'. Yet at the same time he was a man with 'a wonderfull free disposition' which was reflected in the lavish scale of his housekeeping. Perhaps a similar kind of liberal spirit also explains the rich variety of food which was recorded in the household accounts of Sir Robert Harley: in the 1650s, for example, there are references to woodcock, pheasants, partridges, snipe, chickens, turkeys, rabbits, oysters, strawberries, cherries, oranges, raisins and currants, together with cinnamon, cloves and nutmegs.[41]

When expatiating on standards of dress a Puritan divine might concede that it was right that social distinctions should be maintained but at the same time he was adamant that all classes must avoid excess in apparel. In one of their collaborative works John Dod and Robert Cleaver wrote that

> Wantonnesse in things belonging to the bodie is shewed in costly apparell. Not but that there is a diversitie of degrees to be regarded, and every one may be apparelled as it meete and seemely for their estate: but in no estate or degree may one be so excessive as to forget holinesse and Christian sobrietie.[42]

At a time when great importance was attached to the external manifestations of rank and degree and when many persons of quality took a real delight in sartorial splendour it was not easy for the Puritan gentry to adopt the austere standards of dress which were prescribed for those who accepted the necessity of living a godly life. Nevertheless there were some who were prepared to defy social convention and run the risk of exposing themselves and their families to public ridicule. Contemporary portraits sometimes show wealthy squires wearing clothes which closely conformed to the style which the Puritans had made their own; among them we find Sir John Horner, Sir Richard Onslow, Sir John Potts, Sir William Strickland and Brampton Gurdon.[43] The womenfolk, for their part, were under the same obligation: after all, St Paul had emphasised that it was important that women should 'adorn themselves in modest apparel, with shamefacedness and sobriety; not with broided hair, or gold, or pearls, or costly array'.[44] Lady Lucy Jervoise, the wife of Sir Thomas Jervoise, was said to have 'despised the Ornaments of Vanity which other Ladies and Gentlewomen too much delight in and dote upon. Her outward Habit did shew the inward Modesty, Lowliness and Humility of her Mind'. In the light of Harbottle Grimston's very decided views on the matter of dress it is perhaps not surprising to learn that his second wife's clothes were always extremely plain; nor is it difficult to believe the writer of a parliamentary newsletter who commented that Lady Anne Waller 'lookes not so much cloaths as what vertues are convenient for weare; she studies not fashions but graces'.[45]

While some of the Puritan gentry dressed very soberly others seem to have felt themselves under less constraint. As an undergraduate at Cambridge Sir Simonds D'Ewes, who was highly critical of the worldly outlook of his fellow students, must nevertheless have been anxious to dress like a gentleman of fashion since his accounts of expenditure include such items as a French green satin doublet, cloth hose with silver lace and white Spanish leather shoes.[46] In October 1632 Lady Judith Barrington asked the family steward, who was then in London, to order a suit for her stepson John and enclosed with her letter a pattern 'of a good colour and cloth'. Her French tailor, she wrote, had measured him 'and I hope will fitt him better than Pickering did, worse he cannot; three Laces in a Seame I hear now is the best fashion, except we would bestow all lace, which we will not, and besides that is to costly.'[47] Sir Samuel Luke appears to have been not only very small of stature but physically deformed: Samuel Butler, who pilloried him as an archetypal Puritan in *Hudibras*, wrote of him elsewhere that he was an ill-carved urchin who 'looks like a Snail with a House upon his back'. Despite these physical characteristics, or perhaps because of them, Sir Samuel made a point of buying clothes which were anything but sombre. In February 1645 one of his servants wrote to him that in accordance with his instructions he had been to see Mr Blackburne, a London tailor, who had shown him the best French scarlet in the shop and had assured him that it was as good as any to be found in the capital. The cloak and trimming, he added, would cost £30.2s.6d.[48]

Although the great Puritan families might appear to have been sharply divided in their attitude to standards of dress the situation was in fact rather more complex. Faced with this difficult issue some families behaved in a highly ambivalent fashion. Sir Samuel Luke might have had a liking for fine clothes but when they had their portraits painted both he and his wife were dressed in a way which would have been acceptable to the most fastidious Puritan.[49] In December 1638 Lady Brilliana Harley wrote in a letter to her son Edward, who had just begun his studies at Oxford, that it was important that 'you submite to your father's desire in your clothes; and that in a happy temper, both to be contented with plaine clothes and in the weareing of better clothes not to thinke one self the better for them, nor to be trubelled if you be in plane clothes and see others of your rancke in better.' Later, however, she indicated that it was her wish that he should wear handsome clothes and in May 1639 we find her writing to him

I like the stufe for your cloths well; but the cullor of thos for every day I doo not like so well; but the silke chamlet I like very well, both cullor and stuf. Let your stokens be allways of the same culler of your cloths, and I hope you now weare Spanish leather shouwes. If your tutor does not intend to bye you silke stokens to weare with your silke shute send me word and I will, if please God, bestow a peare on you.[50]

Another notable Puritan woman, Lucy Hutchinson, relates of her husband that 'he left off very early the wearing of aniething that was costly, yett in his plainest negligent habitt appear'd very much a gentleman . . . he would rather weare clothes absolutely plaine then pretending to gallantry.' There are indications, however, that John Hutchinson was no doctrinaire in the matter of dress since his wife subsequently refers to him putting on 'a scarlett cloake, very richly laced, such as he usually wore'.[51] In a class which commanded great wealth it was probably inevitable that there should be varying opinions as to what constituted sober apparel and that often it was the more liberal kind of interpretation which prevailed. Many no doubt took the view that it was sufficient to wear clothes which were not unduly elaborate in comparison with the peacock fashions of the age and that given this degree of self-restraint it was unnecessary for them to be lacking in quality or even in colour. At the same time it is clear that the Puritan gentry often followed the practice of dressing to suit the occasion. Plain clothes of a sombre hue would be worn on the Sabbath, on special fast days and at other times when it seemed important to demonstrate that they truly belonged to the household of faith. When the Spanish ambassador had a public audience with the House of Commons in December 1650 John Hutchinson attended in an ordinary black suit because 'he would not appeare offensive in the eies of religious persons'; he was not a little surprised therefore to find that Major General Harrison was sporting a scarlet coat and cloak which were lavishly decorated with gold and silver lace.[52] In other circumstances it might be thought unacceptably demeaning to wear simple clothes which were entirely out of keeping with their owner's social status. Sir John Oglander the diarist was not himself a Puritan but his wife had obviously inherited the Puritan outlook of her father, Sir George More, and in writing of her he makes the revealing comment that she was 'a most Carefull, thrivinge wyfe who was no Spendor, never woore a silke gowne but for her Credite when she went abroad in Companye and nevor to please her selve'.[53]

In the early seventeenth century the wearing of long hair by members of the male sex was frowned upon by many Englishmen, irrespective of their religious convictions. In this respect at least Archbishop Laud was in harmony with some of his bitterest opponents: as Chancellor of the University of Oxford he sought to outlaw both long hair and extravagant dress.[54] In the main, however, the most hostile criticism of this practice came from the Puritan zealots who regarded it as a sign of ungodliness. On one occasion Thomas Pierson, the Puritan rector of Brampton Bryan in Herefordshire, was asked to remonstrate with a young man who had given offence by wearing his hair exceptionally long. Although Pierson clearly disapproved of this brazen effrontery he was one of the mildest of men and would only comment 'let him alone till God Renew his Heart and then he will Reforme his Haire himself.' His dislike of long hair was apparently shared by his patron, Sir Robert Harley, whose portrait by Peter Oliver shows us that he would have been relatively safe from criticism on this account.[55] Other wealthy Puritan squires such as Sir Francis Barrington, a 'patterne of Piety and Good Conscience', and Sir John Cutts also wore their hair short[56] yet they cannot be regarded as typical. John Hutchinson's wife tells us that he had a very fine thickset head of hair which he kept 'clean and handsome, so that it was a good ornament to him, although the godly of those dayes, when he embrac'd their party, would not allow him to be religious because his hayre was not in their cutt nor his words in their phraze'.[57] Leading Puritans like Sir Nathaniel Barnardiston, Sir Arthur Hesilrige and Sir William Armyne also preferred long hair, though Sir Nathaniel's younger son Samuel, who was for some years apprenticed to a London merchant, appears to have had different ideas from his father: according to the traditional story it was Queen Henrietta Maria's remarks about his close-cropped hair which gave birth to the nickname of 'Roundhead'.[58]

The extent to which the Puritan gentry observed the principles of sobriety in their daily lives could vary considerably from family to family but there may also have been regional differences. It is noteworthy, for example, that in Devon there were many landed families whose zeal in religion endowed them with a markedly austere attitude to life which persisted from generation to generation. As an undergraduate Sir Nicholas Martyn was presented by his father with a book of moral precepts which he had written. William Martyn made it clear to his son at the very beginning of the work that God had not placed him in the theatre of the world in order to 'fulfill the lusts thereof nor to embrace these earthly vanities, as chains of pearle and of gold do men's necks'. Self-indulgence, he told him, could have the most serious consequences: 'Now as uncleanesse and lust are augmented by sloth and idlenesse so is it much provoked by superfluitie and excess in diet and by foolish feastings. . . . But most of all is a man provoked to lust by drunkennesse. . . . For drunkenesse . . . maketh him brutish as a beast.' He would therefore be well advised to practise temperance which 'will perswade you in your diet to avoide excesse for your health's sake. In your apparel to be neither garish nor vile but to be in the meane. In wealth not to be prodigall nor in sparing to be miserable.'[59] Other families among the Devonshire gentry were also very much under the influence of this philosophy. The Rolles of Heanton Satchville, recalled the minister of Petrockstow in 1661, had long been noted for their sobriety, temperance and moderation and as evidence of this he could have pointed out the monumental brass in his church which depicts Henry Rolle, the head of the family in Elizabeth's reign, and his numerous sons, all of whom have close-cropped hair. Anxious to ensure that the heir maintained this praiseworthy tradition he offered him some advice drawn from the scriptures: 'Let not the bounty of God towards you in the things of this life be abused to serve either the lusts of the flesh, the lust of the eyes or the pride of life.'[60] The Strodes of Newnham could claim to be one of the leading Puritan families in the county, mainly because of the prestige enjoyed by Sir William Strode who championed the cause of godliness in the House of Commons. At the funeral of his wife Lady Mary in 1619 the minister testified, in words which reflected the influence of St Paul, that 'for her apparell, it was so modest, not with gold put about or broidered haire, that a curious eye could not iustly picke a quarrell at it.'[61] Sir John Northcote wore clothes which were Puritan in style, as did Lady Joan Drake, the mother of Sir Francis Drake the parliamentarian, and her daughter Mary. Sir Francis himself had hair which was so short that there could have been no doubt about his political and religious sympathies. In February 1643 he wrote to John Pym, who was his father-in-law, that the royalist troops were now beginning to scoff at religion and to ask where the God of the Roundheads was; in his case at least the nickname was highly appropriate.[62]

During the early Stuart period the Puritan members of the House of Commons were busily engaged in promoting legislation directed against such evils as extravagance in dress, adultery and fornication, swearing and what was termed 'the loathsome and odious sin' of drunkenness. Among the MPs who served on the committees responsible for processing this legislation there are some familiar names which occur again and again: in particular, Sir George More and Sir Francis Barrington, Sir Thomas Crewe and Sir William Strode. Sir Robert Harley also makes an occasional appearance: in 1610 he was involved in the preparation of a bill for the restraint of swearing while in 1626 he sat on a committee which was considering harsher penalties for those who were guilty of adultery or fornication. These attempts to legislate on matters of personal conduct met with some measure of success. Between 1604 and 1628 three bills for the punishment of drunkards, two bills for preventing and reforming profane swearing and cursing and a bill for the suppression of unlicensed alehouse keepers were passed by both Houses and received the royal assent.[63]

In Puritan circles it was considered that the wealthy gentry who were true professors of religion had a duty to combat sin not only as members of the legislature but as magistrates who were responsible for enforcing the law. When Edmund Rudyerd, a minister of the Word at Uttoxeter, published *The Thunderbolt of God's Wrath* in 1618 he dedicated it to Sir William Bowyer and other justices of the peace whom he counted among his friends, assuring them that it would be

a shrill watch-bell daylie in your eares to waken and stirre you
up more carefully to look into the weightie and burdensome
charge that lyeth upon you, as you are publique magistrates,
and also to your private duties as you are ministers of families,
in both which callings you are most deeply bound to be carefull.

God, he stressed, was likely to take vengeance both on the sinner
and the man who neglected to punish sin. And, putting aside all
false modesty, he entreated them

diligentlie to peruse this little booke with desire to profit by
reading; it will stead you more, to bring a hatred and lothing
of sinne, then any booke that ever you read of the like subject;
yea or of any other except . . . the holy bible; my reason for
this is that it is so full of terror against both the doer and
sufferer of sinne that it will make any Christian heart to feare
and tremble for feare.

Rudyerd's catalogue of sins was very comprehensive and extended
well beyond the realm of legal offences: among other things, it
included idolatry, cursing and swearing, Sabbath-breaking,
dancing, singing wanton songs and usury.[64] In 1632 Edward
Bagshawe, a Puritan lawyer, declared in the course of an epistle
dedicatory addressed to his brother-in-law Francis Nichols, a
Northamptonshire JP, that if ever there was a time for righteous
men in positions of authority to show themselves that time had now
come. A godly magistrate was under an obligation to do good and
had the necessary power to bring it to pass. 'These times have
need of such,' he stressed, 'up therefore and be doing, put on
righteousnesse and let it cloath you.'[65]

Often the Puritan squires who served on the commission of the
peace took it upon themselves to act as strict guardians of morality
and zealously enforced the laws which had particular appeal for
them and which in some cases they had helped to enact as members
of the House of Commons. George Purefoy, one of the principal
landowners in Berkshire, could not stomach either swearing or
debauchery. As a magistrate he was 'an ornament of that order . . .
his grave and regular life was enough to put sin out of countenance'.
In that capacity Sir Robert Harley 'was animated with a most
nimble Soul of Zeale against Sin. He was full of spirits against all
dishonours done to God, he was a Terrour to Evill works, he knew

no Respect of Persons in a businesse wherein God was wronged.'[66]
John Harrington, who was chairman of the Somerset quarter
sessions during Charles I's reign, told his colleagues that 'the
administration of Justice to others should incite us to excell in
righteousnes our selves.' On another occasion he emphasised that
they had much work to do. The increase in the number of alehouses
would be most harmful to the good ordering of the county and
would utterly subvert all peace and quietness. There were many
disorders such as drunkenness, speaking irreverently of the sacrament of communion, vain swearing or cursing, profaning the
Sabbath and practising usury. It was necessary, he concluded, for
the magistracy to take resolute action: 'we cannot doubt but that
we have a calling from God to do this work.'[67]

In 1618 James I granted a patent of monopoly which deprived
the justices of the peace of their power of licensing alehouses. This
decision must have been particularly unpalatable to Puritan magistrates but at least it was still open to them to take action against
those who owned or frequented unlicensed alehouses as well as
those who were guilty of drunkenness. In a letter to his mother-in-
law which was apparently written in 1629 Sir William Masham,
who not long before had been involved in the preparation of an
abortive bill for the suppression of unlicensed alehouses, referred to
the effects of bad weather on the harvest and commented that 'this
hand of god upon the creature (the materialls of drinke) doth pointe
out as it were with his finger the spetiall sinn of our nation, which
is drunkenness.' Sir William, who was on the Essex commission of
the peace, went on to say that the execution of justice against this
sin was the best expiation and gave as his authority Psalm 106, v.
30: 'Then stood up Phinehas and executed judgment: and so the
plague was stayed.' Acting on this maxim he had just punished
four drunkards, four drinkers and two alehouse keepers in one town
and, he added, 'I could wish the like were practised in other places:
we should then have lesse drunkenness.'[68]

Were the Puritan gentry, with their deep sense of commitment
to an austere creed, as dour and humourless as first impressions
might suggest? Undoubtedly there were some individuals who
closely conformed to the traditional image of the straight-laced
Puritan. Sir Nathaniel Barnardiston's discourse was 'so far from
the appearance of lightness or excessive Mirth that in Thirty years
together none ever heard one syllable from his mouth tending to

61

any wanton expression that might offend the most chast Mind or Ear.' If, however, he had a natural gravity his general character was very different from that of Sir Arthur Hesilrige who was described as 'a man of disobliging carriage, sower and morose of temper . . . to whom liberality seemed a vice.'[69] At the same time there were many Puritans at this level of society who, while they were very earnest in their religion, saw no justification for living in a perpetual state of melancholy. Clarendon relates that after John Hampden had settled into a stricter way of life (having previously spent his time in the pursuit of pleasure) he still retained his own natural cheerfulness and affability. Although Sir Henry Vane the younger normally wore a grave expression he was not lacking in humour: his conversation, it was said, was diverting and easy, with a good degree of eloquence and wit, full of facetious and innocent mirth.[70]

Whatever their critics might claim the Puritans often seem to have been convinced that their religion, far from inducing a sense of gloom, was a source of great happiness and joy. While Sir William Waller fully subscribed to the Puritan code of morality he was anxious to stress that it was 'one of the Devil's lyes, and that of which he hath made as great advantage as of any, that Religion is a dull flat melancholy thing, whereas in truth there is no such cleare, defecate mirth as that which cometh from the Springs above'.[71] Sir Simonds D'Ewes, for his part, believed that the professors of religion had a duty to show that they had found true happiness:

> The godlie should endeavour to expresse a cheereful spirit in ther converse with others, because by this they stopp the mouths of such as scandalize religion, alledging that it makes men and women sadd and melancholie; and by this doing alsoe they discourage others from desiring to enter into the way of pietie; as if by that they should be enforced to renounce all mirth, cheerefullnes and lawfull recreation.[72]

CHAPTER FOUR

MARRIAGE AND PARENTHOOD

In their discourses on the subject of marriage the Puritan divines were adamant that religion should take precedence over all worldly considerations when matches were being made. In the choice of a husband or wife, stressed William Perkins, the parents ought to pay greater regard to piety and wisdom than to beauty and riches or any outward blessings.[1] In a sermon which he delivered at a society wedding in Somerset Samuel Hieron lamented that economic motives too often predominated:

> The truth is, generally in matters of choise, religion beareth the smallest stroke . . . the choice of many about wives is like that in use about bargaines and farmes. The questions are (mostly) What is it worth besides the rent? what house upon it, how neere the market, the mill, the sand? When heare you this, How neere the Church or what Minister in the Parish or what good Preacher dwelleth by? Thus is it in this matter also; thus it runneth, what portion, what ioynture, how much money in hand, what securitie for the rest? Not a word, how far religion, what knowledge of God, how disposed in things that concerne the kingdome of God?[2]

Generally speaking, such strictures were well founded yet in the main the Puritan gentry were fully seized of the importance of religious compatibility in marriage. Sir William Masham believed that marriage partners could be brought together through the working of God's will: 'God is the great marriage maker,' he wrote, 'and therefore we must submit to his will . . . who over rules all for

63

the best good of his children.'[3] Sir William Waller relates that
following the death of his first wife in 1633 he prayed to God that
he might be granted another wife who was a religious woman and
that as a result he was directed to Lady Anne Finch, the daughter
of Thomas Finch, Earl of Winchelsea. When the financial arrangements had been settled Sir William and his intended wife agreed
to set a day apart to seek God's blessing on the marriage and

> Itt pleased the Lord to answer our praiers in as full a measure
> of comfort as ever was powred out upon a married couple; and
> though att the first there were some litle differences in our
> natures and judgments . . . yet within a litle while that good
> God wrought us to that uniformity that I may say wee were
> but as one soul in two bodyes.

After the death of his second wife the Lord answered his prayers
again and sent him Lady Anne Harcourt. God, he writes, united
them by this sacred ordinance and made them not only one flesh
but one spirit: one in their affections, judgments, ways, ends. In a
journal which she kept Lady Anne records that Sir William was 'a
religious, wise and faythfull loving husband'.[4]

Sir Simonds D'Ewes observes in his autobiography that when
seeking a wife he put the greatest emphasis on religion though he
was also anxious to enrich his posterity with good blood. In April
1626 he made overtures to his friend Sir Nathaniel Barnardiston
about the possibility of a marriage with Anne Clopton, the daughter
and heir of Sir William Clopton, who had been 'verie religiouslie
educated' under her grandmother Lady Anne Barnardiston.
Although Anne was not yet fourteen years of age Lady Barnardiston
was persuaded to give her consent to the marriage: in September
she wrote to D'Ewes' father that 'the confidence which I have, both
from my Nephew's relations and my owen smale acquaintance, of
the good begininge of grace in your sonn, doe much more incoridge
me to match my Grandechilde with him then all the estate which
you shall leave him.' The wedding took place the following month
and as a result D'Ewes was able to boast to a friend that he was
now 'linked either nearelie or moore remotelie to all or the most
parte . . . of all the ancient nobilitie of England'. In January 1627
he wrote to his wife from the Middle Temple:

> I shall ever account my selfe most happie to see and know you

to grow everie day moore and moore sincere and conscionable in the feare and service of God; that soe yow may gett knowledge and faith sufficient to discerne whether you bee in the estate of salvation or noe: for this will be a greater comfort unto you in life or death then all the honors or wealth of this worlde.

When she was dying in 1641 Lady D'Ewes was plagued with doubts about her spiritual state but Sir Simonds was convinced that she was numbered among the elect; in a letter to his stepmother he wrote that 'her rare death following her exemplarie and holy life hath not only bredd admiration in mee and many others but assurance also that shee now shines in eternal glorie'. In the summer of 1642 he sought the hand of Elizabeth Willoughby, the daughter of a Derbyshire baronet, Sir Henry Willoughby. Sir Henry was not personally acquainted with D'Ewes but Sir John Potts, a Norfolk Puritan, gave him a good account of his friend's character and the marriage negotiations were concluded relatively quickly. During the period of courtship Elizabeth told her sister Lady Aston that D'Ewes had expressed to her 'soe much affection, wisdome and pietie as I verilie beleeve I shall not onlie be trulie happie in him heere, but that hee will be a cheife meanes to further mee in the way to eternall happines heereafter'.[5]

In 1621 it was suggested to Sir Benjamin Rudyerd that he should pay suit to Lady Judith Smith, a young widow who was well born, fair, discreet, religious and virtuous and had property worth £400 a year. Whatever his views on the matter the marriage did not take place: instead she became the wife of Sir Thomas Barrington who at the time the match was first propounded was said to be so in love with her that he would be willing to accept any conditions she might care to insist on. In 1640 Benjamin King, a Puritan minister who had enjoyed their patronage, dedicated to them an expanded version of some of his sermons, explaining that his main reason for doing so was

because this Treatise seemes to be due to you both, who are joyned together not onely in the common bonds of Matrimony, but as Aquila and Priscylla, Zacharie and Elizabeth married together in the Lord and to the Lord Jesus, as to one Husband. This relation to Jesus Christ appeares by that high respect you shew to the spokesmen and faithfull ministers of Jesus Christ, by your Pietie and Zeale for the honour of the Lord Iesus.[6]

Sometimes a Puritan minister might be asked for his views on the character of a possible marriage partner or might even suggest a match himself. In 1628 Robert Bolton wrote to his friend Arthur Hildersham, the celebrated nonconformist, about 'one Mr Sligh who lives at Ash in Derbyshire, some five miles from Derby'. As he understood that Hildersham had been intimately acquainted with the father of 'Mr Sligh' he was approaching him on behalf of a special friend in the hope that he could inform him of 'the outward and spirituall' state of the young man. Sir Samuel Sleigh, as he would become, was the head of a family with strong Puritan connections and it seems likely that Hildersham had no hesitation in rendering a favourable report on him; at all events a marriage was shortly arranged between Sleigh and Judith Boys, who was Bolton's niece and a kinswoman of the Kentish Puritan Sir Edward Boys.[7] Sir William Masham's attempts to find a suitable husband for his stepdaughter Jane Altham led Ezekiel Rogers, who held one of the Barrington livings in Yorkshire, to put forward the name of Henry Slingsby, later to acquire posthumous fame as a diarist. In a letter to Lady Joan Barrington he wrote that Slingsby's father had 'fair lands' in the town of Knaresborough and that he had already passed on his suggestion to her daughter Lady Masham, 'only craving it if God deny a mach so fitt neere hande, she would not suddenly reiect it'. But in the event nothing came of this proposal.[8]

While they tended to look for piety and virtue in prospective marriage partners the wealthy Puritan gentry did not concentrate on this aspect to the extent of disregarding all other factors: on the contrary, they generally had no difficulty in reconciling spiritual and worldly considerations. In theory there should have been no social or financial barriers to marriage among those who belonged to the household of faith; in practice this was very far from being the case. Sir William Waller stressed the importance of consorting with the saints since 'the touch of their conversion will derive vertue to thee',[9] but it is significant that all three of his wives had an impeccable upper-class background. In this context at least the Puritan county families were strongly influenced by the social ethos of their class and, perhaps even more important, were usually determined to protect or advance their financial interests. Both wives of

Sir Simonds D'Ewes were heiresses: his first wife had a right of inheritance in an estate worth £500 a year while his second wife came into possession of property worth £1000 a year on the death of her father. During the negotiations which eventually led to the marriage of Lord Mandeville with his only daughter Sir Christopher Yelverton told the Earl of Manchester, the young man's father, that it was 'your piety . . . your owning of the ways of God' which weighed most heavily with him yet this did not prevent him from waging a long campaign over the terms of the financial settlement.[10]

In the years 1630 and 1631 there were protracted negotiations between the Drydens of Canons Ashby, one of the major Puritan families of Northamptonshire, and the Ishams of Lamport, in the same county, over a projected marriage between John Dryden, the grandson of Sir Erasmus Dryden, and Elizabeth Isham, the daughter of Sir John Isham. The Ishams were not so earnest in religion as the Drydens but they were at least a wealthy family who could afford to provide a handsome portion. As a go-between the Drydens employed John Dod, who had once been their minister at Canons Ashby and was now serving another Puritan family, the Knightleys, at Fawsley, though he had never been formally presented to the living.[11] In April 1630 Sir Erasmus Dryden wrote to Sir John Isham that he had heard both from his friend Richard Knightley and from 'our truly reverensed and worthely beloved Mr Dodd' that he was anxious to match his eldest daughter with his own grandson. He also understood, and for this he expressed his thankfulness to God, that it was Sir John's purpose 'to lay a sound foundacion, namely that you will constantly keepe in your howse such a faithfull mynister as they shall like of to instruct and governe your howse'. If Sir John was willing to provide a portion of £4000 he would allow the young couple £300 a year for their maintenance during his own lifetime and settle a jointure worth £400 a year. Later, in September of that year, John Dod informed the father of the intended bride that Sir Erasmus wanted him to make a down-payment of £1000 as soon as agreement had been reached on the marriage articles. Isham, however, was far from satisfied with the offer which had been made and although both John Dryden and his father were strongly in favour of the match they could not persuade Sir Erasmus to adopt a more generous attitude and the negotiations eventually petered out. In December 1631 the young man died unmarried.[12]

Although this particular match was never concluded it was certainly not unknown for Puritan families to intermarry with families which were not of their persuasion. Sir John Holland, whose religious loyalties are on record in his parliamentary speeches,[13] even went so far as to marry a Catholic, Lady Alathea Sandys, the widow of William Lord Sandys, who had been granted a jointure of £600 a year at the time of her previous marriage. As one of their daughters was later to comment, rather tartly, Lady Alathea's wealth 'made her Religion tolerable'; on the other hand, it was a marriage which was to cause Sir John some embarrassment both as a parliamentary candidate and a member of the Long Parliament.[14]

Although the criterion of religious compatibility was sometimes disregarded the fact remains that in the early seventeenth century there was an extensive network of Puritan marriage alliances which transcended county boundaries. The Knightleys of Northamptonshire were related to the Barnardistons of Suffolk, the Hampdens of Buckinghamshire and the Lukes of Bedfordshire; the Barringtons of Essex to the Bourchiers of Yorkshire, the Gerards of Middlesex and the Lyttons of Hertfordshire as well as the Everards and Mashams of their native county. During the 1630s there were some society weddings which had both religious and political significance. Constance and Susanna Fiennes, two of the daughters of William Lord Saye and Sele, became the wives of Francis Boynton, the eldest son of Sir Matthew Boynton, and Thomas Erle, the heir to Sir Walter Erle, while Dorothy Greville, a sister of Robert Lord Brooke, married Sir Arthur Hesilrige who was no doubt responsible for the comment on her tomb that she 'did much good in her generation'. These marriages, which took place in the years 1634 to 1639, cemented relations between families which were heavily involved in Puritan colonisation schemes, which were strongly opposed to the government of Charles I and which in 1642 would take the side of Parliament against the Crown. When Sir Francis Goodwin, another Puritan squire, drew up his will in 1634 he expressed the wish that his grand-daughter Jane (the only child of his son Arthur, the future parliamentarian) should marry a son of Lord Saye and Sele whom he named as an executor; in the event she was married to another Puritan nobleman, Philip Lord Wharton, who in due course inherited the estate.[15]

When discussing the responsibilities of parents the Puritan divines were emphatic that it was one of their primary duties to inculcate in their children, both by their teaching and example, a genuine love of piety and true religion. Parents, stressed William Perkins, must 'endeavour to sowe the seeds of godlinesse and religion in the heart of the child so soone as it comes to the use of reason and understanding'.[16] William Gouge wrote in his treatise *Of Domesticall Duties* that 'Pietie is the best thing that a parent can teach his childe . . . learning, civilitie, calling, portion are all nothing without pietie. . . . Parents, by teaching their children pietie, are an especiall meanes of propagating true religion from age to age and from generation to generation.' Children should be encouraged to read the Bible as soon as possible, should be catechised day by day and should be taught about the mysteries of preaching, baptism, communion, the strict observance of the Sabbath and other elements of religion. When the day of the Gunpowder Plot was solemnised parents should explain the background to their children who should also be instructed, as the occasion arose, about the causes of a great famine or plague and, on the other hand, of the blessings of victory, plenty or peace.[17]

Among the Puritan gentry such advice was generally followed. Sir Simonds D'Ewes, who owned a copy of Gouge's treatise, wrote in his commonplace book that 'Parents are . . . especiallie bound to instruct the children, pray for them and traine them upp in the feare of God because they drew originall corruption from ther loines.'[18] Often the head of the household took a close personal interest in the religious upbringing of his children, explaining to them the meaning of scriptural passages, supervising their reading of spiritual works and regularly catechising them, perhaps with the aid of one of the many Puritan manuals which were produced for this purpose. According to his biographer Sir Nathaniel Barnardiston showed great solicitude for his children's souls 'by a constant and serious study for their Education in the most exact and strict way of pure and paternal Religion, one testimonial of which was his continual bestowing on them spiritual Counsels and gracious Instructions, the grand scope and end of which was to incite and stir them up to a strict watchfulness over themselves and a close walking with God'.[19] In an epistle addressed to his wife and children which appears among his published writings Sir James Harrington refers to his weekly catechising, morning and evening, expounding the scriptures 'and praying with you besides my constant Repetition of Sermons, preparation and particular examination of you on the

Lord's Day, and Monthly Sacraments'. This type of religious instruction, he adds, had been carried on for over twenty years.[20]

While the father often played a part in the religious education of the children it was usually the mother who had the key role. Lady Anne Waller, we are told, was an excellent mother who brought up her children in the nurture and fear of the Lord and walked before them as an example of piety and humility. Every week she catechised both the children and the servants.[21] According to Sir William Springett's wife his mother had a special regard for the well-being of her children both in the inward and the outward condition and took great pains to educate them in the fear of the Lord. She was 'constant in morning and evening prayer by herself and often with her children, causing them to repeat what they remembered of sermons and scripture'. Similarly, Lady Elizabeth Alston is reported to have been a most tender and careful mother who did not consider it sufficient to have given birth to her children, but in the words of St Paul, travailed again with them that Christ might be formed in them.[22]

In contrast, Sir William Drake can have owed very little of his religious zeal to the care and influence of his mother, Joan Drake, who had been married against her will, was the daughter of religious but over-indulgent parents. In 1616 the author of a spiritual treatise called her 'worthy with the worthiest' but for many years she was sunk in a state of deep melancholy in which she believed that 'it was in vaine for her either to use any meanes for salvation or hope for it; and therefore that it was fruitlesse and in vaine for her to heare the word, read, pray and the like.' So strong was this belief that for a time she refused either to go to church or receive communion. Among the ministers who were called in to offer her counsel and encouragement was John Dod who on one occasion stayed for a month. All this effort, however, was ill-rewarded and it was not until the very end of her life that she began to take a more optimistic view of her spiritual condition. In this kind of domestic situation the religious upbringing of the children might easily have been neglected but their father was a godly man and for some years there was a Puritan minister, Thomas Hooker, living in the household.[23]

With the spread of Arminian beliefs both within the Church and the universities it must have seemed to Puritan parents that it was even more important to ensure that their children were introduced to at least the basic elements of Calvinist doctrine as soon as their understanding permitted. No doubt the Barrington family continued to make use of the catechism prepared for them by one of their chaplains, Ezekiel Rogers, which contained a number of references to the elect:

Q. What is the invisible Church?
A. The number of the Elect who have communion together, whether Militant or Triumphant.

Q. How doth Christ govern the visible Church?
A. First, by a generall calling of all. Secondly, by an effectuall calling of the Elect whereby the benefits of his mediation are applied to them.

Q. By what means doth he apply these benefits to the Elect?
A. Ordinarily by the outward preaching of the Law and Gospel and the inward working of the Spirit.[24]

At the funeral of Sir Francis Pile the preacher stressed that he had not only trained up his children

in secular learning and other qualities befitting ther ranke and condition but he was also carefull . . . to have them sanctified and seasoned with the grounds of the Orthodoxe faith professed in our Church (of which himselfe was ever a constant professour) and to avoid the bypathes of that new learning that some have turned aside into.

The year was 1635 and with Archbishop Laud in control of the Church it did not pay to be too outspoken on doctrinal issues but there can be no doubt that the point which the minister was seeking to put across was that Sir Francis had taken special precautions to prevent his children from being infected with Arminian tenets. The indications are that this grounding in Calvinist doctrine proved effective: when the heir, another Sir Francis, drew up his will in 1647 he followed the usual Puritan practice of expressing his conviction that he was numbered among the elect.[25] Religious instruction of this type must have been very common among the Puritan gentry yet not all of them considered it right that their children should be denied the opportunity to make up their own minds on such important matters. Sir Thomas Hutchinson, who had a profound knowledge of school divinity, declined to reveal his personal views on the doctrine of predestination or indeed on any other doctrinal

71

question 'least a father's authority might sway against his children's light who he thought ought to discerne things with their own eies and not with his'. Although his son John eventually became a convinced Calvinist this was not due to any paternal influence but to his own study of school divinity.[26]

In the early seventeenth century there was a wide measure of agreement among Englishmen over the need for firm discipline in the upbringing of children. It was a time when the head of a family had sovereign authority within his own household, when children were expected to be deferential and obedient to their elders at all times and when schoolmasters and even college tutors often felt it necessary to resort to corporal punishment.[27] Among the Puritan divines there was a strong body of opinion in favour of maintaining a strict discipline, primarily for the good of the soul. William Perkins declared that if children did amiss either during their lessons or while at play 'they are to be restrained by the bridle of discipline. First, by reproofe in word, and when that will not helpe, by the rod of correction.' Having made this point he added that the parent must be neither too severe nor too indulgent.[28] In a work which appeared in 1612 John Brinsley, a Puritan schoolmaster at Ashby-de-la-Zouch, assured his readers that the use of physical punishment had divine approval. God had 'sanctified the rod and correction to cure the evils of their conditions, to drive out that folly which is bound up in their hearts, to save their soules from hell and to give them wisdome. . . . To spare them in these cases is to hurt them.' A decade later William Gouge was advising parents in similar terms:

The better and more proper kinde of correction which is by stripes and blowes is also a meanes afforded by God to helpe the good nurture and education of children. . . . Correction is as physicke to purge out much corruption which lurketh in children and is a salve to heale many wounds and sores made by their folly.[29]

Not surprisingly, in view of the importance which they attached to the Ten Commandments, the Puritan gentry considered that children had an essential duty to honour and obey their parents. Adam Winthrop, the father of the first Governor of Massachusetts, made much of this point in some verse which he addressed to his

72

newly born nephew Henry Mildmay, the son of Sir Henry Mildmay of Graces Hall in Essex:

> And to thy mother be deere
> Obedient be and kinde
> Give eare unto her loveing words
> And print them in thy mynde.
>
> Thy father also love
> And willingly obey
> That thou mayst longe possesse those lands
> Which he must leave one daye.[30]

If, however, the need for obedience was regarded as self-evident there seems to have been no unanimity of opinion over the question of what was required or justified in the matter of parental discipline. In his treatise on the duties of a Christian Harbottle Grimston, who in his private life was noted for his kindness and compassion, advised his readers to 'Discipline thy children . . . if thy children and servants offend grievously, correct and chastise them severely.'[31] According to one of his daughters Sir John Holland was an earnest Protestant who was determined to prevent his children from embracing the faith of their Catholic mother. He therefore assumed personal responsibility for their religious education, offering them 'very excellent Maxims', giving them 'very good moral Instructions' and catechising them himself. At the same time he was a severe father and as she was a wayward child he often chastised her: if she failed to learn her catechism he 'debarred me from my Meat, and if I remembered not the Sermons I was made to write them down'.[32] Contrary to what might be expected some of the most zealous Puritan gentlemen were very benevolent fathers. Richard Sibbes said of his friend Sir Thomas Crewe, the Northamptonshire lawyer, that for 'his conversation in his Family, hee was very milde and gentle at all times: not as some who being sweetened with a Fee are wonderfull milde and calme to their Clients but are Lions in their owne Houses; his carriage was not such'.[33] Although Sir Nathaniel Barnardiston took great pains over his children's religious upbringing he was not disposed to follow the advice of Puritan divines like William Gouge. When his children displeased him, we are told, his moderation and wisdom towards them was so great that 'he would never correct them, nay, not so much as reprove them in his displeasure but still waited the most cool and convenient time wherein they seldom discovered that he was angry by any other effect but his silence'.[34] If Sir Robert Harley and his wife Lady Brilliana had what the Puritans termed a well-ordered family it was also a family in which parents and children were closely bound together by bonds of love. In 1650 the heir, Edward Harley, expressed his thankfulness to God that

> my parents were noble, wise and, above all, godly. That they instructed mee in the feare of God and never cockered [indulged] me in any evill but alwaies corrected it. . . . That the Lord gave my parents hearts to give mee liberall education and inclined their affection to be very tender towards me. That my brethren and sisters and I love one another which, oh Lord, he pleased to continue as becomes Christians, specially to watch against the sins of each other.

At Sir Robert's funeral the preacher, who had known him for many years, emphasised that he was both a strict and a kind father: he 'loved his children most tenderly, I think no man in the world carried more of a Father's dearnesse in him that he did; yet he would never bear with any Evill in any of his children: he would often say to them, I desire nothing of you but your love, and that you keep from Sin'.[35]

It was perhaps symptomatic of a changing attitude to children that in the early seventeenth century there was a growing fashion for group portraits depicting noblemen or gentlemen with their whole families. Among those who commissioned such pictures were a number of Puritan squires as, for example, Sir Thomas Burdett and Sir John Curzon of Derbyshire and Sir Matthew Boynton of Yorkshire. Sir John, who had married Patience Crewe, a daughter of Sir Thomas Crewe, is shown holding the hand of one of his children in an attitude of fatherly affection.[36]

As a general rule the intensive schooling in the principles of religion, together with the personal example of the parents, the daily routine of household prayers and the regular exposure to godly preaching, guaranteed the emergence of another pious and sober generation with an authentic Calvinist outlook. A notable example of this process is afforded by a prominent Bedfordshire family, the Burgoynes of Sutton: in 1644 the editor of a spiritual treatise wrote in the epistle dedicatory which was addressed to Sir John Burgoyne that he would find in himself and his family 'a great instance of that truth in this book asserted, I meane a gracious covenant made, and made good in your family, from parents to children, to severall generations'.[37] On the other hand, some young men brought up in Puritan households conducted themselves in a way which made it difficult to believe that, in words used of Sir Nathaniel Barnardiston's children, they were 'approved vessels of grace'.[38] Sir Benjamin Rudyerd had a younger brother who disgraced himself while serving as a captain in the expeditionary party which first established a settlement on Providence Island: in 1632 a report was received by the Providence Island Company that he had been charged with drunkenness, swearing and insubordinate behaviour towards the Governor.[39] During the early part of his life Sir Poynings More failed to live up to the strict moral standards of a family which had long been noted for its zeal in religion. Some time after the death of his father, which occurred in 1626, his mother sent him a letter in which she warned him to beware of the company he kept and in particular of an associate of his who was not

a gentleman borne as your self well knows and therfore no Creddit to make him your compannion. I hear when you fell you were scars sobber which trobuls me much to think that you should live so besly a life that the countrie should take notis of it and so soon to forgeatt thos good instrouctions that your blessed father which is in heaven taught, so praying god to give you his grace to amend your life.

After running into debt More took himself off to France without telling his family of his intentions. In July 1630 Sir Nicholas Carew commented in a letter to his son Francis, who was travelling with him, that the fear had been expressed that as More 'was a companion here in your unthrifty and carelesse courses so likewise he will be there'. Such were the salad days of a man who was the grandson and heir of Sir George More, that powerful advocate of sobriety, and who would later serve as a Presbyterian elder.[40]

According to a Puritan chronicler Sir William Armyne was 'a vigerous Suppresser of vice and debauchery, a Religious Gentleman and one that kept a very well Ordred family'. From the very first he was determined that his son William, the future parliamentarian, should be 'good as well as great' and indeed he took special care over the upbringing of all his children. In 1613 a neighbouring

Puritan minister praised them for their virtue and religion and paid particular tribute to the character of the heir. In the event Sir William the son proved to be a worthy successor to his father while his brother Eure was described as 'a very Religious Gentleman and a Puritan'. The new head of the family approached the task of rearing his own children in the same spirit as his father: he was careful, it was said, 'to maintaine a hopeful nursery of vertue in his children'. His eldest son William, however, does not appear to have gained a great deal of benefit from this schooling. 'At my first coming to him', related Christopher Shute in the sermon preached at his funeral in 1658, 'I found him deeply toucht with a serious apprehension of the former errours of his life, how far he had provoked a good God by the many sins which his Conscience then charged him with.' Full of repentance for his misdeeds, the young man had told him that if God were to grant him a further lease of life 'I would not for the gain of the whole world live such a life as I have done.' In dedicating the printed version of his sermon to Michael Armyne, the deceased's brother, Shute felt obliged to draw his attention to the family motto which can be seen prominently displayed on the monument in Lenton church which the first Sir William had erected in 1605: *Mallem mori, quam foedari* or, as he translated it, 'I had rather die than defile my Name and Honour with Sin.'[41]

While the Puritan divines were insistent that it was primarily the responsibility of the parents to give their children a thorough grounding in religion they also emphasised that it was essential to keep this requirement well in mind when making arrangements for their formal education. 'Let religious schoole-masters be chosen,' exhorted William Gouge who saw it as the duty of schoolmasters and tutors to give instruction in true piety and religion as well as learning, civility and good manners.[42] In the early seventeenth century there was no lack of proficient teachers who in Puritan terms were sound in religion. Many of the public grammar schools were under the control of town corporations, livery companies or members of the local gentry whose preference was for Puritan masters; many private schools were run by Puritan ministers who found it necessary to supplement the income from their livings or who were debarred from performing any ecclesiastical functions because of their reluctance to conform to the orders of the Church; and many Puritan graduates first obtained employment as tutors to the children of noblemen and gentlemen who were well disposed towards men of their persuasion.[43]

The safest course, if the parents could afford it, was to secure the services of a domestic tutor since his activities could be closely supervised and there was less danger of the children being corrupted by outside influences than when they were put out to school. In his report for the year 1639 Laud told the king that in the Diocese of Peterborough (which embraced the counties of Northamptonshire and Rutland) some knights and esquires 'keepe Schoole-masters in theyr houses or Schollers to converse with' and there is also evidence of this practice in East Anglia: indeed Stephen Marshall, that great Puritan firebrand, had once been a private tutor to a gentleman in Suffolk.[44] When Edward Hartopp, the son of Sir Edward Hartopp of Leicestershire, was admitted to Christ's College, Cambridge in 1624 it was noted in the register that he had previously been educated at home under Mr Valentine. Henry Valentine, who was a graduate of the same college, was later to become a lecturer in the City of London and, in 1630, rector of Deptford in Kent. In 1634 his views were sought on the character of his former pupil who was then being considered as a possible husband for Mary Coke, a daughter of Sir John Coke, one of the Principal Secretaries of State. In what was described as 'a singular good report' Valentine testified that Edward had loved both his studies and a country life, took no interest in gaming, seldom drank any wine and while under his tuition had avoided strong beer.[45]

In the latter part of 1631 Sir Robert Harley was looking for a competent teacher with the right kind of religious background who would be willing to come and live at his Herefordshire mansion, Brampton Castle, and serve as tutor to his children. In October Thomas Pierson, the Puritan minister of Brampton Bryan, wrote to Sir Robert, who was then in London:

And for a schoolmaster to your children, till you can light on one to your content, I thinke (if you lyke to have our new clerke Wilcocks imployed that way) that Mr Froyzell[46] and my self affording some certayne hours each day, to take notice and accompt of their performing, may for a tyme serve the turne.

The following month Sir Robert asked Thomas Hill, one of the Puritan fellows of Emmanuel College, Cambridge, whether he could reommend a good scholar to instruct his children, making it clear that he would prefer someone 'in whose socyetie I may have cause to reioyce and make to my selfe some advantage'. As for his terms of employment he was prepared to deal generously with him: he would be provided with his board and lodging at Brampton Castle 'and I shall hardly deny him the exhibition that you shall reasonably propose'. At the same time, he told him, the company of worthy Mr Pierson would be 'able to supply more defects than I hope he will find in that place'. Sir Robert's papers do not reveal whether his quest met with immediate success but what we do know is that his eldest son Edward went to school at Shrewsbury and Gloucester and that in 1636 a resident schoolmaster was being employed at Brampton Castle. Subsequently Richard Symonds, a minister who had been suspended for nonconformity, joined the household as tutor to the two youngest sons, Robert and Thomas, and we also hear of another Puritan divine, Richard Blinman, who deputised for him when he was ill. In the event the appointment of Symonds proved to be a major blunder: his views on religion were in many ways too extreme for Lady Harley who became increasingly concerned at the influence which he was exercising over the minds of her children. Eventually the situation reached breaking-point and in November 1639 we find her writing to her son Edward, who by then was a student at Oxford: 'I have not hard of anny yet to supply Mr Simmons place in teacheing scoule. I am halfe of an opinion to put your brothers out to scoule. They continue still stife in theare opinions; and in my aprehention upon smale ground.' Later that month she asked him to see whether his tutor could recommend a good schoolmaster and on 6 December she wrote that Mr Symonds 'makes hast away; they grow deeper and deeper in theare opinions so that he now thinkes it is not fite to ioyne with us in the publicke fast.' Clearly there were risks involved even when the children were committed to the care of a domestic tutor.[47]

In Essex there were a number of private schools which had special appeal for Puritan families, though some were relatively short-lived. Sir Thomas Barrington sent his sons John and Oliver to live as boarders with Samuel Collins, the vicar of Braintree, who would subsequently be described as one of those ministers 'whose Names God had made precious among his Saints'. During the course of his long ministry, we are told, he normally preached three times a week and was responsible for laying 'the foundations of Religion and godliness' among the people of Braintree. The patron of the living was Robert Earl of Warwick, the lord lieutenant of the county, who was a great favourer of Puritan divines and a man whose friendship was highly prized by the Barrington family.[48] In the accounts of Sir Thomas Pelham, the Sussex baronet, for the years 1636 to 1640 there are references to payments made to Mr Clutterbuck and Mr Hampden for the board and schooling of his son John. The former was Samuel Clutterbuck, the rector of Dinton in Buckinghamshire who had once been a fellow of Magdalen College, Oxford. According to a contemporary account he was a diligent Bible scholar, an accomplished preacher and a man of true piety whose religious conversation made his house a temple and his family a church. He was also so skilful in teaching children the grounds of literature that 'he did oblige some of the best Families in the Nation by that troublesome Employment'. The latter was John Hampden, now becoming a national figure, whose mother had presented Clutterbuck to the living. In 1639 Sir Thomas paid a visit to Great Hampden where he was no doubt involved in some interesting discussions about the current political situation. Significantly, John Hampden's heir and Thomas Clutterbuck, the minister's son, were both admitted to Emmanuel College, Cambridge, in the autumn of 1639 and John Pelham followed them there in 1640.[49]

Sir Simonds D'Ewes relates in his autobiography that he had been educated at a number of schools in Dorset, London and Suffolk. In the years 1615 and 1616 he was under the tuition of a London schoolmaster, Henry Reynolds, who ran a private establishment in the parish of St Mary Axe. Here D'Ewes studied, among other things, Latin, Greek and French and also began to take a serious interest in godly preaching. The first school in Suffolk which he attended was at Lavenham where one of his fellow pupils was Giles Barnardiston, a younger brother of Sir Nathaniel Barnardiston. Later on it was agreed, at his own entreaty, that he should go to the public grammar school at Bury St Edmunds where some years previously Richard Sibbes and Sir Edward Peyton had both been scholars. This decision owed much to the reputation of the headmaster, John Dickenson, whom he describes as 'an excellent and mild teacher', though there was also the consideration that the school was only a few miles from his father's country seat. D'Ewes remained at Bury until his admission to Cambridge and clearly found it a rewarding experience both in a scholastic and a religious sense: 'for my encrease in the knowledge of divine truths and my practice of pietie it was little inferior during my stay heere to my progresse in learning.'[50]

If the Puritans had ever compiled a directory of public grammar schools which could be recommended to godly parents they would no doubt have included such names as Northwich in Cheshire, Beverley and Hull in the East Riding of Yorkshire, Doncaster and Sheffield in the West Riding, Repton in Derbyshire, Lincoln and Boston in Lincolnshire, Oakham and Uppingham in Rutland, Northampton and Oundle in Northamptonshire, Felsted in Essex, Gloucester, and Dorchester and Blandford in Dorset. The free schools of Oakham and Uppingham had been founded by Robert Johnson, a minister with nonconformist leanings who had at one time been chaplain to Sir Nicholas Bacon, Elizabeth's Lord Keeper and a leading authority in the field of education. When drawing up the statutes for these schools Johnson had included the provision that the masters should be 'painful in the educating of children in good learning and religion' and it is significant that Oakham School had a succession of Puritan masters, men such as James Wadeson, John Wallace and Jeremy Whitaker. Among the local gentry who were closely associated with this school were the Harringtons of Ridlington, a family which was very forward in religion; when the foundation charter was granted in 1587 Sir James Harrington was named as one of the governors along with other members of the family. In view of the great care which he took over the religious upbringing of his children it seems entirely appropriate that Sir William Armyne, who lived in the neighbouring county of Lincolnshire, should have sent both his sons to the school. In August 1607 James Wadeson told him that his son William was full of gratitude to him for his bounty and favours and above all for the way in which he had raised him. In a further letter Wadeson expressed the hope that he would be able to take on responsibility for the tuition of his other son Eure when he had completed his studies under Hugh Tuke, the nonconformist minister of Silk Willoughby, a Lincolnshire living which was in Sir William's gift. Eure did eventually become a boarder at Oakham School but only after John Wallace was appointed master in 1612.[51] John Seaton, who served as usher under Jeremy Whitaker, subsequently taught at Felsted School in Essex and in 1630 was described as 'a bold boy and unlicensed'. At this time the headmaster of Felsted School was Martin Holbeach, a man with pronounced Puritan sympathies

who had been nominated by the Earl of Warwick on the recommen-
dation of John Preston. Such was the reputation of the school while
Holbeach was in charge that it attracted scholars from a very wide
area. Four sons of Oliver Cromwell were educated there, as was
Henry Mildmay, the son of Sir Henry Mildmay of Graces Hall in
Essex, who was to show great zeal for the cause of Parliament. Sir
John Bramston, the ship-money judge, writes that Mildmay 'was
bred a Puritan in blood and education too. . . . He was bred under
Holebech, scholemaster of Felstead, whoe scarce bred any man that
was loyal to his prince.'[52]

Taken as a whole, the Puritan country squires displayed no
marked preference as between private schooling and the public
grammar schools, though they were much more likely to board out
their sons than keep them at home. Whatever the form of schooling
they were usually careful to choose schoolmasters whose religious
sympathies were basically in accord with their own. Since a schoolmaster required a licence from the diocesan authorities and was
liable to come under scrutiny during an ecclesiastical visitation
there was a danger that with Laud in control of the Church their
range of choice might be severely curtailed. In his account of the
metropolitical visitation of 1635 Sir Nathaniel Brent, Laud's Vicar-
General, recorded that he had given Samuel Cobb, the master
of Oundle School who had a considerable reputation among the
Northamptonshire gentry, a canonical admonition for instructing
his children out of a wrong catechism and expounding the Ten
Commandments to them out of the writings of a silenced minister
who may be identified as John Dod. At Gloucester Sir Nathaniel
called before him John Langley, the master of the college school,
who was 'a very good Schoolemaster but thought to be puritanicall';
a determined nonconformist, Langley found himself under suspension and apparently relinquished his appointment.[53] In the Diocese
of Norwich Bishop Wren noted on one occasion that a schoolmaster
was employing a catechism compiled by Dr John Mayer, a Suffolk
minister who enjoyed the patronage of Maurice Barrow, the most
substantial Puritan squire in the county.[54] In some parishes the
deprivation of a nonconformist minister involved the loss not only
of a diligent preacher but of a competent schoolmaster so that the
local Puritans in particular sustained a double blow. Nevertheless,
when everything has been said, the impact of Laudianism was no
more than marginal. For the most part the Puritan gentry seem to

have had little difficulty in securing for their children the kind of schooling which satisfied their religious as well as their academic requirements.

CHAPTER FIVE

THE PURITAN UNDERGRADUATE

During the early seventeenth century the state of the English universities[1] was causing some concern among the propertied classes and
not least in those sections where godliness had taken root. In the
first place, there was a feeling that inadequate discipline was helping
to promote a general laxity of morals. Thomas Hobbes comments
that he had often heard parents complaining that during their time
at university their children had been initiated into such vices as
drunkenness, wantonness and gaming. Sir Simonds D'Ewes, who
was a student at St John's College, Cambridge in the years 1618
to 1620, writes that 'the maine thing which made mee even wearie
of the Colledge was that swearing, drinking, rioting and hatred of
all vertue and pietie under false and adulterate nicknames did
abound ther and generallie in all the universitie.' When Sir Nicholas
Martyn was an undergraduate at Oxford in the reign of James I
his father warned him to be careful in his choice of companions, to
avoid at all costs the evils of drunkenness, lust and gaming and to
refrain from indulging in lascivious, light and wanton speech. It
should be 'your chiefest study and your daily practice,' he told him,
'First of all to serve God, then to feare him and (in fearing of him)
to abhor sinne as the greatest enemy to vertue and the death of
your immortall soule'. Ironically, it was Laud who was responsible
for the most systematic and thoroughgoing attempt to tighten up
discipline at Oxford and curb the excesses of the student body:
writing of his admission to Balliol in 1637 John Evelyn remarks
that the university was then exceedingly regular under the exact
discipline of Archbishop Laud.[2] Secondly, there was the tendency

for more and more colleges to fall under the control of men who
were hostile to the Calvinist dogma which had long held sway in
both universities and who in some cases introduced more elaborate
ceremonial and furnishings into their college chapels. At Oxford
these developments, which the Puritans were apt to describe collec-
tively (but imprecisely) as the growth of Arminianism, owed much
to the driving force of Laud, first as Master of St John's College
and later, from 1629 onwards, as Chancellor of the university.
During the reign of Charles I many of the Oxford colleges were
governed by Laudian divines, men like Accepted Frewen of
Magdalen College, Richard Baylie of St John's, Christopher Potter
of Queen's and Thomas Jackson of Corpus Christi. The Arminians,
declared William Prynne, grew very numerous at Oxford and only
John Prideaux, the Rector of Exeter College, and a few others dared
oppose them.[3] At Cambridge there was a similar trend in evidence
though Laud's influence was not so strong here as it was at Oxford.
Sir Simonds D'Ewes relates that during his undergraduate days no
Anabaptist (by which he meant Arminian) or Pelagian heresies
'weere then stirring but the Truth was in all publike sermons and
Divinitie acts asserted and maintained. None then dared to committ
idolatrie by bowing to or towards or adoring the altar, the communion table or the bread and wine in the sacrament of the Lordes
supper.' In February 1624, however, he noted in his diary that he
had heard a very bad sermon savouring of Arminianism, 'a verie
dangerous heresie, being but refined pelagianisme or rather revised,
which was first broached in the Low Countries and had now of late
spread exceedinglie in Cambridge and in most partes of England'.[4]
From the Puritan standpoint the situation deteriorated rapidly over
the next decade. Writing about Cambridge in the 1630s William
Prynne lists a number of heads of colleges who in his estimation
were professed Arminians and creatures of Laud: these include
Samuel Brooke of Trinity, William Beale of St John's, Edward
Martin of Queens' and John Cosin of Peterhouse. In the autumn
of 1636 Laud received a report on the college chapels in which St
John's, Queens', Peterhouse, Pembroke and Jesus were particularly
commended: 'they endeavor for order', it was noted, 'and have
brought it to some good passe.'[5] In spite of its successes, however,
the Laudian party never achieved the commanding position which
it enjoyed at Oxford and during the early seventeenth century

Cambridge was generally considered to be the more Puritan of the two universities.

At this time geography played a major part in determining where a young man received his university education. Apart from the fact that for most inhabitants of England one university was more accessible than the other there were a number of colleges at both Oxford and Cambridge which had special links with particular regions or even with particular schools.[6] Sometimes the choice of college was attributable to a family association; sometimes it was the academic reputation of a college head or one of the fellows which carried most weight. For the Puritan gentry, however, there was the additional factor that in the early Stuart period, and particularly in the reign of Charles I, it was becoming more difficult to find colleges which satisfied their requirements in terms of doctrine and worship. In these circumstances they often switched their allegiance from one college to another, though only occasionally was there a transfer of loyalty from Oxford to Cambridge.

During the reign of Elizabeth the most important centre of Puritanism in the university of Oxford was Magdalen College which mainly owed its reputation to Laurence Humphrey, a former Marian exile who held the office of President from 1560 to 1589. Humphrey was not only a leading Calvinist theologian who wielded great influence within the university but, in the words of Thomas Fuller, 'a conscientious and moderate Non-conformist'. In all probability he had made a profound impression on such men as Sir Erasmus Dryden, a major figure among the Northamptonshire Puritans, and Sir Ralph Winwood, one of James I's Secretaries of State and a religious zealot, who in their younger days had been closely associated with him as fellows of the college.[7]

Peter Heylyn, the Laudian divine, observes that Humphrey stocked the college with 'such a generation of Non-conformists as could not be wormed out in many years after his decease.' In the reign of James I there were still a considerable number of fellows who shared his religious outlook, among them Richard Capel who 'was resorted to by noted men, especially of the Calvinian party', and had many pupils under his care, and Thomas Bayley, a man 'zealously inclin'd to the puritanical party'.[8] Because of this the college retained its popularity with the Puritan gentry virtually until the accession of Charles I. The parliamentarian squires who had studied there had been drawn from various parts of the country:

they included Sir Richard Ingoldsby, Arthur Goodwin and John Hampden of Buckinghamshire, Sir John Curzon and Sir John Gell of Derbyshire, Sir William Masham of Essex, Sir Robert Cooke of Gloucestershire and John Crewe of Northamptonshire.[9]

During his time at the college Richard Ingoldsby presented his Puritan father with an account which he had prepared of the lives and sayings of the ancient philosophers, 'collected out of sundrie authors, as well Latin as English, at idle night-houres'. To judge from the epistle dedicatory which he prefixed to this essay he was a serious-minded youth who was determined not to squander the opportunity he had been given. Having been placed in a learned university, he told his father, 'I account my selfe in the schoole of wisdome where not to gaine wisdome is to reape follie and whence yf I returne not better I shall shurelie worse, with losse of my time and your hopes.' The work which he was offering for his consideration had been undertaken in order that 'I might seeme to bestow my time and not to spend it, to use good houres in laudable actions and not to abuse your great cost to litle purpose.[10]

Robert Cooke was a contemporary of John Hampden and Arthur Goodwin at the college and like them contributed to a book of commemorative verse which was produced in 1612 following the death of Prince Henry who had been highly esteemed in Puritan circles. His father, Sir William Cooke, placed him under the care of Thomas Bayley and appears to have been well satisfied with the tuition which he received. When Thomas Gataker, who had once served as Sir William's chaplain, published *The Spirituall Watch* in 1619 he recalled in the dedication which he addressed to Robert Cooke that his late father had settled near him his former tutor, whom he described as a man of singular parts, and expressed his confidence that he would continue to perform the role of counsellor: through his advice and assistance he would have 'plentifull meanes of furtherance in that godly course that by God's gratious goodnes you have already made entrance unto.'[11] Bayley was one of a number of Magdalen fellows who obtained preferment from wealthy Puritans. Robert Barnes was instituted in 1612 to two livings, Rotherfield Greys in Oxfordshire and Silchester in Hampshire; in 1626 he recalled that in the latter case his benefactors had been 'those blessed servants of God' Mr Edmund Dunch, a Berkshire squire who had once been a student at the college, and 'his religious daughter in law, the Lady Mary Dunch, now both with the Lord'.

William Langton, who was a notable preacher, became chaplain to Sir Ralph Winwood when he was sent as ambassador to the Low Countries. Richard Capel returned to his native county of Gloucestershire where Nathaniel Stephens presented him to the rectory of Eastington. Here his preaching earned him great popularity: 'He could be a Boanerges,' wrote his friend Valentine Marshall, 'but his bent was most to be a Son of Consolation.'[12]

With the election of Accepted Frewen, once a pupil of Richard Capel but now a disciple of Laud, as President of Magdalen College in 1626 the final curtain came down on the long history of the college as a Puritan academy. At Magdalen Hall, on the other hand, there was a very different situation which was largely due to the influence and authority of a man who had begun his academic career as a fellow of Magdalen College. John Wilkinson, a Yorkshireman who held the office of Principal during the years 1609 to 1643,[13] was a staunch Calvinist whose relations with Laud were less than cordial. In his account of the college Anthony Wood writes that under his government in 1624 or before there were '300 Students in this Hall, of which number were 40 (or more) Masters of Arts, but all mostly inclining to Calvinism'.[14] Among the Magdalen Hall tutors there were many Puritans, men such as William Pemble, Thomas Ford, John Oxenbridge, John Tombes, Henry Wilkinson, who was styled 'Long Harry' to distinguish him from another tutor of the same name, and Edward Perkins. William Pemble, who is described by Anthony Wood as an expert mathematician and a skilful linguist as well as a zealous Calvinist, delivered a series of lectures in which he mounted a powerful attack on Arminian theology. In 1623 he died at Eastington while staying with Richard Capel, who had been his tutor at Magdalen College, and four years later Capel published these lectures, emphasising on the title-page that in them 'the maine sinews of ARMINIUS doctrine are cut asunder.' In 1640 Henry Wilkinson condemned some of the Church's ceremonial requirements in what Sir Simonds D'Ewes describes as an honest sermon and in consequence the Vice-Chancellor forbade him to exercise his priestly function within the university and its precincts; before the end of the year, however, the House of Commons decided that his suspension should be lifted.[15]

John Oxenbridge found himself in trouble with the university authorities for requiring some of his students to sign an undertaking to submit to his government not only in their academic work but in such matters as hair, clothes, recreation and the performance of religious duties. So far as religion was concerned they promised 'To read a certaine portion of Scripture, seconding it at least twice every day by Prayer' and 'To take the Heads of Sermons and repeat them when and where you please'. In answer to the interrogatories which were administered to him he listed the books which he normally prescribed for the study of religion. These largely consisted of works by Puritan authors: the *Seven Treatises* of Richard Rogers, John Ball's *A Short Catechisme* and tracts written by William Bradshaw and William Pemble which may be identified, respectively, as *A Proposition Concerning Kneeling in the Very Act of Receiving* and *An Introduction to the Worthy Receiving the Sacrament*. He had also set his students the task of translating and analysing Calvin's *Institutes* but this had proved too difficult for them; consequently he had recently discontinued this particular exercise. As regards other types of literature he had not discouraged them from reading any authors 'unlesse such as tende to lasciviousnesse or Atheisme, such indeed I have taken from them'.[16]

In the reign of Charles I Magdalen Hall appears to have been almost as highly regarded in Puritan circles as Magdalen College had formerly been. Some gentlemen like Sir Richard Ingoldsby, Sir John Gell and Sir Robert Cooke who had been undergraduates at Magdalen College preferred to send their sons to Magdalen Hall and others who had sons there included Sir Walter Erle, Sir Robert Harley and Sir John Wray.[17] Sir Robert Harley, who had himself been educated at Oriel College, may possibly have decided in favour of Magdalen Hall on the advice of his friend John Tombes who in 1630 had become vicar of Leominster in Herefordshire. In the summer of 1638 he asked another of his Puritan friends, John Workman, once a lecturer but now a schoolmaster, to make some inquiries about the character of Henry Wilkinson and Edward Perkins. In reply Workman told him that he had been informed that 'they were both honest men and good tutors as the times goe.' He also reported that there was another Henry Wilkinson, a nephew of the Principal, who had just been made a Master of Arts and intended to become a tutor. The young man had once lodged with him and during that time had shown himself to be very studious and religious. In the event Sir Robert arranged for his eldest son to be placed with Edward Perkins, a 'very ready and well study'd

Divine, especially in School-Divinity' who had a marked aversion
to episcopal government. The relationship between tutor and pupil
appears to have been a happy and productive one: in November
1638 Edward Harley's mother informed him that she counted it a
great blessing that 'your worthy tutor gives so good a testimony of
you and that you esteme him so highly.'[18]

About the time of Edward's departure for Oxford Lady Harley
presented him with a memorandum of advice in which she coun-
selled him to live a holy life and choose his companions accordingly:

> Nowe I feare you will both see And heare Men of Nobillity
> and of Excelent parts of nature Abandon Themself to swereing
> and that odious sin of Drunckenness and To scorne at Religion
> ... take heede of Theaire temtations and suttelty. Be not
> provocked to sweare: Remember it is A grevious sinne. The
> Command we have from the Lord is sweare not at all.

At the same time he should also avoid the pernicious sin of drunkenness which was the sin of the age, for as St Paul had said, no
drunkard would enter into the kingdom of heaven.[19] During his
time at the college he continued to receive an abundance of moral
advice both from his mother and from Stanley Gower, the minister
at Brampton Bryan. On one occasion Gower warned him that he
was among people who were skilful in dressing up vice as virtue
and advised him to emulate the saints of old. He went on to say
that it was gratifying to hear of his rejection of academic vanities
and added, 'you have some good helpes from your tutor and some
private Christians.' Perkins himself took a close personal interest in
his spiritual progress. In a letter which he wrote to him while
staying at Reading he exhorted him 'to keepe closse to your God
especially in the private intercourse with him and even in these
declining dais to improve your interest you have in him; it will
stand you in stead when all the world will prove but vanitie and
vexation'. In December 1640 he was again pursuing this theme:
'my soule longs after the prosperity of your soule and I know you
would be found not onely to have a name but to live the life of
Godlinesse. Sweet Sir, increase your Communion with God ... doe
what you can to improve your time every way.' In common with
John Oxenbridge's students Edward Harley does not seem to have
read any of Calvin's works until he became an undergraduate,
though in fact there was an English translation of the *Institutes*

available. In January 1639 his mother wrote to him: 'I beleeve, before this, you have read some part of Mr Calvin; send me word how you like him.'[20]

In accordance with the advice which he had received Edward Harley was very particular in his choice of companions. One of his closest friends at the college was Michael Broughton who wrote to him in May 1639:

> May your inner man bee soe replenisht and fortifyed with spirituall graces, that impenetrable armour of the true regenerate, that it may bee surrounded with as much difficulty of surprising, by any of our capitall Antagonists, as the City of the Anakims by the faynt assault of the naked Israelites . . . may yow take direction from God and resolution from him, proceeding to leade on others your subsequents the neerest way to perfection. All which shall adde to the immortall honour of your thrice renowned Parents, the lasting creditt of our amiable and endeared Tutor and the unspeakeable comfort and joy of your deerest intimats.

In 1650 Harley would record his gratitude to God for ensuring that he remained uncontaminated by the evils of Oxford.[21]

One of the Oxford colleges with strong regional links was Exeter, which primarily served the needs of the West Country. Sir Anthony Ashley Cooper, who was admitted to the college in 1637, comments that it was famous for the courage and strength of the tall raw-boned Cornish and Devonshire gentlemen who flocked there in great numbers.[22] Between 1592 and 1641 Exeter was governed in turn by two distinguished Calvinist divines who were noted not only for their learning but for their insistence on strict discipline. Thomas Holland, who was a member of the committee which produced the Authorised Version of the Bible, was 'a man mighty in the Scriptures . . . a faithful Preacher of the Truth and one that adorned it by his holy life and conversation; a zealous defender of the true Religion and a great hater of superstition and Idolatry'.[23] John Prideaux, who succeeded him in 1612, was determined that whatever fate might befall the other Oxford colleges his own college should not surrender to the forces of Arminianism: in the words of Peter Heylyn he was 'a vehement assertor of all the Calvinian Rigours in the matter of Predestination and the Points depending thereupon'. On the other hand, his attitude to the Sabbath was by no means as austere as the doctrine which had been propounded by such men as Greenham and Bownd. In a lecture delivered in 1622 he maintained that works of necessity and charity could legitimately be performed on the Lord's Day and that there was also nothing wrong in engaging in those forms of recreation which served lawfully 'to refresh our spirits and nourish mutuall neighbourhood amongst us'. Shortly after Charles I issued his Declaration of Sports Heylyn took obvious delight in publishing an English translation of the lecture, which had originally been in Latin, for what he termed 'the benefit of the common people'.[24]

While Prideaux was in charge of its fortunes the college had a considerable number of Puritan fellows, among them George Kendal, John Conant and his nephew of the same name, Matthias Styles, William Hodges, Robert Snow and Henry Tozer. William Hodges found himself involved in disciplinary proceedings for attacking Arminianism in his public preaching and on this occasion Prideaux was himself reprimanded for encouraging dissent.[25] Henry Tozer was a strict Puritan who revealed himself as such not only in his sermons, which were very popular among the godly of Oxford, but in his appearance and daily living. Some idea of the kind of influence which he exercised over his pupils may be gained from his *Directions for a Godly Life*, a work which was first published in 1628 and subsequently went through a number of editions. There were some persons, he lamented, who preferred to read 'vain and idle discourses which are so farre from furthering us in the way of Salvation as that (like Tares) they choak the Word of God and hinder the growth thereof'. In conversation it was necessary to follow the counsels of St Paul to the Ephesians 'that we avoid in our talk all filthiness, all foolish talking and jestings which are not convenient'. Such evils as idleness, lasciviousness, drunkenness and gaming must be eschewed at all costs. It was better to be considered precise, he told his readers, than to offend a righteous God 'and though others account it too much preciseness yet do thou not so'.[26] John Conant the younger, who became a fellow in 1633, believed that his first duty was to plant the fear of God in the undergraduates (many of them from the best families in Devon) who were placed under his care. When he took up office as Rector of the college in 1649 he made it his business, we are told, to restore that ancient and wholesome discipline for which it had been so famous under Dr Holland and Dr Prideaux.[27]

Since Devon was one of the most Puritan counties in England it is not surprising that many of the gentry who lived there were educated at a college which not only had strong West Country connections but offered some degree of assurance that its students would return home sober and godly young men who were fortified in their Calvinist beliefs. Four of the richest Puritan landowners in the county – Sir Francis Drake, who was a nephew of the great sea captain, Sir John Davie, Sir Samuel Rolle and John Bampfield – had been contemporaries at the college in the early years of James I's reign while Sir John Northcote and Sir John Yonge had been students under Dr Prideaux.[28] With so many Devonshire gentlemen attending the same college and coming into contact with the same kind of religious and moral influences it was perhaps inevitable that a certain uniformity of outlook should develop among the ruling families of the county. At the same time this process was assisted by the frequent intermarrying which took place.

Besides Exeter College and Magdalen Hall there were several other colleges which offered Laud little grounds for satisfaction, in particular Brasenose under Samuel Radcliffe, Lincoln under Paul Hood and New Inn Hall under Christopher Rogers.[29] Brasenose had special links with Cheshire and Lancashire but also drew students from other parts of the kingdom. Many Puritan gentry were educated there, among them Sir Francis Nichols, who eventually became the patron of his tutor Robert Bolton; Sir William Brereton, who was said to have 'seen more of God' than any of the other parliamentary commanders in the Civil War; and Richard Norton, a Hampshire squire who declined to receive communion in a kneeling position.[30] One of the fellows of Lincoln College, Thomas Knightley, was a nephew of Sir Richard Knightley, that great patron of Northamptonshire Puritanism. He acted as tutor to John and Richard Eliot, the sons of Sir John Eliot, and it was no doubt because of him that such Northamptonshire gentlemen as Sir John Dryden, Sir Francis Nichols and Richard Knightley sent their sons to the college.[31]

At Cambridge the two Elizabethan foundations of Emmanuel and Sidney Sussex retained their popularity with English Puritans throughout the early Stuart period. The first Master of Emmanuel College, 'that happy Seminary both of Piety and Learning',[32] was Laurence Chaderton who was one of the most respected Puritan figures in the university. Anxious to forestall the possibility of the college falling under Arminian control, he resigned in 1622 in order to make way for John Preston who was elected in conditions of great secrecy. This change of Master, declared William Bedell, once a fellow of the college, in a letter written at Bury St Edmunds, 'was altogether unexpected in these parts: whereof I doubt not but there were some secret motives and perhaps conditions more then the world knowes of'. Ironically, Preston was soon engaged in a quarrel with the fellows over their privileges.[33] During Chaderton's lifetime there were two other Masters, William Sandcroft and Richard Holdsworth, whose succession ensured that the college maintained its reputation as the foremost Puritan academy in England. From the outset it was always well stocked with Puritan fellows, men such as Samuel Ward, John Cotton, John Stoughton, Thomas Hooker, Anthony Tuckney, Thomas Hill, Thomas Ball, Anthony Burgess and Samuel Bowles.[34] In the preface to one of his biographical works Samuel Clark tells us that at Cambridge he studied under Thomas Hooker of Emmanuel 'which was the Puritan Colledge, and Mr Hooker one of the choicest Tutors in the University'. Some years later Hooker opened a school in the Essex village of Little Baddow where the local magnate was Sir Henry Mildmay of Graces Hall, a benefactor of the college.[35] When Anthony Tuckney delivered the sermon at the funeral of his friend Thomas Hill in 1653 he testified that he had been a diligent and successful tutor of very many pupils 'and divers of them of quality who have proved great blessings both in Church and Commonwealth'. Like his colleagues he was an exponent of Calvinist doctrine: in Tuckney's words he firmly adhered to 'the good old doctrine of the Church of England, that which in this our University our famous Whitaker, Perkins, Davenant, Ward and others maintained in their times'.[36]

Under Chaderton's government the services in the college chapel brought the students into contact with a thoroughgoing Puritan form of worship. In 1603 it was reported that at Emmanuel 'they do follow a private course of publick prayer after their own fashion' and received the sacraments 'sitting upon Forms about the Communion Table and doe pull the loafe one from the other'.[37] No doubt as a result of this report Chaderton found himself under pressure to bring the college into a state of conformity and in December 1604 he assured the Vice-Chancellor that the fellows and scholars now used the communion book daily, received the bread and wine in a kneeling position and also wore surplices in accordance with the statutes of the university.[38] To judge from later evidence, however, the college continued to engage in public worship in its own way.

Unlike many of the Cambridge colleges Emmanuel had no strong links with any particular region; indeed it was expressly laid down in the foundation charter that the college should not have two or more fellows from the same county at any one time.[39] Students who came to the college were drawn from a wide range of counties. Among the wealthy Puritans who had been undergraduates during Chaderton's reign there were such men as Sir Edward Rodes of Yorkshire, Sir Anthony Irby of Lincolnshire, Sir Francis Thornhagh of Nottinghamshire, Sir John Burgoyne and Onslow Winch of Bedfordshire, Sir William Lytton of Hertfordshire, Sir Robert Brooke and John Gurdon of Suffolk, Sir Henry Mildmay (the Master of the Jewel House) and Harbottle Grimston of Essex, Sir Samuel Owfield of Surrey and Sir Thomas Pelham of Sussex.[40] Sir Robert Brooke had been admitted in the year of the Armada, four years after the foundation of the college, and could therefore claim to have been one of Chaderton's earliest pupils. Many years later he appointed John King, a graduate of Emmanuel, as his household chaplain. Sir Henry Mildmay was a grandson of the founder, Sir Walter Mildmay, and a friend of Joseph Hall, the Calvinist divine, who had once been a fellow of the college. As one of the founder's kin he took a close interest in the fortunes of the college and seems to have been regarded as a zealous and understanding patron by those who were anxious that its Puritan character should be preserved. When the rectory of Wanstead fell vacant he presented Humphrey Maddison, 'an able godly preaching minister', who had been a contemporary of his at Emmanuel.[41] Sir Anthony Irby, who had a succession of Puritan chaplains in his household, belonged to a family which had strong connections with, and often resided in, the Lincolnshire town of Boston. His admission to the college in 1620 may have owed something to the influence of John Cotton who in 1612 had left Cambridge to become vicar of Boston. Subsequently Cotton wrote that 'There were some scores of godly persons in Boston . . . who can witnesse that we entered into a Covenant with the Lord, and one with another, to follow after the Lord in the purity of his Worship' and it seems likely that the Irbys were members of what was in effect a congregation within a congregation.[42] John Gurdon, who would later be described as 'an honest religious Gentleman, but a Presbyterian throughout',[43] was the eldest of four sons of Brampton Gurdon who were admitted to the college between 1611 and 1619. His brother William died in 1620 while in residence there and in the best Puritan tradition it was thought fitting to record the final hours of this 'most hopefull young gentleman'. The night before his death, it was recounted, he 'intreated his Tutor (as he had often done before) to pray with him' and praised God for the assurance he had received that his sins would be pardoned.[44]

As a fellow of Queens' College John Preston had been inclined, when choosing his pupils, to display a preference for the heirs to great estates. Sir Christopher Yelverton and Sir William Roberts had both been favoured in this way and indeed the latter was one of the students who went with Preston when he became Master of Emmanuel in 1622. Among the young men who were admitted to Emmanuel we find Gilbert Pickering, the son of Sir John Pickering; Philip Wodehouse, the son of Sir Thomas Wodehouse; and Richard Roberts, a younger brother of Sir William Roberts, who subsequently entered the ministry and was ejected in 1662 for nonconformity. When Sir John Pickering made his will in 1627 he committed the education of his son to the 'religious care' of his wife and it may be inferred from this that he was anxious to ensure that Gilbert completed his studies at Emmanuel where he was under the direct tuition of the Master. A few years later, in July 1633, one of the Emmānuel fellows, Thomas Hill, was presented to the Northamptonshire living of Titchmarsh which was in the gift of the Pickering family.[45]

Following Preston's death in July 1628 Nathaniel Ward, a Puritan divine who was a graduate of Emmanuel, wrote to William Sandcroft in an attempt to persuade him to stand for election as the next Master. 'It is meete', he told him, 'that some who are able and called thereto should stepp forth and arme themselves with an holy forwardness' in order to frustrate the designs of Satan's instruments. And he went on, 'I coulde wish Sir Henry Mildmay . . . were well possessed of the matter and requested to stand closse freind to the Colledge in promoting and securing their proceedings.'[46] Sandcroft was duly elected and under his government the college retained its traditional character. In September 1636 Laud was informed that at Emmanuel their Chappell is not consecrate ... they sing nothing but certain riming psalms of their owne appointment instead of the Hymnes between the lessons. And lessons they read not after the order appointed in the Calendar but after another continued Course of their owne.... The Students are not brought up nor accustomed to answere any verse at all. ... Their Seates are placed round about and above the Communion Table. When they preach or common place they omit all Service after the first or 2nd lesson at the furthest.

Significantly, the point was also made that many more students were admitted to the college than it could conveniently hold.[47]

In March 1631 the Master received a letter from Sir William Spring, who wanted to know whether he would be willing to accept his son as a student. By way of introduction Sir William recalled that he had been 'an unprofitable member' of the college when Sandcroft had been a relatively junior fellow but thought it unlikely that he would remember him as on the one hand he had achieved no distinction and on the other had not been 'soe Notorious in Evill or any Publique offence that you may call mee to minde by any Record of my shame there remayning'. He now wished to place his only son under Sandcroft's government and he was also hoping that he would recommend an able and honest tutor

to undertake the peculiar Care and trust of a Jewell, soe deare to mee, in whose well or ill doeing consists the sole hopes, or feares, of my happy or miserable age. All I will say of him is that yett I knowe him not (in the least) soyled with the black marke of these times nor unacquainted with those Principles which (through God's Blessing in the farther growth of Grace) I hope may direct his stepps out of that Common Roade, or broade way, wherein the youth of these dayes too loosely wander.

Sir William would shortly be coming to Cambridge with his son in order to make arrangements for his admission to the college 'where I cheifley begg of God hee may above all learne to bee goode and religious and so the better able to doe good service to God and his Country'. The son, William, was soon in residence at Emmanuel but his father did not live long enough to see him become a member of the Long Parliament, a Presbyterian elder and a parliamentary committeeman for Suffolk.[48]

Cases in which father and son both went to Emmanuel College were not uncommon. Before the time of the Civil War William Sandcroft and Richard Holdsworth were receiving into their charge the sons of men like Sir John Burgoyne, Sir Samuel Owfield, Sir Thomas Pelham and Sir Henry Mildmay who had themselves been undergraduates in Chaderton's time. Sir John Burgoyne, whose principal seat was at Sutton in Bedfordshire, owned the patronage rights in the parish which in the years 1607 to 1645 was in the spiritual care of Oliver Bowles, 'a very godly learned man' who had been John Preston's tutor at Queens' College. Samuel Bowles, the minister's son, was placed under Preston's tuition at Queens' College, accompanied him when he moved to Emmanuel and was elected to a fellowship there in 1628. Perhaps predictably, Sir John's eldest son was also educated at Emmanuel. Roger Burgoyne, who was admitted in 1634, would later be praised by a clerical friend for having in him 'a rare mixture of true piety and the highest civility' together with 'a most sweet, affable and obliging temper'.[49]

Emmanuel College took in far more students from the Puritan gentry than any other college at either Oxford or Cambridge. But although Sidney Sussex, which was one of the smaller Cambridge colleges, could not match this degree of popularity it was not without justification that Laud bracketed it with Emmanuel as a nursery of Puritanism.[50] In the statutes of the college it was laid down that the fellows must above all be professors of true religion and among the first to be nominated after its foundation in 1596 were such men as Thomas Gataker, one of the ablest preachers of his generation, and William Bradshaw, the nonconformist divine who was the author of the treatise entitled *English Puritanisme*. Samuel Ward, who was Master during the years 1610 to 1643, was a leading Calvinist theologian. His dislike of the ceremonial aspects of worship, including the wearing of the surplice, earned him the reputation of being a Puritan and it is significant that the report on the state of the university which was drawn up in 1636 contains the comment that at Sidney Sussex 'they have no consecrated Chappell, they read the lessons after an order of their owne and not as they are appointed in the Kalendar. Are much like Emanuel for the rest.' He was also very much of a disciplinarian: there is a story that Sir Francis Clerke, a great benefactor of the college, decided that it would be a worthy recipient of his bounty when, during a private visit to Cambridge, he saw how closely Ward supervised his scholars, how conformist they were in the matter of dress and how diligently they performed their exercises.[51]

Sir Edward Harrington, the leading parliamentarian in Rutland, had been one of the very first pupils to be admitted to the college, having moved there from Christ's College when it opened its doors in 1598. He was related both to James Montagu, the first Master, and Sir John Harrington, later Lord Harrington of Exton, a zealous Puritan who was one of the executors of the foundress and as such responsible for bringing the college into being. Through Sir John's influence Sidney Sussex had special ties with the county of Rutland and, more specifically, with Oakham School of which he and Edward's father were governors.[52] As we have seen, Sir William Armyne, who entered the college in 1610, had previously been a pupil at Oakham School under James Wadeson. No doubt this course of education at school and university made a significant contribution to his religious knowledge which was described at the time of his death as 'both great and growing; the first appeared by the faire choise of his principles in Religion and in the Worship of God, which were alwayes to the most spirituall.'[53] Another Lincolnshire squire, Sir Edward Ayscough, was admitted to the college in 1612 and subsequently, in 1635, he demonstrated his confidence in Dr Ward by arranging with him to take his son Edward who had been a pupil under Lambert Osbaldeston, a man of Puritan sympathies, at Westminster School.[54] Two other Puritan landowners who sent their heirs to Sidney Sussex were Sir Richard Buller and Sir William Lytton. When Rowland Lytton arrived in 1632 he was placed under the tuition of Richard Dugard, one of the most celebrated of the fellows and an intimate friend of John Milton.[55]

During the reign of Elizabeth Christ's College had been very highly regarded in Puritan circles, mainly because the great William Perkins was one of the fellows there. Towards the end of 1609 Archbishop Bancroft forced the college to accept Valentine Cary, a vigorous opponent of Calvinism, as its new Master and Samuel Ward, then a fellow at Emmanuel, lamented in his diary 'Woe is me for Christ's College. Now is one imposed upon who will be the utter ruin and destruction of that College. . . . Lord, my God, take some pity and compassion upon that poor college.' During the next few years some of the Puritan fellows were forced out of the college but they were never completely purged: when Thomas Goodwin, who would later become well known as a nonconformist divine, was admitted as an undergraduate in 1613 there still remained six fellows 'that were great Tutors who professed Religion after the strictest sort, then called Puritans'.[56] In 1620 Cary became Bishop of Exeter and was succeeded by Thomas Bainbrigg who had been put under house arrest in 1609 for attempting to procure the election of a rival candidate. Bainbrigg was a moderate in matters of religion, a gifted preacher and a strict disciplinarian. During his tenure of office, which lasted until 1646, the Puritan element among the fellows grew stronger and there was an upsurge in the number of students, particularly from families which would have regarded Valentine Cary's doctrinal views as wholly unacceptable.[57]

One of the most highly respected of the Christ's College fellows was William Chappell whose career as a tutor spanned the years 1607 to 1633. William Prynne depicts him as 'the most notorious seducing Arminian in the whole University of Cambridge' but if it is true that he abandoned his Calvinist principles this can only have occurred in the latter part of his life.[58] John Shaw, a Puritan divine who had studied under him, considered him to be 'a very acute learned man and a most painfull and vigilant Tutor'. Thomas Fuller writes that he was a great tutor who was remarkable for the strictness of his conversation and was generally accounted a Puritan.[59] His pupils, for their part, were regarded as being too precise and were often called Puritans. They included John Mainwaring whose father, Edward Mainwaring, was 'a pious and much esteemed Gentleman' and whose mother was 'an unparallel'd Gentlewoman for holy tendernesse and exactnesse in Religion'; Gervase Sleigh, a younger brother of Sir Samuel Sleigh who may also have been one of Chappell's pupils; and Edward Hartopp, the son of Sir Edward Hartopp, whose schoolmaster, Henry Valentine, had himself been a student at the college.[60]

When Sir Simonds D'Ewes entered St John's College in 1618 it no longer had the great reputation which it had enjoyed during the Mastership of William Whitaker, the celebrated Calvinist theologian,[61] but he had the good fortune to be placed under the tuition of Richard Holdsworth, the future Master of Emmanuel, who seems to have had an affectionate regard for him. D'Ewes, for his part, thought very highly of his tutor, describing him as one of the most

eminent scholars in the university. In 1620 he recorded in his
expenditure accounts that he had spent 7s 6d. on the purchase of
a pair of gloves for him; in 1641 he proposed in the Commons that
he should be made a bishop, explaining that 'I know him to be a
most learned man and I am confident that hee would [be] most
readie to further a reformation in the church'. Holdsworth was a
strict Calvinist who took great pains in the religious instruction of
his pupils, recommending to them the works of such authors as
Joseph Hall, Richard Sibbes, John Preston, Robert Bolton, John
Davenant and William Perkins. Characteristically, D'Ewes shunned
'the unnecessarie societie of all debauched and atheisticall
companions' who, he maintains, swarmed within the university.
During his time at the college he continued to take notes of sermons
and read a portion of the scriptures as a daily routine, attended the
public lectures of John Davenant, the Lady Margaret Professor of
Divinity, who was highly critical of Arminian doctrine, and came
to the conclusion that the strict observance of the Lord's Day was
an essential feature of true religion. For his recreation he sometimes
played tennis and was even prepared to wager money on the result.[62]
When the Mastership fell vacant in 1633 the fellows elected Holdsworth as the new head of the college but Laud, who suspected him
of having Puritan sympathies, persuaded the king to appoint
William Beale, who was a man of a very different character. Dr
Beale, writes D'Ewes, 'caused such a generall adoracion to and
towards the Altar and sacraments to be practiced as manie godlie
fellows and schollers of the house left ther places to avoid the
abomination'.[63]

While Cambridge Puritanism was generally declining in strength
there was one college where events followed an opposite course.
When Thomas Goodwin was admitted to St Catharine Hall in 1619
its fortunes were at a very low ebb, 'there being no more than 16
Scholars, and few Acts or Exercises of Learning had been perform'd
for a long time.'[64] During the reign of Charles I, however, it was
completely revitalised under the Mastership first of Richard Sibbes,
who took up office in 1626, and then of Ralph Brownrigg, who
succeeded him in 1635, and as a result it acquired great popularity
among the Puritans. Once installed as head of the college Sibbes
made it his business 'to establish learned and Religious Fellows
there insomuch as in his time it proved a very famous Society for
Piety and Learning'. Not long after his death Laud was informed

that there was some uncertainty about 'what they do in the Chappell now. Of late they were as irregular as any, and most like Emmanuel.'[65] For his part Brownrigg was an extremely capable and diligent Master who examined even the younger scholars 'that they might be incouraged in Learning and Piety'. At the time of his election Walter Yonge called him 'a greate antiarminian' and he was also described as 'a strong and zealous defender of the purity and Doctrine of Religion . . . publickly and privately, both against the Arminians and the Papists'; on the other hand, he had a genuine respect for the liturgy and felt it necessary to discourage nonconformity.[66]

According to Thomas Fuller the college had six fellows and about a hundred students. During the years 1626 to 1642 the fellows were virtually all Puritans: they included Thomas Goodwin, who had been chiefly responsible for securing the election of Richard Sibbes; John Arrowsmith and Andrew Perne, who would subsequently be nominated as members of the Westminster Assembly; William Spurstowe who in 1638 was presented by John Hampden to his Buckinghamshire living of Great Hampden; John Knowles, who emigrated to New England the following year; and William Strong, who resigned his fellowship after being accused of uttering scandalous words against Laud and the late Archbishop of York, Samuel Harsnet.[67]

In view of the esteem in which Richard Sibbes was held it is not surprising that following his arrival the Puritan gentry began to look with favour on what had hitherto been one of the least fashionable of all the Cambridge colleges. Among the students who were enrolled during his Mastership were sons of such wealthy Puritans as Sir Nathaniel Barnardiston, Sir Robert Brooke, Sir John Potts, Sir William Masham and Sir Gilbert Gerard. As we have seen, Sibbes was on close terms with the Brooke family and Sir Robert's wife prepared the manuscript of *A Fountaine Sealed*.[68] Sir Nathaniel Barnardiston was another friend and it is noteworthy that several of the womenfolk in his family were benefactors of the college. Sir Gilbert Gerard, for his part, was clearly not unaware of the Master's ability as a preacher since in September 1631, not long before his son Francis entered the college, we find him enthusing about a sermon which he had heard Sibbes deliver.[69] Sir Simonds D'Ewes writes that in 1632 he arranged for the admission of his brother Richard to St Catharine Hall and provided him with 'a verie reli-

gious Tutor' called John Knowles. A man who had strong reservations about the Book of Common Prayer and the Church's ceremonial requirements, Knowles's reputation as a tutor was such that
he had no fewer than forty pupils at a time. On his return from
New England he found that about a dozen of his former students
were serving as members of the Long Parliament while another
thirty had become eminent preachers.[70]

In December 1635 Ralph Brownrigg, who had just taken over
the Mastership, told Sir Simonds D'Ewes that 'as I account it my
duty to promote a peaceable conformity to the orders of our church
so I shall undertake that service in the spirit of love and lenity, being
assured that I am amongst those whose dispositions ar tractable.'[71]
Despite his unwillingness to resist the pressures for uniformity in
the matter of worship the college continued to attract students
from Puritan families, primarily no doubt because of the Calvinist
teaching which it offered. The wife of Sir William Springett writes
that his mother sent him to Cambridge 'as being accounted more
sober than Oxford' and placed him in a Puritan college called St
Catharine Hall 'where was a very sober tender master of the house
and a grave sober tutor'. The young man, who would emerge as a
religious extremist, was admitted to the college in 1637 and was
subsequently joined there by his brother Herbert.[72]

Writing to his patron, Sir Robert Harley, in January 1641 Stanley
Gower told him that he was sure that the fountain of the present
impieties lay in the universities.[73] That Puritanism or godliness was
in decline both at Oxford and Cambridge during the reign of
Charles I was a fact which was generally acknowledged; but despite
this the inflow of students from wealthy Puritan families continued
unabated. On the whole, the changing face of religion at the universities did not present any overwhelming problems for such families.
While they had much less freedom of choice in the reign of Charles
I than in the two previous reigns there were still a number of
colleges which found favour in their eyes: in particular, Exeter,
Magdalen Hall, Brasenose and Lincoln at Oxford, and Emmanuel,
Sidney Sussex, Christ's College and St Catharine Hall at
Cambridge. Under the censorship arrangements in force the opportunities to hear Calvinist doctrine expounded in formal lectures and
sermons were severely curtailed but there were many fellows who
were determined to give their students the kind of religious and

moral instruction which Puritan parents regarded as an essential feature of university education.

When John Hutchinson went to Cambridge in 1632 he was admitted to a college, Peterhouse, where High Church practices were flourishing and placed under the tuition of William Norwich who was a notable scholar but a man of Arminian principles.[74] In the main, however, the sons of Puritan squires were educated at colleges which were 'sound' in terms of both doctrine and worship. Despite all the distractions and temptations of life in the university towns the experience may often have done much to strengthen the religious convictions which they owed to their parents. After studying at Oxford or Cambridge a Puritan gentleman was usually well acquainted with the works of both the classical authors and the leading English exponents of Calvinist doctrine; and indeed he might even have been taught by a famous Puritan author such as John Preston, Richard Sibbes or Robert Bolton. The literary activities of Harbottle Grimston are a faithful reflection of the type of education to which he had been exposed as an undergraduate at Emmanuel College. The religious treatise which appeared in 1644 under the title *A Christian New-Year's Gift* had originally been written in Latin. In addition, he was responsible for a translation of a Latin work by Samuel Ward of Ipswich, a Puritan minister whom he esteemed 'for his integrity of life and eminency of learning'. If the use of Latin had been less common among the educated classes it might have struck him as somewhat ironical that the language of the Roman liturgy should be associated in this way with what he regarded as the principles of true religion.[75]

CHAPTER SIX

RICHES AND MORALITY

When Puritan divines pleaded the cause of godliness they were often moved to offer the assurance that it would bring material as well as spiritual benefits. 'Wouldest thou then be wise?' asked John Barlow in the course of a lecture at Plymouth. 'Then know God and serve him. Wouldest thou grow in wealth? Why, set upon all good actions.'[1] The godly, it was argued, were able to prosper not only because they were under God's patronage but because of the special characteristics which they owed to their religion. In one of their collaborative works John Dod and Robert Cleaver emphasised that 'They are sure to speed well which deale for God and depend upon him in their affairs. . . . Sound Religion and pietie in the soule will make men circumspect and prosperous in their waies . . . the Lord doth blesse their waies and make them fortunate in their workes.' Those who were 'most religious and godly wise . . . will be prudent and faithfull in the managing of those matters which they take in hand and God will bee mercifull and gracious in prospering of them.'[2]

Since self-denial and diligence were held to be essential attributes of the godly there was some credibility in the claim that zeal in religion could open the door to material advancement. Yet Puritan ministers were faced with obvious difficulties in expounding the virtues of diligence to wealthy landowners who could afford to employ stewards and bailiffs to manage their affairs and were under no financial compulsion to follow a professional or commercial career. What they did was to exhort the gentry to avoid self-indulgence in their leisure pursuits, to devote as much of their time as possible to religion and good works and, if they held public office, to spare no effort in performing the duties of their calling. Miserable and damnable, declared William Perkins, was the condition of those with great livings and revenues who spent their days in eating and drinking, in sports and pastimes, 'not imploying themselves in service for Church or Commonwealth'.[3]

Among the Puritan gentry there were many who subscribed to the view that diligence was a Christian duty which had relevance at all levels of society. William Martyn, who was recorder of Exeter, told his son that 'none must be idle but every man must diligently imploy himselfe in such affaires and business as God (his master) hath committed to his care'. Apart from anything else idleness could be a breeding ground for sin: when a man was idle his mind was encumbered 'with many variable cogitations and sundrie thoughts, but not with any which are vertuous and good'.[4] In a book of verse which he called *The Abortive of an Idle Houre* Sir Thomas Wroth offered the comment that

> The world is full of prodigall expenders,
> The borrowers are more then the lenders;
> Those Prodigalls commit the highest cryme,
> Who wast their lives in vaine expence of time.

Sir Thomas himself could not be accused of indolence: he took an active part in local government, served as recorder of Bridgwater and was 'an affecter and favourer of the Muses' whose literary works included a translation of Virgil's account of the destruction of Troy.[5] Another Puritan squire with the same kind of outlook was Sir William Waller, who wrote 'what doth the Lord require of thee; not to lie still but to arise and be doing'. In his 'Daily Directory' he observes that he rose in the morning as early as he could 'that course being most profitable for Soul, body and estate. In Summer time I would be up by five; in winter by six or soon after, as my health would permit, and if nothing intervene of necessity to hinder me.' Similarly, John Hutchinson liked to rise early and go to bed late; and we are assured that 'he never was at any time idle, and hated to see any one else soe.' It was an attitude of mind which would have delighted Richard Bernard, the Puritan divine, who in a treatise published in 1629 emphasised that the masters of households 'must keepe all from idlenesse, the nurse or rather mother of all wickednesse'.[6]

Sir Simonds D'Ewes considered that too many were 'prodigall of ther time, squandering it away upon trifles'. God, he stressed, had commanded men to labour six days, not to live idly, slothfully and unprofitably. He was doubtful whether persons who preferred a leisured existence could belong to the privileged minority of God's elect. On hearing of the death of a friend his first concern was whether he was saved or not, 'because I know hee had manye good desires and inclinations accompanied with a firme and full adhering to the true religion but withall I feared that his course of life, living idlie for the most parte about London, was not compatible to a man trulie pious'. D'Ewes himself had once thought of taking up a legal career, despite the fact that he was the heir to an estate worth £1500 a year, but he tells us that on contemplating the dangers which threatened the Protestant religion both at home and abroad he had decided to abandon the idea; instead he devoted much of his time to antiquarian pursuits. Such was his addiction to historical and genealogical research that in 1634 Sir Nathaniel Barnardiston, whom he regarded as a special friend, felt obliged to write to his wife that 'I should be hartely glad if your knight would spare so much tyme from his studies as that we might inioy both your sweet companyes hear. It is very much that we living so neere together in the same country [county] should not have leysure once in two or three yeares to visit one an other.'[7]

Although it was possible for the wife of a well-to-do squire to enjoy a life of leisure many of the Puritan womenfolk at this level of society preferred to busy themselves in the running of the household, the performance of religious duties, including the instruction of the children and servants, and the relief of the poor and sick.[8] Following the death of his wife, Lady Margaret, in 1635 Sir Thomas Wroth related that she had been 'very discreet, prudent and active . . . in the conduct of her family, setting forth with her own hands divers workes and businesses in her house; always doing some good, protesting that she could not endure idleness'. And in some elegiac verse he wrote

> Neatness she highly prized, and hated sloth,
> As did her word and actions all express
> She had no warrant – often would she say –
> To spend a minute idle of a day.[9]

Much to her husband's satisfaction a Puritan wife often proved to be highly capable and frugal in her housekeeping and might even assist him in matters of business. Bulstrode Whitelocke comments in his autobiography that when he was away from home his second wife carefully and prudently managed his affairs 'and I found none so good stewards as my wives'.[10] In some cases the wife appears in fact to have been more business-minded than the husband. In the autumn of 1632 Lady Judith Barrington, the wife of Sir Thomas Barrington, drew up detailed instructions for the family steward, who was then in London with his master, about the payment of debts and annuities and the collection of rents. 'I think it wear very fitt', she told him, that 'you gett your Master to begin a suite with John Smyth about his spoyling Cottingham Woods.' Sir Thomas was seeking to acquire some Crown property and in another letter to the steward she wrote that 'I doubt he wilbe slow in goeing to my Lord Treasurer and my Lord of Holland; I would not have him complement awaye his £300 charges that he hath been att over and above the £2500 for the purchase.' Lady Judith was clearly a woman who knew her own mind, though to Sir John Bramston, the ship-money judge, she was merely 'that impertinent everlasting talker'.[11]

Some Puritan squires settled so much property on their younger sons that they became major landowners in their own right; others considered it important that with the exception of the first-born their sons should take up careers in the outside world. After telling his children about the time he entered his pedigree at a heraldic visitation Bulstrode Whitelocke emphasised that he did not mention this

to cause any high thoughts of antiquity of pedigrees or of bloud in any of you . . . or to discourage you from honest or lawfull callings which are most becomming and not neglected by the best gentlemen, and I would have you the more humble and the more industrious to preserve yourselves in the quality of gentlemen, and know that where means is wanting gentility proves butt a scorne and will buy no bread.[12]

It was a point of view which was shared by Zouch Tate, who commented in his will that he desired above everything else that his children should be brought up in honest callings in the nurture and admonition of the Lord.[13]

Among the Puritan gentry it was relatively common for younger sons to be apprenticed to city merchants, often when the family had no mercantile background. Sir Nathaniel Barnardiston was 'ever importunate to have all his Sons employed, not taking it as becoming to have any of his line out of useful Callings': of his numerous progeny Samuel, Nathaniel, Pelatiah, William and Arthur all went into commerce. Sir Nathaniel was one of a number of Puritan squires who entered into apprenticeship agreements with members of the Skinners Company; others who did so included Sir Richard Darley, Sir William Armyne and Sir Richard Ingoldsby.[14] Naturally enough, the father of an apprentice expected a reasonable return for the money he had laid out but there could be disappointments. Although his master was supposed to act *in loco parentis* a country boy learning his trade in the metropolis could find himself exposed to many temptations. Sir John Gell had a younger son, William, who while apprenticed to a London merchant was drawn into 'lewde howses to play at dice and cards and soe to neclect his master's busines'. What seems to have particularly horrified Sir John was the fact that his gaming activities had brought him into contact with 'a woman of lewd life and meane condition'. In order to pay his gambling debts William began to steal money from his master and when this came to light he hastened off to the Continent, leaving his father to make recompense.[15]

The links between the Puritan gentry and the legal profession had always been very strong. A number of families, among them the Bacons, the Wrays and the Yelvertons, owed both their wealth and their religious loyalties to Elizabethan forbears who had been successful lawyers. Many Puritan squires sent their sons to the Inns of Court, often with the intention that they should enter the legal profession. Sir Thomas Crewe, who is described as 'a very Learned Lawyer, a serious Christian, and a great promoter of the Reformation', represents a particularly striking example of a younger son who as the result of a profitable career in the law was able to build up a large estate. In December 1623 John Chamberlain commented in one of his news-letters that the king had knighted Everard Digby, who was a Catholic, and Thomas Crewe, the new king's serjeant, who was 'of a quite contrary faction'. When Sir Thomas drew up his will he recalled with gratitude that God had directed his father not to breed him in idleness 'but to bring me up at learning and to sett me in a calling which under god hath bene the meanes to rayse my estate'. At his funeral in 1634 the preacher, Richard Sibbes, recalled that he had been a practitioner in his calling for forty years and that during that time God had blessed him with a great increase in his estate. And he went on to explain that 'God sometimes doth delight to make good his temporall Promises to a religious, industrious and faithfull man, and that in the eyes of the World.'[16]

In a sermon published in 1607 Richard Bernard wrote that the nobility and gentry would rather their sons became anything so long as they did not take holy orders.[17] Even among the Puritan squirearchy there were relatively few younger sons who entered the ranks of the parish clergy, despite the fact that these families had a large number of benefices in their gift. One of the most notable of upper-class divines, Francis Bampfield, tells us that he was born of religious parents 'who gave him up to the LORD for the Ministerial Office and Work; and accordingly he had his Education in the Families of Professors of Religion'. In 1639 his father, John Bampfield, presented him to the rectory of Rampisham in Dorset and eventually he became one of the most celebrated preachers in the West Country. Because of his refusal to conform Bampfield fell victim to the Act of Uniformity and among those who suffered with him were Hugh Everard, a son of Sir Richard Everard; William Gerard, who in 1631 had been presented to the Buckinghamshire rectory of Aston Clinton by his brother Sir Gilbert Gerard; and Richard Roberts, a brother of Sir William Roberts.[18]

As a general rule it was considered unnecessary for the heir to take up a career: after leaving university or one of the Inns of Court he might travel for a time on the Continent or help his father to manage the family estates. There were some, however, who were practising lawyers or civil servants. Sir Henry Yelverton, who was the son of a judge, served as Attorney General to James I and later (after a period of disgrace) as a judge of the Court of Common Pleas; in the parish church of Easton Mauduit, the Northamptonshire village where the Yelvertons were seated, both father and son are depicted in their legal robes. Although Sir Henry observed in his will that God had wrought in him a contempt of the world the fact remains that a lucrative career in the law, together with a large estate revenue, enabled him to maintain a very high standard of living.[19] Since Bulstrode Whitelocke was an only son it was perhaps understandable that his father, who was a judge of the County Palatine of Chester, should encourage him to follow his example and enter the legal profession. As he explains in his autobiography, Whitelocke had a powerful incentive to work hard in his calling: in

1630, he writes, his growing indebtedness encouraged him to display greater industry in the practice of the law in order to satisfy his creditors.[20] His friend Harbottle Grimston, who became recorder of Colchester in 1638, had decided to abandon his legal studies when the death of his elder brother left him heir to an estate worth £2000 a year. That he went back on this decision was due to an ultimatum from Sir George Croke, one of the judges in the Hampden case, who refused to allow him to marry his daughter unless he resumed his studies. The marriage negotiations were successfully completed and, as Whitelocke testifies, Grimston 'tooke to the profession of the lawe and prospered in it'.[21]

In 1626 Sir Robert Harley obtained a grant for life of the office of Master of the Mint. The total revenue from the Harley estates amounted to £1500 a year but since the bulk of the property only came into his possession in 1631 the annual pension or salary of £500 which he received was a very important contribution to his income; on the other hand, the duties which went with the office meant that for several months each year he was living apart from his wife, who remained at home in Herefordshire with their children. Shortly after his appointment Sir Robert became involved in a dispute with Sir Randall Cranfield, who claimed that he was entitled to the office by virtue of a grant from James I. The affair dragged on for years and in 1633 we find the family praying that 'God in mercy will be pleased to give a blessed issue to the buisines with Sir Randall Cranfield'; two years later, however, the office was out of Harley's possession.[22] In some cases an office of profit passed from father to son. When drawing up his will in 1613 Sir William Cooke put it on record that under arrangements which he had made with the Crown the Clerkship of the Liveries would be inherited by his eldest son Robert. Similarly Sir Gilbert Gerard succeeded his father in the office of Clerk of the Council of the Duchy of Lancaster.[23]

In the main the wealthy Puritan gentry were dependent on the revenues from their landed property. As landowners some of them took a close interest in the running of their estates, keeping their own accounts, engaging in commercial farming when the economic circumstances were favourable and superintending improvement programmes which were aimed at increasing their revenue; the same can be said, however, of many country squires who were not of their religious persuasion, among them Catholics as well as

Protestants.[24] Relatively few of the major Puritan families owned estates in regions which offered the possibility of industrial development: such counties as Buckinghamshire, Essex and Suffolk, for example, were not noted for their mineral wealth. Sir Thomas Pelham was a leading industrialist whose iron forges in the Sussex Weald were producing a gross income of some £3600 a year in 1640;[25] but in this respect he was by no means typical of the great Puritan squires.

While the Puritan divines saw nothing wrong in principle with the acquisition of riches they roundly condemned the sin of covetousness, by which they meant the pursuit of financial gain without regard to moral constraints or the interests of others. In a sermon preached at the Northampton assizes Robert Bolton told his listeners, who would have included representatives of many of the richest families in the county, that the covetous man 'begins first (if he be of power and place) to grind the faces of the poore, then to pluck of their skins, then to tear their flesh, then to break their bones and chop them in peeces as flesh for the pot, and at last even to eat the flesh of GOD's people'. Other godly preachers condemned usury, excessive profit-making, rack-renting, depopulating enclosure and indeed any kind of economic activity or transaction which involved injustice or hard dealing.[26]

The godly, declared Sir Simonds D'Ewes, must be careful that what they possess is 'acquired and gotten in a iust and lawfull way . . . wee must beware of covetousness'. Sir William Waller believed that covetousness could provoke divine retribution: in a book of recollections he wrote, 'When out of a covetous desire to gaine a good bargaine upon Mr Price his lease by Winchester, I laid down five hundred pounds as a claw upon itt, by way of morgage, God justly punished me both in the loss of the lease and of my mony too.'[27] Such sentiments were common but economic self-interest was a powerful force even among the godly. During the 1630s a number of Puritan squires were fined for carrying out depopulating enclosures, among them Sir John Wray of Lincolnshire, Sir Edward Hartopp and Sir Arthur Hesilrige of Leicestershire, Richard Knightley of Northamptonshire and Sir John Cutts of Cambridgeshire. Sir Arthur was seated in the parish of Noseley which, apart from the great house, was almost completely uninhabited by the time of the Civil War. Sir John Cutts had evicted his tenants in the parish of Childerley in order to enlarge and improve his park; as a result

111

Childerley Hall was the only building left standing.[28] Another Puritan landowner whose activities brought him to the attention of the depopulation commissioners was Sir William Armyne, who in 1638 was fined £200. Some years later, however, his parish minister was emphatic that he would be remembered as a benevolent landlord: 'For the good he did to the outward man for others . . . his workes will praise him in the gate; and tell how good a Land-lord and benefactor he was; every Tenant and every poor body will be his Orator to set forth his goodnesse of this kind'.[29] Whatever Sir William's attitude to his tenantry it is certainly the case that there were good landlords as well as bad landlords among the Puritan gentry. Sir Francis Barrington was said to 'have ever bene reckned in the number of the better sort of landlordes'.[30] And at a time when rack-renting was prevalent Bulstrode Whitelocke deliberately refrained from overburdening his tenants: after inheriting his father's estate, he writes, 'I held it fitt to be continued in the same way and course that he left it, the same leaseholders and coppyholders and the same rents without any alteration.'[31]

One form of covetousness which was of particular concern to the Puritan clergy was the rapacious attitude displayed by many of the lay patrons of church livings.[32] Where a rectory was impropriate the owner would often take the bulk of the revenue for his own use and allow the minister no more than a modest pittance. Even where a patron's interest was limited to the right of presentation it was possible for him to use this as a money-making device though in doing so he could lay himself open to a charge of simony. In a funeral sermon delivered in 1616 Robert Bolton praised the singular integrity of his late patron, Sir Augustine Nichols, and contrasted it with the common practice of the times,

> wherein there is such sinfull and Simoniacall packing together, compacting, secret covenanting with the party or friends for present money or after-gratifications: some part of the tithes or his owne must be reserv'd to the Patron or he must be the Farmer at his owne price.

Subsequently he complained in an assize sermon that too many of the wealthier sort kept possession of the Church's patrimony. Some excellent spirits, he noted, had recently given back to the Church a number of benefices amounting in value to over £700 a year; these, however, were 'onely such as you mis-call Puritan gentlemen (for I neither heare not nor know of any other that stirs this way) and how few such are to be found in a Countrey'.[33]

In Suffolk there were several Puritan gentry who had a reputation for behaving honourably and even generously in the exercise of their patronage rights. Maurice Barrow was described by one of his ministers, John Mayer, as a most liberal and noble-minded patron who was distinguished by his 'immunity from patronall corruption'. Mayer assured him that his life and practice, 'in carefully providing to supply well the Church of God so farre as your power extendeth with able and painefull Pastours, and in ensuing every good and vertuous course, is a continuall lecture reading to others of your rank and quality'.[34] Sir Nathaniel Barnardiston, for his part, was depicted in some verse written after his death as

> An uncorrupted Patron that did hate
> Out of the Churches meants t'augment his state.[35]

In a document entitled *A Certificate from Northamptonshire* which was published in 1641 there was strong criticism of the greed and parsimony of impropriators but two Puritan squires, Richard Knightley, who was seated in that county, and Sir William Doddington of Hampshire, were specially commended for their beneficence.[36] These men also appear in a list of lay patrons who were said to have been influenced by Sir Henry Spelman's *De Non Temerandis Ecclesiis* in which the private ownership of ecclesiastical property had been condemned as a grievous sin. Richard Knightley, it was recorded, had restored two impropriations, Fawsley and Preston Capes, to the Church, 'being a Gentleman much addicted to Works of Piety, Charity and Advancement of Learning, and shewing great Respect to the Clergy'. As for Sir William Doddington, he had restored 'no less than six Impropriations out of his own Estate to the full Value of Six hundred Pounds yearly and more'.[37] Sir William's generosity was also acknowledged by Bartholomew Parsons, the rector of Ludgershall in Wiltshire, who in 1637 dedicated to him a published sermon with the title *Tithes Vindicated to the Presbyters of the Gospel*. Describing him as 'A Mirrour of Pietie and Patience', he stressed that while many had bestowed lavish gifts on the Church for the benefit of ministers of the Gospel he had 'outrunne them all in our parts'. For he had revealed his love of good works in

restoring by way of free-will offering backe againe to the

Church those impropriations of yours of which you might have said, we have a law of our land and by that law I ought to hold them. . . . All which as you have done not out of lightnesse, vaine-glory or to gaine popular applause . . . but out of a conscience truly informed out of the saving word of God, both of the lawfulnesse and necessity of your act.

According to another account Sir William settled three impropriations in Wiltshire on a number of trustees, among them Denzil Holles and Sir John Evelyn, with the intention that they should be used for the support of nonconformist preachers.[38] A more famous Puritan benefactor was John Hampden: when Archbishop Laud's representative was carrying out a metropolitical visitation in Buckinghamshire in 1634 he was informed that Hampden had given to the church of Great Kimble an impropriation worth £120 a year.[39]

Taken by itself such evidence would give an unduly favourable picture of the Puritan gentry as patrons of church livings. Sir George More, who was a great parliamentary champion of the nonconformist clergy, appears to have engaged in simoniacal practices[40] while other men obliged their ministers to demonstrate the virtues of frugality by personal example. In some cases a minister struggling to make ends meet continued to exercise his pastoral charge either out of a sense of loyalty to his flock or because he was able to enjoy some degree of freedom from the attentions of the diocesan authorities.

Usury was another form of covetousness which was strongly condemned in Puritan circles, though there were differences of opinion as to its precise meaning. One of its severest critics was Roger Fenton, the author of *A Treatise of Usurie*, which appeared in 1611. It was his contention that God's abhorrence of usury was fully revealed in the scriptures: 'Let every one therefore who desireth to resolve his conscience for this matter by Scripture . . . let him consider, I say, how neither usurie nor interest, biting usurie nor increase is ever once named in the booke of God but it is condemned.' Basically, he defined usury as the lending of money for financial gain, whether or not it involved the payment of interest as such. 'Men cavill and play with words', he wrote, 'but God admitteth no such sleights. His meaning is simple and plaine, that all increase above the principall is forbidden.'[41] Fenton's hard-line philosophy was taken up enthusiastically by many Puritan divines.

114

In a work published in 1618 Edmund Rudyerd commented gleefully that Mr Fenton had 'stopped all pipes and boulting holes so close that not one of these foxes nor any of their cubbes can creepe out'. Robert Bolton was also familiar with Fenton's treatise and expressed himself in full agreement with his views: 'if we do lend,' he declared, 'we must lend freely.'[42] There were some Puritan ministers, however, who were more willing to countenance exemptions from the general prohibition on usury. In a sermon published in 1619 Thomas Cooper took the line that a more pragmatic approach was justified during the economic depression which the country was then experiencing. In outlining his attitude to usury he argued that

> though covetousness is usually the ground and Broker hereto yet there may be some use therof, upon some necessary occasions and extreamities, in these barren times wherein so few will lend freely and few make conscience to repay what they borrow, as may tollerate the same, and that rather for the borrower's sake then the lender's, so that oppression be hereby avoyded and the rules of equitie be observed.

While recommending Fenton's treatise for more detailed guidance he offered the opinion that this was a matter which in the final resort must be left to the individual conscience.[43]

Clerical condemnation of the evils of usury undoubtedly had some influence on members of the Puritan gentry though it is not always clear from their recorded views what particular definition they favoured. Sir George More spoke critically of usury in the House of Commons in 1621; William Martyn viewed it in the same light as bribery and extortion; while Herbert Springett, the father of Sir William Springett, was said to have 'scrupled putting his money to use'.[44] On his deathbed Sir Samuel Rolle told the minister who was attending him that 'he acknowledged it . . . as an especiall blessing that neither he nor his father nor his Grandfather (notwithstanding their many and great transactions in the world) had ever borrowed or lent upon usury'. In his will he bequeathed £10 to the poor of Petrockstow, stipulating that 'the money shall not be put to use', and also gave direction that if his executors had any money left in their hands they should use it to acquire lands or leases for his younger children, 'that soe the money maie not be put to usury'.[45]

No doubt it was for reasons of conscience that Sir Robert Cooke, who had considerable business interests, preferred to employ his surplus money in the purchase of annuities charged on land. In October 1637 he wrote to his kinsman Sir Robert Harley, who had apparently been seeking a loan of £1000 from him: 'To satisfye my selfe in the reasonablenes of my demaunds I observe that £1000 for 7 yeares affords in interest £560 the principall mainteined which comes to £1560. £200 per annum for 7 years comes to but £1400.' In a postscript he added that 'in these bargains I am not guided by the ways of interest mony but of accustomed rates for such kind of bargains.' This in fact seems to have been his usual method of investment when there was a substantial sum involved since at his death in 1643 he left annuities totalling £460 a year to his wife and daughters.[46]

In his autobiography Sir Simonds D'Ewes describes the implications of his refusal to have anything to do with what he regarded as the sin of usury. Although he was willing to lend money for considerable periods he never charged a penny of interest. When it came to borrowing money he was occasionally able to secure an interest-free loan from an obliging relative. He found it impossible, however, to meet all his requirements in this way and he was therefore forced, 'not without much search and trouble', to borrow from professional moneylenders 'and to pay annuities upon casualties of lives'. In 1627 he was in correspondence with one of his clerical friends, Richard Chamberlain, about the scriptural objections to usury and suggested to him that an annuity for five years represented a means of avoiding the moral dilemma with which he was faced. In January 1641, when the House of Commons was debating a proposal to pay interest at 8 per cent on certain loans which had been advanced for the public good, he argued that it was wrong to use the word 'interest' but that it was perfectly in order to recompense a man for the loss which he had sustained by temporarily abandoning the use of his capital:

I moved that I had never yet either given or taken use in my particular nor I hoped that I never should. And therfore I would bee loath to give it in generall. For to give use or interest hath been alwaies condemned as unlawfull by the church and law of England. That therfore instead of the wordes lawfull interest without anie proviso . . . ther might bee added the wordes damages soe as it exceeded not the rate of £8 per centum.

116

The Commons duly agreed that the words 'interest' and 'forbearance' should be taken out and that the term 'damages' should be inserted in their place.[47]

When all has been said it is clear that there were many Puritan gentry who regarded usury in a different light from such men as Sir Samuel Rolle and Sir Simonds D'Ewes. In a memorandum relating to her husband's financial affairs Lady Judith Barrington reminded the family steward that it would be necessary for Dr Fox, a well-known London moneylender, to be paid interest on a loan of £500 at the rate of 6 or 7 per cent. She went on to say that her brother-in-law Sir Gilbert Gerard, another Puritan, 'must be payed his interest Mony. I know not well what it is.' Similarly, neither Sir Richard Onslow nor his cousin Onslow Winch was a doctrinaire in such matters: in June 1648 we find Sir Richard paying £17 10s 0d interest money on a loan which he had obtained from his kinsman.[48]

The investment of money in joint stock companies did not raise the same moral issues, primarily because there was no lender and borrower relationship in the normal sense. In practice the Puritan gentry who purchased stock in such companies as the Massachusetts Bay and Providence Island Companies seem to have been motivated more by religious than commercial considerations; if they hoped for financial gain they were sadly disappointed. Sir Thomas Barrington was admitted into the Providence Island Company in January 1631 and by November 1633 he had paid a total of £1025 for 'an entire share of adventure'. Before long the company was in serious financial difficulties and it was decided that an attempt should be made to sell the island to the States of Holland. The king, however, refused to authorise the sale and in these cirumstances steps had to be taken to raise more money both from the stockholders and by means of borrowing. In 1645 Sir John Barrington related in a petition to Parliament that for the good of the kingdom and the propagation of the Gospel his late father had become a member of the Providence Island Company and had not only provided money from his own purse but along with his fellow adventurers had borrowed larger sums on behalf of the company. As a result he was now being sued both for his father's debts and for those of the other adventurers.[49]

During the early seventeenth century a number of the leading Puritan squires were in considerable financial straits. At the height of their prosperity Sir Edward Peyton and Sir William Constable both commanded incomes of over £1000 a year but most of their property had been sold off by the time of the Civil War.[50] Others, among them Sir Robert Harley, found themselves heavily in debt. In February 1633 Sir Robert and his family were praying that 'God would sanctify the meanes for deliverance out of debt'. According to a minister who enjoyed his patronage the difficulties which he experienced owed much to his generous disposition:

> in Gospel or Church-work . . . he had an inlarged and a pious heart, together with a liberall hand, however he did streighten himself and his and engage his credit that hee might shew bowell-kindness to the despised but faithfull ministry of the Gospell and to the indigent members of our Lord Christ, not onely in his native country but even to peregrines and exiles.[51]

Sir Thomas Jervoise procured a series of letters of protection which gained him temporary immunity from the attentions of creditors who were anxious to take possession of his estate; that he was in this predicament was due primarily to the fact that he had stood surety for his friend Henry Sherfield, a Puritan lawyer, when he was engaged in borrowing money.[52] For most families, however, it was a time of great plenty; indeed, many of them were not merely holding their own but enlarging their estates. In some cases a rapid accumulation of property was made possible by a successful professional or commercial career; more often it was the product of an advantageous marriage. One Puritan squire whose material advancement was particularly impressive was Maurice Barrow, a Suffolk landowner, who married Lady Mary Poyntz, the widow of an Essex gentleman and, by 1632, the only surviving child of Sir Richard Smith of Leeds Castle in Kent. At his death in 1628 Sir Richard had left an estate worth £4500 a year, together with £60,000 in plate, money and goods, so that through his wife Barrow became one of the richest landowners in England with a total income of £6000 a year.[53]

Whatever its source the possession of wealth, it was held, carried with it an obligation to perform good works. Although it was one of the basic tenets of Calvinism that good works could not earn salvation the Puritan divines maintained that they provided clear evidence that a man was truly religious: indeed William Perkins insisted that 'the decree of election is the cause and foundation of

all good giftes and workes in men.'[54] Good works could take many
forms but particular stress was laid on actions which were aimed
at alleviating human misery and distress. One of the most detailed
expositions of this theme was John Downame's *The Plea of the Poore*,
which appeared in 1616 and was dedicated to senior members of
the Haberdashers Company who had appointed him to a lectureship. The godly, he wrote, 'are imitators of the godly nature but in
nothing doe wee more resemble God then when we imitate the
goodnesse of his name and be bountifull and beneficiall to all that
neede our helpe'. Although there were many ways in which the
wealthy could show their liberality 'yet this onely doth approve a
man to be godly and blessed when as he giveth freely to the poore
and needy'. At the same time he emphasised, as St Paul had done,[55]
that there was a special obligation towards those who were sincere
Christians: 'And though we be liberall in scattering the seede of our
good workes in all grounds which are ready to receive it, yet princi-
pally we must cast it into those which being fertile and fruitful will
yeelde unto us the best increase. Now such are the faithfull.'[56]
Another Puritan minister who wrote at length about the need for
compassion and charity was Richard Bernard. In 1635 he published
The Ready Way to Good Works and dedicated it to Sir John Wray,
entreating him to accept it 'as now it's presented unto you . . . and
let your charitable practice both grace it and therein comfort mee,
as it will your selfe abundantly'. In the course of this lengthy treatise
he made it clear that it was to men of Sir John's persuasion that
he was primarily appealing:

> They that are seasoned and enlivened with the Spirituall vigour
> of saving grace, that make more than a Laodicean profession
> of Jesus Christ, that are transported and inflamed with more
> than an ordinarie zeale for holinesse and religion: these I say
> be the men whom it principally concernes to bee most forward
> and frequent in these duties of Charity.[57]

Among the Puritan gentry it appears to have been generally
accepted that riches were held in trust from God and carried with
them social responsibilities which were divinely ordained. John
Harrington noted in his commonplace book, perhaps after hearing
a sermon based on the first two commandments, that 'Godlines
consists in the love of God and of our neighbour . . . that to our
neighbour must be as we love ourselves.' In a letter to one of his

119

clerical friends he expressed the view that lack of charity could bring down divine retribution: 'If we be niggardly of doeing good to others God will withhold his guifts from us.'[58] Sir Simonds D'Ewes wrote that 'Holiness is cheiflie eminent in positive goodnes and doing well'; the godly must spend their wealth properly, taking care to relieve the poor and needy. Harbottle Grimston stressed the importance of caring for the poor in his treatise on the duties of a Christian: 'Converse willingly with the poore and lowly. Visit Prisons, Hospitalls and Almshouses to do good to them. . . . If thou hast wherewithall, given something daily to the poore.' In practice he seems to have acted in accordance with these sentiments: we are told that he gave great sums in charity every year and that as a judge he discharged many prisoners by paying their debts.[59] Sir Thomas Crewe had the same kind of charitable instincts. In a work which Henry Scudder dedicated to him the point was made that 'A mercifull and conscionable care of our brethren is a true proof that we our selves are truly religious' and in the sermon which he delivered at his funeral Richard Sibbes emphasised that in this respect he was no mean Christian: 'For his disposition toward the poore hee was very mercifull and compassionate. Hee was the poore man's lawyer.'[60]

The concern which the Puritan gentry felt for the poorer members of society was often manifested when they were acting in an official capacity. As a magistrate, it was said, Sir Nathaniel Barnardiston 'never befriended the Great to the prejudice of those that were little and mean in the World'.[61] In December 1630 Sir Thomas Jervoise, a Hampshire deputy lieutenant, declared in a letter to Viscount Conway, the lord lieutenant, that his ears were filled with the complaints of the poor, who were likely to perish for lack of work. They had no money to buy corn and the cloth trade on which they were dependent for employment was at present in the doldrums. Accordingly he hoped that Conway would look favourably on a petition which the clothiers would be submitting.[62] The following month Sir Thomas Barrington, who was on the Essex commission of the peace, suggested to Viscount Dorchester that there would be much advantage in laying in stocks of corn in every parish and abating the price by 18d or 2s a bushel for the benefit of the poor. In March he told Dorchester that unless emergency measures were taken there would be a severe scarcity of corn. He therefore proposed that the price of corn should be fixed and that every community should be required to hold in reserve a reasonable quantity of grain for the poor.[63]

When economic conditions were bad a Puritan squire with a social conscience would sometimes act on his own initiative to relieve the distress of the poorer inhabitants of the neighbouring villages. In 1631 John Brinsley, a noted preacher, commended Sir John Wentworth, one of the wealthiest landowners in Suffolk, not only for setting up a lecture but for supplying food at a time when the poor were particularly hard hit: 'The bellies of the poore of these parts blesse you already in these times of scarcity: I hope some of their soules shall blesse you for the Bread that perisheth not.'[64] Apart from such *ad hoc* assistance many of the Puritan gentry were operating a regular welfare service of a wholly private character. Sir Nathaniel Barnardiston fed and clothed a large number of poor people and left them legacies at his death; so great was his charity that it extended as far as the poor in New England.[65] In 1631 Bartholomew Parsons, a Puritan minister, praised his friend Sir Francis Pile and his wife for 'sowing plentifully and solemnly at the set times weekely the seede of your almes at your gates' to the neighbouring poor. When Sir Francis died in 1635 Parsons elaborated on this theme in the funeral sermon he delivered:

> our noble Baronet walked in the good old way . . . did not eat his morsels alone but was given to hospitality and to doe good amongst his people. . . . And for the poore round about him his heart, his hand and his gate was ever open to them, the widows, the fatherlesse, the lame, the impotent, the poore children of the neighbour parishes were relieved constantly at his gates.[66]

Not infrequently a wealthy Puritan saw it as his duty to provide the local community with educational facilities for the young or housing for the aged. In the Suffolk parish of Little Thurlow Sir Stephen Soame, a London merchant, not only built a mansion for himself but established and endowed both a school and an almshouse. Subsequently his son Sir William invited a Puritan minister, Jonathan Jephcot, to take over the running of the school.[67] Sir John Davie, a Devonshire landowner, made arrangements for the financial support of a schoolmaster at Crediton who was to teach the children of the poor to read and write and to catechise and instruct them in the grounds of religion. John Browne, the Dorset parliamentarian, who left £20 a year for the relief of the poor of Frampton, recalled in his will that he had built a school there for the tuition of both boys and girls. His attitude to the education of children at the lower levels of society may be contrasted with that of another Dorset Puritan, Sir Walter Erle, who in December 1640 commented in a parliamentary speech that 'it was proved that mechanick men's children should not bee brought upp in learning.'[68]

Among the stock characters in John Earle's *Micro-cosmographie* there is a Puritan woman who 'is so taken up with Faith she has no room for Charity and understands no good works but what are wrought on the Sampler'. No doubt this criticism had some foundation in fact yet there were many Puritan gentlewomen who took to heart St Paul's dictum that women professing godliness should adorn themselves with good works.[69] In 1618 Robert Harris, the Puritan minister of Hanwell in Oxfordshire, expressed his gratitude to Lady Anne Cope for the love she had shown to many poor members of Christ, 'to whom it pleaseth you (thorough my hands) to convey yeerely so great reliefe'. Lady Mary Armyne was 'frequent and constant in giving to Charitable uses. She in her life time erected and endowed some Almshouses in three several Counties and upon special occasions gave away many large sums of money upon charitable accounts.'[70]

One form of charity which was the special preserve of the womenfolk (though not only the Puritan womenfolk) was the provision of medical care. Lady Elizabeth Alston supplied the poor with both food and physic while Temperance Crewe was praised for her treatment of the sick in an epitaph which may have been composed by her husband, Sir Thomas Crewe:

> Hir hand which had good blood in every vaine
> Yet was not daintye, nor did disdayne
> Salve to apply to LAZARUS' sore
> And was inlarged to the poore.[71]

During her widowhood Katherine Springett, the mother of Sir William Springett, acquired a great reputation as a medical practitioner. At her clinic she treated cataracts, burns, sores and many other afflictions and her servants were kept busy distilling waters and spirits and preparing oils, salves, balsams, syrups, conserves, purges, pills and lozenges. Half the revenue from her jointure lands was spent in this way yet she declined to charge a penny and often returned the presents which her grateful patients sought to press on her.[72] Lady Lucy Jervoise had a considerable knowledge of surgery and physic 'and was helpful to such as were hurt and maimed, sick and diseased. And as her skill this way was more than ordinary so most ready and willing she was to be at much Charge, to bestow any Pains, to further their Recovery. She was also Christ's Almoner to the poor and needy.' Like Solomon's virtuous woman she 'stretched forth her hand to the poor and reached out both her hands to the needy'.[73]

While exhorting the godly to be charitable John Downame emphasised that they should help only those who were poor through necessity and not out of choice:

> For there are many sturdie beggars and vagrant rogues, the blemish of our government and a burthen to the common wealth, who have nothing in proprietie but their licencious life and lawlesse condition . . . men without religion, Church, baptisme, faith or God in the world, who like idle drones feede upon the common spoyle and live by the sweate of other men's browes: which kinde of poore are not to be maintained in their wicked courses.[74]

In a similar vein Richard Bernard advised his readers not to assist rogues, vagabonds and sturdy beggars who were 'the very ulcers, scabs and vermine of the Commonweale'. To help 'such professed wanderers, who may and can and will not worke were to maintaine a school of roguery'.[75] This belief that charitable giving should not be indiscriminate but should be directed towards those who were truly deserving enjoyed wide currency among the Puritan gentry who, like many of their fellow Englishmen, were inclined to view the itinerant beggar with loathing and suspicion. Sir Thomas Wroth, whose love of diligence has already been noted, expressed his dislike of beggars in particularly caustic terms:

> Ye roaring beggars, tell mee what you meane,
> To spend each Christmas so much winde, to gleane
> Gratuities from men. O come not neare
> Where I abode, or whisper in my eare;
> Be sure your tongues with modestie be tipt,
> And then I'le tell you, beggars must be whipt.[76]

In a lecture or sermon delivered to his family Bulstrode Whitelocke offered the opinion that 'to be helpfull to a man's poor industrious neighbors is more charity then to give to wandering beggars which seems to be rather an incouragement to idleness then an exercise of charity . . . to sett poor labouring men to work for wages is true charity.'[77] Many Puritan benefactions were in fact specifically aimed at encouraging diligence. Sir John Davie left £20 as a contribution towards the cost of a workhouse which he envisaged would have two basic functions: the provision of work for poor tradesmen who were unable to obtain work by other means and the punishment of such 'vagrants, Idle and lewd people as shal be sent thither to be corrected'. Richard Knightley, one of the principal landowners in Northamptonshire, gave direction in his will that the sum of £100 should be lent without interest to the widows, the orphans, the fatherless and such other persons in the parish of Preston Capes as were in most need, subject to an undertaking that it would be repaid within one year. His intention was that the money should be used as an investment in farming activities and that each year following its repayment it should be lent again for the same purpose.[78] Like some of his fellow Puritans Sir William Doddington provided money for the binding of poor children as apprentices. Such children, he stressed, should not be bound to masters who were known to be cruel to their apprentices and servants but should be placed with men who could be expected to treat them well.[79] Sir Francis Barrington bequeathed £10 for the benefit of the poor of Hatfield Broad Oak, stipulating that it should be used 'to sett them to worke, thereby to keepe them from hauntinge Alehouses, breakinge hedges and loppinge trees'. No doubt his charitable instincts were strongly intermixed with a landowner's concern for the well-being of his estate. From this point of view, however, the bequest cannot be regarded as particularly effective. In 1638 his son Sir Thomas was driven to complain to the Privy Council that certain intruders had set fire to some of his coppice hedges within the Forest of Hatfield and committed other acts of destruction on his property.[80]

CHAPTER SEVEN

SOCIAL ATTITUDES AND RELATIONSHIPS

Of the godly attributes which were highly praised by the Puritan divines few received more attention than humility. 'Humility is the very first step unto Christianity,' stressed Samuel Hieron. 'A man that is not humbled and taught to carry even a very meane and base opinion touching himselfe is not fit for any one good duty . . . if we desire to be saved wee must labour for humility: we shall deceive our selves if wee thinke to come to heaven without it.'[1] Whatever his worldly status and achievements a man was a creature of no significance in the face of the awesome majesty of God. Contemplation of the lowliness of his condition induced a proper sense of humility; it could even persuade a man like Sir James Harrington, a Rutland baronet who was one of the wealthiest landowners in England, to write in his will that 'I confesse my self to be a worme and no man Clothed with earth, full of sinne, deserving godes heavy displeasure but comforted in Jesus Christ.'[2] To its Puritan advocates, however, humility was not solely a matter of self-abasement before an omnipotent God: it was also an essential element in human relations. 'Humility', said John Preston, 'keeps a man within his own compasse. . . . It makes a man sociable and usefull and profitable to others.'[3]

As the Puritan divines were well aware, the concept of humility as a soeial virtue did not have obvious appeal for the rich country squires with their extensive power and prestige as landlords and magistrates, their great houses and parks, their large establishments of servants and their handsome coaches which were no less important as a status symbol than their coats of arms. Some of the gentry, declared Robert Bolton, 'thinke to beare downe all before them with an artificiall affected impetuousnesse, as it were, of Coun-tenance; a disdainfull neglect and contemptuousnesse in their Cariage with a kind of outbraving and brow-beating of their Brethren'. And he added, 'Hee's the best Christian which is most humble.'[4] Notwithstanding such criticism, however, there are indi-cations that among the Puritan gentry the restraining influence of religion did much to mitigate any latent feelings of superiority and arrogance which they may have possessed. Some men like Sir William Waller were prepared to accept that piety and virtue were more often to be found at the lower levels of society than among the ruling families. In a passage which revealed his familiarity with the works of St Paul he wrote that 'Not many wise men after the flesh, not many mighty, not many noble are called but God hath chosen the foolish, weak, base inconsiderable things of the world.' It was not flags and pedigrees, he continued, but a noble heart which made a noble person. Although the children of God might not necessarily have their names inscribed in the books of the heralds they were nevertheless written in the Book of Life.[5] Accor-ding to a minister who knew her well Dorothy Hanbury

> would heare a reproofe from the meanest person wisely admini-stered; she would borrow the eyes and tongues of her soule-friends, engaging them to take notice and to declare unto her what they saw in her contrary unto and not beseeming the Gospel of Jesus Christ, being more ready to mend what was amisse then to flie out against the reprover. . . . Her delight was in the meanest Saints, as if they had been persons of the greatest rank.[6]

At the same time there appears to have been a general feeling that it was wrong to adopt a supercilious attitude towards any man, whether he belonged to the household of faith or not. For had not St Paul said 'Mind not high things but condescend to men of low estate'?[7] 'Dispise not your Inferiours', Lady Brilliana Harley told her son Edward when he was commencing his studies at Oxford. Lady Elizabeth Brooke wrote in her commonplace book, 'Treat all Men with Kindness and wish them well. Do them good according to their Necessity and your Power and Opportunity. . . . If they are in Worldly Respects beneath you manifest your Love by Kindness, Affability and vouchsafing an easy Address to you.'[8] Many of the

Puritan gentry were indeed noted for the affability and condescension (still a neutral word at that time) which they showed to those who were socially inferior. Sir Thomas Crewe, the Northamptonshire lawyer, 'did not beare himselfe bigge upon his Offices or Place. . . . Though his parts did raise him up and advance him above the ordinarie sort of men yet his grace levelled him, that hee made himselfe equall to the lower sort.'[9] His friend Robert Bolton's criticism of the gentry was made in the course of a eulogy on his deceased patron, Sir Augustine Nichols, who had served as a judge in the Court of Common Pleas. Sir Augustine, he emphasised, had taken an entirely different attitude: 'An easinesse of accesse, affablenesse of carriage; a faire, loving, kind deportment towards all. I never saw a Man of such worth and greatnesse looke more mildly upon a meane Man in my life.'[10] At the funeral of Sir Francis Pile, a Berkshire landowner, in 1635 the preacher drew the same kind of contrast: 'And whereas many of his ranke stand upon their tiptoes, keepe their distance and look over their inferiours like lions over lambes . . . he was content to make himself equall with those of lowe degree (yet without wronging his ranke).' Another Berkshire squire, George Purefoy, was also credited with possessing what later ages would call the common touch: his speech, it was said, was 'perfumed with lenity and condescension to men of the meanest rank, so far as he could without making himself cheap and exposing his authority to contempt'.[11] Of Sir William Armyne it was related that

> his carriage was so justly contemper'd betwixt a kind of severe bravery and an humble courtesie that he was contentfull to all, grievous to none; in his very countenance and presence was both a checke to the presumptuous and an incouragement to the meanest of wisedome's children to draw near.

As for his wife Lady Mary she was distinguished for her 'Humility and lowliness of mind . . . she obliged all with whome she conversed or had to do.'[12] In the same way Lady Elizabeth Alston was extremely humble and courteous towards all persons with whom she conversed, 'condescending very much towards them of low degree and especially loving those among them in whom she observed but any inclinations to God and Goodness'.[13]

Despite such evidence it would have been surprising, given the environment in which they lived, if the Puritan gentry had been

entirely free from any feelings of class consciousness. Sir Simonds
D'Ewes wrote that humility was a saving grace whereby 'the soule
being made sensible and apprehensive of its owne vileness and
miserie by Nature endeavours to walke humblie both towards God
and man.' Even so, he had a snobbish streak which was clearly
revealed in a letter addressed to his brother Richard when the latter
was a student at Cambridge. 'You are maintained', he told him,
'with the best of your ranke; dehonorate not yourselfe by your
unseemelie associating with pencioners and subsizers though of
other colledges.'[14] Although well-born Puritans might treat their
inferiors with great civility they nevertheless expected them to know
their place and to show them the deference which they considered
to be their due. According to his wife, John Hutchinson

> never disdain'd the meanest person nor flattr'd the greatest; he
> had a loving and sweete courtesie to the poorest, and would
> often employ many spare howers with the commonest souldiers
> and poorest labourers, but still so ordering his familliarity as
> it never rays'd them to a contempt, but entertained still at the
> same time reverence with love of him. He ever preserv'd
> himselfe in his owne rank, neither being proud of it so as to
> despise any inferior, nor letting fall that just decorum which
> his honor oblieg'd him to keepe up.[15]

Ensconsed as they were in the upper reaches of a hierarchical
society the Puritan gentry were inclined to share the view which was
prevalent within their class that status and precedence were matters
of no small importance. Even Sir Robert Harley, that most zealous
professor of religion, considered that social distinctions should be
meticulously observed. When the gentlemen of Herefordshire
decided, at a meeting held in January 1626, to support his candidature at the forthcoming county election his main concern was to
ensure that he would be returned as the first of the knights of the
shire, a form of precedence which was widely regarded as conferring
great prestige. As a knight of the bath, he stressed, it would be a
dishonour for him to take second place to Sir Walter Pye, who was
only a knight bachelor, and rather than suffer this indignity he
would prefer to withdraw. In the ensuing correspondence Sir Walter
confirmed that he had no objection to Sir Robert being returned
first but made it clear that he was not prepared to acknowledge
this as a right. While expressing his gratitude for this gesture Sir

Robert felt obliged to take issue with him on such an important point of principle. It was not his intention, he wrote, to suggest that either of them had any right to be a knight of the shire or 'to have precedencie in that troublesome honor, both depending on the Publicke suffrage of our Countrey'; if, however, Sir Walter was unwilling to accept that he had a right of precedence by virtue of his order of knighthood 'yow will then give me leave to iustifie it in such a way as shall maintaine my honor and not impaire yours.'[16]

One of Sir Robert's ministers wrote of him that

Ignobled greatness had no value in his heraldry; he well foresaw that a Saint hath the richest coat and that nothing in heaven or earth doth so honour and enoble a family, or person, as true Religion, as God in Covenant, as Christ in chief . . . all the titles of honour and embellishments of the world's glory [are] but sublunar, and stained vanities; all whose tendency is towards the dust.

What may be termed the formal Puritan attitude to titles of honour was endorsed by Sir James Harrington in a book of spiritual meditations:

The highest favours of Princes, from whom flow Earthly dignities, are but shadowes of true honour. . . . My honour is more surely fixt than by Man or Devil to be extirpated or extinguisht. Can all thy power, O Enemy of Man, frustrate my Election, whereby from Eternity I am enroll'd a Peer of Heaven?

In answering charges of hypocrisy Sir James could rightly have pointed out that he had merely inherited his baronetcy which had been acquired by his grandfather; on the other hand, he would have found it more difficult to explain away his knighthood.[17] Another Puritan gentleman who entertained such sentiments was John Hutchinson who, in the words of his wife, 'was above the ambition of vaine titles and so well contented with the even ground of a gentleman that no invitation in the world could have prevail'd with him to advance one step that way; he lov'd substantiall, not ayrie, honor.'[18] In the main, however, the great Puritan squires were only too anxious to acquire titles for themselves; indeed there were very few Puritan landed families with incomes of £1000 a year or more which were not possessed of baronetcies or knighthoods during the early Stuart period. When the order of baronetcy was instituted in

1611 the first man to purchase this honour was Sir Nicholas Bacon, one of the leading patrons of Suffolk Puritanism, and he was soon followed by others of his persuasion, among them Sir Francis Barrington and Sir William Constable.[19] Sir Simonds D'Ewes appears to have acquired his knighthood at the insistence of Lady Anne Barnardiston, who was the grandmother and guardian of his first wife, Anne Clopton. In September 1626 she wrote in a letter to his father that

> as I hope shee shall finde a Religious loving husband of him (if God shall please for to unite them) so my desyer to you is ... that he might undergoe that ordinary stepp of honor ... that so shee might avoyde the contempte of some ill willers to these proceedeings and he gaine further respecte amonkst her kindred by these little additions.

The knighthood was conferred within a short while after the marriage and D'Ewes recorded in his account book that he was 'compelled to bee at the greater charge in obtaining it, the king being verie sparing in making any'. The total cost of this transaction amounted to £364, which was more than the devalued price at which baronetcies were then being offered. In July 1641 he was made a baronet and his Puritan brother-in-law Sir William Eliott wrote to him 'I congratulate the addition to your title and the rather as a reward of merritt.'[20]

If the Puritan gentry were inclined to attach considerable value to earthly titles they usually had nothing but contempt for the contemporary fashion for ostentatious funerals which were as much a form of conspicuous consumption as great houses and large collections of plate. Such an attitude was by no means confined to the godly: even Matthew Wren, the Laudian bishop who was one of their main antagonists, felt it necessary to stipulate that at his funeral care should be taken 'to avoid that pomp and vanity which is now too much in use'.[21] Nevertheless the fact remains that it was customary for a Puritan squire when drawing up his will to make it clear that he wished to be buried without pomp or solemnity or unnecessary expense. This kind of testamentary provision was entirely consistent with the Puritan attitude to church worship in general; it reflected a concern for the financial well-being of the family after the testator's death; but perhaps above all it represented a last act of humility and an affirmation that worldly values counted for nothing in comparison with the blessings of everlasting life.

What many Puritan gentlemen were anxious to forestall was the type of elaborate and costly funeral which the heralds took delight in organising. Sir William Doddington specifically directed that his funeral should be 'without herauld or pompe', while Sir Humphrey Winch expressed the wish that he should be buried in a private and decent fashion without any heralds or escutcheons.[22] The heralds, however, could be very importunate. In 1602 John Chamberlain wrote in one of his news-letters that the funeral of Anne Lytton, the wife of Rowland Lytton, had been performed 'very orderly and with good solemnitie' and the more so because of the presence of William Camden, Clarenceux King of Arms, 'who came from the buriall of the Lady Barrington unlooked for and unrequested but went not empty away as he pretended and wold needes have done'.[23] If the heralds were allowed a completely free hand the expenditure could be very heavy indeed. When Sir Martin Lumley, a former Lord Mayor of London, died in 1634 he was given a magnificent funeral which was supervised by Sir Henry St George, Sir William Le Neve and other officers of the College of Arms and later his son, another Sir Martin, was to say that the funeral charges had amounted to no less than £2300.[24]

While the Puritan gentry usually had a preference for simple funerals, with the preaching of a godly sermon as the principal feature, they were more disposed to follow the well established practice of commissioning church monuments which were a public testimony to family pride, if not to self-esteem. Some professors of religion were critical of memorials which depicted the deceased on the grounds that they represented a form of idolatry. Sir Simonds D'Ewes, however, did not subscribe to this view. In October 1641 he complained in the House of Commons about the excessive zeal of a London churchwarden who by virtue of a parliamentary order for the removal of idolatrous pictures from churches had defaced the figures on the tombs for which he was responsible. This action, D'Ewes argued,

> had brought a great scandall upon the howse of Commons as if wee meant to deface all Antiquities. That when we had prepared a statute to passe to this end and purpose for the

removing of all offensive pictures yet wee had speciallie provided that noe tombs should be medled withall.

In part D'Ewes was influenced by his love of antiquarian pursuits but at the same time it cannot have escaped his memory that in 1624 his father had arranged for the erection of a marble and alabaster tomb with pictures of himself and his wives and children.[25] During the seventeenth century many Puritan squires commissioned monuments either for themselves or in memory of their parents or made provision for this purpose in their wills, in some cases specifying how much was to be spent. After the death of his father in 1600 Sir George More paid for a large tomb to be set up in the church of St Nicholas at Guildford. This has full-size effigies of both his parents and an inscription composed by Sir George himself which records 'their vertuous and godlye life, Hee beyng ever more a zealous Professor of true Religion and a favourer of all those whiche truelye were Religious'.[26] Sir James Harrington, the Rutland squire who likened himself to a worm, had been one of the first gentlemen in England to secure a baronetcy. In his will, which was drawn up in 1613, he observed that he had erected a little memorial to himself and his first wife in his parish church of Ridlington and indicated that he wished to have it inscribed with the date of his death, his new style and an escutcheon with a bloody hand which was the emblem of his baronetcy. As though to counter possible criticism he added that while he took no pride in such matters 'so doe I not disdaine that badge his maiestie hath given to me and my heirs male for ever'. The memorial, which is on the north wall of the chancel, is indeed small, certainly in comparison with many of the church monuments which were going up in this period. Sir James and his wife are shown kneeling in prayer and it is perhaps indicative of their religious sympathies that he has short hair while she is dressed simply in a black gown and white ruff.[27] John Gurdon, a wealthy Suffolk landowner, gave direction in his will that a monument should be put up in his parish church of Assington to the memory of himself, his parents and his wife, leaving it to his grandson to choose a design which he considered 'meete and fitt for our estate, condicion and callinge as wee lived in this worlde'. Following his death in 1623 his wishes were carried out (though the monument is relatively modest in size) and subsequently his son Brampton was commemorated in similar fashion.[28]

In another part of Suffolk the parish church of Kedington contains a whole series of magnificent tombs with effigies of successive heads of the Barnardiston family and their wives. Following the death of Sir Nathaniel Barnardiston in 1653 one of the sons of Samuel Fairclough, the Puritan rector of Kedington, felt it necessary to warn his wife about the sin of idolatry:

> If worship doth offend I thee implore
> And crave a favour, Madam, 'tis this one,
> Adde to his memory no pictur'd stone
> Lest whilst within the Church my vows I pay
> I to the Image of this Saint should pray.

In his will Sir Nathaniel had merely left £40 for the construction of a vault in Kedington church but after the Restoration the family erected an alabaster monument which incorporated effigies of both him and his wife.[29] On the other hand, there were many Puritan squires whose memory is preserved only by simple wall tablets or ledger stones. Perhaps in their case a true sense of humility prevailed.

A form of humility to which the Puritan divines attached particular importance was the readiness of members of the laity to accept their guidance and correction. Looking back on his long career as a minister of the Gospel, Richard Baxter commented with feeling on the self-esteem of the rich who were often reluctant to entertain any criticism of their faults: unless they were guilty of some 'swinish inexcusable sin', he wrote, they could not bear to be told of their transgressions.[30] Among the Puritan gentry, however, such intransigence appears to have been less common. One of Sir Anthony Cope's ministers wrote of him that when he was at family prayers 'hee would shame himself most in his confessions for his owne most speciall sinnes'; and that he particularly respected those preachers 'that least favoured his corruptions, often blessing God for such teachers as would not give him rest in sinne'. George Purefoy, another wealthy landowner, was also commended for the meekness which he displayed: his chaplain testifies that 'when I laid before him his impatiency and fretting, to which he had been prone; with humility he acknowledged his fault, but withall ascribing the praise to the grace of God.'[31] Nevertheless it cannot always have been an easy matter for a well-to-do family to submit to the dictates of a spiritual counsellor who considered that every aspect of their daily living came within his purview.

Evangelical work could be a hard uphill task and some Puritan ministers were almost pathetically grateful for any support which they received from the gentry. When William Attersoll, the rector of Isfield in Sussex, published his treatise *The Conversion of Nineveh* he dedicated it to Sir John Rivers, 'whose good affection to our Tribe (so much scorned and scoffed at in the world) and carefull frequenting the exercises of religion many wayes appeareth'. At the same time he was anxious to express his appreciation of the respect which Sir John had shown him 'in that you disdaine not, but upon every occasion of passing by, to come under the roofe of my poore cottage'.[32] Often, however, the Puritan divines exhibited little of the deference which was usually accorded to persons of wealth and rank. Baronetcies and knighthoods, coats of arms and pedigrees: whatever their importance in worldly terms they could not begin to compare with the everlasting joys which were reserved for the elect. During the course of the sermon which he delivered at the funeral of Lady Mary Strode in 1619 John Barlow made it brutally clear that he was not interested in such matters:

> She, in respect of her birth and pedigree, shall of me receive no praise (though, for any thing I know, in that commendable). We are all of one blood; God little respects to commend that in any; and they are most honourably (as I perswade my selfe she was) descended that are borne againe by the word and spirit, and where the Lord is silent I wish to be silent also.[33]

Many of the godly divines were on terms of easy familiarity with members of the gentry who shared their religious sympathies, often taking a close, and sometimes even a patronising, interest in their spiritual progress. John Clarke wrote in an epistle dedicatory addressed to Sir Edward Ayscough, who had once given him shelter, and his 'religious and noble' wife

> You are happy (Right Worshipfull) above many in that God hath given you a mind to know him, a heart to love him. Presse on still toward the marke: study which way to honour God most and to live to him, this will bring you peace at the last. 'Tis not a forme of godlinesse ... but the power of it in a sanctified life which before God is much set by. Goe on in that

good way you have begun, count all things but dung that yee
may winne Christ and bee found in him. Take up the crosse
which lies in the waies of God. Deny your selves. This doe and
you shall cause the blessing to rest on your house and posteritie
after you, and those Olive plants about your table shall become
trees of righteousnesse.[34]

When one of the works of Richard Stock, a well-known London
preacher, was published posthumously in 1641 the editor, James
Cranford, chose to dedicate it to Lady Anne Yelverton, the wife of
Sir Christopher Yelverton, explaining that he was doing so because
of her goodness which he acknowledged and desired to help. Cranford was a nonconformist divine who held the Northamptonshire
living of Brockhall and was obviously well acquainted with Lady
Yelverton. In the epistle dedicatory he stressed that women were
in as woeful a condition as men and like them could only be saved
by 'repentance towards God and faith towards Christ, the joyning of
knowledge and obedience. . . . Madam, I have heard your Ladiship
plead for these things and know in part your pains and your
progresse in them.' He well knew that she would make good use of
a book of this kind. 'Madam, your growth and increase in these
graces which are already eminent in your Ladiship is the thing I
desire and this book, with God's blessing on it, may procure.' What
Lady Yelverton thought of such a public appraisal is not known.[35]

Lady Joan Barrington was in contact with many godly ministers
who kept up a steady bombardment of advice and exhortation.
Ezekiel Rogers, who served for twelve years as domestic chaplain
to the Barrington family, was eventually preferred to their living
of Rowley in Yorkshire and from here he maintained a regular
correspondence with her. In one of his letters he expressed the hope
that 'you are still growing from strength to strength towards Sion,
that you are dayly more stablished and rooted in faith'; in another,
that 'you are now growne (not full but) exceeding rich in faith and
godlines.' In addition to supplying her with a set of rules for self-
examination he was always ready to offer her advice on such matters
as her choice of friends and servants and her responsibilities in
relation to the spiritual well-being of other members of the family.
In 1631, following a short visit he had made to her house at Hatfield
Broad Oak, he implored her 'not only by your prayers and example
but advise to helpe forwarde your sonne and daughter'. Some years

later Rogers heard that Sir Thomas Barrington was planning to replace him in the living of Rowley with a young man, Thomas White, who was currently employed as his household chaplain. In November 1636, when he was under suspension for nonconformity, he sent Sir Thomas an indignant letter in which he protested that 'I have done yo more service and tooke more paines with yo in one weeke (witnesse at my first coming my watchings with yo in the time of your melancholy and risings at midnight to cherish and comfort yo &c) then he hath done in his whole time.' In the event the patron had his way: Rogers resigned the living and went to New England and White became the new rector of Rowley. Following his arrival in New England Rogers was engaged in some acrimonious correspondence with Sir Thomas over a payment which he claimed was due to him. Writing in September 1641 he complained bitterly about the way Sir Thomas had treated him, an exile for Jesus Christ, and while recording his satisfaction at the events which were taking place in England felt obliged to tell him that 'you have not yet putt of your harnesse; and if you that are Reformers be not exact in your walking with God in holiness and righteousness, my feares wilbe still increased.'[36]

This unseemly episode offers a useful corrective to the general impression fostered by Puritan biographical literature that a common bond of godliness ensured a full and perfect understanding between patron and minister. Nevertheless the fact remains that a special relationship did exist in many cases. Puritan ministers were often treated like close family friends: they acted as executors and trustees and might even play a part in marriage negotiations; they might be asked to advise on, and make arrangements for, the education of the children; and they sometimes received handsome gifts under the wills of their patrons. At the same time there is evidence of a certain amount of intermarriage between the gentry and the brethren of godly divines, a process which was no doubt assisted by the fact that many of the latter came from families of good social standing. Richard Roberts, a brother of Sir William Roberts and himself a Puritan divine, married the eldest daughter of William Gouge, whose treatise *Of Domesticall Duties* laid great stress on the husband's authority over the wife.[37] Jane Browne, the daughter of John Browne, the Dorset parliamentarian, had two clerical husbands: Walter Newburgh, the rector of Symondsbury, who had been presented to that living by Sir Walter Erle, and Dr John

Stoughton, the minister of St Mary Aldermanbury in London, who was a friend of Sir Robert Harley and a man who was frequently in trouble with the church authorities.[38]

In 1629 Roger Williams, who was then domestic chaplain to Sir William Masham, wrote to Lady Joan Barrington about the possibility of a match between himself and a niece who was under her care. 'Obiections have come in', he told her, 'about her Spirit, much accused for passion etc. and hastie, rash and unconstant, other feares about her present Condition, it being some Indecorum for her to condescend to my low-ebb.' Speaking for himself, it was well known how a gracious God and a tender conscience had kept him back from honour and preferment; as for his intended wife he was emphatic that there was no one whom he loved more. Although he addressed her as 'an Angell of God' Lady Barrington viewed the proposal with a distinct lack of enthusiasm and Williams was left in no doubt that his suit was not welcomed. This prompted him to fire off a very different kind of letter in which he assured Lady Barrington that 'We hope to live together in the heavens though the Lord have denied that union on Earth' and proceeded to launch a bitter attack on her, openly questioning the sincerity of her religious beliefs. It was not for nothing, he declared, that she had recently been visited with many troubles, including the loss of her husband: 'the Lord hath A quarrell against you.' He went on:

> I know not one professor . . . whose truth and faythfullnes to Jesus Christ is more suspected, doubted, feared by all or most of those that know the Lord. . . . It hath almost astonisht me . . . that not only inferiour Christians but ministers eagle eyd, faythfull and observant to your Ladiship, after so many yeares of God's patience toward you, so long profession, such helpes and meanes incomparable, should yet be driven to sigh, to say litle, to suspend their Judgments, to hope but feare and doubt.

Three things in particular were causing concern:

> First, feares are that the World hath choakt those blessed seeds that have beene sowne and keepes the fruits from true perfection. . . . A strangenes from the faythfull in spirituall Societie. . . . A stand or stay in the wayes of holynes.

There followed some quotations from the scriptures, among them a passage from the Book of Job which Williams obviously regarded as particularly apposite: in the words of his transcription, 'He with whome we deale excepteth not the persons of Princes nor regardeth the rich more than the poore; for they are all the worcke of his hands.' Not surprisingly, Lady Barrington was deeply shocked and angered by this letter. Although he was her son-in-law Sir William Masham clearly felt under some obligation to defend his chaplain and subsequently he wrote in a letter to her that he now believed that Williams had acted only 'out of love and conscience'. A kind word from her, he suggested, would give him much comfort.[39]

Notwithstanding their dependence on the patronage of wealthy landed families the Puritan divines were often prepared to criticise the way in which they used their leisure. 'What is the pleasure of Hawks and hounds', declaimed a Devonshire parson, 'but a mungril pleasure? What are gamings at Cards and Dice but the firebrands of passion and the consumption of treasure and time?' John Dod, who was acquainted with many of the Northamptonshire gentry, expressed astonishment at the amount of time which was devoted to recreation of a secular kind and made the scathing comment that 'when we see Hounds and Hawks and Cards and Dice we may fear that there is some sick soul in that Family.'[40] Robert Bolton, who was in charge of a Northamptonshire parish for many years, condemned the nobles, knights and gentlemen who were unwilling to forgo their pleasures even for a short while in order to hear the preaching of the Word at the public lectures which were often a feature of market-days in towns where Puritan influences were strong:

> Bowling-greenes, gaming-houses, horse-races, hunting-matches; their curs and their kites; their cock-pits and their covetousnesse ... doe too often eate up and devoure that blessed fat and marrow of time, those golden and goodly opportunities which GOD in great mercy affords them in the Ministry to make their peace with him before they goe into the pit and bee seene no more. For one houre whereof, to heare but one Sermon after the irrecoverable day of visitation is past and expired, they would be content to live as precisely and mortifiedly as ever man did upon earth so long as the world lasts, but it shall not be granted.

As this tirade was delivered in the course of an assize sermon at Northampton it is likely to have had a mixed reception from a gathering which would have included representatives of many of the principal families of the county.[41]

Some Puritan squires took little or no interest in field sports, though this was not necessarily because of the criticism voiced by godly ministers. Many others, however, can be found engaging in such pursuits as hunting, hawking and fishing; and indeed it appears to have been widely held that there was nothing wrong with this type of recreation provided it was not carried to excess. 'It is observed by some', wrote Sir William Waller, 'that hunting hath an ill name in Scripture.' He was satisfied, however, that it was not unlawful in the sight of God and armed with this conviction he offered the prayer 'O my God . . . let me not live to abuse this liberty which thou art pleased to allow, either by our affecting it or by turning my delight in it to a Sanguinary wontonness . . . that it may be my principal end by this exercise to improve my health and strength to the advantage of thy service.'[42] According to his wife Sir William Springett had a great love of fishing and coursing but, she stressed, 'the vanity of these things his mind was out of when he was engaged in religion'.[43] Sir Edward Peyton described hunting and hawking as most commendable exercises. Hunting was 'manly and heroick', a 'virile recreation' which ensured that the participants were not 'enervated by ease, the betraier of corporall and mentall abilities'. In 1623 he obtained a royal warrant authorising him to take a hundred partridges every year in the Isle of Ely and adjoining areas, where gentlemen could not hawk, on the basis that he would 'plant' them at his own charge in open country near his Cambridgeshire seat of Isleham.[44]

In his youth Sir James Harrington was riding at night to a race-meeting when his horse fell into a deep pit and he was lucky to escape with his life. This incident made a profound impression on him and he was later to write

Worldly, yea, too often sinful Pleasure is the Dallilah and flattering Mistriss of our Youth so that slavishly and unweariedly we count it Day and Night; else I would not have lost my sleep, nor travelled all Night, only to see such a transitory delight as a Horse Race; where usually our precious time, our wisdom and our Moneys run faster away from us than our Horses.[45]

Such sentiments may well have been common yet the fact remains that horse-racing had a following among the Puritan gentry. In 1619 a group of landowners in the East Riding of Yorkshire joined together to establish an annual race at Kiplingcotes for 'the continueing of Neighbourhood and societie amongst the Noblemen and Gentlemen of the . . . County of York'. Somewhat surprisingly, this was a sporting association which declined to practise religious discrimination: its membership represented various shades of opinion, ranging from known Catholics like Henry Viscount Dunbar to Puritans like Sir Matthew Boynton.[46]

Like the major field sports the game of bowls was essentially a pastime of the well-to-do; indeed as James I emphasised in his Declaration of Sports it was a recreation which 'the meaner sort of people' were legally forbidden to participate in.[47] Sir William Waller regarded the sport with amused contempt:

> It is a measuring cast whether it is better sport to see the bowling or the bowlers; of the two the last would make one laugh most. . . . Certainly there cannot be a better jeast seen then the antick figures into which they screw themselves; nor a greater absurdity heard then the sensible advice that they cast after their senseless bowles.[48]

It was nevertheless a very popular activity during the early seventeenth century and many of the Puritan gentry seem to have taken pleasure in it. Sir Simonds D'Ewes played at bowls in various towns in the vicinity of his Suffolk home and also while staying with his brother-in-law Sir William Eliott in Surrey; some men like Sir Thomas Pelham had their own bowling greens or alleys; while John Strode, a younger son of Sir William Strode, was reputed to be the most skilful bowler in England.[49] In a number of counties there were bowling clubs which the local gentry used as meeting-places where they could discuss business matters or politics or merely exchange gossip. Some of these clubs even had a religious function: according to Bishop Wren of Norwich, writing in 1636, there was not a bowling green in Suffolk, that great Puritan county, which did not have its lecture or sermon. In June 1636 we find Sir Edmund Moundeford writing to his cousin Framlingham Gawdy to suggest that they should meet at the bowling green in the Suffolk market town of Bury St Edmunds. His brother-in-law William Heveningham would also be there and he hoped that they might be joined by Sir John Holland 'whose company we all wish'. All these men would later support the cause of Parliament, as would Sir Simonds D'Ewes, another of the gentry who played bowls at Bury St Edmunds.[50]

In discussing indoor recreation William Perkins drew a distinction between games of skill such as chess and draughts which he felt able to commend and games of chance which 'by the consent of godly Divines are unlawfull'. His attitude to gambling was quite simple and straightforward: 'It is . . . an abuse of Recreation when it is used to winne other men's money.'[51] In 1661 a Devonshire minister warmly praised the virtues of successive heads of the Rolle family of Heanton Satchville (among whom was Sir Samuel Rolle) and in the process singled out for special mention the contempt which they had for cards and dice. 'The very instruments and occasions of evil', he declared, 'were an offence unto them. Amongst other disorders against which they testified their dislike gamings at cards and dice have not been so much as tolerated in their families (as I have been credibly informed) for well near, if not more then, a full century of years.' Another Devonshire gentleman, William Martyn, was of the same mind: 'no time can be worst spent', he told his son, 'then that which is vainely consumed in such foolish sporting.' Gaming promoted covetousness, discontent and disquiet of mind; it was worse than bribery, extortion and usury.[52] Sir Francis Pile was a man noted for his open-handed hospitality and concern for the poor: in order to perform 'this worthy worke with the greater credit and comfort hee avoyded the vaine and needlesse expenses of dicing, carding, running horses.'[53]

Sir Simonds D'Ewes took a strong dislike to gaming with dice when he was a student at the Middle Temple: though prepared to accept that the game was not unlawful in itself he was appalled by the oaths, execrations and quarrelling that accompanied it. Later on he came to regard both dicing and card-playing as sinful and displeasing to God.[54] At the same time there were some wealthy Puritans who were inclined to take a more favourable view of such forms of recreation without necessarily engaging in any serious gambling. Bulstrode Whitelocke recalls that one Christmas at Fawley Court, his Buckinghamshire seat, 'we had our pleasures of the time within doores, by musicke and playing att Cardes, but not for great somes, only for pastime.' In this he followed his father's rule, 'neither to spend much time nor to hazard much money on gameing butt to use these diversions moderately'. At Hatfield Broad Oak in Essex Sir Thomas Barrington and his family played shovel-

141

board, sometimes in the company of Francis Parker, their parish minister, but as at Fawley Court the sums which changed hands were relatively modest.[55]

When Thomas Shepard, an Essex lecturer, was driven out of the Diocese of London in 1631 he took shelter with Sir Richard Darley, a Puritan squire who lived at Buttercrambe in Yorkshire. Arriving at Buttercrambe Hall on a wet Saturday night he was astounded to find that some members of the family were playing at dice and backgammon and immediately concluded that he was entering a profane house. Eventually he managed to impose his own stringent code of conduct on the household though it is clear from his account that not everyone appreciated his reforming zeal.[56]

In 1619 Sir Robert Harley drew up a list of books which had belonged to his brother James and among the items listed was a volume entitled *Th'overthrow of Stage-Playes*. The author was John Reynolds, a well-known Puritan who had been President of Corpus Christi, Oxford, and the thrust of his arguments may be gathered from an explanatory note on the title-page which assures the reader that the work manifestly proves that 'it is not onely unlawfull to bee an Actor but a beholder of those vanities.'[57] During the early part of his life Robert Bolton 'could not abide their company that were of a strict and holy conversation, such he would fetch within the compasse of Puritans' and one of the manifestations of his ungodly outlook was his love of stage plays. As a minister, however, he viewed them in a very different light: 'let those examine themselves', he thundered, 'who offer themselves to those sinfull occasions, breeders of many strange and fearefull mischiefes, I meane prophane and obscene Playes . . . the grand empoysoners of grace, ingenuousnesse and all manly resolution.' To Bolton it was unthinkable that a godly man should have any liking for stage plays.[58] When Sir James Harrington paid his first visit to London about the beginning of Charles I's reign he decided to go to the theatre as he had heard that stage plays were very popular and 'by the Youth of our Nation preferred above the best of Sermons'. What he thought of this experience was neatly summed up in some verse he wrote:

> Thence to Theatres I went
> Where vain Wits their Poems vent;
> Heard and saw such Ribaldry
> As defiles both Eare and Eye.

Many years later he declared in the course of an exhortatory epistle addressed to the nobility and gentry of Great Britain that at the Day of Judgment they would have to account for

> So many Stage-Playes, the Scoffers of goodness and holiness of conversation; the Consumers of useful time and of the innate Virtue, Modesty and Estates of all kindes of Persons; as also so many Frothy and Airy amorous Verses, Ditties and Songs, the Nurses and Panders of all manner of loosness and uncleanness in all sorts of People.[59]

At Court it was the practice for masques and plays to be staged on Sundays and this inevitably caused offence in Puritan circles. Sir Edward Peyton, however, had more fundamental objections to such official entertainments: writing of the reign of James I he declared that 'sin was hatched from an egg to a Dragon to devour holiness of life; insomuch that the Masks and Playes at Whitehal were used onely for Incentives to lust.'[60]

While some Puritan gentlemen were contemptuous of both stage plays and actors there were others who seem to have taken a more broadminded view. It is apparent from his expenditure accounts that Sir Thomas Barrington sometimes went to the theatre while Sir Benjamin Rudyerd, who was a friend of Ben Jonson, wrote that

> Mine eye hath seen, my heart hath prov'd
> The most and best of earthly joyes,
> The sweet of love, and being lov'd,
> Masks, Feasts and Playes and such like toyes.[61]

Sir Thomas Barrington, who was not averse to using theatrical metaphors in his letters,[62] owned a copy of the Second Folio edition of Shakespeare and it is noteworthy that Sir Robert Harley's library, though consisting mainly of religious works, included a volume of Ben Jonson's plays along with Shakespeare's sonnets and Bacon's essays.[63]

Whatever their attitude to the use of music in church the Puritan gentry usually had no objections in principle to secular music and dancing; and indeed no less an authority than William Perkins had signified his approval of music-making for recreational purposes.[64] The accounts of Richard Shuttleworth, who lived at Gawthorpe Hall in Lancashire, record the payment of gratuities to musicians and pipers who would often, no doubt, provide an accompaniment for dancing. When Sir Oliver Luke was acting as guardian to Elizabeth Eliot, a daughter of his friend Sir John Eliot, he suggested to her father that it would be fitting for her to receive instruction in music; in reply Sir John, who was then a prisoner in the Tower, readily gave his consent.[65] Sir Thomas Barrington employed a music master to teach his daughter Lucy to sing and also arranged for her to have dancing lessons; in addition, there are references in his accounts to payments for wassails, morris dances and 'Loude Musicke'. When Lucy eventually married there were trumpeters, fiddlers and hautboy players on hand to assist in the festivities.[66]

To judge from household inventories and other sources of evidence such instruments as viols and virginals were often to be found in Puritan manor-houses. Sir Thomas Wodehouse had a particularly strong affection for music, a point which is stressed in a seventeenth-century verse chronicle of the family:

> In hounds and horses hee great pleasure tooke
> His home-delights were Musiq and a booke.

When drawing up his will in 1658 he bequeathed to his grandson Thomas his organ, a harpsichord, a chest of viols and all the other instruments in the music room of his house.[67] In this respect he shared a common interest with Bulstrode Whitelocke who had received instruction in both music and dancing at Merchant Taylors School. As an undergraduate at Oxford Whitelocke frequented musical gatherings and eventually, following his admission to the Middle Temple, he 'grew a Master'. During his time at the Middle Temple he and some of his fellow students met every evening at St Dunstan's tavern where they practised galliards, corantoes, French dances and country dances; he stresses, however, that they appeared 'much more like to grave antients in a Councell Chamber then to young revellers in an house of drinking'.[68]

On the whole, the wealthier Puritan families seem to have accepted the validity of the contemporary view that the accomplishments of a proper gentleman must include music and dancing as well as fencing and horsemanship. At the same time there was a feeling, as Bulstrode Whitelocke's comment indicates, that such pastimes should be approached in a sober frame of mind. William Martyn told his son Nicholas, who was then a student at Oxford, that for his 'better and more gentlemanlike sporting and recreation' he recommended dancing and vaulting which were both good for the health. It was important, however, that they should have for their 'chiefest ends comelinesse without Pride, pleasure without wantonnesse, recreation without self-liking, societie without ribaldry, exercise without wearinesse, and contentednesse without covetousnesse'.[69] What mainly worried the Puritan divines (aside from the evil of Sabbath-breaking) was the kind of dancing in which persons of both sexes took part: one of its most forceful critics was Edmund Rudyerd, a Staffordshire minister, who condemned what he described as 'Lascivious and unchast (mixt) dauncings'.[70] Walter Yonge the diarist believed that mixed dancing, like stage plays and masques, 'tended to the high provocation of God's wrath' while Sir Simonds D'Ewes shunned it because he considered it to be a controversial sin. Harbottle Grimston no doubt had mixed dancing in mind when urging the readers of his treatise *A Christian New-Year's Gift* to 'use not idlenesse, wanton Books, lascivious Pictures, nor immodest dances'.[71]

In the stricter Puritan households the most common type of musical activity was the singing of psalms. Among the papers of Sir Simonds D'Ewes there is a book of metrical psalms

> Set foorth and allowed to be sung in all Churches, of all the people together, before and after Morning and Evening Prayer; and also before and after Sermons, and moreover in private houses for their godly solace and comfort, laying apart all ungodly songs and ballades which tend onely to the nourishing of vice and corrupting of youth.[72]

It was the kind of work which a Puritan chaplain would have had no hesitation in recommending to his employer.

CHAPTER EIGHT

GODLINESS UNDER THREAT

During the years between the appointment of George Abbot as Archbishop of Canterbury in 1611 and his loss of effective power after the accession of Charles I[1] the Puritans could regard the situation which existed within the Church of England with reasonable equanimity. Abbot was a strict Calvinist who was involved in a lengthy and bitter feud with William Laud. Sir Simonds D'Ewes describes him as an orthodox and learned divine who was in no way infected with Arminianism.[2] Among seventeenth-century commentators there was general agreement that he was well disposed towards the Puritans. Clarendon compares him unfavourably with his immediate predecessor, Richard Bancroft, stressing that he made little effort to ensure that his clergy observed the discipline of the Church or conformed to the articles and canons. Peter Heylyn comments that he allowed the practice of nonconformity to become so firmly established that subsequent attempts to rectify the situation were interpreted as the bringing in of innovations. Writing from a rather different standpoint Roger Morrice, a nonconformist divine, relates that through the kindness of Archbishop Abbot and others the Puritans gained some ease, quiet and liberty. None of the bishops voluntarily engaged in their prosecution except Richard Neile and John Buckeridge 'so that they were at this time indulged both in Doctrine, Worship and Ceremony'.[3] In the Northern Province Toby Matthew, who was Archbishop of York between 1606 and 1628, followed the same kind of *laissez-faire* policy and under his rule little was done to curb even the most persistent offenders.[4] There were also a considerable number of Calvinistminded bishops who were either in sympathy with or at least unwilling to antagonise the Puritans. They included Robert Abbot, a brother of the Archbishop, John Davenant, Thomas Morton, James Montagu, Nicholas Felton, George Carleton and John Williams. Thomas Morton claimed that his remissness in prosecuting the nonconformists had hindered his career while Robert Abbot was regarded as a Puritan in some quarters. John Williams, who became Bishop of Lincoln in 1621, was a High Churchman yet he was also 'very communicable . . . with dissentient Brethren that did not conform, whom he gain'd first with kindness and then brought over with Argument'. So leniently did he treat the Puritans that Sir John Lambe, whom he had appointed as his Commissary, secretly complained to the Privy Council about his conduct.[5]

As a result of Bancroft's determined efforts to enforce uniformity in matters of worship many of the Puritan clergy had conformed, at least to the extent necessary to avoid deprivation. Before long the term 'conformable Puritan' began to come into use: according to Thomas Fuller it was probably invented by Samuel Harsnet, Bishop of Norwich and later Archbishop of York, who applied it to those ministers who observed the requirement for outward ceremony as an act of expediency 'yet dissented from it in their judgments'.[6] During the period of Abbot's supremacy this pliant attitude was still in evidence yet there was also a good deal of nonconformity, both clerical and lay, which in many dioceses the ecclesiastical authorities either winked at or dealt with very lightly. In parishes which enjoyed some degree of local autonomy in matters of worship a Puritan squire would often be able to receive communion either standing or sitting, to have his children baptised without the sign of the cross and to hear two profitable sermons every Sunday. His minister, who would usually be styled 'pastor', might wear the surplice only occasionally, if at all, and perhaps even abbreviate the Prayer Book services. No doubt the liberal treatment of Puritan divines who drew the line at anything which could be construed as separatism largely explains why there was so little parliamentary interest in liturgical or ceremonial issues during the years 1610 to 1625.

Although the Puritans had reason to be grateful to Archbishop Abbot the more clear-sighted of them could perceive the clouds which were beginning to gather on the horizon even before the accession of Charles I. During the early 1620s there was growing evidence that Arminianism was gaining ground at a comparatively rapid pace. In 1622 one of Buckingham's chaplains caused a stir by preaching an Arminian sermon at Cambridge while two years later Sir Simonds D'Ewes noted in his diary that this 'verie dangerous heresie' was spreading to most parts of England.[7] When the king issued directions for the restraint of preaching in August 1622 he referred to this new development in the covering letter which he addressed to the Archbishop of Canterbury. According to this letter Archbishop Abbot and some of his fellow bishops had informed him that many young students had been broaching unprofitable, unsound, seditious and dangerous doctrines which if allowed to take hold could lead to a schism within the Church. The declared aim of the royal directions was to prevent the dissemination of these unorthodox tenets but in reality they were a double-edged weapon since they also placed severe restrictions on the propagation of Calvinist doctrine. Among other things it was stipulated that no minister below the degree of bishop or dean should preach in any public auditory on the 'deep points' of predestination, election or reprobation or of the universality, efficacy, resistibility or irresistibility of God's grace; such matters, it was stressed, were better left to the divinity schools. Any constraints on godly preaching were naturally repugnant to the Puritans but at least the embargo did not extend to the printed word and over the next few years there was a steady outflow of literature in defence of the Calvinist position. In 1627 Richard Capel, the rector of Eastington in Gloucestershire, published a posthumous edition of certain lectures on the nature of grace and faith which his friend William Pemble had delivered at Magdalen Hall, Oxford. The work contained some sharp criticism of Arminian doctrine and in dedicating it to his patron Nathaniel Stephens he commented that

> Bookes are more necessary in a state than arms. Arms are to defend us from the invasion of foes, bookes are to preserve us from the infection of errors; enemies can but kill the body, errors endanger the soule. There are crepte into the Churches a number of false opinions, some that oppugne, others that obscure the grace of God . . . sith therefore errors are so plenty bookes cannot but be very necessary . . . there are few Schollars or others that minde these matters but doe begin to see thorow the conceipts of the Arminians.

In conclusion he warmly commended the book to his patron as a man whom God had made willing to learn and able to judge.[8]

Despite the fears and anxieties of the godly divines it was not until the Parliament of 1625 that the Puritan members of the House of Commons began to pay serious attention to the problem of Arminianism; before that they had been much more concerned with the threat (as they apprehended it) of Catholicism both at home and abroad. The particular matter which aroused their interest was the publication of certain works by Richard Montague, an ambitious clergyman whose religious opinions earned him the patronage of the new king and the support of such prelates as Laud and Neile. Montague believed that the Church of England was too much under the domination of the Puritans. Writing to his friend John Cosin in October 1624 he expressed the hope that John Prideaux, one of his Calvinist critics, would not be appointed to the vacant see of Gloucester; Bishop Laud, he stressed, 'must nowe and in such cases putt for the Church with the Duke and use his greate Creditt, that we be not swallowed up with a Puritan Bishopriqry'.[9] In July 1625 Walter Yonge noted in his diary that 'Doctor Montague, Canon of Windsor, was questioned in the parliament house concerning a book by him containing many points of popery and other dangerous affections.' The committee which was appointed by the House of Commons to examine his works commented that through his influence the fire kindled by Arminianism in the Low Countries was likely to spread to England, deplored the fact that he had intimated that there were Puritan bishops and described his literary activities as a great encouragement to popery.[10]

The Montague case was still under consideration when Parliament was dissolved on 12 August. In a letter dated 3 December Bishop Davenant of Salisbury told his friend Samuel Ward, the Master of Sidney Sussex, Cambridge, that he was afraid that 'Mr Montague his book will breed himselfe and others much trouble whensoever a Parliament shall bee called. His opinion concerning Predestination and Totall-falling from Grace is undoubtedly contrary to the Common Tenets of the English Church ever since we were borne.'[11] The next Parliament assembled in February 1626 and one of the first actions of the Commons was to set up a committee on religion which included many Puritan members, among them Sir Benjamin Rudyerd, Sir Francis Barrington, Sir Gilbert Gerard, Sir Edward Peyton, Sir Francis Goodwin and Sir

Walter Erle. Sir Edward Peyton was later to write that Charles I had 'from the beginning of his Govornment ... resolved to go a way contrary to the stream of a pious Rule and the command of God'.[12] The committee was given the task of examining Montague's works and concluded that he merited impeachment by the House of Lords. The charges which were framed by the committee reflected the general contention of the Puritans that in seeking to combat Arminianism they were simply defending the *status quo*. Among other things, it was alleged that Montague had expounded doctrine which was contrary or repugnant to the Thirty Nine Articles and that he had attempted to create factions and divisions within the Commonwealth by applying the odious and scandalous name of Puritan to such of the king's subjects as conformed to the doctrine and ceremonies of the Church of England.[13] In the event Montague escaped impeachment and two years later was made Bishop of Chichester, succeeding George Carleton who had been one of his most prominent critics.[14]

Parliament was dissolved on 15 June and shortly afterwards the king issued a proclamation forbidding his subjects, and in particular the clergy, to propagate by writing, preaching or printing any opinions on religion which were not clearly warranted by the doctrine and discipline of the Church of England. John Rushworth comments that 'The effects of this Proclamation, how equally soever intended, became the stopping of the Puritans' mouths and an uncontrolled liberty to the Tongues and Pens of the Arminian Party.'[15] To the more well-informed Puritans the situation was beginning to look very serious. 'Arminianism and Pelagianism', wrote Walter Yonge, 'do much speed abroad in divers parts of this realm and many bishops infected therwith.'[16] Archbishop Abbot was now in disfavour and Laud's influence was growing rapidly. Since Buckingham had become, in the words of a gossip writer, 'the great protector of the Montagutians'[17] it is not difficult to understand why he aroused bitter emotions in Puritan circles.

The growth of Arminianism was not the only development which was worrying the Puritans; they were also deeply disturbed about what they conceived to be a general decline of morals. Sir Edward Peyton thought that one of the factors in this situation was the restraint of godly preaching but mainly attributed it to the example set by the courtiers of James I. The king's favourite nobles, he writes, being addicted more to pleasure and delights then the School of prudence and wisdome, looking more at their own Interest then the common good or piety of life, gave so vast a liberty to their lives as made an abordment of loosness in many; insomuch that strictness of life (which our Saviour requires) was imputed a disgrace and the vainest counted the wisest, the profanest no hypocrite and a Puritan was stiled a Devil.

In addition, he relates that under the early Stuart kings there was a good deal of drunkenness and blasphemous swearing in Court circles. These criticisms appeared in a work published in 1652: not surprisingly, he took a rather different line in an essay entitled 'A Discours of Court and Courtiers' which he presented in 1633 to a cousin of the king, James Stuart, Duke of Lennox. Here he lavishly praised both James I and his son and (continuing his shameless display of sycophancy) claimed that ever since the beginning of Elizabeth's reign the courtiers of England had conducted themselves in a commendable fashion, 'Religion having had a commaund and force over all their actions.'[18] Lucy Hutchinson, for her part, agreed with his later assessment of the Court of James I:

> The Court of this king was a nursery of lust and intemperance. . . . The generallity of the gentry of the land soone learnt the Court fashion and every greate house in the country became a sty of uncleannesse. To keepe the people in their deplorable security till vengeance overtooke them they were entertain'd with masks, stage playes and sorts of ruder sports. Then began Murther, incest, Adultery, drunkennesse, swearing, fornication and all sort of ribaldry to be no conceal'd but countenanced vices, favour'd wherever they were privately practis'd because they held such conformity with the Court example.

Mrs Hutchinson was prepared to concede that after the accession of Charles I the atmosphere of the Court changed for the better: her main criticism of Charles I's Court was that it was permeated with Catholic influences.[19]

One feature of Court life which inevitably aroused concern in Puritan circles was a persistent disregard for the sanctity of the Lord's Day which took such forms as the staging of plays and masques on Sunday evenings. Sir Simonds D'Ewes was frequently amazed and disgusted at the Sabbath-breaking which the Court indulged in and encouraged in others. On 5 May 1622 he wrote in his diary 'This night (the moore the pittye) was the maske at court'; he himself had heard three good sermons that day. In July 1623 he commented on the visit of two Spanish emissaries: 'The blessed Lordes day that should have been spent in God's service was past over in iollitye and feasting . . . the pomp at Court and desire to see it made thousand others to breake the sabbaoth.' When a Russian embassy was welcomed in similar fashion in the spring of 1628 Sir Simonds wrote indignantly to a friend about this 'horrible profanation of Sunday'.[20]

Early on in his reign Charles I's attempts to raise money without parliamentary sanction provided another powerful stimulus to the process of alienation which was now in train. Writing of the forced loan of 1626 Bulstrode Whitelocke remarks, with some justification, that 'The Papists were forward in the Loane and the Puritans were Recusants in it.'[21] Between the end of 1626 and the beginning of 1628 many of the great patrons of 'true religion' were absent from their homes, either because they were in prison or because they were under house arrest in distant counties. In October 1626 two of the leading Puritan squires in Essex, Sir Francis Barrington and his son-in-law Sir William Masham, refused to act as commissioners for the forced loan and were both committed to prison, the former to the Marshalsea and the latter to the Fleet. Sir Francis, who was aged and infirm, felt it prudent to draw up his will and began by quoting the warning which the prophet Isaiah had delivered to Hezekiah, the King of Judah: 'Thus saith the Lord, Set thine house in order; for thou shalt die and not live.' In December 1626 his chaplain, James Harrison, sent him a firkin of Colchester oysters and wrote in the accompanying letter that it was 'noe small mercy to be able to deny ourselves and willingly to take up our crosse and follow the lord in sincerity of heart'; and that 'the patient abideing of the godly shall not be forgotte for ever'. The following month it was reported from London that Sir Francis was still a prisoner in the Marshalsea 'where he hath every Sunday 2 sermons and on Sunday last old Mr Dod preached before him forenoone and after-noone'. John Dod, whose patron, Richard Knightley, would soon find himself in the Fleet, had chosen what must have been regarded as a highly appropriate text from the Book of Revelation: 'Fear none of these things which thou shalt suffer: behold the devil shall cast some of you into prison, that ye may be tried; and ye shall have tribulation ten days.'[22]

Although the resistance to the forced loan was not confined to any one section of the gentry the number of wealthy Puritan squires who were prepared to suffer imprisonment rather than submit to arbitrary taxation was very remarkable. These were men who had no Court connections and who tended to identify themselves with the interests of their counties: they included, for example, Sir William Armyne, who 'was above the corruption of Court-flattery' and who 'hunted all one scent of his Country's welfare and never forsook it'.[23] It was an episode which would not easily be forgotten. According to the Grand Remonstrance of 1641 many of those who were imprisoned 'contracted such sicknesses as cost them their lives';[24] and indeed two of the Puritan prisoners, Sir Francis Barrington and Sir John Pickering, died within a short time after their release.

While the controversy over the forced loan was still raging there was a dramatic development in the struggle which was going on within the Church. In July 1627 Archbishop Abbot, whose critical attitude to the forced loan had earned him the King's displeasure, was banished to one of his houses in Kent and in October was formally suspended from his office. The five bishops who were made responsible for exercising his functions were not noted for entertaining any feelings of sympathy towards the Puritans: besides Laud and Neile they included George Mountaigne of London, John Buckeridge of Rochester and John Howson of Oxford.[25] Although Abbot was allowed to resume his duties in 1628 he enjoyed only the shadow of his former power and it was Laud, now Bishop of London, who effectively controlled the Church through his influence with the king. From this time onwards most (though not all) new bishops were drawn from that faction which had disapproved of Abbot's endorsement of Calvinist doctrine and the indulgence which he had shown towards the Puritans.

Early in 1628 the government decided to call a parliament and order was given for the release of those who had been under constraint for opposing the forced loan. Among the Puritan gentry the sense of outrage occasioned by the forced loan proceedings was intermingled with grim forebodings about the future of the Protestant religion, both on the Continent and at home. In February Sir Simonds D'Ewes lamented in a letter to a friend that when he thought of 'the dreadfull ruine of God's church abroad and the imminent desolation which threatens us at home I could wish even to dipp my penn in teares not inke, nay rather in bloud then teares'. That same month Sir Robert Harley and his household were praying for the good estate of God's Church, the sufficiency of the Gospel and the sanctification of the Sabbath and adding the heart-felt exhortation that 'God would in mercy vouchsafe a happy Parliament'. According to D'Ewes some of those who took their seats in the Commons 'weare farre gone with the new blasphemous fancies of the Anabaptists called by a late and frivolous name Arminians'; on the other hand, there was a large and active group of Puritan members, many of whom had been imprisoned as loan refusers.[26] During the first session of this Parliament the House was more concerned with political and constitutional grievances than with religious issues. The Puritans, however, ensured that religion was not completely neglected and on 20 March it was decided that this weighty subject should be considered by a committee of the whole House. In a debate at the end of March Sir Henry Mildmay mounted a strong attack on the Arminians whom he depicted as agents of Rome: in the course of his speech he declared, 'I will add another to Montague no lesse dangerous and it is Dr Jackson; they would Introduce Popery.' 'New opinions are introduced', complained Sir Robert Harley, 'and every Subdivision in our Religion is a Weapon in our Adversaries hand.'[27] In June Sir William Spring informed his friend Sir Simonds D'Ewes that it had been agreed that the Remonstrance which was being prepared should contain a reference to Bishops Neile and Laud 'by name as suspected for Arminians'. In this Remonstrance the Commons told the king that his subjects were afraid that there was a conspiracy afoot to bring about an alteration in religion. Nothing was being done to combat the increase of popery; on the contrary, its adherents received extraordinary favours and respect at court from persons of great quality and power, including the Countess of Buckingham. Moreover, there was

> a daily growth and spreading of the Faction of the Arminians, that being ... but a cunning way to bring in Popery. . . . And it being now generally held the way to preferment and promotion in the Church, many Scholars do bend the course of their Studies to maintain those Errors; their Books and

Opinions are suffered to be printed and published and on the other side, the imprinting of such as are written against them, and in defence of the Orthodox Church, are hinder'd and prohibited.

At the same time (the Remonstrance went on) attempts were being made to hinder the preaching of the Word, which was the most powerful means of strengthening and propagating true religion.[28]

A new parliamentary session began on 20 January 1629 and shortly afterwards the House of Commons resolved that religion, and more particularly the dangers of popery and Arminianism, should take precedence over all other business. During this session, writes Sir Simonds D'Ewes, the House displayed great zeal for the glory of God and the maintenance of true religion 'that it might not bee intermixed with popish ceremonies or idolatrous actions, nor the pure doctrine of the Church of England bee corrupted with the blasphemous tenents of the Anabaptists', as he preferred to call the Arminians, 'in derogation of God's grace and providence'.[29] In an emotional speech delivered on 27 January Sir Walter Erle expressed the fear that popery and Arminianism, joining hand in hand, would help to bring in a Spanish tyranny. And he went on to make a personal declaration which must have stirred the hearts of his Puritan colleagues:

that which for an undoubted truth I have from the Church of England heretofore received, that will I stand to and forgo my estate, my liberty, yea my life itself rather than forgo it. As for passing of bills, settling revenues and the like, without settling Religion, I must confess I have no heart to it. Take away my Religion, you take away my life; and not only mine but the life of the whole State and kingdom.

In the debate on religion which took place on 29 January Sir Benjamin Rudyerd drew a contrast between the old menace of popery which simply called for the proper execution of the recusancy laws and the more subtle threat of Arminianism which had 'lately crept in and crept upp into highe places'. In the light of this threat he proposed that the House should consider the Thirty Nine Articles, the ancient catechism which appeared in the Book of Common Prayer and the Lambeth Articles of 1595. Sir Robert Harley attributed much of the blame for the increase of Arminianism to the writings of such men as Richard Montague, Thomas Jackson and John Cosin and suggested that the Lords should be asked 'to joyne with us in a Remonstrance to the King that he would be pleased to cause these persons . . . to be punished and their bookes to be publiquely burnt'. The House was also concerned about the setting up of altars and the introduction of new ceremonies into public worship, though these developments had not yet reached significant proportions. Yet none of the protests about the trends in religion had the slightest impact on the situation and the rumour which Walter Yonge noted in his diary that 'the Kinge inclyneth somewhat to the Puritane faction' proved to be ill-founded.[30]

On 2 March Parliament was suddenly adjourned and that day Sir Thomas Barrington, one of the Essex members, sent his mother a letter which reflected the profound disquiet aroused by the king's intervention. 'God of his mercye looke on us,' he wrote, ''tis farr more easy to speake bravely then to be magnanimous in suffring, yet he whose hart bleedes not at the threates of theise times is too stupid; I pray God send us better grounds of comfort to be armed for the worst that can befall us.' In another letter he expressed the fear that there would be a dissolution. All men who wished well to the Church and Commonwealth were 'mourning for this threatening evell; joye only now appears in those aspects, that while Religion had so faire a way to advaunce in, were then no way pleased.'[31] His forebodings were fully justified: the king had already decided to dissolve Parliament and on 10 March the decision was formally announced. Writing some years later Sir Simonds D'Ewes declared that this was 'the most gloomie, sadd and dismall day for England that happened in five hundred yeares space last past'. The dissolution, he emphasised with the benefit of hindsight, had the most serious consequences for both Church and Commonwealth.[32]

Shortly after the dissolution a number of Puritan ministers drew up a petition in which they sought authority to preach against the Arminian errors. As a result of the royal proclamation of 1626, they complained, it was no longer possible to expound the saving doctrines of election and predestination as enshrined in the seventeenth Article of Religion. In the event the petition was blocked by Laud, who some time before had told the Duke of Buckingham that the doctrine of predestination was one of the cardinal features of Puritanism.[33] Under his direction considerable efforts were made to restrain public criticism of Arminian doctrine or the propagation of

Calvinist doctrine by applying a more rigid censorship and disciplining parish ministers and university fellows who were felt to have gone too far in their preaching. When considering books for publication, writes William Prynne, the authorities made a special point of taking out passages in which it was argued that men might be assured of their salvation and that such knowledge was attainable in this life. Moreover, there appears to have been some attempt to prevent the dissemination of works which had already been published: in January 1630, for example, Walter Yonge recorded in his diary that Archbishop Harsnet of York had forbidden the books of William Perkins to be sold within his province.[34] At the same time the Arminians were generally allowed much greater latitude both in the pulpit and in their published writings. In February 1631 Thomas Gataker told his friend Samuel Ward, the Master of Sidney Sussex, Cambridge, that 'ffor the points of Arminianisme publiquely preached, it is commonly bruited that few come up either at Court or Crosse', meaning St Paul's Cross, 'but that touch upon them'; and later that year Bishop Davenant of Salisbury, who had been reprimanded for preaching a Calvinist sermon in the presence of the king, commented in a letter to Ward that 'since the books of the Arminians are common amongest the learned I think it may proov preiudicial in time yf wee shall utterly give over our own Defence.' During the reign of Charles I, relates Sir Simonds D'Ewes,

> many wicked Anabaptisticall or popishlie affected divines and schollers in both universities and elsewheere mainteined in the schooles and pulpits justification by workes, free-will, christ's bodilie presence in the sacramente of the Lord's supper and a world of other corrupt and noisome tenents.[35]

Laud's attempts to restrict the propagation of Calvinist beliefs were by no means ineffective: it is significant, for example, that the authors of the Root and Branch petition of 1640 alleged that the doctrines of predestination and free grace had been generally withheld from the people's knowledge and criticised the faintheartedness of ministers who, afraid of displeasing the prelates, had neglected to preach such doctrines.[36] Yet in some parishes it was still possible to hear sermons with a Calvinistic flavour, though the harsher or more complex doctrinal points might be deliberately omitted.[37] At the upper levels of society there were still ample opportunities for acquiring a knowledge of Calvinist doctrine since it could be taught in conditions of privacy by a household chaplain, a resident schoolmaster or a university tutor. Moreover, the libraries of wealthy Puritans were usually well stocked with books which provided guidance on the concepts of predestination, election and assurance. Many of these books had been published in the reign of James I or earlier but even when the Laudian form of censorship was in operation men like Sir Simonds D'Ewes and Sir Thomas Barrington were able to purchase copies of works by Richard Sibbes and John Preston which had been printed in the Netherlands and smuggled into England.[38] Despite the attitude of the church authorities the Puritan gentry continued to claim in their wills that they had received assurance of their election. When Sir William Doddington, a Hampshire squire, drew up his will in September 1638 he indirectly revealed his lack of sympathy for the new Arminian tenets. In making financial provision for the curate of Fordingbridge he inserted the condition that he should be a constant preaching minister who taught no other doctrine than that which was consistent with the Articles of the Church of England approved in 1562.[39]

In December 1629 the king, acting on Laud's advice, issued directions requiring the bishops to exercise much tighter control over lecturers and private chaplains. Afternoon sermons, it was decreed, were to be turned into catechising and the employment of a domestic chaplain was to be permitted only in the case of noblemen and persons with a strict legal entitlement. Subsequently, in the autumn of 1633, a further blow was struck when the bishops were instructed not to ordain any man unless he intended to take on responsibility for a cure of souls, though an exception could be made for university fellows and certain other special categories.[40]

As Walter Yonge noted in his diary, Laud himself took a strong line with the lecturers in his Diocese of London. In Essex a number of Puritan ministers were forced to relinquish or found themselves suspended from their lectureships, among them John Rogers of Dedham, Thomas Hooker of Chelmsford, Thomas Shepard of Earl's Colne and Daniel Rogers of Wethersfield.[41] In 1629, the year he was suspended, John Rogers published a treatise entitled *The Doctrine of Faith* which contained a preface written by his friend Thomas Hooker. Rogers dedicated the work to some Puritan gentlewomen who must often have heard him preaching: Lady Anne Mildmay, the wife of Sir Henry Mildmay who was seated at Graces Hall in

Essex; Helen Bacon, the wife of Nicholas Bacon of Shrubland Hall
in Suffolk; and Meriell Gurdon, the wife of another Suffolk squire,
Brampton Gurdon of Assington. 'God', he told them, 'hath neerely
joyned you all together by many bonds, both Civill and Religious,
both of Nature and Grace, and hath given you to be all of one
minde in the Lord.'[42] In November 1629 Sir Richard Everard wrote
to his mother-in-law, Lady Joan Barrington, that he had heard that
Thomas Hooker's case would go very hard with him as the Bishop
was extremely hostile. Another preacher (who may be identified as
Nicholas Beard) had recently moved to Ipswich so they were likely
to sustain a double loss. In an accompanying letter Lady Everard
complained that 'we are left in a pitifull condition and may well
say with Jehesaphat we know not what to doe but our eyes are
upon the Lord for the means that we have is very pore and we have
litell hope of any other.'[43] When Thomas Shepard was driven out
of Earl's Colne in 1630 he was given shelter by Sir Richard Darley
at his Yorkshire manor-house where he served for some time as his
chaplain. The flight to Yorkshire had been organised by Ezekiel
Rogers, who had once been chaplain to Sir Francis Barrington and
had been presented by him to the living of Rowley in the East
Riding. His brother Daniel, who was suspended from his lectureship
in 1629, also had close ties with the Barrington family. When he
published his *Treatise of the Two Sacraments of the Gospell* in 1633 he
dedicated it to Lady Joan Barrington, acknowledging the love and
respect which many of his name and tribe had received from her.
Another lecturer who enjoyed the support of the Barrington family
was James Harrison, one of their chaplains, whose sermons were
regularly attended by Sir Thomas Barrington. When the metropolitical visitation of the Diocese of London was carried out in 1636 Sir
Nathaniel Brent, the Vicar-General, reported that Mr Harrison, a
lecturer in the parish where Sir Thomas Barrington lived, had
prayed and preached above three hours at the time of the fast and
curtailed the prayers set out by authority.[44]

In December 1636 Bishop Wren of Norwich told Laud that when
he had first arrived in the diocese 'Lectures abounded, especially
in Suffolke. Not a Market or a bowling greene or an Ordinary
could stand without one, and many of them were set up by private
Gentlemen at their pleasure.' One Suffolk landowner, Sir William
Spring, had insisted that his minister at Cockfield should deliver a
Thursday lecture and within the last few years had established

another lecture at Ixworth. The origins of the lectureship at Ixworth had in fact been described in a letter which Sir William had sent to his friend Sir Simonds D'Ewes in February 1633. The minister of the parish, he wrote, had been holding a prayer meeting every Friday and

> some neighbor ministers happening to bee present, on or other hath offered themselves to bestow some pertinent and necessary directions unto the people, by which Course thus by accident begun there hath bin soe goode liking taken of itt and soe greate a desire of the Continuance, both by the Inhabitants and neighborhoode as wee are all of one hert and purpose to supplicate to authorety for the allowance of an establisht lecture.

It would be necessary, Sir William went on, to provide the bishop with two lists, one of the ministers who would participate and the other of the laymen who were willing to contribute money for the support of the lecture. To Wren the proliferation of lectures was a situation which could not be tolerated; when Laud presented his annual report to the king in January 1638 he was able to assure him that in the Diocese of Norwich there were now only six lectures, all of which were performed by neighbouring ministers who were conformable to the law of the Church.[45]

The suppression or regulation of lectures was not the only way in which the ecclesiastical authorities struck at godly preaching. Many of the parish clergy who were suspended or deprived for nonconformity were highly regarded in Puritan circles for the quality and relevance of their preaching: in enforcing the Laudian innovations, declared Sir Benjamin Rudyerd in a speech delivered in the Long Parliament, the High Church prelates 'have a minde to worry preaching; for I never yet heard of any but diligent Preachers that were vext with these and the like devices'.[46] Since the preaching of the Word was a matter of supreme importance to the Puritans they would often journey to other parishes for spiritual nourishment if it was not forthcoming in their own parish churches. During the Laudian era serious efforts were made to stamp out this practice, even in parishes where there was no preaching,[47] but it was an activity which the church authorities found difficult to control. In his report on the metropolitical visitation of the Diocese of Lincoln Sir Nathaniel Brent commented that in Bedfordshire and indeed in all the southern parts of the Diocese (which also included Buckinghamshire and Huntingdonshire) the people were 'much addicted' to the habit of travelling beyond their own parishes in order to hear the sermons of preachers who were particularly admired. In Buckinghamshire John Hampden was presented for this offence and on making his appearance gave an undertaking to obey the laws of the Church.[48] Further north, but still in the Diocese of Lincoln, there were reported to be many Puritans at Buckminster in Leicestershire who attended services at Stainby which was just across the border with Lincolnshire. Buckminster Hall was the seat of a Puritan baronet, Sir Edward Hartopp, who was the lord of the manor but not the patron of the living.[49]

Until he inherited his father's Devonshire estates Sir Richard Strode lived at Chalmington in the neighbouring county of Dorset and here he was involved in a bitter feud with John Mayo, the minister of his parish church of Cattistock, which led him to withhold payment of his tithes. In 1634 Sir Richard found himself arraigned in the Court of High Commission which was informed that he 'was and is reputed a schismaticall person and such a one as useth to leave his owne parish church where there is a learned preaching Minister to resort to other churches'. Among other things it was alleged that John Traske, who in 1618 had been deprived of his priestly status for propagating Judaism, had been entertained in his house where he had said prayers *ex tempore* and had expounded chapters or passages of scripture and that his patron had taken him with him into the country to preach in other places. In a certificate which Bishop Hall of Exeter submitted it was pointed out that Sir Richard had long since discarded Traske and had recently begun to frequent his own parish church 'and left gadding abroad to other Ministers'. The Court concluded that there were reasonable grounds for suspecting that he was 'a man ill affected to the State and governement Ecclesiasticall and the orthodox true Religion here by lawe established and professed within this Realme' but merely warned him to conduct himself peaceably and in conformity with the law.[50]

Although Puritan journeyings were repugnant to Laud it was occasionally possible for a wealthy individual to obtain a special dispensation enabling his family to worship in another parish. The Lukes, who were one of the most important Puritan families in Bedfordshire, had several livings in their gift but must have considered themselves unfortunate that they had no patronage rights in either of the parishes where their principal residences were situated. In a petition which he presented to Laud in July 1638 Sir Samuel Luke told him that his house, Wood End, was about a mile from the parish church of Cople and that, especially in winter, the journey was often very difficult because of the heavy flooding which occurred. In view of this he sought a licence for himself and his wife, together with two menservants and a maidservant, to attend church services either at Cardington where he had another house or at Haynes where his father lived or at Northill which was a neighbouring parish. No doubt there was an element of truth in the reason which he gave for his request but it also seems likely that he was at loggerheads with John Gwyn, the vicar of Cople, whose religious sympathies were very different from his own. At the metropolitical visitation earlier in the year two of the inhabitants of Cople had been presented for going from their own parish to attend services at Cardington church and Gwyn had accused another man of commenting at a burial that in his surplice he looked like a morris dancer. It is, moreover, significant that there was a strong Puritan tradition in the parish of Haynes, whose recent incumbents had included Thomas Brightman, the apocalyptic writer, and Walsingham Shirley, who in 1634 had been called a nonconformist. Taking the petition at its face value, Laud authorised the grant of a licence with the proviso that Sir Samuel, his wife and his servants should receive communion at their own parish church and discharge all other duties that were fitting. In the final analysis it is perhaps a reflection on the standard of efficiency of the Laudian bureaucracy that such a concession should be made to a man whom Sir John Lambe, one of its chief officials, was to describe in 1641 as a deadly enemy who sought his ruin.[51]

In the Canons of 1604 the stipulation had been made that except in times of necessity no minister should preach or administer holy communion in any private house unless it had a chapel which could lawfully be used for divine service. Even where such a chapel existed there was no automatic right to keep a resident chaplain since this was a privilege limited by statute to archbishops, bishops, peers, knights of the garter, judges and senior officials of the Crown.[52] In practice, however, these restrictions were often disregarded and so long as Archbishop Abbot remained in effective control of the Church little effort was made to enforce them. At the same time the right to employ a chaplain was sometimes exercised in a way which was contrary to the spirit, if not the letter, of the law: Thomas Gataker, for example, writes that Sir Henry Hobart, the celebrated judge, gave him the title of his chaplain, 'being but a titular matter, requiring no constant attendance, onelie a visit now and then and a Sermon sometime upon some special occasions, the rather that by his power and countenance I might sit the more quietlie and exercise my Ministerie more freelie'.[53] Laud, for his part, was determined to curb the employment of private chaplains and from 1629 onwards he sought to ensure that the law was strictly observed. One Puritan minister, John Davenport, believed that Magna Carta was not without relevance in this context: in a letter to Lady Mary Vere he claimed that it was not in the power of the bishops to 'take from you what is settled upon the Nobility and others by magna charta, the right and power of intertaining chaplaines'.[54] According to William Prynne the restrictions on the ordination of priests which were introduced in 1633 prevented many young divines from securing employment as chaplains in the households of religious gentlemen.[55] Even so, the practice of maintaining a chaplain, whether ordained or otherwise, was widespread throughout the reign of Charles I with Puritan landowners frequently defying or attempting to circumvent the law. In the annual report on his province for the year 1636 Laud told the king that the Bishop of Norwich had asked 'what he shall doe with such Schollers (some in holy Orders and some not) as knights and private gentlemen keepe in their houses under pretence to teach their children. As alsoe with some divines that are beneficed in Townes or neare but live in gentlemen's houses.' Laud considered that the latter should be required to live where their cures were; as for the rest, the king had already given direction that no one should be allowed to keep a chaplain unless he was legally entitled to do so. In endorsing these comments the king stressed that it was also necessary to make sure than even those who were qualified by law employed only conformable men.[56]

In his companion report Archbishop Neile of York was more reassuring or complacent. Some knights and gentlemen in his diocese, he wrote, had curates living in their houses because the stipends which they allowed them out of their impropriations were extremely modest; these ministers, however, were orthodox and conformable and their prayers and catechising were in accordance with the Book of Common Prayer. On the other hand, the situation in the Diocese of Peterborough, as revealed in Laud's report for the year 1639, gave more cause for concern:

> some knights and Esquires keep Schoolemasters in theyr houses or Schollers to converse with or dyet the Vicar where his Maintenance is little. And this they saye is not to keepe a Chaplaine . . . yet most of these read or saye Service in theyr Houses (which is the Office of a Chaplaine) but they read not the Prayers of the Church according to the Liturgye established.[57]

In the same report the archbishop also commented that the Bishop of Ely had informed him that at Childerley, near Cambridge, Sir John Cutts maintained a chaplain in his household although he was not qualified by law. Sir John (whose family motto was *Spero in Deo*) had recently depopulated the township in order to extend his deer park and now only Childerley Hall remained standing. There had once been two parishes, Great and Little Childerley; the latter still existed but the church was in ruins and on its decayed walls stood 'meane houses of Office, as Brewhouse, Stable &c'. As the patron of the living Sir John had presented Edward Rainbowe, a fellow of Magdalene College, Cambridge and household chaplain to the Earl of Suffolk, who was clearly no more than the titular incumbent. In addition, there was a resident minister whom Sir John described as a curate though in practice he fulfilled the role of a domestic chaplain. 'The knight and his ffamily', wrote Laud, 'goe to noe other church but he hath a Chappell which he saith was consecrated by Bishop Heton', who had occupied the see from 1599 to 1609, 'and produces an Instrument with Seale.' In conclusion he assured the king that it was his intention to look further into the matter.[58] Elsewhere in the country there were other parishes where depopulating enclosures, sometimes as far back as the early sixteenth century, had brought about major demographic changes; where as a result the parish church had ceased to have any real parochial functions and in some cases had been allowed to fall into ruin; and where a Puritan squire had in effect converted the cure of souls into a domestic chaplaincy. A traveller who passed through the Leicestershire village of Noseley in 1645 recorded in his journal that besides the manor-house there were not above two cottages in the parish. The owner of the manor-house was Sir Arthur Hesilrige who, it was reported in 1634, had declined to present a minister to the living and had instead taken a Puritan chaplain into his household.[59]

Some young men who became domestic chaplains saw this as a stepping-stone to more lucrative employment. Sir Thomas Barrington foresaw difficulty in persuading ministers or scholars to come and live in his household unless he was prepared to put them into the livings in his gift as and when these fell vacant; thus in June 1638 he presented Thomas White, who had been serving as his chaplain, to the Yorkshire rectory of Rowley.[60] In the main, however, the chaplain in a Puritan household was a man who found it difficult to stomach the Church's ceremonial requirements and who valued the liturgical and doctrinal freedom which went with such a position, even though his stipend might be small. During the reign of Charles I Sir William Masham of Essex, who was described in 1636 as 'a very factious Puritan', employed two chaplains whose names are known to us. Roger Williams joined the household after graduating from Pembroke College, Cambridge in 1627 but left for New England in 1630. His successor was John Norton who, since leaving Cambridge, had been earning a living as a curate and schoolmaster at Bishops Stortford in Hertfordshire but had been unwilling to accept a benefice because of his reluctance to subscribe to the Articles of Religion. The new chaplain was a man of considerable ability, though of irritable temper. During his sojourn at Otes Hall he not only served the household but went about preaching in the neighbourhood until he was eventually silenced by the church authorities. In October 1635 he and his wife arrived in New England. No doubt Sir William had a whole series of chaplains: it is significant, for example, that when drawing up his will in 1656 he stipulated that the minister who was living with him at the time of his death should be paid the sum of £3 to enable him to buy books.[61]

According to a contemporary account of his life Henry Jessey, who left St John's College, Cambridge in 1624, was first entertained by Brampton Gurdon at Assington Hall in Suffolk. In 1627 he entered holy orders but because of the growing emphasis on the ceremonial aspects of public worship he chose to remain with the Gurdons as their chaplain, carrying on 'his labours thereunto and to the Neighbourhood thereabouts, teaching more privately and distribuiting Godly practical books among them'. During his residence at Assington Hall he declined several offers of preferment but eventually, in 1633, he moved to Yorkshire where he served as assistant to William Alder, the nonconformist vicar of Aughton. The following year, however, Jessey was forced to leave the parish because of his resistance to the Laudian innovations and was then taken in by Sir Matthew Boynton of Barmston, who employed him as chaplain and lecturer. The Boynton and Gurdon families were both involved in Puritan colonisation schemes and during the time that Jessey was living with him Sir Matthew was making plans to emigrate to southern Connecticut. As a preliminary step the Boyntons moved to London and later, in the summer of 1636, they took a house near Uxbridge in Middlesex. In August 1637 Jessey, who by this time had left their service, wrote to John Winthrop in New England that Sir Matthew, having found a new chaplain, 'one of the same heart, mind and spirit', and 'remaining this 12 month within 20 miles of London, in a place 5 miles from the Parish Church, hath enjoyed great freedome but now of late the clouds gather fast towards a storme'.[62]

Between 1633 and 1637 Thomas Cawton served as chaplain to Sir William Armyne who, though his main estates were situated in Lincolnshire, was then living at Orton Hall in Huntingdonshire. Cawton's son writes that he had a free and clear call to that place and that he was much beloved

> for his abilities, faithfulness and plain dealing with that Family, from the highest to the lowest. A Papist could say that few rich men's Confessors should be saved, that is, that few great men's Chaplains should go to Heaven, because they were so apt to flatter their Masters; but he would neither smother faults nor smooth them over in the greatest but would so sweetly reprove and admonish all sorts according to their qualities that though he were so honest as to be plain yet he was so discreet as to be pleasing in his reprehensions. . . . He was ever taking occasion to do good in that Family, more especially in his solid, sound and plain Exposition of Scripture, in his profitable and clear way of principling, catechising and building them up in their most holy faith, and in his Family and private prayers with and for them . . . by which means he so effectually wrought upon that Family that many have cause to be thankfull they ever were of that Family for his sake.[63]

Among the Puritan gentry there were many who had private
chapels in their houses, some of recent origin and others which
dated back beyond the Reformation. Sometimes an ancient chapel
had been given over to secular uses, perhaps as a store-room or a
farm building. If a Puritan owner wanted to bring it back into use
as a place of worship he might seek permission from the diocesan
authorities to have it reconsecrated, even though such a ceremony
would be repugnant to him; on the other hand, he might choose to
disregard this requirement. In proceedings which were started in
1639 the High Commission heard how Sir Henry Rosewell of Forde
Abbey, which was then in a detached part of Devon, had reinstated
a chapel or oratory which had once belonged to the former Cister-
cian monastery. Sir Henry, who was noted in Puritan circles for his
'true love to Religion', had at one time kept lambs, cattle and
poultry in the chapel but had never asked for it to be reconsecrated.
Now it was used for services conducted by a domestic chaplain
and attended not only by the household but by persons from the
surrounding district: indeed on some occasions as many as twenty
or thirty outsiders had been present, giving rise to the suspicion
that conventicles were being held under Sir Henry's patronage. In
recent years he had often been presented for staying away from the
parish church of Thorncombe and had eventually been excommunicated. In his defence Sir Henry claimed that he and his family had
frequently resorted to Thorncombe church before the arrival of the
present incumbent, Robert Gomersall (who had become vicar in
1628) and that his subsequent conduct was due not to any schis-
matic opinion but to his personal differences with the vicar which
had been the subject of earlier proceedings in the Court of High
Commission; it seems likely, however, that his strong Puritan
sympathies were an important underlying factor in this situation.
When the High Commission considered the charges on 30 January
1640 there was some difference of opinion as to whether such a
chapel could have retained any kind of ecclesiastical status following
the dissolution of the monasteries, but they were generally agreed
that it would need to be reconsecrated before any further services
were held there and that even then the household should not be
entirely absolved from the requirement to attend public worship at
the parish church. Characteristically, Laud threw in the additional
point that an examination should be made to see whether Sir Henry
was entitled to keep a chaplain. In the event the High Commission

decided that he should pay a fine of £100 together with the costs of the action. At the same time it was agreed that after being reconsecrated the chapel should be used only by the household; that the choice of minister to officiate there would require the specific approval of the Bishop of Exeter; and that the bishop should also determine how often Sir Henry should go to his parish church. Subsequently it was reported that Rosewell was refusing to pay the costs of the suit and on 25 June 1640 order was given for an attachment to be issued.[64]

To Sir Henry these proceedings must have seemed an appalling invasion of privacy; hitherto such treatment had been reserved for Catholic landowners. The ecclesiastical authorities, however, could hardly have ignored such a blatant case of religious particularism. Given reasonable circumspection a Puritan squire who employed a household chaplain had little cause to fear that his domestic arrangements would come under scrutiny.

CHAPTER NINE

GODLY PATRONAGE

In seeking to enforce uniformity within the Church an archbishop like Bancroft or Laud was confronted with a situation in which the patronage rights in a very large number of parishes were in the hands of laymen who were altogether out of sympathy with his aspirations. The commonest type of cure was the presentative living which could be either a rectory, if the incumbent was entitled to take the revenue from the great tithes, or a vicarage which had been endowed out of the temporalities where these were impropriate. When the patron presented a new minister it was necessary for the bishop of the diocese to satisfy himself not only that the nominee had been properly ordained but that he was a man of good character and sufficient learning to perform the duties of the cure. For his part the minister was under a formal obligation to take the oath of canonical obedience and to subscribe to the Three Articles set out in the Canons of 1604. By virtue of this subscription he acknowledged that the sovereign was the Supreme Governor, that the Book of Common Prayer contained nothing contrary to holy scripture and that each and every one of the Thirty Nine Articles was agreeable to the Word of God.[1] Provided these conditions were fulfilled the bishop had no choice but to proceed with the institution and induction of the nominee and in practice it appears to have been relatively uncommon for the patron's wishes to be frustrated.

In certain circumstances the Crown became entitled to exercise the right of presentation, in particular when the patron failed to nominate a new minister within six months after the living fell vacant, when the previous incumbent had been deprived on a charge of simony or when there was a minority and the estate was under the control of the Court of Wards. Although there was usually no lack of applicants if the incumbent was guaranteed a reasonable income a patron who had very exact requirements might sometimes be hard pressed to find a suitable minister within the prescribed time-scale. Sir John Horner, a Somerset landowner, experienced this problem when seeking a new rector for Pudimore Milton: in December 1632 he presented John Strickland, an assistant to the famous John White of Dorchester, who according to an acquaintance accepted the living 'to preserve it from the lapse'.[2]

Presentative livings were subject to full diocesan control which was primarily exercised through the visitation machinery. There were, however, certain other types of cure which were largely exempt from episcopal supervision and interference. In the case of a peculiar or a donative cure[3] the lay owner could appoint a stipendiary curate without any form of presentation, institution or induction. Since the curate's stipend was entirely a matter for the patron it could often be relatively modest, but some Puritan ministers were willing to put up with this because of the degree of freedom which they were able to enjoy. It was for this reason that Francis Drake, an outspoken critic of Arminianism, managed to recruit Thomas Hooker for his donative cure of Esher in Surrey. Another Puritan divine writes that Hooker, 'being a Nonconformitan in judgement, not willing to trouble himself with Presentative Livings, was contented and perswaded . . . to accept of that poore living of £40 per annum, Mr Drake . . . being a worthy wel-beloved Gentleman and able to procure his liberty and retaine him still in the same'.[4]

One of the main reasons for Laud's unpopularity with sections of the propertied classes, both Puritan and otherwise, was the fact that he was not prepared simply to adopt an acquiescent attitude towards a system which permitted so great a degree of lay encroachment on the Church's powers and revenues. Although his approach to the problem was less radical than some of his critics alleged he was determined that at the very least the laity should not benefit to any greater extent than they were strictly entitled in law. Peculiars and other privileged churches received special attention and in some cases had their status challenged, and it was apparently at his instigation that in 1632 the king ordered a full-scale investigation aimed at recovering the many advowsons which local magnates, it was claimed, had usurped from the Crown since 1588. In addition,

Laud prevailed upon the king to let him have the disposal of livings
which were temporarily under the control of the Court of Wards
and sought to take full advantage of vacancies occurring through
lapse of time or as the result of simony proceedings.[5]

In practice the effectiveness of Laud's campaign for a general
conformity to a more High Church concept of public worship
depended to a very great extent on the character of the bishops in
the various dioceses. When a bishopric fell vacant the question of
who would take over the see was the subject of both prayer and
speculation in Puritan households. In June 1631 Sir Thomas
Barrington wrote to his mother that the Archbishop of York and
the Bishops of Ely and Worcester had all lately died and there was
therefore a need for some new actors to take the stage. 'Our prayers
to God', he told her, 'are and ought to be that the next scene may
be better performed, especially by those that shall be destined to so
large a part as the Northerne See. We heear of Morton and wish
him.' In a further letter to her he commented that the see of York
was still empty: 'we looke at Lincolne and Coventry, being both on
the way Northward.' This, however, proved to be wishful thinking
for the Archbishopric of York was granted neither to John Williams
of Lincoln nor to Thomas Morton of Coventry (both of whom were
well regarded in Puritan circles) but to Richard Neile, who was
later to remark in correspondence with Laud that he was regarded
as 'a great adversary of the puritane faction'.[6] In his account of the
reign of Charles I Clarendon relates that most of the bishops were
supporters of Laud but others who had not been beholden to him
nor had any hope of being in that position were content to give
perfunctory orders for the execution of his policy.[7] There were in fact
a number of Calvinist bishops (mainly survivors from the previous
regime) who deplored the growth of Arminianism and who in their
attitude to the Puritans had more in common with Abbot than with
Laud; during the mid-1630s, when this group was at its fullest
strength, they were exercising authority over one-quarter of all the
parishes of England. As Bishop of Lincoln John Williams held an
appointment which was of the greatest strategic importance since
he was in charge of the largest diocese in England, a diocese which
embraced the counties of Bedfordshire, Buckinghamshire, Huntingdonshire, Leicestershire and Lincolnshire and parts of Hertfordshire; indeed some of the most Puritan counties in the kingdom.

Joseph Hall, who became Bishop of Exeter in 1627, subsequently wrote that

> I entered upon that place not without much prejudice and suspicion on some hands: for some . . . had me in great jealousy for too much favour of Puritanism. . . . I took the resolution to follow those courses which might most conduce to the peace and happiness of my new and weighty charge. Finding, therefore, some factious spirits very busy in that diocese I used all fair and gentle means to win them to good order and therein so happily prevailed that, saving two of that numerous clergy who continuing in their refractoriness fled away from censure, they were all perfectly reclaimed; so as I had not one minister professedly opposite to the anciently received orders (for I was never guilty of urging any new impositions) of the church in that large diocese.[8]

Other factors which helped to soften the impact of the Laudian version of Thorough were the power and influence of wealthy patrons, the ingenuity and resource which were often displayed by both patrons and ministers, the venality or inefficiency of some diocesan officials and the degree of protection, admittedly not amounting to total immunity, afforded by privileged churches. At the same time it is clear that many Puritan ministers were willing to conform sufficiently to gain admission to the livings which they had been offered and, once installed, to avoid suspension or deprivation.

One region where there were many benefices under Puritan control was East Anglia with its thriving cloth industry and its strong connections with the University of Cambridge. Thomas May, the historian of the Long Parliament, described the Diocese of Norwich, which embraced the counties of Norfolk and Suffolk, as 'a Diocese in which there were as many strict Professors of Religion (commonly called Puritans) as any part of England'. When Henry Jessey left Cambridge in 1624 he was anxious, his biographer tells us, to settle in Suffolk or Essex 'in regard that he had sometime been there and heard famous Preachers and found many precious Christians'.[9] Suffolk, like Essex, was one of the most Puritan counties in England. In the account which he wrote of his native county during the reign of James I Robert Reyce, the Suffolk antiquary, referred to 'the great number of religious, grave, reverend and learned ministers of God's holy word which are planted in this shire, travelling to the Lord's harvest, with sound doctrine and upright life'. At the same time he noted with approval that many of the gentry were 'crowned with the purity of true religion and godly life'.[10]

While Suffolk was well stocked with Puritans the Diocese of Norwich had a succession of bishops who viewed them with varying degrees of repugnance. During the time when George Abbot was Archbishop, however, the situation remained relatively peaceful and Richard Corbet, who occupied the see between 1632 and 1635, was too easy-going to be an effective instrument of Laud's ecclesiastical policy. The storm broke with the arrival of Matthew Wren, described by Clarendon as 'a man of a severe, sour nature', who had the same kind of energy and singlemindedness as Laud himself. Although he only held the bishopric from 1635 to 1638 his activities played a major part in alienating public opinion in East Anglia during the later years of Charles I's personal government. Early in 1636 he began a general visitation of the diocese which was conducted with great thoroughness and no little severity. Church-wardens, wrote Sir Simonds D'Ewes, were examined upon many new and strange articles which were so objectionable that some godly, learned and orthodox ministers resigned their livings while others were suspended or deprived for refusing to yield to them.[11] Laud naturally saw the situation rather differently: in January 1637 he informed the king that there were about 1500 clergy in the diocese and many disorders yet less than 30 of them had been excommunicated or suspended.[12] Among other things Wren sought to impose tighter control over the preaching of sermons on weekdays and Sunday afternoons and it was through his insistence that the communion tables in many East Anglian churches were moved to the east end and enclosed with rails. When impeachment proceedings were brought against him in 1641 he was described as 'a compleate mirrour of innovation, superstition and oppression' who had waged a war against 'good and well disposed people', using as his weapons 28 injunctions and 139 articles containing 879 questions.[13] On his translation to Ely in 1638 there was no doubt much rejoicing but his successor was Richard Montague, already a notorious figure in Puritan eyes, who was determined to carry on the policy which he had inherited. In August of that year Sir Simonds D'Ewes wrote in a letter to his brother, who was then abroad, that 'wee have a new Bishopp but noe remission yet of our olde burthens'.[14]

According to a contemporary Sir John Wentworth, who had succeeded to the Somerleyton estate in 1618, 'brought good preachers in to the Island of Lovingland and there was the cheife patron of Religion and honesty in his tyme; he shewed a very free and noble disposition.' Lothingland, one of the old hundreds of Suffolk, is the northernmost extremity of the county, lying between the towns of Great Yarmouth and Lowestoft; bounded by the North Sea and the River Waveney, it must have seemed far more like an island at that time, particularly in winter when the river was in full spate. Here Sir John was not only the principal landowner but the patron of a number of benefices: Ashby, Bradwell, Flixton, Lound and Somerleyton.[15] The most notable of his ministers was John Brinsley, the author of various theological works and a great preacher whose powerful and lucid sermons gained him a considerable following. In the pulpit, we are told, none had a more reverend aspect or discovered a greater degree of seriousness; nothing that he said had the least show of levity. Sir John first became acquainted with him when he was serving as a lecturer at Yarmouth. Brinsley's activities there brought him under increasing pressure from the church authorities and it was in these circumstances that he began to receive invitations to preach at churches which were under Wentworth's patronage. On 11 March 1631 he delivered a sermon at the 'consecration or restitution' of Flixton church which Sir John had rebuilt at his own expense. That same year he also published a sermon which he had preached at the inauguration of a public exercise begun, he explained on the title-page, for the benefit of the island of Lothingland. In the dedication he told Sir John that the sermon represented

> the first fruits of your owne; your owne by countenance, your owne by maintenance. What you heard with attention I question not but you will willingly review and in what concernes you readily practise. . . . This religious exercise which God hath made you the instrument to erect, and I hope to continue, shall honour you in the eyes of God and his Saints.[16]

By this time Brinsley was evidently beginning to think about the possibility of seeking employment elsewhere for in December 1631 Sir Robert Harley was in correspondence with him about a living which had fallen vacant at Montgomery. In March 1632 the Privy Council stopped him preaching at Yarmouth and after a while he accepted an offer of preferment from Sir John Wentworth, who presented him to the livings of Somerleyton and Ashby.[17] During the course of Wren's visitation it was reported that a conventicle had been held in a barn at Somerleyton and Sir John was asked to investigate the matter. Some of those who had been present claimed that they had merely been repeating one of Brinsley's sermons; Brinsley himself refused to tell the commissioners anything about the episode. Suspecting that he was a nonconformist, the commissioners ordered him to read morning service in their presence and after a good deal of hesitation he eventually complied, 'looking pittyfully as a man that did penance' and bowing 'litle at the name of Jesus'. In the visitation court Brinsley was told that he deserved to be suspended but in the end he was sent away with a caution; as one of the commissioners later recounted, 'I prayed God make him an honest man . . . and lett him goe.'[18]

Sir John had a number of Puritan relatives, among them Sir Philip Parker, who lived at Erwarton in the coastal area to the south of Ipswich and, Sir Nathaniel Barnardiston, who was seated at Kedington in the south-west corner of the county. In some rough jottings made by Bishop Wren there is a reference to the christening of one of Sir Philip's children in Erwarton church. On this occasion, he noted, the minister delivered a long sermon, wore no surplice and neglected to use the sign of the cross when baptising the child. The rector of Erwarton at this time was Robert Wickes, whom Sir Philip had presented to the living in 1622; according to the official record of Wren's visitation he had promised to conform and read the Book of Sports.[19] In the early seventeenth century the Barnardistons had four church livings in their gift, Kedington, Barnardiston and Great Wratting in Suffolk and Great Coates in Lincolnshire. When Sir Nathaniel succeeded his grandfather in 1619 the incumbent at Kedington was Abraham Gibson, the author of a work entitled *The Lord's Mourning for Vain Swearing*. Sir Simonds D'Ewes recalls in his autobiography that during a visit to Kedington Hall in 1624 he heard two excellent sermons by Gibson and that in addition there was 'much religious and solid conference in the private, by which I learned moore touching the Nature, signes, causes and effects of Faith, that principal Christian grace, then ever I had done before'.[20] When any of Sir Nathaniel's benefices fell vacant it was his practice to 'spend many daies in Fasting and Prayer to invite the Direction of God to guide his bestowing thereof'. The most famous of his ministers was Samuel Fairclough who, according to a fellow divine, 'was a Boanerges in the pulpit, an admirable preacher, both very judicious and moving. . . . He was mighty in the scriptures, fervent in spirit, serving the Lord night and day with incessant prayer.' Early on in his career he had preached in some of the principal towns of East Anglia and had earned the disapproval of Bishop Harsnet for neglecting to use the sign of the cross. Sir Nathaniel had frequently heard him preach and found his sermons extremely rewarding. When the need arose for a new minister at Barnardiston there were many applicants for the living but he was determined to appoint Fairclough so that he could be 'his constant Auditor, once every Lords-day' since the church was only a short distance from Kedington. Sir Nathaniel offered him the living on the understanding that he would be granted one of his more lucrative benefices when a vacancy occurred; Fairclough accepted the offer and in June 1623 the formalities were completed. Although Harsnet was still Bishop of Norwich Sir Nathaniel managed to arrange for his nominee to be instituted without being required to take the oath of canonical obedience, to subscribe to the Three Articles or even to appear before the diocesan in person. Early in 1630, following the death of Abraham Gibson, he presented Fairclough to the rectory of Kedington, a living worth £200 a year, and as before he was able to secure his institution without the usual preliminaries.[21]

At Kedington the new incumbent preached four sermons a week, two of them every Sunday, one every Thursday and the other every Saturday night in his own house. The Thursday sermon was a public lecture, 'the licence whereof was purchased at a great rate', and such was his reputation that his audience often included a number of scholars from Cambridge as well as many clergymen. His attitude to the Prayer Book services was one of outward conformity: it was said of him that he 'could and did submit to the use of the Liturgy, though he made it not matter of his choice'. Since, however, he could not accept either the contents of the Book of Sports or the Laudian innovations he was frequently summoned to appear before the archdeacon and commissary at Bury St Edmunds, but 'return and answer was always given that by reason of his Distemper', which was occasioned by a fall, 'he was unable to Ride so far'. At length the commissary, no doubt growing impatient with all this prevarication, decided to hold his court at the parsonage house of Kedington and in these circumstances it seemed likely that the errant minister would find himself suspended; in the event, however, the court merely took note of his infirmity and allowed him to continue his pastoral work. Sir Nathaniel, for his part, always entertained the highest regard for Fairclough: when drawing up his will he expressed the wish that he would afford his children 'his best help and assistance in the waies of God'.[22]

Another of Sir Nathaniel's ministers was Christopher Burrell, the rector of Great Wratting, who was Fairclough's brother-in-law. Like Fairclough he was a nonconformist who declined to read the Book of Sports: as a result he was suspended by Wren's commissioners and later deprived of his living by Bishop Montague. Following his ejection Sir Nathaniel chose as his successor a young man called John Owen who was Fairclough's assistant at Kedington. Owen would subsequently write of his patron

> Mushrooms of Gentry can streight from a blew
> Be dipt in scarlet, which is honour's hue,
> Yet in his birth and bloud he found a staine
> Till 'twas innobled and he born again.

In January 1641 Lady Anne Barnardiston (the second wife of Sir Nathaniel's grandfather) sought to enlist the help of her grandson, Sir Simonds D'Ewes, on behalf of Burrell, whom she still considered to be the rightful incumbent. In her letter she expressed the hope that Sir Nathaniel was 'earnest to have him restored as well in living as libertie' but clearly felt that a greater sense of urgency was required since she asked him to let Barnardiston know in forthright terms 'that he will suffer much in the opinion of his country neighbors in these parts; many looke upon the successe of this busines and surely as this man speeds Sir Nathaniel wilbe censured if it be not fully evidenced to them that he desired and indevoured to have him restored to both.' Obviously it was important that Sir Nathaniel's reputation as a champion of godliness should not be impaired as a result of this episode.[23]

Among the wealthy Puritans in Sir Nathaniel's circle of friends was Brampton Gurdon, who lived at Assington Hall. In January 1631 the living of Assington fell vacant with the death of Thomas Chambers who, according to the parish register, had served the cure faithfully and diligently since 1598 and during that time had preached two sermons every Sunday. As his successor the Gurdons chose Nathaniel Rogers, who had recently been dismissed as curate in the Essex parish of Bocking for performing a burial service without a surplice. An accomplished preacher, he was soon attracting a considerable following: indeed his popularity was so great that Assington church was often unable to accommodate all who wanted to hear him preach. Early in 1635, however, he decided to give up his living rather than wait for the ecclesiastical authorities to silence him. When Sir Nathaniel Brent visited Bury St Edmunds in April, during the course of his metropolitical visitation, he noted that Rogers was 'an absolute inconformitan. I am told he hath resigned his Benefice purposing to goe into New England. Howsoever I have suspended him de facto.' The next vicar of Assington was Thomas Walker who, like his predecessor and the sons of Brampton Gurdon, had once been a student at Emmanuel College, Cambridge. Within two years of his admission to the living he found himself under suspension for nonconformity but eventually he was allowed to resume his duties.[24]

In the Midlands the reputation of Northamptonshire as a Puritan county was comparable to that which Suffolk had acquired. During the early years of James I's reign Bishop Dove of Peterborough acted with great severity against the nonconformist clergy but after the appointment of George Abbot as Archbishop of Canterbury the situation became more peaceful, though the conduct of John Lambe, who was Chancellor of the Diocese, aroused a good deal of discontent. In May 1621 the House of Commons discussed a petition in which Lambe was accused of corrupt and oppressive practices. The petition had been forwarded by the mayor and corporation of Northampton but Lambe told the king that the complaints had been 'underhand sett on and countenaunced by greater persons in this Countye that thorough me ayme att your Majesty's Ecclesiasticall Jurisdiction'. Among other things he had been criticised for dealing harshly with those who journeyed to other parishes to hear sermons; in fact, he stressed,

I punishe none but where I find either manifest contempt of the lyturgie of the Church or of their owne Minister. The fault is now growne too common. The Puritans goe by troupes from their owne parishe Church (though there be a Sermon) to heare another whom their humour better affecteth.[25]

According to a seventeenth-century writer such Northamptonshire families as the Drydens of Canons Ashby and the Knightleys of Fawsley worked in close association with Viscount Saye and Sele, who lived at Broughton Castle in Oxfordshire, and the Copes of Hanwell, another Oxfordshire family, in providing support and protection for godly ministers in that part of the Midlands where the two counties shared a common border.[26] The most celebrated of these ministers was John Dod, a determined nonconformist, who served at one time or another at Hanwell, Canons Ashby and Fawsley. Another Northamptonshire squire who was associated with this group was Sir John Pickering of Titchmarsh; when some sermons of Robert Bolton were published in 1632 the editor commented in his account of the author that he could never think of Sir John (who was a friend of Bolton) except in the words of St Paul, 'The world was not worthy of him.'[27] In December 1615 Sir John executed a deed conveying to William Lord Saye and Sele, his father-in-law Sir Erasmus Dryden and his brother-in-law Robert Horsman the 'first and next avoidance' of his living of Titchmarsh. On the death of the incumbent, Robert Williamson, the trustees were to select a fit person (obviously meaning a godly preaching minister) to succeed him. When Sir John himself died in 1628 his son Gilbert was still a student at Emmanuel College, Cambridge and in accordance with the provisions of his will a group of relatives and friends who included Dame Susan the mother, Sir Erasmus Dryden, Robert Horsman and another Puritan squire, Francis Nichols of Faxton, obtained a grant of the young man's wardship from the Crown. Three years later Robert Williamson resigned the living and the Crown, which enjoyed the patronage rights during the minority, presented his son and namesake to the rectory. No doubt it was the intention of those who were looking after the ward's interests that this should be merely an interim arrangement: at all events the new incumbent tendered his own resignation in 1633, not long after the ward's coming of age, and the way was then clear for the surviving trustees, Lord Saye and Sele and Robert Horsman, to exercise the power vested in them by the deed of 1615.[28]

Now that their opportunity had finally arrived the trustees decided to offer the living to Thomas Hill, a Puritan fellow of

Emmanuel College who must have been well known to Gilbert Pickering. Hill was renowned not only for his abilities as a tutor but for the quality of his preaching which was described as 'plain, powerful, spiritual, frequent and laborious'. If, as seems likely, the trustees had high expectations of him they were not to be disappointed: 'partly by preaching and conversing up and down with others but especially . . . with his own Parochial charge he proved a great blessing not onely to that Town but also to the whole Countrey.'[29] On the eve of the metropolitical visitation of 1635 Sir John Lambe commented in some preparatory notes that Hill was a nonconformist who had not yet read the Book of Sports to his congregation. So popular was his preaching, he went on, that people from all over the county flocked to hear him. What was worse, his sermons were often highly inflammatory: at Kettering and Pytchley, for example, he had declared that the righteous were under persecution and must arm themselves against the threat which confronted them. Sir John seems to have been putting the worst possible construction on some words which were potentially ambiguous yet despite his adverse comments Hill managed to avoid deprivation and was still serving as rector of Titchmarsh in September 1640 when his name appeared in a list of Puritan divines who were alleged to have held a conventicle at Kettering.[30]

When Sir Gilbert Pickering married Elizabeth Montagu, the daughter of Sir Sidney Montagu, in 1638 the right of presentation to the rectory was considered to be important enough to justify special provision in the settlement which was made. On 28 April he conveyed the advowson to trustees chosen by himself and his father-in-law for a period of eighty years. As and when the living became vacant the trustees were to present such minister as Sir Gilbert would nominate and after his death this right of choice was to pass to his wife, assuming that she survived him.[31]

After serving for many years as rector of Hanwell John Dod was suspended in 1604 for nonconformity. Subsequently, we are told, he received a call to be minister of Canons Ashby where he lived quietly for a time under the protection of Sir Erasmus Dryden, 'in whom there was a rare mixture of Piety and Learning'. When Dod and his colleague Robert Cleaver, who had also been silenced, published one of their collaborative works in 1609 they dedicated it to Dryden, expressing their appreciation of his kindness towards them and referring to his 'godlie wife and hopefull familie'.[32] The

Drydens maintained that their church at Canons Ashby was a peculiar and therefore exempt from the jurisdiction of the Bishop of Peterborough. On the occasion of a parliamentary survey in 1656 testimony was produced that Canons Ashby had once been a priory and had been purchased from the Crown after the dissolution of the monasteries: 'it was then and now is a Peculiar. And the Bishopps of that Diocese had never Institution or Induction there.'[33] If, however, the church was legally immune from diocesan control it was still subject to the authority of the Archbishop of Canterbury and in any event Dod was flouting the law by preaching without a licence. In 1611, after Richard Neile, then Bishop of Coventry and Lichfield, had complained about Dod's activities, James I instructed the archbishop to take action against him. As a result he was forced to leave Canons Ashby, yet in September 1614 we find the archbishop writing to Bishop Dove that the king wished to know whether there was any truth in a report that several silenced ministers, among them Dod and Cleaver, were continuing to preach in his diocese.[34]

John Winston, who edited a number of Dod's sermons for publication, appears to have been serving as stipendiary curate at Canons Ashby at least as early as 1629 and was still there in 1651.[35] In March 1635, when preparations were being made for a metropolitical visitation, Archbishop Laud told his Vicar-General that Canons Ashby, Adstone and Harrington, all in Northamptonshire, claimed to be subject only to the authority of the Metropolitan and that it was reported that through lack of ecclesiastical censure the inhabitants were very unchaste, their churches much profaned and their ministers out of all order. The whole matter, he stressed, should be thoroughly investigated and the situation at Canons Ashby, where the patron was Sir John Dryden, required particular attention.[36] A hostile account of Sir John which was written some years later depicts him as a man who was noted for his weakness and simplicity and as 'a Puritan by tenure' who was 'very furious against the Clergy'. At Canons Ashby, it was alleged, he had converted most of the church to profane uses, 'the Chancel to a Barn, the Body of it to a Corn-Chamber and Store-House, reserving one Side-Isle of it only for the publick Service of Prayers, &c.'.[37]

In his report on the metropolitical visitation Sir Nathaniel Brent noted that the parishes of Canons Ashby and Adstone each had one house, in the former case belonging to Sir John Dryden and in the latter to a gentleman by the name of John Harby; that there were no churchwardens in either parish though the churches were undoubtedly parochial; that one of the ministers was leaving England because he felt unable to conform and that the other had been suspended for nonconformity. Both patrons had appeared before him and had undertaken to appoint conformable ministers and arrange for churchwardens to be sworn. Satisfied that his intervention had achieved the desired results he added with a touch of complacency that 'I make noe doubt of a perfect reformation in these two places.'[38]

At Fawsley, which is not far distant from Canons Ashby, Sampson Wood was deprived of his living for nonconformity during the purge conducted by Bishop Dove in 1605. The patron, Sir Richard Knightley, then presented Christopher Spicer, a Puritan minister who from 1608 onwards was also rector of Cogenhoe, another Northamptonshire parish; in practice, however, Wood continued to serve the cure and to enjoy all the profits until his death in 1625. The success of this subterfuge may have been due in some measure to the geographical remoteness of the parish and the fact that it had relatively few inhabitants which meant that the church resembled a family chapel. There may, however, have been another reason since a Puritan chronicler relates that Richard Knightley, who succeeded to the estate in 1619, bought some immunity for his ministers by sending gifts of venison to Sir John Lambe.[39]

According to the same writer, Richard Knightley was 'a very eminent Christian and a great Countenancer and Protector of the Puritans'. Every morning he heard a sermon in the church 'and then afterwards Feasted such Auditors as would stay and all Gentlemen and others that came to dinner', frequently observing that it was more necessary to feast men's souls than their bodies.[40] When Sampson Wood died in 1625 there was no formal change of incumbent but Knightley entrusted the cure of souls to John Dod, who had been living under his protection for some years, and procured a licence which enabled him to preach in public. At Fawsley, we are told, Dod 'preached twice every Lord's day. There he went over the gospel of John, the Epistle to the Colossians and other Scriptures.' As at Canons Ashby 'he had quietnesse from the Courts . . . for in neither of these places was there any Churchwardens.'[41] In the notes which he prepared for the metropolitical visitation of 1635 Sir John Lambe described how the Knightleys had hoodwinked the church authorities and stressed that while Christopher Spicer was nominally vicar of Fawsley it was Dod who actually performed the duties of the cure. Mr Dod, he wrote, had long since been deprived of his living at Hanwell and was still 'inconformed'. In the course of this visitation Sir Nathaniel Brent sat at Northampton and noted in his report that Mr Dod of Fawsley 'appeared not; he is 85 yeares old, and faith was made that he was very sicke'.[42] The same year Dod published some sermons on the Lord's Prayer which he had preached over twenty years before. In the dedication he told Richard Knightley that he prayed daily for him and felt obliged to leave some testimony behind 'of mine unfeined and hearty thankfulnesse for all your favours and goodnesse to mee and mine'.[43] When Spicer, the titular incumbent, died in 1637 Knightley presented John Wilkins, a man of many talents who was then a tutor at Magdalen Hall, Oxford. Wilkins, who was Dod's grandson, appears to have been vicar of Fawsley in little more than name. Not long after his institution he became chaplain to Viscount Saye and Sele and his grandfather continued to serve the cure till his death in 1645.[44]

In the neighbouring county of Warwickshire there was an exempt church which provided shelter for many nonconformist divines over the years. Wroxall, writes Edmund Calamy, was a place 'where Puritanism had taken Root'; where the Burgoynes 'shelter'd many an Hunted Deer, both in the days of Queen Elizabeth and in the two succeeding Reigns'. According to Victorian legal opinion Wroxall church was a public chapel which had a parochial function. Strictly speaking, it was neither a peculiar nor a donative cure but it was nevertheless free from diocesan jurisdiction and the appointment of a curate was entirely a matter for the patron. When Simeon Ashe was deprived of his Staffordshire living in the reign of Charles I Sir John Burgoyne gave him sanctuary at Wroxall where he probably acted as assistant to Ephraim Huitt, who was already serving as minister there in 1634. In his report for the year 1638 Laud told the king that Huitt had taken it upon himself to hold public fasts in his parish without authority and had condemned the decent ceremonies prescribed by the Church. He went on to say that the Bishop of Worcester had informed him that he was proceeding against Huitt and intended either to reform him or punish him. In the event Huitt was suspended and took himself off to New England. Subsequently, in 1641, Sir John entrusted the curacy to William Cooke, 'a man of a most godly, mortified life' who had a marked dislike of prelacy and ceremonial requirements. When a treatise which he had written was published in 1644 the editor dedicated it, at his request, to the patron who was 'the chiefe meane to opening a doore to him for the exercise of his Ministerie'. After the Restoration Cooke's successor, Luke Milbourne, was ejected for nonconformity and a fellow divine made the significant comment that he 'might have kept in by a little Conformity, at least till a metropolitical visitation', as his predecessors Mr Huitt and Mr Cooke had done.[45]

In Lincolnshire there were two landed families which were particularly renowned for their patronage of godly ministers, the Wrays of Glentworth and the Armynes of Osgodby. In 1603 Sir William Wray was described by a Puritan divine as 'a principal professor and protector of religion' to whom a multitude of ministers were indebted.[46] At one time he had no fewer than eight ministers under his patronage, among them Robert Atkinson, a popular preacher and hardened nonconformist who served as vicar of Glentworth between 1600 and 1626.[47] His son Sir John assigned the living of Blyton to Thomas Coleman, who was to become well known as an exponent of Erastian principles in the Westminster Assembly and who is said to have viewed with equal repugnance both prelacy and Presbyterianism. For his own parish of Glentworth Sir John chose a young Puritan divine who was a graduate of Emmanuel College, Cambridge and already had a considerable record of nonconformity. During the latter part of his time at the university John Ashburne had acted as curate at St Andrew's church in Cambridge, 'not being licensed and seldom wering the surplesse'. After leaving the university he had been employed for some years as curate of St Mary Tower at Ipswich. During the course of Bishop Wren's visitation in 1636 it was revealed that Ashburne had never been licensed for that purpose by the ordinary of the diocese and that he had conducted services in a way which was contrary to the orders of the Church. He was suspended by Wren's commissioners at the beginning of April, sought unsuccessfully to obtain reinstatement and on 11 September was instituted by Bishop Williams to the living of Glentworth on the presentation of Sir John Wray.[48]

Sir William Armyne, whose Elizabethan mansion was situated in the parish of Lenton, is said to have been 'eminently virtuous and religious' and one 'that gave great encouragement and Countenance to the Puritans and a further Reformation in the Church'. He owned the patronage rights in three Lincolnshire parishes, Lenton, Silk Willoughby and Pickworth, and was for many years the patron of Hugh Tuke, who was frequently in trouble with the church authorities over his nonconformity. Sir William's son and namesake, who succeeded in 1622, was

> very carefull to provide such helpes and guides for the soules as might be most usefull to the faith and salvation of the people ... in all these places in his dispose he planted men of very good reputation and abilities to preach the Gospell and gave proportionable encouragement both for countenance and maintenance; and the assurance that the people had of his severity to any known evill was as good as an use of reproofe to them.[49]

Although Sir William always filled his livings with Puritan ministers, men like Matthew Lawrence and Seth Wood, it is significant that none of them suffered deprivation while he was their patron. According to Seth Wood 'he was to such good men as lived under his wing and protection a shadow from the heat and a refuge from the storme of that persecution which scorched others very sore, for though the times knew he was not too great to crush yet he was too wel beloved to provoke'. But perhaps the most important factor was the *laissez-faire* attitude of Bishop Williams, with whom he and his wife appear to have been on good terms.[50]

In the remote border county of Herefordshire there was only one Puritan patron of any standing during the early seventeenth century. In the sermon preached at the funeral of Sir Robert Harley in 1656 the minister declared that

> He was the First that brought the Gospell into these parts. This Country lay under a Vaile of darknesse till he began to shine ... as God removed godly Ministers by Death he continued still a succession of them to you, not onely Brampton-Brian but Ye also of Wigmore and Ye of Leyntwardine owe your very souls to Sir Robert Harley who maintained your Ministers upon his own cost that they might feed you with the Gospell of Jesus Christ. . . . This Planting of godly Ministers, and then Backing them with his Authority, made Religion famous in this little corner of the world.[51]

Under the terms of a marriage settlement Sir Robert had the right of presentation to the rectory of Brampton Bryan while his father was still alive and in 1612 he installed Thomas Pierson, who had been a close friend of William Perkins at Cambridge. According to Edmund Calamy, writing in 1647, Pierson 'was so famous in his generation, such a burning and shining light, and so instrumentall to the good of the Church, both by his own indefatigable labours in the Ministery of the Gospel, as also by the publishing of divers Treatises of Mr Perkins and Mr Brightman'. From another account we learn that he had no objections to the liturgy and was prepared to kneel when receiving communion; on the other hand, he had scruples about wearing a surplice and using the sign of the cross in baptism, though he was willing to let his curate follow his own conscience in these matters. From time to time Sir Robert's father would complain about Pierson's nonconformity to the Bishop of Hereford but in these circumstances he was always able to count on the full support of his patron. In September 1615 Sir Robert emphasised in a letter to the bishop that while his pastor could not conform in all respects he was nevertheless content to remain silent about the points of contention as he regarded the maintenance of peace within the Church as second only in importance to the satisfying of his conscience. Despite all the complaints and the questioning which he had to endure Pierson was able to hold on to his living:

> although he was generally Reputed . . . a Non-Conformist . . .
> he always carryed himself so discreetly with such Reverend
> Respect unto those in Authority that he was well accepted of
> by them and never in all his Time was so much as once Silenced
> or suspended either ab officio or Beneficio but Alwayes enjoyed
> the Liberty of the Ministry.

With Sir Robert's active encouragement Pierson turned Brampton Bryan into a thoroughgoing Puritan parish with two sermons every Sunday, weekday lectures and a regular programme of spiritual exercises. Every quarter he kept an ember day fast which attracted many godly persons from far and wide 'as the Flight of Doves to the Windowes of Holy Light'.[52]

Following Pierson's death in October 1633 Sir Robert made extensive enquiries among his clerical friends with a view to recruiting another minister who was cast in the same mould. This proved

to be a lengthy process and in January 1634 we find the household
at Brampton Castle praying, with perhaps a hint of desperation,
that 'God would in riche mercye restore the Gospell to us by one
after his owne heart and continew our exercises'. One of the Puritan
divines whose help was sought was Thomas Hill who had recently
left Emmanuel College to take up his pastoral charge in
Northamptonshire. In a letter dated 21 November 1633 he told Sir
Robert that when writing to John Knowles of St Catharine Hall,
Cambridge he had suddenly thought of another possible candidate
and was confident that 'he will every way answere your desire
and I beleeve exceed your expectation.' This individual was David
Ensigne, a fellow of Emmanuel College and subsequently vicar of
Preston Capes in Northamptonshire, where the patronage rights
were in the hands of Richard Knightley. Ensigne had already
declined several offers of preferment but 'Meethinkes I knowe some-
things in his spirit and your place that will sweetly sute.' Hill went
on to say, however, that if Sir Robert would allow him further time
he would 'procure such a one as may be fitt to succeed that worthy
man of God and serve you for your salvation'. Another correspondent mentioned the names of several nonconformist ministers,
among them Julines Herring, a lecturer at Shrewsbury who was
already well known to Sir Robert, but in conclusion recommended
either Thomas Porter of Hanmer in Denbighshire or Thomas Fisher
of Whitchurch in Shropshire who were 'singular for parts and piety,
life and doctryne'.[53] Sir Robert also had the assistance of Dr John
Stoughton who was minister of St Mary Aldermanbury, the church
which he attended when residing in London. Stoughton wrote on
his behalf to Peter Thatcher, the rector of St Edmund's, Salisbury,
offering him the vacant living and explaining that Sir Robert was
exercising particular care in choosing a new minister

> the rather because it is the place of his owne abode and there-
> fore concerning him more neerely both in regard of the benefit
> of the publick ministery and the comfort of his owne private
> society, and because he hath lost a worthy man, Mr Pierson,
> the losse of who he desires to repaire in a worthy successor.

He then proceeded to describe the attractions of this particular
living:

> I assure my selfe you shall find a worthy, Religious and loving

Patron and frend of Sir Robert, and such as I have not found many like in all these respects, and beside potent in his country . . . sweet and humble in his conversation for your comfort and converse, and free of his heart and purse, and I heare his Lady . . . rather transcends him.

Thatcher, however, was unwilling to desert his flock at Salisbury and gracefully declined the offer.[54]

In March 1634 Sir Robert secured the institution of William Brice, an 'eminently godly and very learned Man', who had been serving as minister at Henley in Oxfordshire. His former parishioners, however, were so reluctant to lose him that they sent a deputation to his new patron, who in response to their entreaties allowed him to return.[55] In the end Sir Robert had to look to Yorkshire for a suitable minister who was willing to settle in Herefordshire. Stanley Gower, a curate at Sheffield parish church, received an invitation which was couched in such forthright terms that it would have caused a considerable stir had it fallen into the wrong hands. First of all it was made clear that he was being called by the parish:

> wee will owne you, as our Minister, not quatenus sent by the Prelate of this Diocese but quatenus consented unto as our Minister and consenting to be our Minister. Thus Mr Dod told me was he clearly called to Fawsley, where now he our worthy Knight as the chiefe member of the Congregation chose you, the parish consenting unto him.

As regards the pastoral needs of the congregation they wanted a minister who would not only expound the scriptures but also abridge the Prayer Book services: 'if you read not the Confession you incurr the danger of the Statute;[56] the rest is cut of in many scores of Congregations in England who yet have no such to play the Nehemiah as wee, by God's grace, have.' While the person deputed to send the invitation said nothing about the administration of holy communion he noted with satisfaction that Gower dispensed with the sign of the cross in baptism. On the subject of episcopal authority he was terse but unequivocal: 'Submission to the English Bishops in any thing wee cannot yeeld to.'[57]

On 21 June 1634 Thomas Toller, the vicar of Sheffield, and two neighbouring ministers, William Carte and John Newton, signed a certificate testifying that they could see no reason why Stanley Gower should not 'remove thence to any place whereunto by God his providence he shall be lawfully called'. It was not a certificate which would have passed close scrutiny since all three ministers were nonconformists; nevertheless Gower was admitted to the living of Brampton Bryan in the following September.[58]

In the event the new rector proved to be a good choice. In January 1635 Sir Robert wrote to James Usher, the Archbishop of Armagh, that God had provided Mr Gower (who had once been the archbishop's chaplain) as a means 'to hold out his holy light againe amonge us'; more prosaically, he added that he had first made diligent inquiry of him and 'his owne worth perswaded mee to geve hym a free and cheerfull call.'[59] In February 1638 it was alleged that Stanley Gower and Richard Symonds, a schoolmaster living in Sir Robert's house,[60] had been guilty of Puritan practices and that Harley himself had given them his support and encouragement. According to these charges the rector never read the absolution or the litany, seldom wore a surplice and in his preaching criticised the veneration shown to places of worship and stressed that the times were dangerous. Symonds, for his part, was a suspended priest who was in the habit of repeating Gower's sermons, spiced with his own comments, for the edification of the household at Brampton Castle. In addition, there were private fasts during which Gower prayed and preached *ex tempore* for the greater part of the day. Despite these serious accusations he was allowed to retain his living and a year later Sir Robert's daughter Brilliana was writing to her brother Edward, who was then at Oxford, that he was preaching better and better every day. The only action which the bishop appears to have taken was to forbid him to hold special fasts on ember days.[61] While Gower was highly regarded by the Harley family his relations with Nathaniel Cradock, another Puritan divine who was living at Brampton Castle, did not betray much evidence of godliness. In January 1641 Cradock was reported to have spoken very reproachfully of Gower, calling him a base, filthy fellow and a drunkard and claiming that he had never preached anything worth a pin.[62]

In Dorset the chief centre of Puritanism was the county town of Dorchester whose religious loyalties owed much to the personality and influence of John White, the long-serving minister of Holy Trinity.[63] In the neighbourhood of Dorchester there were two major

Puritan families, the Brownes of Frampton and the Trenchards of Wolfeton House in the parish of Charminster. In 1634 John Browne was involved in a curious transaction in his capacity as patron of the church of Frampton: Bernard Banger, the vicar of Frampton, exchanged livings with William Clifford, the rector of Yarlington in Somerset. The reasons for this exchange are by no means clear but it may not have been unconnected with the fact that Clifford had been in trouble with the High Commission earlier that same year. In the autumn of 1635 Browne, White and Clifford were subjected to questioning about some money which had been sent to Dr John Stoughton of St Mary Aldermanbury. The authorities apparently suspected that the money was intended for the support of Puritan ministers in New England; Browne, however, insisted that it was the portion of his daughter Jane who in January 1636 would be married to Stoughton in the church at Frampton. In the end the matter was quietly dropped.[64]

According to one of his fellow gentry Sir Thomas Trenchard, who was the patron of several livings, was 'a very honest well-natured worthy man, a favourer of the Puritans'.[65] The parish church of Charminster, which is only a short distance from the Tudor mansion of the Trenchards, enjoyed the status of a peculiar and was exempt from the jurisdiction of the Bishop of Bristol. As owners of the impropriation the family employed a stipendiary curate who in return for a modest allowance read the Prayer Book services in the churches of Charminster and Stretton. In July 1634 Sir Nathaniel Brent undertook a metropolitical visitation of the Deanery of Dorchester and its peculiars and the following month John Browne wrote in a letter to Dr Stoughton that the Vicar-General had pressed the use of the ceremonies and that Richard Dike, the curate of Charminster, had told his parishioners that he had given direction that all members of the congregation should bow at the name of Jesus. As we learn from another source, Sir Nathaniel had also offered the tendentious comment that in the matter of the ceremonies the archbishop was not insisting on anything more than had been required ever since the Reformation.[66]

In October 1634 Robert Tutchin, an unbeneficed Puritan minister, came to live at Charminster, where Sir Thomas provided him with a house and an allowance of £40 a year. Tutchin, who was 'one of the Primitive Simplicity and Integrity, Purity and Piety', was probably unwilling to accept a living because of the strains this might impose on his conscience; Dike, on the other hand, was condemned as a scandalous minister when the Puritans were in power.[67] It seems likely therefore that Tutchin was assigned the major role of preacher while Dike performed the more routine duties of the cure and no doubt his presence helped to foster the illusion that despite its privileged status Charminster was a parish in which order and conformity prevailed. Another Puritan divine who was living at Charminster before the Civil War was Jerome Turner, a former schoolmaster whom Sir Thomas employed as his domestic chaplain: in Anthony Wood's estimation he was 'a fluent preacher but too much addicted to Calvinism'.[68]

Sir Walter Erle, who was seated at Charborough in the eastern part of the county, was Governor of the short-lived Dorchester Company whose members included John Browne and John White. The church, which stood near Charborough Hall, was technically a public chapel annexed to the church of East Morden but in practice it was probably more in the nature of a domestic chapel. During the years 1617 to 1654 Charborough and East Morden were both served by Nevill Drant who, as a curate at North Mimms in Hertfordshire, had been suspended for nonconformity.[69] Although Sir Walter's main estates were in Dorset he also had property in Devon and here he held the patronage rights in one of the most Puritan parishes in the county. In 1632 he presented to the living of Axmouth a young minister by the name of William Hooke who had previously been serving as rector of Upper Clatford in Hampshire where the patron was another Puritan squire, Sir Thomas Jervoise. Hooke, who had married a niece of Lady Joan Barrington, was described by Anthony Wood as 'a puritanical preacher' who gained notoriety with his seditious sermons and his nonconformity in all particulars. He was undoubtedly one of the two refractory ministers in the diocese who refused to compromise on Bishop Hall's terms[70] and his activities as vicar of Axmouth would almost certainly have led to his deprivation had he not decided to emigrate to New England. Walter Yonge, who had a house in the parish and must often have heard him preach, noted in his diary that on 5 April 1639 Mr Hooke resigned his benefice into the bishop's hands. Before the end of July Sir Walter had presented another minister, Nathaniel Dike, whose family was renowned for the number of godly divines which it had produced.[71]

In the main, the wealthy Puritan gentry were remarkably

successful in ensuring that their parish churches remained in the charge of ministers who satisfied their needs, particularly as regards the type of preaching which was aimed at illuminating the way to salvation. Relatively few lost the services of a godly pastor through deprivation or enforced resignation and even then it was usually possible to put in a suitable replacement. Nevertheless the Laudian era was, generally, a difficult and anxious time for Puritan patrons, who might be put to considerable trouble in defending their ministers in the face of official pressures and who were often able to do little to protect their churches from what they regarded as the rising tide of idolatry and superstition. Much, however, depended on which diocese a church was situated in. The Puritan squires who were seated in the Diocese of Norwich had reason to envy their brethren in the Diocese of Exeter where Bishop Hall behaved as though the latitudinarian philosophy of Archbishop Abbot was still in fashion.

CHAPTER TEN

DESPAIR AND HOPE

During the years 1629 to 1640, writes Clarendon, the kingdom 'enjoyed the greatest calm and the fullest measure of felicity that any people in any age for so long time together have been blessed with; to the wonder and envy of all parts of Christendom'.[1] For most of the leading Puritan families it was a period when, in material terms at least, life went on much as usual. Economic prosperity manifested itself in such ways as the acquisition of land, the rebuilding or improvement of mansion houses, the purchase of coaches, plate and jewellery, and the commissioning of portraits and elaborate pedigrees. There was, however, a feeling in Puritan circles that affluence was breeding self-indulgence and excess of every kind and that before long God would wreak vengeance on a sinful nation. In August 1634 a Dorset squire, John Browne, wrote to his friend Dr John Stoughton, who was the minister of St Mary Aldermanbury in London, to commiserate with him over the death of his wife, and added that she might have been 'in mercy delivered from that evil to come which our sinnes give us iust occasion to feare will speedily overtake us'. Stoughton himself declared in one of his sermons that 'The English nation is most healthfull when it swimmes in teares, and more dangerous to fall into a sicknesse when it overflowes with laughter.' Looking back on this period Bulstrode Whitelocke commented, in a speech delivered in 1642, that God had blessed England with a long and flourishing peace and 'we turned his grace into wantonness, our peace would not satisfy us without luxury nor our plenty without debauchery, instead of sobriety and thankfullnes for our mercyes we provoked the givre of them by our sinnes and wickednes to punish us'.[2]

If the Puritan gentry were concerned about the moral state of the nation this was by no means their only source of anxiety. Many years later Sir Arthur Hesilrige described (with some rhetorical touches) those features of Charles I's reign which had particularly appalled him. The Privy Council, he related, bit like a serpent and the Star Chamber like scorpions. Two or three gentlemen could not venture out for fear of being charged with committing a riot. Men's souls and consciences were put on the rack by Archbishop Laud; they were not allowed to speak of holy scripture or repeat a sermon at their tables. Many godly ministers were forced to make their bed in the wilderness. Altars were set up and bowing enjoined; pictures were placed in church windows and images were introduced in Durham cathedral and elsewhere. And, he concluded, there were many other excesses both in Church and State.[3]

Sir Arthur himself had been reprimanded by the Privy Council and sent to the Fleet by the High Commission.[4] During the Laudian era a number of Puritan squires were hauled before the High Commission for one reason or another, among them Sir Richard Strode, Sir Philip Parker, Sir Henry Rosewell and Sir John Dryden. In November 1640 it was alleged in the Commons that a Northamptonshire gentleman, Francis Nichols, had been involved in High Commission proceedings for no less than five years merely for wearing a hat in sermon time; in fact he was accused of various offences, including participation in conventicles.[5]

By the time that the Long Parliament was summoned there were not a few Puritan gentlemen who had personal grievances against the Archbishop of Canterbury. Sir Edward Hungerford experienced the rigours of the Laudian censorship system at first hand when attempting to publish a religious testament written by his father. One of Laud's chaplains took exception to certain passages which were critical of Catholicism and insisted that they should be removed; Sir Edward, however, was not prepared to make any alterations and eventually, in 1639, an unabridged version was published at Oxford without the knowledge of the Archbishop.[6] Writing about the loss of his office of Master of the Mint Sir Robert Harley recalled that he had incurred the displeasure of men who were powerful at Court, and in particular Archbishop Laud, 'for that he did appear in the High Commission Court . . . with Dr

Stoughton, preacher att Aldermanbury London, and for entertaine-inge Mr Workman, preacher att Glocester, into his house and visitinge him in the Gatehouse where hee was Imprisoned by sentence of the said High Commission Court'. As a result he had been forced to surrender his office and according to his calculations this had involved a total loss of income of £3875 between the years 1635 and 1642. Such a significant reduction in his annual income could hardly have occurred at a worse time since he had already been experiencing financial difficulties.[7]

To the Puritan gentry it seemed that the government of Charles I was mounting a simultaneous onslaught on liberty, property and true religion. In a work published in 1645 Sir Simonds D'Ewes advanced the thesis that the promotion of idolatry and superstition usually went hand in hand with tyranny:

> Falshood, Heresies, men's Inventions, burthensome Superstitions intermixed with God's Worship and Idolatry or any divine Creature adoration, consisting in men's bowing to or towards Images, Crosses, Altars, Communion-tables, Reliques or the like, can never be generally or publikely established without sharp and cruell persecution be exercised and practised upon the goods, estates, liberties and lives of the godly.[8]

The forced loan of 1626, distraint of knighthood, ship money, fines for depopulations, the revival of the forest laws: such extra-parliamentary measures tended to be viewed by those wealthy enough to feel their impact as a scandalous attack on property rights. While ship money was by no means a heavy burden its constitutional implications were disquieting. In his autobiography D'Ewes comments with feeling that in 1635 'the libertie of the subjects of England received the most deadlie and fatall blow it had been sensible of in 500 yeares last past'. If the levying of money for the ostensible purpose of providing for the defence of the kingdom 'could be done lawfullie then by the same right the king upon the like pretence might gather the same summe tenn, twentie or an hundred times redoubled and soe to infinite proportions upon any one shire when and as oft as hee pleased and soe noe man was in conclusion worth anie thing'.[9] Even before Hampden took his stand in 1637 there were many Puritan squires who refused to pay ship money, among them Sir William Brereton of Cheshire, Sir John Wray and his half-brother Sir Christopher Wray of Lincolnshire,

Sir William Masham of Essex, Sir Gilbert Gerard of Middlesex and Sir Walter Erle, Sir Richard Strode and John Browne of Dorset. In Northamptonshire the Puritans were alleged to be the moving force behind the opposition to ship money. In April 1636 one of the diocesan officials, Robert Sibthorpe, claimed that Sir John Dryden, the high sheriff, was deliberately neglecting his duties in the matter of ship money and that in this respect he was being aided and abetted by his Puritan high constables. The following year there was a report that John Crewe, the son of Sir Thomas Crewe, the former king's serjeant, was busily engaged in organising resistance to ship money.[10]

By the mid-1630s there are clear signs that many Puritan squires were becoming thoroughly disheartened as a result of the trend of events in both Church and State. In a letter written to Dr John Stoughton in September 1635 Sir Thomas Wroth expressed his dismay about the state of religion, maintaining that there was no hope of any alteration in ecclesiastical affairs and stressing that now was the time for the godly to show their courage. Fearing that the letter might fall into the wrong hands he sent it to a forwarding address in Coleman Street, that great centre of London Puritanism, but shortly afterwards the authorities took possession of it when a search was made of Dr Stoughton's study and adjudged it to be a dangerous and seditious document, mainly no doubt because it contained a reference to the possibility of bloodshed. There is no evidence, however, that the matter was taken further: indeed, Sir Thomas was appointed in August 1636 to the Somerset commission of the peace.[11] A strong feeling of hopelessness also pervaded the letters which John Winthrop and his son, who continued to take a close interest in English affairs after their arrival in New England, were receiving from their relatives and friends in Suffolk. In April 1636 Sir William Spring explained that his letter was being dispatched by a means which Sir Nathaniel Barnardiston had discovered but went on to say that 'the time with us heere' was not 'soe free and sure to us as that I dare write you what I think and would you knew, neyther doe I ever expect a time for itt till wee meete in the haven after our storms are passed'. 'Blessed be our good God,' wrote Sir Nathaniel a year later, 'we all heare inioy our healthes in some competent manor, though accompened with noe smale trobles.' About the same time Brampton Gurdon remarked in a letter to Winthrop that he wished it was possible to write something about the Church or the State which was likely to give comfort to an English mind but the head was sick and all the members out of joint.[12]

To add to the miseries of the English Puritans the Protestant cause in Germany suffered a major setback with the death of King Gustavus Adolphus of Sweden in 1632 and the defeat of the Swedish forces at Nördlingen in 1634. In February 1633 Sir Robert Harley and his family were praying for 'the blessing of unity among the protestant Princes of Germany and for a worthy generall to succeed the King of Sweden'. Similarly, Sir Simonds D'Ewes relates that in these years his soul was filled with 'frequent sorrow and amazement' not only on account of the general hatred of true religion at home but also because of the tribulations of God's Church abroad and in particular the catastrophe at Nördlingen and the consequences flowing from it. To such men it must have seemed that the fate of European Protestantism was hanging in the balance.[13]

From the rural solitude of his manor-house the Puritan squire looked out on a world where, in the words of John Browne the Dorset parliamentarian, 'papisticall heresie' was flourishing;[14] where a government which had broken free from parliamentary constraints seemed bent on destroying local autonomy and individual liberty; and where (as he was inclined to believe) such vices as swearing, drunkenness and fornication were spreading in an alarming fashion. In these circumstances the concept of the godly household assumed even greater significance. To the Puritans the godly household represented a kind of spiritual fastness where the purity of Calvinist doctrine could be preserved, where God could be worshipped without the distraction of ceremonies for which there was no scriptural justification and where virtue could enjoy some immunity from the corrupting influences of a sinful world. The mood of introspection which was developing was very much in evidence in a letter which Sir Robert Harley received from a nonconformist minister, Thomas Wilson, in the spring of 1636:

> I need not commend unto you, one approved in Christ yourselfe, that your house should be a Church for doctrine and discipline, that ther should be morning and evening sacrifice day by day continually ... worship god in spirit and truth, hating vaine fictions and inventions and loving god's law. Shun now as pernicious the errors of the wicked and the spots of the

world and follow truth and holiness. Have the power of godlines by faith to receive life from Christ . . . save your selfe from this untoward generation and build up your selfe dayly by looking on the love of god in Christ . . . 'tis a contending age. Be stedfast in the present truth . . . learne to suffer: mortifyed men will be best martyrs . . . looke at and lay hold on eternall life, love not the world.[15]

As Wilson recognised, Sir Robert was one of the last persons to need such advice. According to another Puritan divine his house, Brampton Castle, 'was an house of Prayer: 'twas the Center where the Saints met to seek God'. Sir Robert was 'one that did Swim deep in the Tide of Fasting and Humiliation' and his household regularly engaged in spiritual exercises throughout the Laudian era. On Wednesday last, wrote one of his sons in February 1639, 'my father . . . kept a fast in the house and I unworthie to be at it was at it.'[16]

While there was a tendency for the godly to become more inward-looking in matters of religion this did not necessarily mean that the Puritan gentry simply retired to their estates and turned their backs on the world. When Sir Robert Harley ceased to have lodgings in London, which one of his ministers had equated with Hell,[17] this was solely because he had been forced out of his office of Master of the Mint; even then he was still anxious to be kept in touch with the latest Court gossip.[18] Many Puritan squires continued to travel up to London on business (in some cases for meetings of such bodies as the Providence Island Company); for medical treatment at the hands of the best or more expensive physicians in the kingdom; or occasionally for purely social reasons. Not infrequently they took their families with them and stayed for months at a time. During the early seventeenth century the Crown regularly issued proclamations requiring members of the country gentry who were sojourning in London to return to their estates but it was sometimes possible to obtain special permission to remain in the capital. A list prepared in February 1633 of persons of quality who had been granted such permission includes the names of several Puritan landowners, among them Sir Thomas Hutchinson, who was awaiting the completion of his new country house, and Sir John Cutts, who had recently been married in London and wished to extend his stay.[19]

If they had moments of despair the Puritan gentry could reassure themselves that they were not entirely powerless in the face of the

Laudian campaign against the cause of true religion since they were both patrons of church livings and justices of the peace. As a Herefordshire magistrate Sir Robert Harley was inspired with

> a most nimble Soul of Zeale against Sin. He was full of spirits against all dishonours done to God, he was a Terrour to Evill works, he knew no Respect of Persons in a businesse wherein God was wronged: among other things, how would he Vindicate the Sabbath from contempt? Prophannesse durst not appear upon the face of it; by this means the Congregations were frequented on the Lord's dayes and many thousand soules prevented from their sinfull sports sate under the droppings of the word.[20]

Sir Thomas Dacres, a Hertfordshire justice, also sought to maintain the sanctity of the Sabbath and as a result incurred the wrath of William Laud, then Bishop of London. One Sunday the churchwardens of Cheshunt parish church informed Sir Thomas, who had just been listening to a sermon, that during service time they had found a number of men drinking in private houses. Sir Thomas was well aware of the relevant statutory provisions: after all, he had been appointed in 1628 to a House of Commons committee which had been responsible for processing a bill for the suppression of unlicensed alehouses. Accordingly he issued a warrant (which was later signed by two of his fellow justices) authorising the levying of fines for running an alehouse without a licence, for drinking in such an establishment and for staying away from church. At the same time he suggested to the churchwardens that it was their duty to present the offenders in the ecclesiastical court for disorderly behaviour on the Sabbath. When Laud heard of the episode he summoned the zealous knight and demanded to know why he, as a mere layman, had been meddling in matters which concerned the Church. Sir Thomas protested that he had only been performing his duty as a justice of the peace and had acted entirely within the framework of statutory authority. Laud, however, brushed aside his arguments and threatened to start proceedings against him; but in the event it was the churchwardens who found themselves in this position.[21]

Lay interference in ecclesiastical matters was particularly likely to occur when there was a close-knit Puritan group on the commission of the peace. In the annual report which he presented to the king at the beginning of 1635 Laud told him that Bishop Montague of Chichester had certified that all was very well in his diocese except for the east part where 'some Puritan Justices of the Peace have awed some of the clergie with like opinions with themselves, which yet of late have not broken out into any publike Inconformity.' Subsequently, in January 1640, he informed the king that Bishop Duppa of Chichester had reported that his diocese was not so much troubled with Puritan ministers as with Puritan magistrates. Such a state of affairs also existed in Buckinghamshire: in June 1636, for example, Laud was told that the clergy in those parts were overawed by the justices and lay gentry.[22] In Northamptonshire, a county which had already gained notoriety in James I's reign with its petitions on religion, there is evidence of concerted opposition to the Laudian version of Thorough which was not confined solely to the magistracy. At the summer assizes in 1639 a number of gentlemen who were 'mett together accidentally' at the sheriff's table decided to send a message to Bishop Towers of Peterborough who was about to inaugurate his first visitation. This was a request that he should modify his visitation articles, some of which they considered to be very strict and unusual, so that 'the officers and ministers under him might not make use of them . . . to presse new things to be practized in the worship and service of God which are not enjoyned by the Rubrick and Cannons of the Church of England'. About the same time it was alleged that John Crewe was supplying money to many of the Puritan clergy, apparently from funds which had been specially collected for this purpose.[23]

Undoubtedly the most dramatic response to Laud's ecclesiastical policy was the exodus of many hundreds of the king's subjects to the New World. Milton wrote in 1641:

> Let the Astrologer be dismay'd at the portentous blaze of comets and impressions in the aire as foretelling troubles and changes to states: I shall beleeve there cannot be a more illboding signe to a Nation (God turne the Omen from us) then when the Inhabitants, to avoid insufferable grievances at home, are inforc'd by heaps to forsake their native Country.[24]

Among these refugees were a considerable number of ministers who in many cases were well known to the Puritan gentry: when, for example, Sir Nathaniel Barnardiston was writing to John Winthrop the younger in April 1636 he asked him to convey his best wishes to John Cotton, Thomas Hooker, John Wilson, Thomas Weld and Nathaniel Ward, all of whom had removed from East Anglia or Lincolnshire to Massachusetts within the previous four years.[25] As for the Puritan gentry themselves they might talk from time to time about the possibility of emigrating but it was a very difficult decision for persons of quality who were accustomed to living in a state of affluence and exercising great power within their local communities; moreover, they were usually in a better position than those of lower degree to ensure that their spiritual needs continued to be satisfied. When Stanley Gower was offered the living of Brampton Bryan in 1634 the letter of invitation which was sent on behalf of the patron, Sir Robert Harley, concluded with the anguished plea 'I beseech you doe what you can for us that wee be not driven to leave our Native countrey and friends and which is more, the stage of Europe, where wee are all to act our partes in the destruction of the great whore.'[26] No doubt this was the kind of sentiment which Sir Robert indulged in when he was in a particularly pessimistic mood but there is nothing to suggest that he ever seriously contemplated uprooting himself and his family. In April 1636 Meriell Gurdon, the wife of Brampton Gurdon, wrote in a letter to Governor Winthrop's wife that it would grieve any Christian heart to hear that in so short a time so many of God's faithful ministers had been silenced and

> that which is worse many that seemed to be zeleous doe yeld obedence to the inventions of men . . . I did thinke befor it had come to this . . . that we should have ben providing to come to you but now I see that my husband in regard of his many years doth rathar thinke he hath a calling to suffar hear then to remove himselfe. The Lord teach us what his will is and giv us harts to submite truly unto it and his holy Spirit to cary us throwe.

Brampton Gurdon would remain at home but he already had two children in Massachusetts, his son Edmund whom Winthrop had taken under his wing and his daughter Meriell who had married Richard Saltonstall, the son of Sir Richard Saltonstall whose own sojourn in the colony had been short-lived.[27]

In September 1635 a correspondent of Lord Deputy Wentworth wrote that Sir Henry Vane the younger had gone to New England for reasons of conscience and intended to stay there for the rest of his days. During the voyage, observes his seventeenth-century biographer, his personal appearance aroused suspicions among the other passengers: 'his honourable Birth, long Hair and other Circumstances of his Person rendered his fellow-travellers jealous of him, as a spye to betray their Liberty rather than any way like to advantage their design.' In May 1636 he was elected Governor of Massachusetts but after stirring up some bitter religious controversies he returned the following year to England, much to the relief of his fellow settlers.[28]

Sir Henry had travelled out to New England with John Winthrop the younger, who had been entrusted with the task of founding the colony of Saybrook in southern Connecticut. There was a clear expectation that before long some of the Puritan nobility and gentry would be going over and accordingly it was decided that houses should be built in readiness for them. In September 1635 Sir Arthur Hesilrige and George Fenwick, two of the members of the Saybrook committee in London, wrote to Winthrop, 'Your abilitie to performe your undertaking we suspect not; only our request is that . . . fitt houses be builded.' The following March we find Emmanuel Downing commenting in a letter to Winthrop that Sir Arthur had refused to deal for Captain Endicott's house because the merchants had told him that it had been built with their money and therefore belonged to them.[29] In Yorkshire two Puritan baronets, Sir Matthew Boynton and Sir William Constable, decided that their future lay in Connecticut and in the course of 1635 they began to make the necessary preparations, though they were forced to move slowly for fear that their intentions might become public knowledge. In February 1636 Sir Matthew wrote to Winthrop:

I shall bringe over a greate ffamilie . . . I pray you advertise me what course I shall take for providinge a house against my comminge over where I may remaine with my ffamilie till I can be better provided to settle my selfe, and lett me have your best assistance; and withall I pray you lett me receyve advice from time to time what provitions are most commodious to be made theyr, or to be sent from hence, that soe I may make the best advantage of my time before I come.

At this stage Sir Matthew was clearly in earnest since he sent over a number of servants, together with some farm stock, and began to sell outlying parts of his estate. In 1637, however, both he and

Constable abandoned their plans for emigrating to New England. Sir William and his wife crossed over to the Netherlands and took up residence at Arnhem where there was an English congregation which practised its religion on lines which were very different from the Laudian form of worship. Towards the end of the year Sir Matthew settled the bulk of his estate on trustees and some time later he and most of his family joined the Constables at Arnhem.[30]

During the period of Charles I's personal rule some of the Puritan noblemen and gentry acquired plantations in New England as an insurance against the possibility that they might eventually be forced to take refuge there. In his autobiography Sir Simonds D'Ewes recalls how he had begun 'to consider that a higher providence might ere long call mee to suffer for his name and gospell or might prepare a way for my passage into America'. As we shall see, he was more optimistic than some of his fellow Puritans about the future of English Protestantism yet he felt it prudent to seek advice from Edmund Browne, a minister residing at Boston in Massachusetts, about the purchase of a plantation. In reply Browne told him that there was a suitable tract of land in the neighbourhood of Ipswich and went on to say that grants of 600 acres had been made to a number of gentlemen and there were many lords who owned plantations. If, however, a gentleman did not come himself, or send an honest friend or choose employees who were skilled in agriculture, there was every prospect that he would suffer financial loss. Should D'Ewes decide not to buy a plantation as a means of making 'provision for harsh times if they should happen in England, my advice is that you would venture some thing by degrees to bee imployed in the breeding of cattle'. Writing to D'Ewes in September 1633 Winthrop stressed that he could not advise him to invest any money in this way unless he dispatched 'some faithfull man' to manage the stock; on the other hand, he observed, 'you may drive a trade with the Lord heere in helping forward the work of the Gospell or sending over some poore godly familyes with a year's provision'. Although D'Ewes apparently concluded that an investment in cattle would be too risky he continued to take a close interest in the affairs of the colony and was able to render it some assistance.[31]

While its objectives were more modest the Providence Island Company[32] brought together a greater number of Puritan notables than either the Massachusetts Bay Company or the Saybrook enterprise. Besides the Earl of Warwick, Lord Saye and Sele and Lord Brooke, its members included John Pym, Sir Benjamin Rudyerd, Sir Thomas Barrington and his brother-in-law Sir Gilbert Gerard, Sir Thomas Cheke, Sir William Waller, Sir Edmund Moundeford, Henry Darley (who was the eldest son of Sir Richard Darley) and John Gurdon (the heir of Brampton Gurdon). When the company was founded in 1630 it is unlikely that those who bought stock had any serious intention of travelling to Providence Island themselves: it was more a matter of enabling others to settle there. In January 1632 Sir Thomas Barrington persuaded a number of poor men living at Braintree in his own county of Essex to enter into agreements in which they undertook to go 'under his name and as of his famyly' to the Island of Providence when the next ship was dispatched by the company and to be ready for the journey when he should call them; there is no evidence, however, that Sir Thomas himself was planning to emigrate.[33] Writing to Sir Simonds D'Ewes in September 1637 Sir Edmund Moundeford laid great stress on the religious aspects of the enterprise: 'I wish they', meaning the adventurers,

> had your advice and societie; I know they would be glad of your company. Many of them I am sure you know; they are men fearing God, desirous to inioy and advance trew religion, which in any place will be hapines and no place but is miserable without it. . . . I know you ar well affected with the best things and I doubt not but this work (thurogh God allmighty his assistance) will be for his glory and the comfort of many if it may be assisted by such as yourself, thus comending my service to you and us and ours to the safe-keeping powere which only can preserve us in these last, worst backsliding tymes.

Early the following year there were some dramatic scenes at meetings of the stockholders when Lord Saye and Sele and subsequently the Earl of Warwick, Lord Brooke and Henry Darley declared their intention of travelling to the island as soon as they had settled their affairs. Sir Edmund Moundeford told D'Ewes that the king had refused to allow the company (which was faced with a financial crisis) to sell the island to the States of Holland; on the other hand, they had obtained from him various privileges including exemption from the travel restrictions imposed by proclamation. In these circumstances it had been decided that three members of the company should go in person to the island, 'no man to refuse', and that they should take a party of 500 men with them. 'Sum of the Lords and others of great qualitie', he went on, 'ar resolved to goe.' On the island there were many good people and highly moral teachers and the place was warmly recommended for health and plenty.[34] In an undated note which has survived among his papers Sir Simonds makes some interesting observations on the subject of emigration, apparently with Providence Island particularly in mind. In his view colonisation was both a remedy for overpopulation and a fulfilment of God's will. The plantation was a means 'to ease England of these exceeding numbers which long peace hath filled her withall'; moreover, it was 'God's generall command to mankind to goe and replenish the earth'. Those who had settled there conceived that 'desolation is comming upon this realme' but they were mistaken because Thomas Brightman (one of the earliest apocalyptic writers) 'saith confidentlie that the plantacion of the Gospell by Queen Elizabeth shall never bee abolished out of England nor shall this realme ever want princes for the maintainance of the truth'.[35]

In March 1638 an attempt was made to obtain the services of Ezekiel Rogers, a Puritan minister who had for some time been under pressure from his patron, Sir Thomas Barrington, to resign his Yorkshire living in order to make way for a young man who was employed as his domestic chaplain.[36] It was explained to him that the company intended that men of quality should be admitted to places of council and magistracy and that every individual who took with him his family and six menservants should have freehold land assigned to him and have a voice in choosing the government and making laws. In the event Rogers went to New England.[37]

The Earl of Warwick and his colleagues had hardly announced their plans before events in Scotland caused them to think again. On 27 February the National Covenant was signed in Edinburgh and the Scots began to make warlike preparations. Before long the Covenanters were in correspondence with some of the disaffected noblemen and gentry in England, among them the senior members of the Providence Island Company who had been talking of emigration. Bulstrode Whitelocke writes that the gentlemen who had been imprisoned as a result of the forced loan proceedings or had been distrained for refusing ship money or had otherwise been disobliged received approaches from the Covenanters and secretly favoured and assisted their designs, as did many others, 'especially those inclined to the presbiterian governement or whom the publique proceedings had any wise distasted'. He himself was solicited on behalf of the Covenanters but he persuaded his friends 'not to foment these growing publique differences nor to be any means of incouraging a forein Nation, proud and subtle, against our natural Prince'.[38]

The stirrings of rebellion in Scotland inevitably aroused expectations that the king might be forced to call a parliament in an attempt to raise money for a military campaign. At the same time they provided new and significant evidence for those who saw the future in apocalyptic terms. Since the early years of Elizabeth's reign many preachers and writers had been prophesying the dawn of a millenial age when, following the destruction of the Church of Rome, the rule of the saints would begin. During the reign of James I Sir Henry Yelverton heard a sermon based on a text about the second coming of Christ which must have been typical of its kind. From the notes which he made it is clear what message was being imparted: 'daies nombred. . . . Signes monstruous merveylous . . . horrible earthquaks, wickednes growen ripe, warres and rumours of warres spread. Gospell preached allmost every where: remaineth but a full Conversion' of the Jews.[39] According to an inventory of his library which was made in 1637 Sir Robert Harley owned a number of apocalyptic works, among them John Napier's *A Plaine Discovery of the Whole Revelation of St John*, Arthur Dent's *The Ruine of Rome*, Hugh Broughton's *A Revelation of the Holy Apocalyps* and Thomas Brightman's *Apocalypsis Apocalypseos*. In addition, he was on close terms with such Puritan divines as John Stoughton, Stanley Gower and John Tombes, who believed that the rule of the saints would shortly be inaugurated. As he revealed in a fast sermon delivered in July 1644 Gower was familiar with the works of Broughton, Brightman and Joseph Mede, the millenarian scholar. For the printed version he produced an appendix giving the sources for some of the passages in his sermon and dedicated it to Sir Robert with the comment that 'These thinges I have annexed for others, not for you, who have diligently sought out the accompts.'[40]

Among the Puritan gentry of Lincolnshire Sir William Armyne, Sir John Wray and Sir Anthony Irby had all been exposed to apocalyptic prophecies. Sir William was the patron of Tempest Wood, one of the very first of the English millenarian scholars, who served as vicar of Lenton between 1601 and 1639. A graduate of Christ's College, Cambridge, Wood engaged in lengthy correspondence with Joseph Mede, a fellow of that college whose own concept of the millenial state was 'Pure and clean . . . altogether free from the least suspicion of Luxury and Sensuality'.[41] Wood's meditations on the Book of Revelation were never published; on the other hand, Robert Parker's treatise *The Mystery of the Vialls Opened* eventually gained him posthumous fame through the good offices of Sir John Wray. When this work appeared in print in 1651 the stationer explained in the preface that the manuscript had been in Sir John's possession for many years, indeed before the Palatinate had been reduced to a field of blood, and that it was he who was responsible for arranging for its publication. 'I conjecture and verily think', declared Parker, 'that all the troubles that shall happen in this western world in these times are only to make way for the ruine of Rome.'[42] Sir Anthony Irby, who was a great patron of Puritan ministers,[43] had a domestic chaplain, Benjamin Stoneham, who was described as a man of 'an unblameable conversation and zealous for the Millenium'. Stoneham entered Sir Anthony's household after graduating from Cambridge in 1637 and seems to have remained with him until the time of the Civil War so that the family may well have been treated to a millenarian commentary on the dramatic events which were taking place in these years.[44] During the same period Christopher Feake, who would become well known for both his millenarian views and his hostility to the established order in Church and State, was enjoying the patronage of Sir Samuel Owfield, a wealthy squire who sometimes resided at Gatton in Surrey and sometimes at Elsham in Lincolnshire. In 1636 Feake was living at Gatton where he appears to have been employed as domestic chaplain to the Owfields and it was here that his interest in the prophecies of the Book of Daniel and the Revelation of St John was first aroused following the news of the anti-Prayer Book riots in Edinburgh.[45]

At Arnhem in the Netherlands John Archer and Thomas Goodwin, who served as pastors to the English congregation there, were busily engaged in expounding chiliastic doctrine. In a treatise entitled *An Exposition of the Revelation* which he was writing in 1639 Goodwin commented that 'we live now in the Extremity of Times . . . we are at the Verge and, as it were, within the Whirle of that great Mystery of Christ's Kingdom which will, as a Gulph, swallow up all Time.' In his estimation the period between 1650 and 1700 would witness the ruin of Rome, the destruction of the Turkish Empire and the beginning of Christ's kingdom on earth. Archer, for his part, envisaged a similar chronology of events in a work which appeared in 1642 under the title *The Personall Reign of Christ upon Earth*. The downfall of the Papacy, he wrote, would occur in 1666 (a year which had special significance for many of the scholars who worked in this field) though he felt it necessary to emphasise that before then 'wee are like to see sad times.'[46] In all probability the members of the English congregation at Arnhem, who included Sir Matthew Boynton and Sir William Constable, were only too willing to accept an apocalyptic interpretation of the political developments which were unfolding across the Channel.

Some Puritan gentlemen such as Sir Henry Vane the younger and Sir James Harrington were convinced that Jesus Christ would reign on earth for a thousand years. Vane, who was familiar with the works of both Brightman and Mede, wrote that 'the time of the End, that is to say, the fore-told-of day, in which Christ is to judge the World in Righteousness . . . is at the very doors, and ready to open it self upon us, as the day of Redemption to the Good, and Terror and Amazement to the Wicked.' Christ would then rule with his saints for a thousand years and the kingdom of Antichrist and the Beast would be brought to final ruin and destruction.[47] In a tract published in 1645 Harrington declared that 'the last dayes foretold and fore-warned of by our Saviour are at hand' and as evidence referred his readers to the judgments of famine and pestilence which God had handed down and the conflict which was raging between nation and nation. He went on to say that the Gospel which at first

> broke out like lightning in the East shall in this last age upon the ruine and through the clouds of spirituall Babilon dart it selfe and shine gloriously in our westerne Churches even to the Indies that the' other paralell prophesie may be fulfill'd by the subjecting and uniting the Kingdomes of the Earth into the Kingdome of the Lord and of his Christ.

In a work which appeared in 1669 he wrote that the saints would enjoy a thousand years of rest and peace upon the earth but only when their 6000 years of trouble, labour and persecution had expired. According to the scriptural chronology a period of about

1213 years would elapse before the second coming of Jesus Christ inaugurated the millenium.[48]

Probably there were relatively few Puritans at the upper levels of society who believed in the concept of a millenial age in which Jesus Christ would personally reign on earth. But in the years immediately preceding the Civil War some at least of the Puritan gentry were convinced that the world was now entering a crucial, and perhaps the ultimate, phase of its history; that through the working of God's will the most momentous events were about to happen; and that although the saints would undergo much suffering they would eventually triumph over the enemies of true religion. As the whole system of Thorough was disintegrating John Harrington wrote in his commonplace book that 'The end of the World is neere and the scripture plainly foreshewes that in these last times shall be granted manifestacion of God's mercy to the godly and his fierce wrath against the wicked.'[49] In February 1639 Lady Brilliana Harley wrote in a letter to her son Edward that

> If ever we had caus to pray it is nowe. Shure the Lord is about a glorious worke. He is refineing his Church and happy will thos days be when shee comes out like gould; and if our wicked men had cause to fear it is nowe, for certainely the Lord will call them to accounte. Theaire day is at hand.

As we have seen, the library at Brampton Bryan contained a copy of John Napier's *A Plaine Discovery of the Whole Revelation of St John*, a work which had first been published at Edinburgh in 1593. In this treatise Napier forecast that in 1639 'the third thundering Angell' would begin; in other words, it would usher in the final stages of the decline and fall of the Roman Antichrist. Probably Lady Harley was alluding to this prophecy when in April she told her son that

> We heare that the kinge of Spaine begins to deale with the monasteries in Spain, as Henry the 8 did in Ingland . . . let me upon this put you in minde that this year 1639 is the yeare in which maney are of the opinion that Antichrist must begine to falle. The Lord say Amen to it: if this be not the year yet shure it shall be in due time.

The following month Edward's sister Brilliana assured him that grace was never more needed than in these declining times and

209

added the ominous comment that they must now learn to lay down their lives for Jesus Christ.[50]

During the 1630s Napier's treatise appears to have aroused considerable interest in Puritan circles, probably because of the significance which he attached to the year 1639. Sir Thomas Barrington purchased a copy in July 1638 when Scotland was on the brink of rebellion.[51] In the library of Sir Simonds D'Ewes there were copies both of Napier's work, which he acquired in 1639, and Thomas Brightman's *Apocalypsis Apocalypseos*. During the years 1592 to 1607 Brightman had served as rector of Haynes in Bedfordshire where 'his daily discourse was against Episcopal Government, which he declared would shortly be pulled down'. Following his death the manuscript of *Apocalypsis Apocalypseos* had been prepared for publication by Thomas Pierson, who was later to come under Sir Robert Harley's patronage. 'Our religion', wrote D'Ewes in a letter to Sir Julius Caesar in March 1629, is 'desolated abroad, assaulted at home and blasphemed by the enemies.' In his 'heavenly' *Apocalypsis Apocalypseos*, which had been written about thirty years before, Brightman had foretold the very judgment now in execution and had warned the Protestant Churches of Britain, France and Germany about the setbacks which they were to suffer. He had also anticipated that the Churches would be able to surmise what was in store for them 'by reason of the contempt of the word of God and the true professors therof, together with the crying sinns and great excesses of all conditions'. According to Brightman's thesis (D'Ewes went on) European Protestants would have to endure 'a long and large persecution, not much inferior to those of the primitive times', but once this storm had passed there would arise

> the most glorious and triumphant times of peace and union to the Church of God following the ruine of Antichrist which hee assignes at furthest to bee then but 50 yeares (now twentie distant) that any former age ever saw. Moore blessed shall those bee whoe shall live to enjoy that time or wee who are likely noe lesse gloriouslie by God's assistance to witnes the truth of the gospell by a cheerefull laying downe of our lives in the power of Faith for that truth.

No doubt D'Ewes considered that the Catholic successes in the Continental war, the Laudian persecution and the general decline in moral standards which the Puritans were constantly bewailing all bore testimony to the validity of Brightman's prophecies.[52]

Some Puritan ministers took delight in the prospect of a heaven on earth in which all men would be equal. When Thomas Goodwin, an Essex minister, published the sermon which he had delivered at the funeral of Lady Judith Barrington he wrote exultantly in the dedication that 'Estates and Honours, Nobility, Gentry, Lords and Ladies are things which shortly will be quite out of Fashion, and Christ will be All in All.'[53] While the wealthy Puritan gentry had a deep longing for the joys of a celestial paradise they may well have been troubled by fears of a social and economic upheaval when they contemplated the possibility of an earthly kingdom of the saints. Significantly, they were much less inclined to talk about the establishment of a new Jerusalem than their clerical associates, and even when they did so they may not necessarily have been envisaging anything more than a reformed and purified Church of England.

Apocalyptic beliefs which had application to the immediate future could breed political radicalism. In a work published in 1652 (and therefore enriched with the benefit of hindsight) Sir Edward Peyton wrote that those who had resisted the tyranny of Charles I had 'fulfilled God's determination upon the seventh Conjunction of Saturn and Jupiter (being Sabbatical) since the beginning of the world to bring down the Mountain of Monarchy which had continued more than five hundred years' and to substitute for it 'an Aristocratical or Plebeian way of rule which will better advance the Kingdom of Jesus Christ thorow the Universe'.[54] In the late 1630s, however, the overthrow of the monarchy, or even a major curtailment of its powers, did not figure among the aspirations of the Puritan gentry, whether or not they had been influenced by apocalyptic prophecies: what they wanted was an end to the system of Thorough in all its forms. Those who were prepared to come out in open defiance refused to pay ship money or deliberately failed to respond to the requests for personal contributions towards the cost of the royal expedition against the rebellious Scots.[55] During the years 1636 to 1639 a considerable number of Puritan magistrates were dismissed from office, mainly because of their opposition to ship money. These included such men as William Viscount Saye and Sele, Sir William Masham, Sir John Wray, Sir Walter Erle, Sir Gilbert Gerard, John Hampden, Nathaniel Stephens and John

Crewe.[56] On the other hand, there is no evidence of any general reluctance on the part of the Puritan gentry to serve as justices of the peace during the period of Charles I's personal rule. In 1637 Sir John Danvers of Northamptonshire and Sir Robert Brooke of Suffolk were removed from the commission of the peace for not appearing before the circuit judges to be sworn, but in Sir Robert's case at least this did not amount to an act of voluntary resignation since he was soon reinstated. Despite their feelings of alienation most Puritan justices continued in office, no doubt fortified by the conviction that the godly magistrate could do much good; and other Puritans, among them Sir Gilbert Pickering, were appointed to the magistracy for the first time.[57]

When the time came for the annual picking of sheriffs in November 1639 the schedule of names which was submitted to the king listed a surprisingly large number of Puritan squires, some of whom had refused to pay ship money or had defied the Crown in other ways. Sir Robert Harley and Sir William Brereton were fortunate enough to be passed over but not a few of the Puritan nominees were chosen, among them Martin Lumley for Essex, Sir Thomas Wroth for Somerset and Sir Simonds D'Ewes for Suffolk. The sheriffs, noted one of the Privy Council officials, were 'ill chosen'.[58]

On 25 November Sir Simonds D'Ewes wrote to his brother, who was then on the Continent:

> It hath pleased God to send an unwelcome preferment upon mee this yeare of the shreivaltie of Suffolke . . . wee are like to have sadd and dismal assizes because all things in Scotland hasten on apace to distraction and tumult. Let us ioine our praiers that God may direct the iudgments that hang over our heads.

The following month it was announced that the king had decided to call a parliament but at the same time new ship-money writs were issued. To D'Ewes the outlook seemed very grim and he was able to draw little comfort from the fact that a parliament was due to assemble within a few months. On 30 December he was confiding to his brother that

> I see noe likelihood but of dismall and intestine warrs if God doe not myraculouslie prevent it. Wee have some assurances of a Parliament and yet shipp-monie being now pressed for

212

alsoe at one and the same time makes all men wonder and makes me despaire of anye happie successe in a publike Councell.[59]

CHAPTER ELEVEN

DOING GOD'S WORK

Although the policy of Thorough had helped to foster a considerable degree of unanimity among the country gentry the elections for the Short Parliament revealed divisions which cannot always be explained purely in terms of local feuds. In Gloucestershire the gentry had agreed beforehand that Sir Robert Cooke and Sir Paul Tracy would be the most appropriate choice as knights of the shire and in the event they were both elected. The election, however, was less of a formality than had been expected because of the intervention of a third candidate, Nathaniel Stephens, who received some votes from Sir Robert's tenants, contrary to the understanding between the other two candidates. All the evidence suggests that religion was the primary factor in this challenge to Tracy's candidature. Both Cooke and Stephens were zealous Puritans and a number of godly divines were actively involved in the campaign, among them Henry Stubbes, Sir Robert's domestic chaplain, and William Mew, a former London lecturer who had been presented by Stephens to the rectory of Eastington. Significantly, one of Tracy's supporters told Cooke that he would never again trust any man who wore his hair shorter than his ears.[1] In Essex there were also three candidates in the county election: Sir Thomas Barrington and Sir Harbottle Grimston, both of whom were Puritans, and Henry Neville who was favourably regarded by the Laudian clergy. The Earl of Warwick, who was lord lieutenant of the county, exerted all his influence on behalf of the Puritan baronets and further support was provided by Stephen Marshall, the vicar of Finchingfield in Essex, and other ministers who frequently preached outside their parishes during the weeks immediately preceding the election. When the voting took place at Chelmsford the result was a victory for Barrington and Grimston.[2]

Writing to John Winthrop the younger in March 1640 Sir Nathaniel Barnardiston, who was returned for Suffolk, characterised his election as a divine summons:

> and now the Lord hath put me upon a tryall by calling of me, with Sir Phillip Parker, (alltogether unsought for) to serve for my countrey in the Parliament which is to begin the 13th of Aprill next. I have nothing to supporte me in this great busines, being contious to my self of my most unfitnes every way, but the all suffitience of Hym that caled me cann inable me, who deliteth to manifest this powre by contemtable and weake meanes. . . . This parlament will beget a resolution in us but I fear I could wish sume of you wear hear before it endeth.[3]

In Herefordshire the gentry agreed among themselves, as they had done before, that Sir Robert Harley and Sir Walter Pye, a courtier who lacked the religious commitment of his associate, were the most suitable candidates for the county seats. Fears that a third candidate might appear on the day of the election led to correspondence over the tactics to be adopted but the outcome was never really in doubt. Sir Robert, wrote Nathaniel Cradock, a minister who enjoyed his protection, had 'the generall good will and cheife consente of his cuntry. . . . God hath made him so usefull for upphoulding of his true worship and service and for the curbing of the ungodly and worser sorte.'[4]

Among the papers of Sir Robert Harley there is a list of grievances which he appears to have taken with him to Westminster. This refers, among other things, to the suppression of lectures and the silencing of ministers who were 'men of unblameable life and doctrine (only for being nonconformists)'; the punishment of Christians who met together to fast and pray on the grounds that they were taking part in conventicles; the calling in and burning of pamphlets which favoured the sanctification of the Sabbath; the harsh treatment meted out to godly persons who travelled to another parish to hear a sermon when there was no sermon in their own parish; the introduction of altars, pictures, crucifixes and other church furnishings, and the proceedings of the bishops in the ecclesiastical courts. There are also suggestions that as the king was short of money he should annex all the bishoprics to the Crown; that there was no need for deans, prebendaries, canons and archdeacons; and that the ecclesiastical laws should be purged.[5] Although many leading Puritans were elected to the Short Parliament there is very little evidence of religious radicalism either in the petitions which they presented or in the speeches which they delivered.[6] Not surprisingly, it was the abandonment of the Laudian policy of repression (as the Puritans regarded it) which was considered to be the most immediate requirement and indeed there were sound tactical arguments for this method of approach since Laud had managed to offend a wide cross-section of the laity. In addition, the Puritan divines were not so well organised as a pressure group at this stage as they would be during the time of the Long Parliament. Had the Short Parliament not been dissolved so quickly the situation might have been different. As a foretaste of what was to come the Commons decided on 23 April to invite Stephen Marshall to preach on the occasion of a fast day and nominated Sir Thomas Barrington, a close friend of his, and Sir William Masham to serve as churchwardens.[7]

When the Short Parliament was dissolved on 5 May all the grievances which had been aired remained unremedied. On 13 May Brampton Gurdon wrote in a letter to Governor Winthrop that 'We are hear in verry hard condicyon in regard our parlament is desolved but . . . it comforteth the hartes of the honest men of both housen' that they refused to give a penny to help the king in his intended war against the Scots.[8] After the dissolution the resistance to ship money seems, if anything, to have hardened. On 9 May an officer employed by Sir Simonds D'Ewes for the collection of ship money arrived at Kedington Hall, the seat of Sir Nathaniel Barnardiston, where 'his request met with an unenthusiastic response. Lady Barnardiston told him that her husband was a parliament man and as he was away from home she did not know what to say. Samuel Fairclough, the Puritan rector of Kedington, was no less evasive: while claiming that he did not object to paying his assessment he begged to be allowed more time to find the money. In July the sheriff of Cheshire wrote to a relative that at the next quarter sessions the Puritan faction on the bench of magistrates intended to prefer bills of indictment against him and those of his officers who had been active in levying ship money. The most prominent of these refractory justices, he went on, was Thomas Stanley of

216

Alderley, who had threatened to shoot anyone who attempted to distrain his goods.[9] For the sheriffs it was not an easy situation. Threatened with Star Chamber proceedings over his poor performance in executing the ship-money writ Sir Simonds D'Ewes sat down to compose a vindication of his conduct. Among other things he stressed that for nearly twenty years he had been a gownman (meaning a scholar) and for virtually all that time had been 'whollie sequestred to his studies'; consequently there were very few parts of the county which were known to him.[10]

During the course of the summer there were also reports that many were refusing to pay coat and conduct money for the support of the new expedition against the Scots. In Middlesex the opposition was led by two wealthy Puritans, Sir William Roberts and Sir Gilbert Gerard, while in London Sir Edward Hungerford was named as a refuser.[11] Not all the Puritan gentry, however, felt bold enough to defy the Crown in this manner: in August, for example, Sir William Eliott, a deputy lieutenant in Surrey, told his brother-in-law Sir Simonds D'Ewes that 'we have had a great deale of Conduct money brought in and for my parte I have payd both that and the ship money lately.'[12]

To the godly the situation within the Church now appeared even more serious than it had before the meeting of the Short Parliament. Shortly after the dissolution Convocation had approved new Canons which formally endorsed the Laudian innovations and required the clergy to take an oath which contained the pledge that they would never consent to any alteration in the government of the Church 'as it stands now established and as by right it ought to stand'. Walter Yonge noted in his diary that the bishops of the various dioceses were directed

> to administer an oathe unto the clergie that bishops are *Jure divino* and that they will not give consente that the government by Bishops ever shalbee altered. Many ministers contested against the said oathe in every dioces and subscribed petitions to his majestie against the said oathe. The like did many gentlemen subscribe.

Had the Canons been put into effect, declared Sir Simonds D'Ewes, they would have 'banished first our godly ministers and then made us all that had any care of preserving our soules . . . to have changed out habitations and to have left our native Countries and all that had been neare or deare unto us only to preserve our soules'.[13]

With the unhappy experience of the Short Parliament still fresh in their minds some at least of the Puritan gentry seem to have been determined that the next parliament should be an effective instrument of change. On 30 October, a few days before its opening, Sir Nathaniel Barnardiston wrote to his kinsman Sir Simonds D'Ewes, who had been returned for Sudbury, that he hoped that 'we shall not now lopp the branches but stub up the rootes of all our mischifes, which wilbe as the safer, so the shorter worke.' This type of biblical language, which foreshadowed the emergence of the Root and Branch party, may possibly have owed some of the popularity which it acquired to the influence of Thomas Brightman's treatise on the Book of Revelation; in referring to the forthcoming downfall of Antichrist he had prophesied that 'All the boughes and branches shall be overthrown together with the tree it self.'[14] Many of the godly were convinced that the Long Parliament had a divinely ordained mission. 'I can onely bring Straw or Stubble to this greate woork,' wrote Sir John Dryden, a Northamptonshire MP, on 26 November, 'but God bee praised heere want not skilfull agents for this great woorke.' Despite the hindrances which had been encountered 'the walls goe up fast, though they cannot be sudenly finished; the ruines are such both in Church an Common welth that soom yeares will hardly repair all breaches.' In March 1641 Sir Simonds D'Ewes was told by his aunt Hanna Brograve that he must labour to the utmost of his power to advance the sceptre of Christ 'and be not content with a modest way but let us have the holle way of God . . . study the word to find out the way of Christ and then take heed of balking any treuth'. The following month Lady Brilliana Harley wrote to her husband, 'I hope the Lord will still be with you to suport you that you may Cheerefully undergoo the greate worke you are aboute. When I Consider that it is the Lord's worke you are in I am well Pleased to under goo all that is of discomfort in it.'[15]

Among the Puritan divines there were high hopes of a thorough reformation of religion and MPs who were known to be sympathetic to their cause were bombarded with advice and encouragement. Sir Robert Harley, who was later to be described as 'a man truely zealous of Reformation',[16] was the recipient of a number of letters of exhortation from his clerical associates and acquaintances. Stanley

Gower, his parish minister in Herefordshire, told him in November that the ceremonies and the obligation laid on ministers to subscribe to the Articles of Religion must be swept away and that he was expecting that episcopal government would be utterly overthrown or at least radically overhauled. Another of Sir Robert's ministers, William Doyle, informed him that he was looking forward to a major alteration in religion which would go beyond the moderate reforms inaugurated at the beginning of Elizabeth's reign. William Browne wrote from Manchester:

> Very glad am I that God hath called you to that Honourable Assembly. . . . There is divers things amisse with us as Organs, Altars, gestures, vestures, crosses, &c, which I hope you will remove, as also some scandalous persons. . . . I doubt not but you are resolved to remove whatsoever savours of Anti-Christ from amongst us. But because there will be some difference betwixt the conformists and others what discipline shall be raysed I think you may doe well to conforme the same to the Apostles' times, whereof we have presidents in France, Geneva, Scotland, and other reformed Churches.[17]

According to Richard Baxter the Long Parliament consisted of two sorts of men, those who were primarily concerned with civil liberty and those who were more mindful of the interest of religion and inveighed against the innovations in matters of worship, the Book of Sports, the casting out of ministers, the High Commission, the suppression of lectures and 'such other things which they thought of greater weight than ship money'.[18] Baxter was drawing too sharp a contrast: Puritan MPs tended to be strongly in favour of public liberty in all its forms while many of their colleagues shared their dislike of the Laudian ceremonies. Yet the fact remains that it was the Puritan members who took the lead in the campaign for ecclesiastical reform and the proceedings against Laud and his associates; and indeed this is hardly surprising, given their deep sense of commitment to a form of religion which Laud had seemed determined to destroy and the extent to which they had personally felt the impact of his version of Thorough. Some, like Sir Nathaniel Barnardiston and Sir Thomas Wodehouse, had been deprived of the services of godly ministers who had enjoyed their patronage; others, like Sir Arthur Hesilrige and Sir John Dryden, had found themselves involved in proceedings in the High Commission.[19]

During the early weeks of the Long Parliament a number of Puritan MPs voiced the prevailing discontent about the state of religion. 'Judges', declared Harbottle Grimston, 'have overthrowne the Lawe and Bishops Religion.' The Laudians, argued Sir Benjamin Rudyerd, 'have a minde to quell preaching and to drawe the Religion to olde Ceremonies'. Some of the prelates and their adherents, Sir John Holland told the Commons, had imposed many innovations in the doctrine, discipline and government of the Church. The number of Catholics had dangerously multiplied, idolatry had increased and as a result God's heavy judgments had been 'highly provoked'. Although there were many grievances in regard to both Church and Commonwealth he considered that religion should be given priority: 'I desire wee may proceed with all true piety well grounded and right guyded zeal towards God, his Howse, his truth.' Sir John Wray expressed the hope that it would be 'our constant Resolution . . . to settle Religion in itts Splendor and pyety, by pulling down Dagon from the Altar and whippinge the buyers and sellers out of the Temple'. Parliament, he stressed, had been called to do God's work: 'And for what ends came wee hyther if not to propagate and advance his glory and Gospell?' In these early speeches the language was often faintly menacing (or at least it must have seemed so to the more conservative elements in the Commons) but little indication was given as to the kind of reformation the Puritan members had in mind. At this stage they do not appear to have had any clear-cut objectives beyond the sweeping away of the Laudian innovations, though it is noteworthy that as early as 24 November Sir Edmund Moundeford moved that a day should be set aside for considering objections to the Book of Common Prayer while the following day Sir William Brereton, who in Clarendon's words was noted for his 'averseness to the government of the Church', mounted an attack on the powers of the High Commission.[20]

When the Commons discussed a report from the Grand Committee for Religion (which had been established as a committee of the whole House) on 25 November Sir John Wray voiced his concern at the evidence which he found in it of the striking growth of popery. 'What must we do then', he asked,

> to preserve our Religion safe and sound, to us and our posterity, that our golden Candle-stick be not removed? Why, the only

way is to fall to our work in earnest and lay the Axe to the Root, to unloose the long and deep Fangs of Superstition and Popery, which being once done the Bark will soon fall down. . . . I shall humbly move that the Groves and high places of Idolatry may be removed and pulled down, and then God's wrath against England will be appeased.[21]

Sir John's choice of phraseology is interesting not only because of the use of Root and Branch language but because of his identification of the Church of England as one of the seven golden candlesticks which figure in the Book of Revelation. As we have seen, the manuscript of Robert Parker's *The Mystery of the Vialls Opened*, which was based on the Book of Revelation, had been in his possession for many years,[22] and in addition it is likely that he was familiar with Richard Bernard's treatise *The Seaven Golden Candlestickes* since the author had benefited from the generous patronage of the Wray family and in 1635 had dedicated another of his works to Sir John and his wife.[23]

On 11 December the delivery of the London or Root and Branch petition brought it home to the Commons that there were vigorous pressure groups outside Parliament which were impatient for a major alteration in religion. Shortly afterwards Sir Simonds D'Ewes wrote to his wife that 'On Friday morning last wee entred upon the waightiest matter that ever was yet handled in the House: for there came a petition to us from the Cittie of London . . . desiring, amongst other particulars, that the verie government by Archbishopps and Lord Bishopps in the Church, with all their ceremonies and courts, might be abolished.' After all the general rhetoric in which they had indulged the radical demands set out in the petition must have done much to concentrate the minds of the Puritan members. Probably very few of them had been seriously contemplating the possibility of abolishing episcopacy: hitherto they had tended to think more in terms of good bishops and bad bishops. Sir Simonds D'Ewes had referred approvingly in his autobiography, which he had written during the 1630s, to such bishops as George Abbot the previous Archbishop of Canterbury, James Montagu and Nicholas Felton; John Williams was described by Bulstrode Whitelocke as a very great friend and indeed he was on good terms with many Puritans; while Sir William Brereton's decision to call on Thomas Morton when visiting Durham in 1635 was no doubt prompted by his reputation as a prelate who declined to be an

221

instrument of Laud's ecclesiastical policy.[24] Those who spoke in the debate on the Root and Branch petition were generally in favour of entertaining it, though this did not necessarily mean that they supported everything it contained. At this stage D'Ewes wished only to deprive the bishops of their secular powers: in his speech, as recorded in his journal, he emphasised that in his view the House

> ought to proceed with great moderation. For doubtles the goverment of the church of God by godlie, zealous and preaching Bishops had been most ancient, and I should reverence such a bishop in the next degree to a King . . . but . . . if matters in Religion had gone on but 20 yeares longer as they had done of late yeares ther would not in the issue soe much as the verie face of Religion have continued amongst us but all should have been overwhelmed with idolatrie, superstition, ignorance, profanenes and heresie. As I allowed ancient and godlie Bishopps soe I disliked their baronies and temporall Honours and imploiements.[25]

A few days later Sir John Wray told the Commons that there were two aspects of the government of bishops which he, like Francis Bacon before him, regarded as unsatisfactory: first, the sole exercising of their authority and, secondly, the deputation of that authority to diocesan officials. He made it clear, however, that he desired 'rather their Reformacion than their Ruine'.[26]

On 12 December the Grand Committee for Religion established a sub-committee to inquire into the decay of preaching, the growth of popery and the increasing numbers of 'scandalous' ministers. At the same time it was agreed that all members of the Commons should report to this body within six weeks on the state and condition of the preaching ministry in their respective counties. The sub-committee, which was enlarged a week later, consisted very largely of Puritan MPs, among them John Hampden, Sir Arthur Hesilrige, Sir Thomas Cheke, Sir Gilbert Gerard, Sir John Franklin, Sir Gilbert Pickering, Sir Oliver Luke, John Bampfield, Sir William Masham, Sir Thomas Pelham, Arthur Goodwin, Sir Edward Hungerford, Sir Robert Harley, Sir William Brereton, Sir Thomas Barrington, John Crewe and Sir John Wray.[27] On 16 December the Commons appointed a committee to draw up charges against Archbishop Laud. One member, Harbottle Grimston, revealed his attitude in the comment that 'the roote and ground of all our miseries and calamities both in Church and Commonwealth weere originallie proceeding from him'; another, Bulstrode Whitelocke, had been involved in a private quarrel with Laud but declined to serve on the grounds that he had been a student of his at St John's College, Oxford.[28] On 19 December Laud was committed to the Tower.

Early in the New Year John Bampfield, one of the leading Puritan squires in Devon, wrote euphorically about the activities of the Long Parliament of which his eldest son was a member:

> The news of these times are so excellent that he deserves not to breathe this British air who prayeth not god heartily for them. . . . For ever be this Parliament renowned for so great achievements, for we dream now of nothing more than of a golden age. . . . It is the nature of freedom, or the freedom of our own nature, that so pleaseth.[29]

So far the Commons had done little more than talk about the need for church reform but already some of the Puritan divines were taking matters into their own hands, abandoning any pretence of conforming to the Church's ceremonial requirements and preaching with greater boldness than at any time in the previous decade. In May 1641 John Tombes, the vicar of Leominster in Herefordshire, told Sir Robert Harley that in December he had arranged for the communion table, which had been turned altar-wise when Matthew Wren was Bishop of Hereford, to be restored to its original position and had also begun to dispense with the surplice and the cross in baptism, much to the indignation of the ignorant and superstitious. On the other hand, some of the bishops and parish clergy continued to act as though Laud was still at the helm. On 13 January 1641 Sir Philip Parker, one of the knights of the shire for Suffolk, presented a petition from the Puritan ministers of that county in which they asked to be relieved of the burdens and superstitions introduced by Bishop Wren and called for a reformation of the Book of Common Prayer and a diminution of the ceremonies. In the debate which ensued Sir Simonds D'Ewes complained about the unsatisfactory state of religion in the course of a diatribe against the Laudian party: 'wee see the Lordes day still profaned, their adorations still practiced and ther hereticall preachings dailie exercize.'[30]

Many of the parish clergy who remained faithful to the Laudian regime found themselves under attack in petitions which some of their parishioners submitted to Parliament; according to D'Ewes no fewer than 900 petitions of this kind had been received by June 1641.[31] Even so, it was not necessarily an easy matter to secure the removal of such a minister. In the Surrey parish of Godalming Sir William Eliott was one of the main instigators of a petition which was framed against the vicar, Nicholas Andrews, who had been appointed by the Dean of Salisbury in 1635. Shortly before it was submitted he wrote to his brother-in-law Sir Simonds D'Ewes that 'our vicar hath now by all the wayes he can sought a Reconciliation with me . . . our Articles ar now ready for the howse, 11 in number but very fowle and yet strongly proved, and the peticyon subscribed by the hands of above 100 parishioners.' The actual charges were both numerous and varied. Among other things, it was alleged that he was zealous in 'pressinge and urginge of Ceremonies and Innovations'; that he was contemptuous of the doctrine that the greater part of mankind would be denied salvation; and that he frequented taverns 'and useth gameinge both at cards and Tables, as well uppon the Lord's dayes as others'. To Sir William there were two aspects of the vicar's behaviour which were particularly disturbing. In the first place, he was 'an enemy to Preachinge, denyinge unto his parishoners Sermons which were gyven by will and alsoe denyinge Sermons at the buriall of the deade and at the christeninge of Children and sometimes at the administracion of the Sacrament of the Lord's Supper'. He himself was inclined to preach only infrequently, 'and then but in a verie fruytlesse and unprofitable manner'. At the same time he had refused to allow a lecturer to be brought in and had threatened to present some of his parishioners who had been travelling to other parishes to hear the Word of God. Secondly, he had stopped the practice of permitting communicants to receive the bread and wine while remaining in their seats; this was in spite of the fact that he had often been requested to continue the arrangement for the benefit of persons who had seats adjoining the chancel and who, because of physical infirmity, could not 'well endure to sitt soe longe out of theire seates in cold weather'. No doubt the main consideration here was the fact that Sir William did not take kindly to the idea of kneeling before an altar to receive communion. Such a petition might have been expected to meet with a sympathetic response from the Puritan MPs but Andrews had friends in high places. In July 1641 Sir

William told D'Ewes that he was treating the parliamentary proceedings with contempt and had

> lately putt one from the Communion because his Conscience
> would not suffer him to kneele. For Affternoone sermons we
> can have none, and weakly it is performed at the best by a
> Curatt as bad as himself, for the vicar himself is not able to
> preach above once in a quarter . . . he is so great an Enimye
> to preaching and goodnes.

His wife was also becoming increasingly concerned at the lack of
progress in obtaining a change of minister and in March 1642 we
find her writing despairingly to her brother 'o how happy were I
to have the society and godly counsels of a faithfull minister who
might instructe us both in life and doctrine; it were to tedious to
wright how much I suffer by this want.' After what must have
seemed like an eternity Andrews was finally deprived of his living
and committed to prison where he died.[32]

At the beginning of 1641 Stanley Gower declared in a letter to
his patron Sir Robert Harley that the bishops were the cause of all
the ills within the Church. Both they and the cathedral men, whom
he termed 'Abbey lubbers', should be swept away: they were
worthless usurpers of the Church's revenues and the devil's proctors
whose purpose was to uphold Antichrist. On 23 January Sir Robert,
who was now emerging as one of the leading parliamentary
representatives of the Puritan divines, presented a petition in favour
of a reformation of episcopal government which bore the signatures
of nearly 1000 ministers. The same day Gower wrote to him about
a petition which was circulating in Herefordshire. 'I was ashamed',
he told him, 'to see the causles timidity of the Justices of our
Countrey to subscribe the petition against Episcopacy.' James
Kyrle, who was one of the few Puritan gentlemen in the county,
'was the sole man that subscribed it'. About the same time Kyrle
himself was writing to Harley:

> The Lord prosper your paynes and holye indevoures in his
> worke that we maye se the reformation we hope and pray for.
> I cam to oure sessions with a petition of oure grevances in
> matters of religion but could not procure the subscription of
> anye one of oure Justices, yet I have sent it abroade the shire
> soe that if we can in any time, with a convenient number of

handes, be readye I shall trouble you with it; but soe unworthye are we in Herefishire of such a mercy that I am a feard it will fall to nothinge.[33]

The campaign for the abolition of episcopacy was being orchestrated by a group of Puritan ministers in London who were working in close conjunction with their brethren in the counties. This group included such men as Stephen Marshall, Cornelius Burgess, Edmund Calamy and William Spurstowe, who were also promoting the cause of reformation in the fast sermons which they preached before members of the Long Parliament.[34] Marshall, vicar of Finchingfield, was acquainted with Sir Thomas Barrington and other Puritan MPs representing Essex; Calamy was a friend of Sir Simonds D'Ewes, who had often heard him preach at Bury St Edmunds; while Spurstowe had been presented by John Hampden to the rectory of Great Hampden in 1638. Significantly, both Marshall and Calamy were in attendance when Sir Robert Harley delivered in the ministers' petition on 23 January.[35]

To the Harley family the issue was entirely straightforward: it was God's will that episcopacy should be totally abolished. On 28 January Lady Harley wrote in a letter to her son Edward that 'Munday, as I heard from you and others, was to be the day of debate about bischops. We at Brounton keep the day to shue to our God for his derection of the parlament. I beleefe that herarchy must downe, and I hope now.'[36] If, however, this goal was to be achieved it would be necessary first of all to win over the House of Commons.

During the early months of 1641 the Commons received a whole series of petitions calling for the abolition or radical alteration of episcopal government. For the most part the knights of the shire who presented these petitions were thoroughgoing Puritans, men such as Sir William Masham for Essex, Sir Oliver Luke for Bedfordshire, Sir Philip Parker for Suffolk, John Potts for Norfolk and Sir William Brereton for Cheshire.[37] In some counties the petitions aroused considerable dissent and attempts were made to organise counter-petitions. Such a division was in evidence in Devon where the benign rule of Bishop Hall of Exeter had given the Puritans little cause for dissatisfaction: on 19 February a petition which was hostile to episcopacy was presented to the House of Commons by John Northcote and the same month Sir Samuel Rolle wrote in a letter to one of the knights of the shire that another petition had been drawn up in support of the hierarchy. He went on to say that 'diverse ministers as I heere have papers to which they gett hands of diverse men who never see the petition'; in fact such practices were common at this time and the Puritans appear to hav been no less guilty than their opponents. On 15 February Lady Harley asked her son Edward to send her word

> wheather thos that have put in the petitions against bishops have taken the hands of all such as doo not understand what they have put theaire hands to. I am toold it is the way in all cuntrys. . . . To me it does not sound reasonabell; for, in my opinion, such hands should be taken as understand it, and will stand to what they have down.[38]

The first opportunity for MPs to have a full-scale debate on the issue of church government occurred on 8 February when they turned their attention to the London petition which had been presented in December. A number of Puritan MPs who spoke were in favour of referring the petition to a committee for further consideration. There were other Puritan MPs, however, who were openly hostile to the idea of abolishing episcopal government. Sir Benjamin Rudyerd, an apostle of moderation in all things, advocated a form of limited episcopacy with the bishops stripped of their secular authority and under an obligation to take advice from representatives of the diocesan clergy on important ecclesiastical matters: in essence it resembled the system propounded by Archbishop Usher who enjoyed considerable respect in Puritan circles. Harbottle Grimston also thought it desirable to deprive the bishops of their temporal powers but was strongly opposed to any more radical solution. A new form of church government, he stressed, might prove unpopular with the people and incompatible with a monarchical system and once established it might no longer be amenable to parliamentary control.[39] The following day the Commons decided to remit the London petition and part of the ministers' petition which had been presented on 23 January to a committee known as the Committee of Twenty Four. This committee, which now had a further six MPs added to it, had been set up on 10 November with the task of reporting periodically to the House on the state of the kingdom. Half its members were Puritans, among them Sir Robert Harley, John Pym, Harbottle Grimston, Sir Walter Erle, John

Hampden, John Crewe, Sir Thomas Barrington, Sir Benjamin Rudyerd and Sir Henry Vane the younger. During the next few weeks the committee met regularly and, among other things, took evidence from Cornelius Burgess, who acted as spokesman for the clerical pressure group which sought the overthrow of episcopal government.[40]

Before long the bishops found themselves under attack in two parliamentary bills, one for their removal from the House of Lords and the Privy Council and the other for the total abolition of episcopacy. The Root and Branch Bill was introduced on 27 May, the same day as Sir Edward Ayscough presented a Lincolnshire petition which was very close to it in spirit. Although the bill stood in the name of Sir Edward Dering it was largely the work of Sir Henry Vane the younger, whose antipathy to the Laudian Church had led him to go into exile in New England. After the bill had been read for a first time the Commons decided, by 139 votes to 108, that it should be given an immediate second reading and it was then remitted to a committee of the whole House.[41]

On 8 June the Lords rejected the Bishop's Exclusion Bill and Sir Simonds D'Ewes wrote in a letter to his brother that this would 'certainly make us proceed in the other Bill for rooting them out utterly'. Two days later some of the Puritan MPs, among them Sir Robert Harley, John Pym and John Hampden, met together to take stock of the situation. At this meeting, which was also attended by Stephen Marshall, it was decided to press ahead with the Root and Branch Bill and the following morning Sir Robert Harley moved that it should forthwith be considered. Sir Simonds D'Ewes, who played an important part in the ensuing debate, records that Pym, Hampden and some others preferred to remain in the background and leave it to him to make the running: probably they felt it prudent to wait and see what kind of reception such a potentially controversial measure would have. 'Wee desire', D'Ewes declared, 'to entaile True Religion to us and our posteritie for ever.' In his view episcopal government was not of apostolical origin nor did he believe there were any dangers involved in establishing a radically new form of church government. The speech, he notes, was received with great acclamation and Sir Walter Erle, who sat behind him, took him in his arms and embraced him. Other Puritan members who spoke included Sir Henry Vane the younger, Sir Thomas Barrington and John Crewe. Sir Henry wanted to sweep away the whole system: 'For the whole Fabrick of this building is so rotten and corrupt, from the very foundation of it to the top, that if we pull it not down now it will fall about the eares of all those that endevour it within a very few yeares.' Barrington was also in favour of a fundamental change. The episcopal hierarchy, he maintained, resembled an 'exorbitantly growne Tree whose Topp and Master boughs have much overswelled and overswayed'. The only means of remedying the present evils and allaying anxieties about the future was to lay the axe to the root of this tree and cut it down. Crewe, on the other hand, expressed his opposition to the abolition of bishops and suggested instead that there should be a bill for restraining their powers. That a man of his religious persuasion should take such a moderate line caused some surprise among his colleagues yet he was by no means the only Puritan member to have reservations about the objectives of the Root and Branch party.[42]

On 12 June the House agreed, without a division, that the bill should make provision for the abolition of episcopacy. This does not necessarily mean, however, that the Root and Branch party had a solid majority in the Commons, and indeed the evidence of contemporary opinion suggests otherwise. Sir Simonds D'Ewes comments in his journal that the episcopal party in the House was 'strong'. Clarendon, for his part, writes that Nathaniel Fiennes and young Sir Henry Vane and shortly afterwards Mr Hampden were believed to be for Root and Branch but Mr Pym did not share their views nor did Mr Holles nor any of the northern men or those lawyers who drove most furiously with them.[43] Richard Baxter observes that the great majority of those who remained with the Long Parliament in 1642 were 'moderate Episcopal Conformists' and cites as examples Arthur Goodwin, Thomas Grantham, Sir John Bampfield and Sir William Constable. Other parliamentarians such as Ferdinando Lord Fairfax, Sir John Gell and Sir William Waller were 'conformable to Episcopacy and Parochial Worship and some of them so Zealous for the Liturgy and Diocesanes that they would not hear a Man as a Minister that had not Episcopal Ordination'. Among others who might have been included in his list was Sir Christopher Yelverton, who gave shelter to Bishop Thomas Morton, a man highly regarded in Puritan circles, during the Commonwealth period and allowed him to ordain ministers according to the orders of the Church of England.[44] Probably it could be said of this type of Puritan as it was said of Sir Thomas Fairfax the parliamentary general that he was 'no enemy to episcopacy if a good choice had been made of them'.[45]

The division within the ranks of the Puritan MPs over the issue of ecclesiastical government does not appear to have been a reflection of differences in social and economic status. Although the wealthier sort had good reason to adopt a cautious attitude there were nevertheless a considerable number of major Puritan landowners who supported the Root and Branch programme. Sir John Wray, who was one of the richest baronets in England, had originally expressed himself in favour of reform rather than abolition but had finally come round to the view that a more radical solution was necessary. A factor which weighed heavily with him was the conviction that there was no scriptural justification for the concept of episcopal government. In the course of a parliamentary speech which was published in May 1641 he declared that unless the bishops could

justifie by the holy Scriptures that such Rights and Liberties as they pretend for their spirituall Primacy over the Ministers of Christ be in deed and truth inferred unto them by the holy law of God I suppose the King's Highnesse . . . by the words of the great Charter and by his oath is bound utterly to abolish all Lordly Primacy, as hitherto upheld and defended, partly by ignorance and partly by an unreasonable and evill Custome.[46]

In contrast, Clarendon writes that many believed that John Hampden's aversion to episcopal government was attributable to his dislike of certain Churchmen and of the innovations which they had brought in.[47] Significantly, some at least of the well-to-do members of the Root and Branch party had apocalyptic expectations, as indeed had some of the ministers who were engaged in the same cause. Sir Henry Vane the younger thought that the day was fast approaching when Jesus Christ would reappear on earth and begin a thousand-year reign with all his saints. Sir Robert Harley, Sir Simonds D'Ewes and Sir John Wray, and perhaps also Sir Thomas Barrington, had been influenced by the prophecies of such authors as John Napier, Thomas Brightman and Richard Bernard. A man who had no liking for bishops, Brightman had declared that the downfall of episcopacy was part of God's purpose and it is noteworthy that in July 1641 a tract was published which purported to show that everything he had predicted concerning Germany, Scotland and England had been fulfilled. Bernard, who was familiar with the works of Napier and Brightman, had claimed in a treatise published in 1617 that the events foretold in the Book of Revelation were in train and the seventh trumpet had already sounded. At the beginning of 1641 we find him launching an attack on episcopacy in a pamphlet entitled *A Short View of the Prelaticall Church of England*.[48] To those MPs who were convinced that God was about to inaugurate the rule of his saints it might well have appeared that the abolition of episcopal government was a necessary and even inevitable stage in the process of liberating religion from the thrall of the Roman Antichrist, and that in supporting the Root and Branch programme they were simply acting as instruments of God's will.

When the Root and Branch Bill was further considered on 15 June Sir Simonds D'Ewes stressed that it was the intention 'to reduce things to the best and primitive condition'. Later on he was to explain to his fellow MPs that to reduce the bishops 'to the primitive use', as he was advocating, was 'to take them cleare away as they now are'. Another Puritan member, Sir Benjamin Rudyerd, conceded that some of the bishops had ambitious and dangerous aims but went on to say that he disagreed with those who believed that there was an innate ill quality in episcopacy. Bishops had governed the Church for 1500 years and he had no wish to see them disappear: 'Let them be reduced according to the usage of ancient Churches in the best times, so restricted as they may not be able hereafter to shame the calling.' To D'Ewes this attitude was much too faint-hearted.[49]

On 21 June a Puritan minister, John Hall, sent Sir Robert Harley an effusive letter in which he commended him for his efforts in the cause of religion: 'Many spirits have you inlarged that was straitned, yea many Congregations give abundant thanks to God on your behalf . . . now the Lord increase your peace, preserve your health, fill you with length of dayes that you may live to see Syon's glory and Antichrist's fall.' The same day Thomas Harley, one of Sir Robert's younger sons, wrote in a letter to his brother Edward, who was then in London, that he had heard that the bill for the extirpation of all the archbishops and all the cursed (and here he resorted to the use of cypher) had been passed in the Commons; but his joy was premature.[50]

It was on 21 June that the Commons, sitting as a committee, first began to consider what provision should be made in the Root and Branch Bill for an alternative system of church government. Sir Simonds D'Ewes records in his journal that Sir Henry Vane the younger proposed the addition of a clause empowering some of the clergy and laity in each county to exercise ecclesiastical jurisdiction 'for a time'. 'Divers spake to it', he writes, 'and some would have a constant president in the presbiterie, others would have him but temporarie ... at the will of the presbiterie.'[51] Although Vane's proposal might be construed as embryonic Presbyterianism Clarendon, who was in the chair when the Commons debated the Root and Branch Bill in committee, assures us that Sir Henry equally hated episcopacy and presbytery.[52] Richard Baxter recalls that a member of the Long Parliament had often told him that before the outbreak of the Civil War he had known only one Presbyterian in the House of Commons, Zouch Tate the Northampton MP, 'it being not then known among them'. Presbyterianism had been a considerable force in Northamptonshire during the reign of Elizabeth and had apparently survived, in the form of an underground movement, until at least the 1590s: it is possible therefore that Tate, who was the head of one of the leading Puritan families in the county, had ideas on church government which were rooted in Elizabethan practice.[53] Whether, as Baxter suggests, he was the only genuine Presbyterian in the Commons when the Root and Branch Bill was under consideration is difficult to determine: Sir Robert Harley, for example, was described at his death as 'Earnest for Presbytery'[54] but it is not clear how long he had held this conviction. What is certainly true is that in 1641 there was little enthusiasm among MPs for a Presbyterian system in the full sense, despite the lobbying of the Scots Committee in London.

On 16 July Lady Brilliana Harley wrote in a letter to her eldest son that she wished 'to give our gracious God the glory of thos great things that has bine doun in the parlament'. In particular she was delighted that the bill for the abolition of the Court of High Commission had received the royal assent and that the Commons 'have proceeded so fare against the bischops. The Lord our God, who can doo great things, I hope will perfect that great worke.'[55] By this time it had been decided that the Root and Branch Bill should include a clause providing for ecclesiastical jurisdiction to be exercised by commissions consisting entirely of laymen; in other words, the country gentry.[56] The Commons had rejected Presbyterianism but in any case other matters were now beginning to overshadow the issue of church government. Before the end of the summer the bill had disappeared without trace.

Despite all the external pressures the Long Parliament had so far done little to advance the cause of ecclesiastical reform. On 13 February a bill for the abolition of superstition and idolatry had been referred to a committee which included a number of Puritan MPs, among them Sir Richard Buller, Sir Anthony Irby, Sir Simonds D'Ewes, Sir Robert Harley and Sir Edmund Moundeford,[57] but other legislative measures were given precedence and it was eventually allowed to expire. In September, however, the Commons made partial amends by approving two orders of some importance, one authorising the establishment of lectureships at the expense of the parishes which wanted them and the other directed against the Laudian innovations. Under the terms of this latter order the churchwardens of every parish were required to move the communion table from the east end of the church and take down the altar rails; all crucifixes, scandalous pictures, candlesticks and other idolatrous objects were to be removed; bowing at the name of Jesus was no longer to be permitted; and the Lord's Day was to be duly observed and sanctified, with dancing and sports giving way to afternoon sermons.[58] Responsibility for publishing the order in the various counties was assigned both to the knights of the shire and the representatives of the boroughs and some Puritan MPs and magistrates displayed great zeal in seeking to enforce its provisions. On 8 October Sir Robert Harley, who had played a major part in guiding the order through the Commons, sent a sharp letter of rebuke to the churchwardens of the parish church of Leominster, accusing them of failing to act in accordance with the obligations imposed on them. On returning from the quarter sessions at Hereford he had visited the church and had seen

one Crucifix uppon the great stone crosse there and another Crucifix of stone over the Church Portch and in the great window in the West end of the Church two Crucifixes painted and other scandalouse pictures of the persons of the Trinity and in the great window in the East end of the Church one other Crucifix painted, all which I doe require you to abolish,

233

according to the Order of the House of Commons which I send you herewith.

As already noted, Sir Robert was a friend of the vicar, John Tombes, and on 24 November the latter preached a sermon in which he condemned not only the Laudian innovations but such features of public worship as the playing of organs, the wearing of surplices and the use of the sign of the cross in baptism. Although, he declared,

> I know Ceremonies invented by men are pretended to serve for edification, yet I must professe that I never found in my reading or experience that ever any person by such rites or observances was wonne to the profession of Christ or brought to any spirituall knowledge of Christ, any true faith or sincere obedience to him.

Those who had been most forward in imposing ceremonial burdens had also shown themselves

> adversaries to the constant and fruitfull preaching of God's word, sanctifying of the Lord's day, exercising of the duties of Religion in private houses, as prayer, repeating of God's word, praysing of God, Godly conferences of Scripture, reformation of prophane swearing, excessive drinking, gaming, sporting and the like palpable sinnes.

In short, they were antagonistic to virtually everything which the Puritans considered important.[59]

At the end of 1641 the situation in the ecclesiastical field was viewed with mixed feelings in Puritan circles. Archbishop Laud and, more latterly, twelve of his bishops had been imprisoned; the Court of High Commission had been abolished; godly preaching was flourishing, and some attempt had been made to eradicate the Laudian innovations. So far, however, the reforming zeal of the House of Commons had not had any great impact at the parish level and the Laudian clergy were still, for the most part, holding on to their benefices: indeed Sir William Eliott could write from Surrey that 'These popish and proud Cleargye were never at a greater heighte.'[60] Above all, the major issue of church government remained completely unresolved, though it had been intimated in the Grand Remonstrance that it was the intention to remit this

234

question to a general synod of ministers. In a petition which they
delivered to the House of Commons in January 1642 Sir Richard
Everard, Sir John Barrington and other Essex gentlemen revealed
the sense of frustration which they felt: 'wee doe apprehend a great
stop of Reformation in matter of Religion.'[61] Some Puritan squires
like Sir Robert Harley and Sir Simonds D'Ewes were still fervently
hoping that episcopacy would soon be abolished.[62] Many more
wanted a religious settlement which curtailed the powers of the
bishops and their diocesan officials, guaranteed the supremacy of
Calvinist doctrine and entrusted the parochial work of the Church to
a godly preaching ministry which had been relieved of 'ceremonial
burdens'. At the same time there was growing concern among the
Puritan gentry over the breakdown of ecclesiastical discipline and
the proliferation of religious sects to which it was giving rise. This
anxiety was reflected in a parliamentary speech prepared by Sir
William Drake, one of the Buckinghamshire MPs, but apparently
never delivered:

> what Superstition and Innovations have bin brought in upon
> our Religion of late times by ambitious, heady and passionate
> men? And from this fountaine originally as I conceive flowes
> most part of our present distractions. . . . I shall never expect
> to see the quiet setled state of this kingdome till there be some
> course taken to settle Religion to some rule and uniformity and
> not to be thus suffered in an uncertaine condition, betweene
> illegall Innovations and superstitions on the one side and
> Irregular confusion on the other.[63]

The Long Parliament would eventually make a settlement of religion but not until it had fought and won a civil war.

POSTSCRIPT

Most Puritan squires sided with Parliament during the Civil War.
In the main, however, they were reluctant to go to war and in 1642
at least had no wish to overthrow the monarchy or stage even a
'gentleman's revolution.'

Once the Civil War began the Puritan gentry, many of whom
had been appointed deputy lieutenants under the Militia Ordinance, played a leading part in advancing the cause of Parliament
in the counties. A number of these Roundheads were particularly
active, among them Sir Richard Onslow, 'a person of great spirit
and abilities' who 'bore the principal sway' in Surrey; Sir Gilbert
Pickering of Northamptonshire who was described by a royalist as 'a
most furious, fiery, and implacable Man'; Sir John Gell, 'a singular
christian' who was said to be 'a man beloved of his Countrey',
meaning Derbyshire; and Sir William Brereton who completely
transformed the situation in Cheshire.[1]

Such men seem generally to have believed that Parliament was
fighting for Religion and Liberty. Some put the main emphasis on
the defence of true religion, others on the defence of the laws and
liberties of the kingdom. What was regarded as beyond doubt was
that God was on their side.

APPENDIX

A List of the Puritan Gentry Families appearing in this Study

The list contains a total of 123 families. In all, thirty-five counties are represented.

SYMBOLS The letter A denotes that the family had a landed income of at least £1000 a year at some point between 1603 and 1642.

The numerals indicate

1 patronage of Puritan incumbents or lecturers.

2 employment of Puritan chaplains.

3 represented among dedicatees of Puritan works.

–1–	Alston of Odell, Bedfordshire
A123	Armyne of Osgodby, Lincolnshire and Orton Longville, Huntingdonshire
A123	Ayscough of South Kelsey, Lincolnshire
A123	Bacon of Redgrave, Suffolk
A1–3	Bacon of Shrubland Hall, Suffolk
A12–	Bampfield of Poltimore, Devon
A1–3	Barnardiston of Kedington, Suffolk
A123	Barrington of Hatfield Broad Oak, Essex
A1–3	Barrow of Barningham, Suffolk
A1–	Bourchier of Beningbrough, Yorkshire
A1–3	Bowyer of Kynpersley, Staffordshire
A12–	Boynton of Barmston, Yorkshire
A123	Boys of Fredville in Nonington, Kent
A123	Brereton of Handforth, Cheshire
A123	Brooke of Cockfield Hall, Yoxford, Suffolk

237

A12–	Browne of Frampton, Dorset
A——	Buller of Shillingham, Cornwall
A123	Burdett of Foremark, Derbyshire
A1–3	Burgoyne of Sutton, Bedfordshire and Wroxall, Warwickshire
A1–3	Cheke of Pirgo, Essex
A——	Constable of Flamborough, Yorkshire
A123	Cooke of Highnam, Gloucestershire
A123	Cope of Hanwell, Oxfordshire
A1–3	Crewe of Steane, Northamptonshire
–1–3	Curzon of Kedleston, Derbyshire
A12–	Cutts of Childerley, Cambridgeshire
A——	Dacres of Cheshunt, Hertfordshire
–1—	Danvers of Culworth, Northamptonshire
A12–	Darley of Buttercrambe, Yorkshire
A1—	Davie of Creedy in Sandford, Devon
A1—	D'Ewes of Stowlangtoft, Suffolk
A1–3	Doddington of Breamore, Hampshire
A1–3	Drake of Buckland Abbey, Devon
A123	Drake of Esher, Surrey and Shardloes, Buckinghamshire
A123	Dryden of Canons Ashby, Northamptonshire
A1–3	Dunch of Little Wittenham, Berkshire
–1—	Eliott of Busbridge, Surrey
A1–3	Erle of Charborough, Dorset
A1—	Evelyn of West Dean, Wiltshire
–123	Everard of Langleys in Much Waltham, Essex
A12–	Franklin of Willesden, Middlesex
A1–3	Gee of Bishop Burton, Yorkshire
A12–	Gell of Hopton, Derbyshire
A1—	Gerard of Flambards, Harrow on the Hill, Middlesex
A1—	Goodwin of Over Winchendon, Buckinghamshire
A–2–	Grantham of Goltho, Lincolnshire
A1–3	Grimston of Bradfield, Essex
A123	Gurdon of Assington, Suffolk
A1—	Hampden of Great Hampden, Buckinghamshire
–1–3	Hanbury of Kelmarsh, Northamptonshire
A123	Harley of Brampton Bryan, Herefordshire
–1—	Harrington of Kelston, Somerset

A123	Harrington of Ridlington, Rutland
A12–	Hartopp of Buckminster, Leicestershire
A1–3	Hele of Gnaton Hall, Newton Ferrers, Devon
A–2–	Hesilrige of Noseley, Leicestershire
A123	Hobart of Blickling, Norfolk
A123	Hoby of Hackness, Yorkshire
A12–	Holland of Quidenham, Norfolk
A1—	Honywood of Marks Hall, Essex
A1–3	Horner of Cloford and Mells, Somerset
A123	Hungerford of Corsham, Wiltshire
A–2–	Hutchinson of Owthorpe, Nottinghamshire
A–23	Ingoldsby of Lenborough, Buckinghamshire
A–23	Irby of Boston and Whaplode, Lincolnshire
A1—	Jervoise of Herriard, Hampshire
A123	Knightley of Fawsley, Northamptonshire
A1–3	Lucy of Broxbourne, Hertfordshire
A1–3	Luke of Wood End in Cople, Bedfordshire
A—	Lumley of Great Bardfield, Essex
A—	Lytton of Knebworth, Hertfordshire
A12–	Mainwaring of Whitmore, Staffordshire
—3	Martyn of Oxton in Kenton, Devon
A123	Masham of Otes Hall, High Laver, Essex
–1–3	Mildmay of Graces Hall, Little Baddow, Essex
A1–3	Mildmay of Wanstead, Essex
A–23	More of Loseley Park, Surrey
A–2–	Moundeford of Feltwell, Norfolk
–1–3	Nichols of Faxton, Northamptonshire
A1—	Northcote of Hayne in Newton St Cyres, Devon
A1—	Norton of Southwick, Hampshire
A12–	Onslow of Knowle in Cranleigh, Surrey
A123	Owfield of Gatton, Surrey and Elsham, Lincolnshire
–1—	Parker of Erwarton, Suffolk
A1–3	Pelham of Laughton, Sussex
A1—	Peyton of Isleham, Cambridgeshire
A12–	Pickering of Titchmarsh, Northamptonshire

A–23   Pile of Compton Beauchamp, Berkshire
–1—   Potts of Mannington, Norfolk
A12–   Purefoy of Wadley, Berkshire

A—3   Rivers of Chafford in Penshurst, Kent
A——   Roberts of Neasden House, Willesden, Middlesex
–12–   Rodes of Great Houghton, Yorkshire
A1–3   Rolle of Heanton Satchville, Devon
A123   Rosewell of Forde Abbey, Devon
A123   Rous of Rous Lench, Worcestershire
–1–3   Rudyerd of West Woodhay, Berkshire

–1—   Saltonstall of Huntwick Grange, Wragby, Yorkshire
——   Shuttleworth of Gawthorpe, Lancashire
–12–   Sleigh of Ashe, Derbyshire
A1—   Soame of Little Thurlow, Suffolk
A1—   Spring of Pakenham, Suffolk
—2–   Springett of Langley, Kent
–1—   Stanley of Alderley, Cheshire
–1–3   Stephens of Eastington, Gloucestershire
——3   Stephens of Little Sodbury, Gloucestershire
A12–   Strickland of Boynton, Yorkshire
A–23   Strode of Newnham, Devon

A1—   Tate of Delapré Abbey, Northamptonshire
A——   Thornhagh of Fenton, Nottinghamshire
A12–   Trenchard of Wolfeton House, Charminster, Dorset

A12–   Vane of Fairlawne, Kent and Raby Castle, Durham

A–23   Waller of Winchester Castle, Hampshire
A1–3   Wentworth of Somerleyton, Suffolk
A–2–   Whitelocke of Fawley, Buckinghamshire
A——   Winch of Everton, Bedfordshire
A12–   Winwood of Denham in Quainton, Buckinghamshire
A1—   Wodehouse of Kimberley, Norfolk
A–2–   Wray of Barlings Abbey, Lincolnshire
A1–3   Wray of Glentworth, Lincolnshire
A–2–   Wroth of Petherton Park, Somerset

A1–3   Yelverton of Easton Mauduit, Northamptonshire
A——   Yonge of Stedcombe House, Axmouth, Devon

NOTES

Introduction

1 The most thoroughgoing attack on the concept of Puritanism as a separately identifiable trend is to be found in Charles H. George and Katherine George, *The Protestant Mind of the English Reformation 1570–1640* and the former's article on 'Puritanism as History and Historiography' in *Past and Present*, no. 41, 1968.

2 For another discussion of the problem of definition see Christopher Hill, *Society and Puritanism in Pre-Revolutionary England*, ch. I.

3 Samuel Fairclough, *The Saint's Worthinesse and the World's Worthlesnesse*, 12.

Chapter 1   God's Elect

1 Francis Bampfield, *A Name, an After-one*, 2.

2 J. R. Tanner (ed.), *Constitutional Documents of the Reign of James I*, 82. Dorothy Gardiner (ed.), *The Oxinden Letters, 1607–1642*, 265.

3 In the words of Sir Simonds D'Ewes (BL, Harleian MSS 646, f. 51).

4 *Gentleman's Magazine*, new series, xxxvi, 371. BL, Harleian MSS 593, f. 56. The scriptural passages are Isaiah, ch. 5, vv. 20 and 23; and Proverbs, ch. 17, v. 15.

5 BL, Additional MSS 53,726, ff. 7, 8, 40, 59, 68.

6 BL, Harleian MSS 389, f. 314. Cf. Henry Parker, *A Discourse Concerning Puritans*, 10.

7 See Patrick Collinson, *The Elizabethan Puritan Movement*, 120. In pt. 8, ch. 4 and 5 of this standard work there is a valuable account of the

transition from the Puritan movement of Elizabeth's reign to the more diffuse type of Puritanism of the early seventeenth century.

8 This work, which was entitled *The Nobles*, is discussed in H. F. Kearney, *Scholars and Gentlemen*, 39–41. See also Albert Peel (ed.), *The Seconde Parte of a Register*, ii, 53–4, 195, 219.

9 W. Haller, *The Rise of Puritanism*, 117–23. For the activities of the Puritan group in the House of Commons see below, 59.

10 Bodleian: Tanner MSS 72, f. 298. See also the distinction which Peter Heylyn draws between Puritans and Calvinists in *Cyprianus Anglicus*, 124.

11 William Bradshaw, *English Puritanisme*, 1.

12 Thomas Goodwin, *A Fair Prospect*, epistle dedicatory.

13 J. R. Scott, *Memorials of the Family of Scott*, 196. *C. S. P. Dom., 1603–10*, 177.

14 *Hutchinson Memoirs*, 44.

15 Thomas Gataker, *Two Sermons Tending to Direction for Christian Cariage*, epistle dedicatory.

16 Richard Baxter, *The Saints Everlasting Rest*, 540–1.

17 *Hutchinson Memoirs*, 44.

18 Baxter, *op. cit.*, epistle dedicatory to Sir Thomas and Lady Jane Rous, and 541.

19 John Dod and Robert Cleaver, *A Plaine and Familiar Exposition of the Fifteenth, Sixteenth and Seventeenth Chapters of the Proverbs of Salomon*, 70. Robert Bolton, *Mr Bolton's Last and Learned Worke of The Foure Last Things*, 244.

20 Sir William Waller, *Divine Meditations*, 91, 92.

21 *Hutchinson Memoirs*, 35.

22 John Wing, *The Saint's Advantage*, epistle dedicatory. Jeremiah Dyke, *Good Conscience*, epistle dedicatory. BL, Egerton MSS 2644, ff. 275, 279.

23 BL, Portland MSS, BL Loan 29/172, f. 346. Timothy Woodroffe, *A Religious Treatise upon Simeon's Song*, epistle dedicatory (addressed to Edward Harley, the eldest son of Sir Robert).

24 Dr Williams's Library: Morrice MSS, J, no pagination.

25 *Surtees Society*, lii, 156, J. T. Rutt (ed.), *Diary of Thomas Burton*, iv, 77. *C.S.P.Dom., 1635–6*, 405.

26 Dr Williams's Library: Morrice MSS, J.

27 Sir John Neale, *Elizabeth I and her Parliaments 1559–1581*, 202–3, 210, 212. BL, Sloane MSS 271, ff. 20–1 and Additional MSS 48,109, f. 14.

28 Samuel Clark, *The Lives of Sundry Eminent Persons*, pt ii, 109.

29 Neale, *op. cit.*, 57, 59, 292.

30 Samuel Clark, *A Collection of the Lives of Ten Eminent Divines*, 133, 134. PRO, Wills, PROB 11/133/32 (will of Sir William Cooke). Thomas Gataker, *Discours Apological*, 15 and *The Spirituall Watch*, epistle dedica-

tory. Dr Williams's Library: Morrice MSS, I, 373(6). N. E. McClure
(ed.), *The Letters of John Chamberlain*, ii, 220.

31 BL, Portland MSS, BL Loan 29/122 and Lansdowne MSS 721, ff. 93–5.

32 Thomas Park (ed.), *Nugae Antiquae*, ii, 21. BL, Additional MSS 46,381,
ff. 135–7, 143–4 and Egerton MSS 2711, f. 74.

33 See below, 23, 104.

34 PRO, Wills, PROB 11/142/130.

35 John Barlow, *The True Guide to Glory*, 40.

36 BL, Egerton MSS 2650, f. 213.

37 St John, ch. 3, v. 3.

38 John Barlow, *The Good Man's Priviledge*, 5.

39 BL, Harleian MSS 227, f. 1.

40 William Dillingham, *A Sermon at the Funeral of the Lady Elizabeth Alston*,
40.

41 Sir James Harrington, *Horae Consecratae*, 369.

42 Samuel Fairclough, *The Saint's Worthinesse and the World's Worthlesnesse*,
13. The passage in question is Psalm 51, v. 5.

43 George Sikes, *The Life and Death of Sir Henry Vane*, 8. J. H. Adamson
and H. F. Folland, *Sir Harry Vane. His Life and Times 1613–1662*, 28, 32.

44 BL, Portland MSS, BL Loan 29/84.

45 BL, Additional MSS 28,008, f. 26. Thomas Gataker, *Two Sermons:
Tending to Direction for Christian Cariage*, epistle dedicatory.

46 John Collinges, *Par Nobile*, treatise on the life of Lady Frances Hobart,
2, 4, 13. Samuel Otes, *An Explanation of the Generall Epistle of Saint Jude*,
epistle dedicatory.

47 William Prynne, *Canterburie's Doome*, 167.

48 William Perkins, *A Christian and Plaine Treatise of the Manner and Order of
Predestination and of the Largenes of God's Grace*, 6–7, 31, 33.

49 Thomas Cawton the younger, *The Life and Death of that Holy and Reverend
Man of God Mr Thomas Cawton*, 3. A. W. Harrison, *Arminianism*, 142,
152–5. A. G. Matthews, *Calamy Revised*, 227. *DNB*.

50 BL, Portland MSS, BL Loan 29/172, no pagination.

51 See H. C. Porter, *Reformation and Reaction in Tudor Cambridge*, 334, 335,
371.

52 Richard Sibbes, *A Fountaine Sealed*, 210–11.

53 BL, Harleian MSS 374, ff. 61–3 and 646, ff. 81, 127.

54 Derbyshire Record Office: Chandos-Pole-Gell MSS, Box 31/21.

55 William Earl of Pembroke, *Poems*, 47 (this contains a number of poems
by Rudyerd).

56 BL, Additional MSS 53,728, no pagination.

57 BL, Egerton MSS 2650, f. 308 and Lansdowne MSS 721, f. 109.

58 John Ley, *A Patterne of Pietie*, epistle dedicatory. Edmund Calamy, *The*

Happinesse of Those who Sleep in Jesus, 27–8. E. W. Harcourt, *The Harcourt Papers*, i, 174.

59 BL, Egerton MSS 2645, ff. 142, 232 and 2650, f. 211. Daniel Rogers, *Treatise of the Two Sacraments of the Gospell*, epistle dedicatory. PRO, Wills, PROB 11/187/151.

60 Richard Sibbes, *A Fountaine Sealed*, 243–4.

61 *Hutchinson Memoirs*, 34–5. See also Lucy Hutchinson, *On the Principles of the Christian Religion*, 24–5.

62 John Preston, *An Abridgement of Dr Preston's Works*, 169, 686.

63 William Martyn, *Youth's Instruction*, 3. Devon County Record Office: Orphans' Court Wills, Book 144, f. 151.

Chapter 2 A Life of Piety

1 Sir James Harrington, *A Holy Oyl*, 21.

2 William Bradshaw, *English Puritanisme*, 17.

3 *C.S. P.Dom., 1634–5*, 22–3.

4 For the lecturers see Christopher Hill, *Society and Puritanism in Pre-Revolutionary England*, ch. III and Paul S. Seaver, *The Puritan Lectureships. The Politics of Religious Dissent 1560–1662*.

5 John Barlow, *The Good Man's Priviledge*, epistle dedicatory.

6 *Camden Society*, xli, 24–5. William Gouge, *Of Domesticall Duties*, 521.

7 PRO, Wills, PROB 11/244/101.

8 Thomas Gataker, *A Good Wife God's Gift, and a Wife Indeed*. Richard Sibbes, *The Bride's Longing for her Bride-Groomes Second Comming*. Robert Bolton, *Mr Bolton's Last and Learned Worke of The Foure Last Things*.

9 BL, Egerton MSS 2646, f. 162 and 2650, f. 177. Benjamin King, *The Marriage of the Lambe*, epistle dedicatory. Calamy, *Account*, 544.

10 BL, Additional MSS 48,016. Edward Phillips, *Certaine Godly and Learned Sermons*. Essex County Record Office: Hatfield Broad Oak MSS, D/DBa/F5/1 and 2.

11 BL, Harleian MSS 339, ff. 4–27; 379, ff. 1–5; 486, f. 83; 593, ff. 163–74; 646, f. 28. The text taken for the sermon of December 1615 was St Matthew, ch. 8, v. 32.

12 John Barlow, *The True Guide to Glory*, 48. Edmund Calamy, *The Happinesse of Those who Sleep in Jesus*, 28.

13 Nathaniel Parkhurst, *The Faithful and Diligent Christian Described and Exemplified*, 51–2.

14 BL, Additional MSS 48,016, f. 77.

15 *Gentleman's Magazine*, new series, xxxvi, 367, 371. Mary Penington, *A Brief Account of My Exercises in My Childhood*, 5.

16 Sir William Waller, *Vindication of the Character and Conduct of Sir William Waller*, 237 and *Divine Meditations*, 107–8. St Paul refers to 'psalms and

hymns and spiritual songs' in Ephesians, ch. 5, v. 19.

17 Mary Penington, *A Brief Account of My Exercises in My Childhood*, 5.

18 *Camden Society*, lviii, 69. *C.J.*, iii, 57,259. For nonconformity in the church at Brampton Bryan see below, 186, 188, 189.

19 Thomas May, *The History of the Parliament of England*, 39.

20 See below, 160–2, 178–9.

21 Paybody had been serving as chaplain to Sir Thomas Grantham's wife, Lady Lucy. In 1631 she presented him to the Lincolnshire rectory of Panton (Francis Peck, *Desiderata Curiosa*, ii, 291. PRO, Institution Books, Series A, iii, f. 103).

22 Sir Edward Peyton, *A Discourse Concerning the Fitnesse of the Posture Necessary to be Used in Taking the Bread and Wine at the Sacrament*, 1–2, 4, 7.

23 Seth Wood, *The Saint's Enterance into Peace and Rest by Death*, 18.

24 Sir Edward Peyton, *The Divine Catastrophe of the Kingly Family of the House of Stuarts*, 49–50. BL, Harleian MSS 646, f. 162.

25 Samuel Ainsworth, *A Sermon Preached at the Funerall of that Religious Gentlewoman Mrs Dorothy Hanbury*, 28.

26 For a general account of the spiritual household see Christopher Hill, *Society and Puritanism in Pre-Revolutionary England*, ch. 13.

27 William Perkins, *The Workes*, iii, 698.

28 Richard Bernard, *Iosuah's Resolution for the Well Ordering of his Household*, 24 and epistle dedicatory. For the proceedings in the High Commission see below, 167–8.

29 Harbottle Grimston, *A Christian New-Year's Gift*, 64.

30 For Lady Honywood's days of humiliation see A. Macfarlane (ed.), *The Diary of Ralph Josselin, 1616–1683*, 15, 24, 29, 64.

31 BL, Portland MSS, BL Loan 29/27. David, ch. 9, vv. 3–5.

32 BL, Harleian MSS 227, f. 5; 339, f. 38 and 646, ff. 104–5, 108, 111, 122, 126, 128, 159, 161.

33 John Dod and Robert Cleaver, *Three Godlie and Fruitful Sermons*, 49–50.

34 John Collinges, *Par Nobile*, treatise on the life of Lady Frances Hobart, 16–17, 22. Samuel Clark, *The Lives of Sundry Eminent Persons*, pt ii, 194.

35 Thomas Froysell, *The Beloved Disciple*, 102–3. BL, Portland MSS, BL Loan 29/121 and 124.

36 Samuel Ainsworth, *A Sermon Preached at the Funerall of that Religious Gentlewoman Mrs Dorothy Hanbury*, 29. Edmund Calamy, *The Happinesse of Those who Sleep in Jesus*, 28, 30. Sir William Waller, *Divine Meditations*, 179.

37 Samuel Clark, *The Lives of Thirty-Two English Divines*, 158. C. E. Vulliamy, *The Onslow Family 1528–1874*, 6–8. HMC, *Fourteenth Report*, Appendix, ix, 476.

38 Samuel Clark, *The Lives of Sundry Eminent Persons*, pt ii, 111–13. Samuel Fairclough, *The Saint's Worthinesse and the World's Worthlesnesse*, 17.

39 John Dod and Robert Cleaver, *Three Godlie and Fruitful Sermons*, 51, 53.

40 Norfolk Record Office: Kimberley MSS, Box 14, 111.

41 John Barlow, *The True Guide to Glory*, 48–9. William Dillingham, *A Sermon at the Funeral of the Lady Elizabeth Alston*, 41. Samuel Clark, *The Lives of Sundry Eminent Persons*, pt ii, 194. Nathaniel Parkhurst, *The Faithful and Diligent Christian Described and Exemplified*, 49–52, 81. John Wilford, *Memorials and Characters*, 624–5. Duke of Manchester, *Court and Society from Elizabeth to Anne*, i, 344.

42 BL, Egerton MSS 2711, f. 74.

43 Edmund Calamy, *The Nonconformist's Memorial* (ed. Samuel Palmer), ii, 335. BL, Harleian MSS 646, f. 159.

44 Second Epistle to Timothy, ch. 3, v. 15.

45 A. G. Watson, *The Library of Sir Simonds D'Ewes*. BL, Portland MSS, BL Loan 29/202 (between ff. 230 and 231) and Hargrave MSS 107. Although the catalogue of the Yelverton library in the Hargrave MSS is dated 1694 it lists many works published in the early seventeenth century and earlier. Further information about books belonging to Sir Robert Harley, and also to his brother James, appears in BL Loan 29/124. Other sources of evidence include a list of books purchased by Sir Thomas Barrington between 1635 and 1639 (*Library*, fourth series, xviii, 417 seq.)

46 Richard Baxter, *The Saints Everlasting Rest*, dedication to the inhabitants of Kidderminster.

47 See the comprehensive list of religious authors in John Wilkins, *Ecclesiastes*.

48 PRO, Wills, PROB 11/164/103.

49 BL, Portland MSS, BL Loan 29/202 (between ff. 230 and 231) and Hargrave MSS 107, f. 7. Watson, *op. cit.*, 99. *Fawsley Park, Northamptonshire. Catalogue of the Library* (auction, 1914), 118. PRO, Wills, PROB 11/192/45. William Perkins, *The Works* (1605), 'A Faithfull and Plaine Exposition upon the Two First Verses of the Second Chapter of Zephaniah', epistle dedicatory, and *The Workes* (1608, 1609), i, 'A Treatise Tending unto a Declaration Whether a Man be in the Estate of Damnation or in the Estate of Grace', epistle dedicatory, and ii, 'The Arte of Prophecying', epistle dedicatory. Dr Williams's Library: Morrice MSS, M, xi, 16.

50 Henry Scudder, *A Key of Heaven*, epistle dedicatory.

51 See also below, 92.

52 John Dod and Robert Cleaver, *A Plaine and Familiar Exposition of the Fifteenth, Sixteenth and Seventeenth Chapters of the Proverbs of Salomon*, epistle dedicatory.

53 Samuel Clark, *The Lives of Thirty-Two English Divines*, 145. Nathaniel Parkhurst, *The Faithful and Diligent Christian Described and Exemplified* 45–6, 74. Richard Sibbes, *A Fountaine Sealed*, epistle dedicatory.

54 *DNB* (Nicholas Byfield). *C.S.P.Dom.*, *Charles I, Addenda, 1625–49*, 75. Nicholas Byfield, *The Rule of Faith*, epistle dedicatory.

55 Samuel Hieron, *The Minoritie of Saints, Three Sermons, A Helpe unto Devotion* and *The Spiritual Tillage*, epistles dedicatory. Benjamin Brook, *The Lives of the Puritans*, ii, 270–3.

56 Sir William Waller, *Divine Meditations*, 29.

57 George Sikes, *The Life and Death of Sir Henry Vane*, 50. Samuel Fairclough, *The Saint's Worthinesse and the World's Worthlesnesse*, 14, 22. BL, Additional MSS 37,343, f. 164. Thomas Adams, *The White Devile*, epistle dedicatory.

58 John Wilford, *Memorials and Characters*, 625.

59 Sir James Harrington, *A Holy Oyl*, 333–45.

60 See Patrick Collinson, 'The Beginnings of English Sabbatarianism', in *Studies in Church History*, i (ed. C. W. Dugmore and C. Duggan), 207–21, and Christopher Hill, *Society and Puritanism in Pre-Revolutionary England*, ch. V.

61 Robert Bolton, *Mr Bolton's Last and Learned Worke of The Foure Last Things*, 162.

62 *Camden Society*, lviii, 69.

63 BL, Additional MSS 53,726, f. 89.

64 Thomas Fuller, *The Church-History of Britain*, xi, 146.

65 BL, Portland MSS, BL Loan 29/202 (between ff. 230 and 231). Thomas Froysell, *The Beloved Disciple*, 106.

66 Richard Sibbes, *The Bride's Longing for her Bride-Groomes Second Comming*, 117. Robert Cleaver, *op. cit.*, epistle dedicatory.

67 BL, Additional MSS 35,331, f. 62.

68 BL, Additional MSS 27,400, f. 13. Sir Edward Peyton, *The Divine Catastrophe of the Kingly Family of the House of Stuarts*, 31.

69 *C.J.*, i, 511, 521, 522, 523, 524. W. Notestein, F. H. Relf and H. Simpson (ed.), *Commons Debates, 1621*, ii, 34, 82, 95 and iv, 33, 52–3, 62–5.

70 *Camden Society*, xli, 75, 118. *C.J.*, i, 671, 677.

71 *C.J.*, i, 799, 800. Statute 1 Charles I, cap. i.

72 *C.J.*, i, 877, 880. Statute 3 Charles I, cap. ii.

Chapter 3   Holiness and Sobriety

1 BL, Harleian MSS 227, f. 8.

2 PRO, Wills, PROB 11/205/142.

3 See William Haller, *The Rise of Puritanism*, 117–18.

4 BL, Portland MSS, BL Loan 29/172, f. 34, and 202 (between ff. 230 and 231). Thomas Taylor, *The Progresse of Saints to Full Holinesse*, epistle dedicatory. See Paul S. Seaver, *The Puritan Lectureships*, 135, 137–8.

5 BL, Egerton MSS 2711, f. 73.

6 *Essex Archaeological Society Transactions*, new series, ii, 33. BL, Egerton MSS 2645, f. 142.
7 Samuel Ainsworth, *A Sermon Preached at the Funerall of that Religious Gentlewoman Mrs Dorothy Hanbury*, 29–30.
8 BL, Harleian MSS 227, ff. 3, 22.
9 See below, 63–6, 68.
10 John Frewen, *Certaine Sermons upon the 2, 3, 4, 5, 6 7 and 8 Verses of the Eleventh Chapter of St Paule his Epistle to the Romanes*, twelfth sermon, no pagination.
11 Seth Wood, *The Saint's Enterance into Peace and Rest by Death*, 16–18.
12 Thomas Froysell, *The Beloved Disciple*, 99. Timothy Woodroffe, *A Religious Treatise upon Simeon's Song*, epistle dedicatory. BL, Harleian MSS 227, ff. 3, 7 and 646, f. 105.
13 Samuel Fairclough, *The Saint's Worthinesse and the World's Worthlesnesse*, 24. *Suffolk's Tears*, 6.
14 Henry Scudder, *A Key of Heaven*, epistle dedicatory. John Bridges, *The History and Antiquities of Northamptonshire*, i, 198, 200.
15 Duke of Manchester, *Court and Society from Elizabeth to Anne*, i, 347. Lord Nugent, *Some Memorials of John Hampden*, i, 208.
16 Thomas Hobbes, *Behemoth* (ed. Ferdinand Tonnies), 25.
17 Sir Edward Peyton, *The Divine Catastrophe of the Kingly Family of the House of Stuarts*, 60.
18 Sir James Harrington, *Holy Oyl*, 234. Daniel Lysons, *The Environs of London*, ii, 815. John Collinges, *Par Nobile*, life of Lady Frances Hobart, 13.
19 BL, Portland MSS, BL Loan 29/27. See also *H.M.C.*, *Fourteenth Report*, Appendix, pt ii, 171.
20 PRO, Wills, PROB 11/154/70 and 247/217.
21 Sir Edward Peyton, *The High-way to Peace*, 8 and *The Divine Catastrophe of the Kingly Family of the House of Stuarts*, 60–1. PRO, Chancery Proceedings, C.3/397/118.
22 BL, Harleian MSS 387, f. 47.
23 *Herald and Genealogist*, iv, 133. PRO, Chancery Proceedings, C.10/27/101.
24 BL, Portland MSS, BL Loan 29/172, ff. 181, 240, 259, 271, 273.
25 Epistle of Paul to Titus, ch. 2, vv. 11 and 12. This saying is embedded in the General Confession in the Book of Common Prayer. See also Bartholomew Parsons, *Dorcas*, 19.
26 *Leicestershire Archaeological Society Transactions*, ii, 269, 270.
27 *The House of Mourning*, 255.
28 John Preston, *Grace to the Humble*, 4, 5, 21, 107. Richard Sibbes, *A Fountaine Sealed*, 174–5.
29 Norfolk Record Office: Kimberley MSS, Box 14, 111, no pagination. First Epistle of John, ch. 2, v. 16. Nathaniel Parkhurst, *The Faithful and*

Diligent Christian Described and Exemplified, 101. BL, Egerton MSS 2711, f. 115. Harbottle Grimston, *A Christian New-Year's Gift*, 67, 76, 104, 112.

30 Sir Thomas Wroth, *The Abortive of an Idle Houre*, 15.

31 *The Poetry of Anna Matilda*, 131 (the *Recollections* of Sir William Waller are printed at the end of this volume).

32 *Hutchinson Memoirs*, 13.

33 See J. T. Cliffe, *The Yorkshire Gentry from the Reformation to the Civil War*, 115–17.

34 Sir William Waller, *Divine Meditations*, 43–4.

35 Thomas Case, *The Vanity of Vaine-Glory*, 83.

36 Waller, *op. cit.*, 180.

37 BL, Harleian MSS 593, f. 56 and 379, f. 65.

38 *C.J.*, i, 532.

39 Sir James Harrington, *A Holy Oyl*, 371.

40 See Sir George More, *A Demonstration of God in his Workes*.

41 W. H. Long (ed.), *The Oglander Memoirs*, 141. BL, Portland MSS, BL 29/274.

42 John Dod and Robert Cleaver, *A Plaine and Familiar Exposition of the Ten Commandements*, 287.

43 David Underdown, *Somerset in the Civil War and Interregnum*, facing p. 167. C. L. Vulliamy, *The Onslow Family 1528–1874*, facing p. 20. R. W. Ketton-Cremer, *Norfolk in the Civil War*, facing p. 148. Sir James D. Legard, *The Legards of Anlaby and Ganton*, facing p. 198. National Portrait Gallery: photograph of Brampton Gurdon's portrait painted in 1649.

44 First Epistle to Timothy, ch. 2, v. 9.

45 John Wilford, *Memorials and Characters*, 625. Gilbert Burnet, *History of his Own Time*, ii, 70. *The Spie*, no. 14, 110.

46 BL, Cotton Charter xvi, 13, ff. 6, 8.

47 BL, Egerton MSS 2646, f. 46.

48 Samuel Butler, *The Posthumous Works of Mr Samuel Butler*, ii, 91. H. G. Tibbutt (ed.), *The Letter Books 1644–45 of Sir Samuel Luke*, 438.

49 National Portrait Gallery: photographs of portraits of Sir Samuel Luke and his wife Lady Elizabeth.

50 *Camden Society*, lviii, 16, 22, 50.

51 *Hutchinson Memoirs*, 12, 203.

52 *Ibid.*, 197.

53 Francis Bamford (ed.), *A Royalist's Notebook*, intro. xxv.

54 H. R. Trevor-Roper, *Archbishop Laud*, 118.

55 BL, Lansdowne MSS 721, f. 110. Oliver Millar, *The Age of Charles I: Painting in England 1620–1649*, 113.

56 National Portrait Gallery: photographs of portraits of Barrington (c.1605) and Cutts (1607).

57 *Hutchinson Memoirs*, 63.

58 National Portrait Gallery: photographs of portraits of Barnardiston, Hesilrige and Armyne. *DNB* (Sir Samuel Barnardiston). Sir Nathaniel is depicted in Samuel Clark, *The Lives of Sundry Eminent Persons*, pt ii, 105.

59 William Martyn, *Youth's Instruction*, 1, 64, 65, 68, 69.

60 William Trevethick, *A Sermon Preached at the Funeral of the Honourable Colonel Robert Rolle of Heanton Sachville*, epistle dedicatory.

61 John Barlow, *The True Guide to Glory*, 49–50.

62 National Portrait Gallery: photograph of engraved portrait of Sir John Northcote. Lady Eliott-Drake, *The Family and Heirs of Sir Francis Drake*, i, plates facing pp. 250, 276, 394. BL, Harleian MSS 164, f. 298.

63 *C.J.*, i, 434, 830. Statutes 1 James I, cap. ix, 4 James I, cap. v, 21 James I, cap. vii and xx, 3 Charles I, cap. iv and v.

64 Edmund Rudyerd, *The Thunderbolt of God's Wrath*, epistle dedicatory and *passim*.

65 Robert Bolton, *Mr Bolton's Last and Learned Worke of The Foure Last Things*, epistle dedicatory by the editor, Edward Bagshawe.

66 John Hinckley, *A Sermon Preached at the Funerals of that Worthy Personage George Purefoy the Elder*, 29. Thomas Froysell, *The Beloved Disciple*, 105–6.

67 BL, Egerton MSS 2711, ff. 24, 70.

68 BL, Egerton MSS 2650, f. 318. *C.J.*, i, 841.

69 Samuel Clark, *The Lives of Sundry Eminent Persons*, pt ii, 112. Sir Charles Firth (ed.), *The Memoirs of Edmund Ludlow*, ii, 133.

70 Clarendon, i, 245. Violet A. Rowe, *Sir Henry Vane the Younger*, 278.

71 Sir William Waller, *Divine Meditations*, 34.

72 BL, Harleian MSS 227, f. 17.

Chapter 4   Marriage and Parenthood

1 William Perkins, *The Workes*, iii, 693.

2 Samuel Hieron, *The Bridegroome*, 12–13.

3 BL, Egerton MSS 2645, f. 96.

4 *The Poetry of Anna Matilda* (annex containing the *Recollections* of Sir William Waller), 127–9. E. W. Harcourt, *The Harcourt Papers*, i, 171, 173, 179.

5 BL, Harleian MSS 379, ff. 16, 89, 94, 99, 101; 383, f. 105; 384, ff. 21, 36; 386, ff. 55, 233; 646, ff. 88, 91–4, 96.

6 N. E. McClure (ed.), *The Letters of John Chamberlain*, ii, 340. Thomas Birch (ed.), *The Court and Times of James I*, ii, 467–8. Benjamin King, *The Marriage of the Lambe*, epistle dedicatory.

7 BL, Additional MSS 4275, f. 48.

8 BL, Egerton MSS 2644, f. 240.

9 Sir William Waller, *Divine Meditations*, 39.
10 BL, Harleian MSS 98, f. 36; 386, f. 218 and 646, ff. 88, 91, 93. PRO, Chancery Proceedings, C.7/424/11. Duke of Manchester, *Court and Society from Elizabeth to Anne*, i, 381–92.
11 See below, 182–3.
12 Northamptonshire Record Office: Isham Correspondence, IC/182, 184, 187, 188, 193, 197, 199. See also Mary E. Finch, *The Wealth of Five Northamptonshire Families 1540–1640*, 34–5.
13 See below, 220.
14 C. S. Durrant, *A Link Between Flemish Mystics and English Martyrs*, 272–3. PRO, Court of Wards, Decrees, Wards 9/xcviii/ff. 153–55. Bodleian, Tanner MSS 321, ff. 3, 5–6. *C.J.*, ii, 35.
15 J. T. Cliffe, *The Yorkshire Gentry from the Reformation to the Civil War*, 308, 310 (a memorandum relating to the Boynton-Fiennes marriage settlement is in the possession of the author). Dorset County Record Office: Lane MSS, D60/F2. Leicestershire Record Office: MSS of Lord Hazlerigg, 55. *Leicestershire Archaeological Society Transactions*, ii, 270. PRO, Wills, PROB 11/166/72 (Sir Francis Goodwin) and 192/1 (Arthur Goodwin). C. Oscar Moreton, *Waddesdon and Over Winchendon*, 135.
16 William Perkins, *The Workes*, iii, 694.
17 William Gouge, *Of Domesticall Duties*, 498, 536–42.
18 A. G. Watson, *The Library of Sir Simonds D'Ewes*, 168. BL, Harleian MSS 227, f. 14.
19 Samuel Clark, *The Lives of Sundry Eminent Persons*, pt ii, 110.
20 Sir James Harrington, *A Holy Oyl*, 259.
21 Edmund Calamy, *The Happinesse of Those who Sleep in Jesus*, 30.
22 *Gentleman's Magazine*, new series, xxxvi, 366. William Dillingham, *A Sermon at the Funeral of the Lady Elizabeth Alston*, 40. Epistle to the Galatians, ch. 4, v. 19.
23 John Hart, *The Burning Bush Not Consumed*, epistle dedicatory to Mrs Joan Drake, and *Trodden Down Strength, by the God of Strength, or Mrs Drake Revived*, passim.
24 Ezekiel Rogers, *The Chief Grounds of Christian Religion, Set Down by Way of Catechizing*. This work was not published until 1648 but it is clear that Rogers had produced it while serving as chaplain to Sir Francis Barrington during the years 1609 to 1621.
25 Bartholomew Parsons, *A Sermon Preached at the Funerall of Sir Francis Pile Baronet*, 34. PRO, Wills, PROB 11/207/57.
26 *Hutchinson Memoirs*, 16, 34–5.
27 See Lawrence Stone, *The Family, Sex and Marriage in England 1500–1800*, 162–78.
28 William Perkins, *The Workes*, iii, 694.

29 John Brinsley, *Ludus Literarius*, 290. William Gouge, *Of Domesticall Duties*, 552–3.

30 BL, Harleian MSS 1598, f. 13.

31 Harbottle Grimston, *A Christian New-Year's Gift*, 52–3. Sir Henry Chauncy, *The Historical Antiquities of Hertfordshire*, ii, 318.

32 C. S. Durrant, *A Link between Flemish Mystics and English Martyrs*, 273–5.

33 Richard Sibbes, *The Bride's Longing for her Bride-Groomes Second Comming*, 122.

34 Samuel Clark, *The Lives of Sundry Eminent Persons*, pt ii, 110.

35 *HMC, Fourteenth Report*, Appendix, pt ii, 190. Thomas Froysell, *The Beloved Disciple*, 103–4. See also the letters of Lady Harley in *Camden Society*, lviii.

36 National Portrait Gallery: photograph of group portrait of the Burdett family (c. 1620). The Curzon portrait (1633) is at Kedleston Hall, Derbyshire and the Boynton portrait (after Van Dyck) at Burton Agnes Hall, Yorkshire.

37 William Cooke, *A Learned and Full Answer to a Treatise Intituled, The Vanity of Childish Baptisme*, epistle dedicatory by Francis Woodcock.

38 Samuel Fairclough, *The Saint's Worthinesse and the World's Worthlesnesse*, epistle dedicatory.

39 PRO, Colonial Entry Books, Bahamas, C.O.124/ii/f.30.

40 Guildford Muniment Room: Loseley MSS, More Letters. BL, Additional MSS 29,599, ff. 36, 38. W. A. Shaw, *A History of the English Church 1640–1660*, ii, 435. Sir Poynings More seems to have owed his appointment as a Presbyterian elder in the county of Surrey to the fact that he was an MP: see Stephen Foster, 'The Presbyterian Independents Exorcized', *Past and Present*, no. 44, 63–4.

41 Dr Williams's Library: Morrice MSS, I, 697(12) and (16), and M, xi, 4. Seth Wood, *The Saint's Enterance into Peace and Rest by Death*, 23. Christopher Shute, *Ars piè Moriendi: or The True Accomptant*, epistle dedicatory and 25, 26, 29.

42 William Gouge, *Of Domesticall Duties*, 541, 586.

43 See, for example, J. T. Cliffe, *The Yorkshire Gentry from the Reformation to the Civil War*, 264–7.

44 Lambeth Palace Library: MS 943, f. 295 and Register Laud, i, f. 255. T. W. Davids, *Annals of Evangelical Nonconformity in the County of Essex*, 391.

45 J. Peile (ed.), *Biographical Register of Christ's College, 1505–1905*, i, 312–13, 361. Dorothea Coke, *The Last Elizabethan: Sir John Coke, 1563–1644*, 183.

46 Thomas Froysell, a Puritan divine, served for some years as vicar of Clun in the neighbouring county of Shropshire. See Calamy, *Account*, 562.

47 BL, Portland MSS, BL Loan 29/121 and 123. *C.S.P.Dom., 1635–6*, 440. *Camden Society*, lviii, 37, 55, 69, 74, 76, 77.

48 *Essex Archaeological Society Transactions*, new series, xii, 207–9. Matthew Newcomen, *A Sermon Preached at the Funerals of . . . Mr Samuel Collins*, 49, 50, 51, 53.

49 BL, Additional MSS 33,145, ff. 89, 105, 108, 118, 123, 129 and 36,776, f. 81. John Wilford, *Memorials and Characters*, 518–20. W. D. Macray (ed.), *A Register of the Members of St Mary Magdalen College, Oxford*, new series, iii, 145. *Al. Cant.*, i, 359; ii, 296; iii, 336.

50 BL, Harleian MSS 646, ff. 9, 10, 12, 15, 19, 20, 21, 28–30, 149. *Biographical List of Boys Educated at King Edward VI Free Grammar School, Bury St Edmunds*, 351. Sir Edward Peyton, *The Divine Catastrophe of the Kingly Family of the House of Stuarts*, 139.

51 W. L. Sargant, *The Book of Oakham School*, 5, 7, 9, 14, 15, 17, 55, 58, 74. Dr Williams's Library: Morrice MSS, M, xi, 8, 10, 11, 16.

52 Sargant, *op. cit.*, 15. *V.C.H., Essex*, ii, 534. F. S. Moller (ed.), *Alumni Felstedienses*, intro. xi, xxv, 2. *C.S.P.Dom., 1629–31*, 391. *Camden Society*, xxxii, 123–4.

53 PRO, S.P.Dom., Charles I, S.P.16/ccxciii/128. *V.C.H., Gloucestershire*, ii, 324, 326. John Dod and his friend Robert Cleaver were the authors of *A Plaine and Familiar Exposition of the Ten Commandements*.

54 Bodleian: Tanner MSS 68, f. 209. PRO, Institution Books, Series A, iii, f. 231. The work in question was *The English Catechisme* which went through five editions between 1621 and 1635.

Chapter 5   The Puritan Undergraduate

1 The most important general works on this subject are M. H. Curtis, *Oxford and Cambridge in Transition 1558–1642*, H. F. Kearney, *Scholars and Gentlemen* and Lawrence Stone (ed.), *The University in Society*, vol. i.

2 Thomas Hobbes, *Behemoth* (ed. Ferdinand Tonnies), 147. BL, Harleian MSS 646, f. 47. William Martyn, *Youth's Instruction*, 8, 12, 37, 64, 65, 92, 98. H. R. Trevor-Roper, *Archbishop Laud*, 118. John Evelyn, *Diary and Correspondence of John Evelyn* (ed. William Bray), 7.

3 William Prynne, *Canterburies Doome*, 176.

4 BL, Harleian MSS 646, f. 47. *The Diary of Sir Simonds D'Ewes* (ed. Elizabeth Bourcier), 181–2.

5 Prynne, *op. cit.*, 177. BL, Harleian MSS 7033, f. 165.

6 See Lawrence Stone (ed.), *The University in Society*, i and in particular Stone, 'The Size and Composition of the Oxford Student Body 1580–1909' and Victor Morgan, 'Cambridge University and "The Country" 1560–1640'.

7 Thomas Fuller, *The Church-History of Britain*, ix, 233–4. W. D. Macray

(ed.), *A Register of the Members of St Mary Magdalen College, Oxford*, new series, ii, 193 and iii, 87–8. N. E. McClure (ed.), *The Letters of John Chamberlain*, i, 528, 530–1.

8 Peter Heylyn, *Cyprianus Anglicus*, 50. Anthony Wood, *Athenae Oxonienses*, iii, 422, 633. Macray, *op. cit.*, iii, 133, 136.

9 *Al. Oxon.*, 321, 349, 364, 556, 584, 641, 787, 982.

10 BL, Lansdowne MSS 724.

11 *Luctus Posthumus*, 50, 52, 54. Thomas Gataker, *The Spirituall Watch*, epistle dedicatory. Samuel Clark, *A Collection of the Lives of Ten Eminent Divines*, 133, 134.

12 Macray, *op. cit.*, iii, 115, 123 and vi, 194. *Al. Oxon.*, 431. Sir Robert Atkyns, *The Ancient and Present State of Glocestershire*, 219. Richard Capel, *Tentations*, preface by Valentine Marshall, no pagination.

13 He also had a second term from 1646 to 1648.

14 Thomas Fuller, *The Church-History of Britain*, xi, 142. William Laud, *The Works*, v. 56. Anthony Wood, *The History and Antiquities of the Colleges and Halls in the University of Oxford*, iii, 686.

15 Anthony Wood, *Athenae Oxonienses*, ii, 330–1 and iii, 1033. William Pemble, *Vindiciae Gratiae*. William Laud, *The Works*, v. 50–1, 56, 58, 287–9, 297. W. H. Coates (ed.), *The Journal of Sir Simonds D'Ewes*, 150, 182.

16 PRO, S.P.Dom., Charles I, S.P.16/cclxvi/19,20,43. BL, Additional MSS 5831, f. 60. William Laud, *The Works*, v. 98.

17 *Al. Oxon.*, 320, 464, 556, 651, 787, 1683.

18 BL, Portland MSS, BL Loan 29/81, 121 and 122. *DNB* (John Tombes). Calamy, *Account*, 469. *Camden Society*, lviii, 13.

19 BL, Portland MSS, BL Loan 29/78. First Epistle to the Corinthians, ch. 6, vv. 9 and 10.

20 *Camden Society*, lviii, 8, 10, 13, 15, 16, 20, 28. BL, Portland MSS, BL Loan 29/81 and 172, f. 203.

21 BL, Portland MSS, BL Loan 29/73. *H.M.C.*, *Fourteenth Report*, Appendix, pt ii, 190.

22 W. D. Christie (ed.). *Memoirs, Letters and Speeches of Anthony Ashley Cooper, First Earl of Shaftesbury*, 15, 16.

23 Samuel Clark, *The Marrow of Ecclesiastical History*, pt i, 439.

24 Peter Heylyn, *Cyprianus Anglicus*, 68. John Prideaux, *The Doctrine of the Sabbath*, 39–40. Dr Williams's Library: Morrice MSS, G, 889.

25 William Laud, *The Works*, v. 56–8, 66–7, 70.

26 Benjamin Brook, *The Lives of the Puritans*, iii, 112–16. Henry Tozer, *Directions for a Godly Life*, 164–5, 169–70, 176–7, 186, 189–90. The saying of St Paul was drawn from the Epistle to the Ephesians, ch. 5, v. 4.

27 John Conant, *The Life of the Reverend and Venerable John Conant*, 4, 11. See also Calamy, *Account*, 76.

28 *Al. Oxon.*, 65, 377, 422, 1077, 1278, 1704.

29 Anthony Wood, *Fasti Oxonienses*, i. 347 and *The History and Antiquities of the Colleges and Halls in the University of Oxford*, vol. ii, pt i, 424. William Prynne, *Canterburies Doome*, 176. William Laud, *The Works*, v. 182. Sir Charles Mallet, *A History of the University of Oxford*, ii, 14–15, 302, 304.

30 Robert Bolton, *Mr Bolton's Last and Learned Worke of The Foure Last Things*, epistle dedicatory and biographical account by the editor, Edward Bagshawe, no pagination. Thomas Case, 'God's Rising, His Enemies Scattering', *The English Revolution. I. Fast Sermons to Parliament*, iv, 173. Anthony Wood, *Athenae Oxonienses*, iii, 252–3. *Camden Fourth Series*, xxi, 288. *Al. Oxon.*, 146, 176, 1068, 1079.

31 A. B. Grosart (ed.), *The Letter-book of Sir John Eliot*, 105–7, 146, 164–5, 170–2. *Al. Oxon.*, 427, 863, 864, 1068.

32 Samuel Clark, *A Collection of the Lives of Ten Eminent Divines*, 56.

33 Bodleian, Tanner MSS 73, f. 129. BL, Harleian MSS 3783, f. 47.

34 For a list of fellows see BL, Harleian MSS 7033, ff. 86–8.

35 Samuel Clark, *The Lives of Sundry Eminent Persons*, 3. T. W. Davids, *Annals of Evangelical Nonconformity in the County of Essex*, 162. Thomas Fuller, *The History of the University of Cambridge*, 147.

36 Anthony Tuckney, *Death Disarmed*, 48, 56. The persons named are William Whitaker, William Perkins, John Davenant and Samuel Ward.

37 BL, Harleian MSS 7033, f. 98.

38 *HMC, Hatfield MSS*, xvi, 378, 381, 382.

39 *V.C.H., Cambridgeshire*, iii, 474.

40 *Al. Cant.*, i, 227, 258; ii, 269, 275, 450; iii, 92, 187, 278, 336, 447; iv, 231, 435.

41 *A True Picture of the Much Honoured and Reverend Mr John King*, 3. A. G. Matthews, *Calamy Revised*, 309. Joseph Hall, *Contemplations*, vi, book 17, epistle dedicatory. BL, Harleian MSS 3783, f. 17. *Al. Cant.*, iii, 125. H. Smith, *The Ecclesiastical History of Essex under the Long Parliament and Commonwealth*, 247.

42 Matthews, *op. cit.*, 82, 102, 120, 265. P. A. Irby, *The Irbys of Lincolnshire and the Irebys of Cumberland*, pt i, 26, 37, 122. John Cotton, *The Way of Congregational Churches Cleared*, 20. Larzer Ziff, *The Career of John Cotton. Puritanism and the American Experience*, 43, 49, 51. I. Morgan, *Prince Charles's Puritan Chaplain*, 18–19. Benjamin Brook, *The Lives of the Puritans*, iii, 151–60. Calamy, *Account*, 77.

43 *Vindiciae Veritatis*, 138.

44 *Al. Cant.*, ii, 275. BL, Harleian MSS 1598, ff. 1–2.

45 Morgan, *op. cit.*, 30–3. *Al. Cant.*, iii, 359, 466, 467; iv, 459, 489. Matthews, *op. cit.*, 412. Epistle to the Hebrews, ch. 11, v. 38. PRO, Wills, PROB 11/153/19. For the presentation of Thomas Hill see below, p. 179–80.

46 BL, Harleian MSS 3783, f. 11.

47 BL, Harleian MSS 7033, ff. 164–5.

48 BL, Harleian MSS 3783, f. 22. *Al. Cant.*, iv, 138. D. Brunton and D. H. Pennington, *Members of the Long Parliament*, 109. *The County of Suffolke Divided into Fourteene Precincts for Classicall Presbyteries*, 7. Sir Charles Firth and R. S. Rait (eds), *Acts and Ordinances of the Interregnum, 1642–1660*, i, 94, 115, 140, 150, 168.

49 *Al. Cant.*, i, 192, 258; iii, 188, 278, 336. Samuel Clark, *The Lives of Thirty-Two English Divines*, 76. Edward Stillingfleet, *Origines Sacrae*, epistle dedicatory.

50 William Prynne, *Canterburies Doome*, 369.

51 C. W. Scott-Giles, *Sidney Sussex College*, 26, 33, 37, 40. David Lloyd, *Memoirs*, 164. BL, Harleian MSS 7033, f. 165 and Lansdowne MSS 887, f. 44. John Walker, *Sufferings of the Clergy*, pt ii, 158.

52 *Al. Cant.*, ii, 310. Scott-Giles, *op. cit.*, 10, 12, 13, 26, 29. W. L. Sargant, *The Book of Oakham School*, 55.

53 *Al. Cant.*, i, 39. Seth Wood, *The Saint's Enterance into Peace and Rest by Death*, 18.

54 *Al. Cant.*, i, 61. G. F. Russell-Barker and A. H. Stenning (eds), *The Records of Old Westminsters*, i, 37.

55 *Al. Cant.*, i, 251; ii, 72; iii, 92. Thomas Fuller, *The History of the University of Cambridge*, 58.

56 J. Peile (ed.), *Biographical Register of Christ's College, 1505–1905*. i, 183. M. M. Knappen (ed.), *Two Elizabethan Puritan Diaries*, 130–1. Thomas Goodwin, *The Works*, v, account of his life, ix, x.

57 *HMC, Hatfield MSS*, xxi, 144. Peile, *op. cit.*, i, 207, 213.

58 Peile, *op. cit.*, i, 232. William Prynne, *Canterburies Doome*, 178. See also *HMC, House of Lords MSS*, new series, xi, 440.

59 BL, Additional MSS 4460, f. 3. Thomas Fuller, *The Worthies of England*, (ed. J. Freeman), 455. David Lloyd, *Memoirs*, 607.

60 Peile, *op. cit.*, i, 209, 312–13, 343–4, 349, 361. Samuel Clark, *The Lives of Thirty-Two English Divines*, 148, 149.

61 See J. B. Mullinger, *St John's College*, 51, 72, 96, 108.

62 BL, Harleian MSS 386, f. 60 and 646, ff. 38, 42, 46–7; Cotton Charter xvi, 13, ff. 6, 7. W. H. Coates (ed.), *The Journal of Sir Simonds D'Ewes*, 53. M. H. Curtis, *Oxford and Cambridge in Transition 1558–1642*, 124.

63 Mullinger, *op. cit.*, 110, 111. BL, Harleian MSS 646, f. 162.

64 Thomas Goodwin, *The Works*, v, account of his life, v.

65 Samuel Clark, *op. cit.*, 144. BL, Harleian MSS 7033, f. 165.

66 David Lloyd, *Memoirs*, 404–6. BL, Additional MSS 35,331, f. 64. Dr Williams's Library: Morrice MSS, J, no pagination.

67 Thomas Fuller, *The History of the University of Cambridge*, 84. Thomas Goodwin, *The Works*, v, account of his life, v and xiv. A. G. Matthews,

Calamy Revised, 311–12, 457. Calamy, *Account*, 605–8. BL, Egerton MSS 784, f. 106. Benjamin Brook, *The Lives of the Puritans*, iii, 196–200, 315–18.

68 *Al. Cant.*, i, 92, 227; ii, 207; iii, 155, 385. For the connection with the Brooke family see above, p. 38.
69 Fuller, *The History of the University of Cambridge*, 83, 84. PRO, Wills, PROB 11/163/25 (will of Dame Katherine Barnardiston). BL, Egerton MSS 2645, f. 290. In his will, which is dated 4 July 1635, Sibbes refers to his friends Sir Nathaniel Barnardiston, Sir William Spring and Sir Robert and Lady Brooke (PROB 11/168/80).
70 BL, Harleian MSS 646, f. 149. Calamy, *Account*, 605, 607. D'Ewes and Sibbes had both been pupils at the grammar school at Bury St Edmunds: see above, p. 79.
71 BL, Harleian MSS 374, f. 84.
72 *Gentleman's Magazine*, new series, xxxvi, 367. *Al. Cant.*, iv, 138.
73 *HMC, Fourteenth Report*, Appendix, pt ii, 71.
74 *Hutchinson Memoirs*, 24–5. T. A. Walker (ed.)., *Admissions to Peterhouse 1615–1911*, 46. See also W. Notestein (ed.), *The Journal of Sir Simonds D'Ewes*, 58.
75 The English version of Ward's treatise, which was published in 1640, was entitled *The Wonders of the Load-Stone*.

Chapter 6   Riches and Morality

1 John Barlow, *The Good Man's Priviledge*, 21.
2 John Dod and Robert Cleaver, *A Plaine and Familiar Exposition of the Fifteenth, Sixteenth and Seventeenth Chapters of the Proverbs of Salomon*, 52, 88–9.
3 William Perkins, *The Workes*, i, 733.
4 William Martyn, *Youth's Instruction*, 59.
5 Sir Thomas Wroth, *The Abortive of an Idle Houre*, 22 and *The Destruction of Troy*. Richard Niccols, *The Cuckow*, epistle dedicatory addressed to Wroth.
6 Sir William Waller, *Divine Meditations*, 17, 170–1. *Hutchinson Memoirs*, 5. Richard Bernard, *Iosuah's Resolution for the Well Ordering of his Household*, 27.
7 BL, Harleian MSS 227, ff. 15, 16; 384, ff. 63, 198; and 646, ff. 73, 74, 91, 96.
8 See below, p. 122–3.
9 Duke of Manchester, *Court and Society from Elizabeth to Anne*, i, 344, 347.
10 BL, Additional MSS 37,343, ff. 13, 138.
11 BL, Egerton MSS 2646, ff. 44–5, 46. *Camden Society*, xxxii, 94. *Essex Archaeological Society Transactions*, new series, xii, 206.

12 BL, Additional MSS 37,343, f. 144.

13 PRO, Wills, PROB 11/215/41.

14 Samuel Clark, *The Lives of Sundry Eminent Persons*, pt ii, 110. Samuel Fairclough, *The Saint's Worthinesse and the World's Worthlesnesse*, epistle dedicatory. *Miscellanea Genealogica et Heraldica*, third series, i, 42, 43, 102, 152.

15 Derbyshire Record Office: Chandos-Pole-Gell MSS, Boxes 41/31, 56/36 and 60/68.

16 Dr Williams's Library: Morrice MSS, I, 373(16). Thomas Birch (ed.), *The Court and Times of James I*, ii, 438, PRO, Wills, PROB 11/165/45. Richard Sibbes, *The Bride's Longing for her Bride-Groomes Second Comming*, 126. *DNB*.

17 Richard Bernard, *The Faithfull Shepheard*, quoted in I. Green, 'Career Prospects and Clerical Conformity in the Early Stuart Church', *Past and Present*, no. 90, 71.

18 Francis Bampfield, *A Name, an After-one*, 2. PRO, Institution Books, Series A, ii, f. 8. Calamy, *Continuation*, 411. A. G. Matthews, *Calamy Revised*, 26, 186, 219, 412. Sir Charles Firth and R. S. Rait (eds), *The Acts and Ordinances of the Interregnum, 1642–1660*, i, 93, 114, 149, 232.

19 Sir Gyles Isham, *Easton Mauduit and the Parish Church of SS. Peter and Paul*, PRO, Wills, PROB 11/157/55.

20 BL, Additional MSS 53,726, ff. 32, 53.

21 Anthony Wood, *Athenae Oxonienses*, iii, 27. BL, Harleian MSS 991, f. 14 and Additional MSS 53,726, f. 83.

22 BL, Portland MSS, BL Loan 29/27, 122 and 124. *Camden Society*, lviii, 230.

23 PRO, Wills, PROB 11/133/32. *C.S.P.Dom.*, *1603–10*, 15. M. F. Keeler, *The Long Parliament, 1640–1641*, 141, 185–6. Sir Robert Somerville, *History of the Duchy of Lancaster*, ii, 5, 53, 62 and *Office-Holders in the Duchy and County Palatine of Lancaster from 1603*, 29, 30.

24 See, for example, J. T. Cliffe, *The Yorkshire Gentry from the Reformation to the Civil War*, chs II and III.

25 BL, Additional MSS 33,145, ff. 84–5, 87–91, and Additional MSS 33,154. See also Anthony S. Fletcher, *A County Community in Peace and War: Sussex 1600–1660*, 13–14.

26 Robert Bolton, *Mr Bolton's Last and Learned Worke of The Foure Last Things*, 231–2. For similar indictments see W. K. Jordan, *Philanthropy in England 1480–1660*, 191–3.

27 BL, Harleian MSS 227, f. 16. *The Poetry of Anna Matilda* (appendix containing Sir William Waller's *Recollections*), 130.

28 PRO, Chancery, Petty Bag Office, Miscellaneous Rolls, C.212/20. *Camden Society*, lxxiv, 185. Lambeth Palace Library: MS 943, f. 293. *V.C.H., Cambridgeshire*, ii, 26.

29 PRO, Chancery, Petty Bag Office, Miscellaneous Rolls, C.212/20. Seth Wood, *The Saint's Enterance into Peace and Rest by Death*, 21.

30 BL, Egerton MSS 2644, f. 173.

31 BL, Additional MSS 53,726, f. 81.

32 For a general account of the lay ownership of church property see Christopher Hill, *Economic Problems of the Church*.

33 Robert Bolton, *Mr Bolton's Last and Learned Worke of The Foure Last Things*, 161, 178–9.

34 John Mayer, *A Commentarie upon the Foure Evangelists and the Acts of the Apostles*, i, epistle dedicatory.

35 *Suffolk's Tears*, 13. See also Nathaniel Parkhurst, *The Faithful and Diligent Christian Described and Exemplified*, 56.

36 *A Certificate from Northamptonshire*, 9–10.

37 Sir Henry Spelman, *The English Works*, preface to *De Non Temerandis Ecclesiis*, lxiii.

38 Bartholomew Parsons, *Tithes Vindicated to the Presbyters of the Gospel*, epistle dedicatory. Dr Williams's Library: Morrice MSS, J, no pagination.

39 PRO, S.P.Dom., Charles I, S.P.16/cclxxiv/12.

40 Guildford Muniment Room: Loseley MSS 1654, f. 169.

41 Roger Fenton, *A Treatise of Usurie*, 11, 28, 35, 48.

42 Edmund Rudyerd, *The Thunderbolt of God's Wrath*, 85. Robert Bolton, *A Short and Private Discourse Betweene Mr Bolton and one M.S. Concerning Usury*, 36, 40, 68–9.

43 Thomas Cooper, *The Worldling's Adventure*, 63–4.

44 W. Notestein, E. M. Relf and H. Simpson (eds), *Commons Debates, 1621*, iii, 184 and v. 148. William Martyn, *Youth's Instruction*, 93. *Gentleman's Magazine*, new series, xxxvi, 366.

45 William Trevethick, *A Sermon Preached at the Funeral of the Honourable Colonel Robert Rolle of Heanton Sachville in the County of Devon*, no pagination. PRO, Wills, PROB 11/204/58.

46 BL, Portland MSS, BL Loan 29/172. M. F. Keeler, *The Long Parliament, 1640–1641*, 141. PRO, Wills, PROB 11/194/142 and Chancery Proceedings, C.8/101/47.

47 BL, Harleian MSS 339, f. 37 and 646, ff. 96, 105, 145, 157. W. H. Coates (ed.), *The Journal of Sir Simonds D'Ewes*, 213.

48 BL, Egerton MSS 2646, f. 45. Guildford Muniment Room: Onslow MSS, 110/10/6.

49 Essex County Record Office: Hatfield Broad Oak MSS, D/DBa/02/ 1,16,17,23,25. A. P. Newton, *The Colonising Activities of the English Puritans*, 238–9. *HMC, Sixth Report*, Appendix, 71.

50 *Sir Edward Peyton*: PRO, Chancery Proceedings, C.3/397/118 and C.10/13/ 86; Chancery, Close Rolls, C.54/3215; and S.P.Dom., Committee for

Compounding, S.P.23/cxi/865,867 and cxcii/889, 891–2, 897. R. E. C. Waters, *Genealogical Memoirs of the Extinct Family of Chicheley*, i, 238. *Sir William Constable*: BL, Additional MSS 40,135, f. 23. PRO, Chancery, Close Rolls, C.54/2746 and S.P.Dom., Committee for Compounding, S.P.23/clxxxviii/328,360,456,462. Humberside County Record Office: Harford of Holme MSS, H1/22,32,37. Yorkshire Archaeological Society Library: MD 59/19.

51 BL, Portland MSS, BL Loan 29/27. Timothy Woodroffe, *A Religious Treatise upon Simeon's Song*, epistle dedicatory.

52 Hampshire Record Office: Jervoise of Herriard Park MSS, 44 M69/F9 and F10. *C.S.P.Dom., 1635–6*, 258.

53 PRO, Chancery Proceedings, C.8/42/83. BL, Harleian MSS 383, f. 61 and Additional MSS 15,520, f. 74.

54 William Perkins, *A Christian and Plaine Treatise of the Manner and Order of Predestination*, 23.

55 Epistle of St Paul to the Galatians, ch. 6, v. 10.

56 John Downame, *The Plea of the Poore*, epistle dedicatory and 7, 11–12, 35.

57 Richard Bernard, *The Ready Way to Good Works*, epistle dedicatory, and 87. See also W. K. Jordan, *Philanthropy in England 1480–1660*, ch. VI.

58 BL, Egerton MSS 2711, ff. 70, 74.

59 BL, Harleian MSS 227, ff. 8, 16. Harbottle Grimston, *A Christian New-Year's Gift*, 72,93. Gilbert Burnet, *History of his Own Time*, ii, 69–70.

60 Henry Scudder, *A Key of Heaven*, 251. Richard Sibbes, *The Bride's Longing for her Bride-Groomes Second Comming*, 124.

61 Samuel Clark, *The Lives of Sundry Eminent Persons*, pt ii, 108.

62 *C.S.P.Dom., 1629–31*, 403.

63 *Ibid.*, 476, 532.

64 John Brinsley, *The Preacher's Charge and People's Duty*, epistle dedicatory.

65 Clark, *op. cit.*, pt ii, 114. PRO, Wills, PROB 11/232/376.

66 Bartholomew Parsons, *Dorcas*, epistle dedicatory, and *A Sermon Preached at the Funerall of Sir Francis Pile Baronet*, 35, 36.

67 BL, Additional MSS 19,103, f. 271. Calamy, *Account*, 113–14.

68 PRO, Wills, PROB 11/244/101. Dorset County Record Office: Browne of Frampton MSS 7582. W. Notestein (ed.), *The Journal of Sir Simonds D'Ewes*, 98–9.

69 John Earle, *Micro-cosmographie*, 75. First Epistle of Paul to Timothy, ch. 2, v. 10.

70 Robert Harris, *Samuel's Funerall*, epistle dedicatory. Samuel Clark, *The Lives of Sundry Eminent Persons*, pt ii, 194.

71 William Dillingham, *A Sermon at the Funeral of the Lady Elizabeth Alston*, 41. John Bridges, *The History and Antiquities of Northamptonshire*, i, 200.

72 *Gentleman's Magazine*, new series, xxxvi, 366.

73 John Wilford, *Memorials and Characters*, 625.

74 John Downame, *The Plea of the Poore*, 38.

75 Richard Bernard, *The Ready Way to Good Works*, 412–13.

76 Sir Thomas Wroth, *The Abortive of an Idle Houre*, 23.

77 BL, Additional MSS 53,728, no pagination.

78 PRO, Wills, PROB 11/244/101 and 181/186.

79 PRO, Wills, PROB 11/179/49.

80 PRO, Wills, PROB 11/154/70. *C.S.P.Dom.*, *1637–8*, 610. *C.S.P.Dom.*, *1639*, 257. Essex County Record Office: Hatfield Broad Oak MSS, D/DBa/ L25.

Chapter 7   Social Attitudes and Relationships

1 Samuel Hieron, *All the Sermons of Samuel Hieron*, 30, 31.

2 PRO, Wills, PROB 11/123/9.

3 John Preston, *The Golden Scepter*, 113–14.

4 Robert Bolton, *Mr Bolton's Last and Learned Worke of The Foure Last Things*, 167.

5 Sir William Waller, *Divine Meditations*, 35–6. First epistle of Paul to the Corinthians, ch. 1, v. 26.

6 Samuel Ainsworth, *A Sermon Preached at the Funerall of that Religious Gentlewoman Mrs Dorothy Hanbury*, 17, 29.

7 Epistle of Paul to the Romans, ch. 12, v. 16.

8 BL, Portland MSS, BL Loan 29/78. Nathaniel Parkhurst, *The Faithful and Diligent Christian Described and Exemplified*, 147.

9 Richard Sibbes, *The Bride's Longing for her Bride-Groomes Second Comming*, 122–3.

10 Robert Bolton, *Mr Bolton's Last and Learned Worke of The Foure Last Things*, 166.

11 Bartholomew Parsons, *A Sermon Preached at the Funerall of Sir Francis Pile Baronet*, 35. John Hinckley, *A Sermon Preached at the Funerals of that Worthy Personage George Purefoy the Elder*, 27.

12 Seth Wood, *The Saint's Enterance into Peace and Rest by Death*, 16–17. Samuel Clark, *The Lives of Sundry Eminent Persons*, pt ii, 193, 195.

13 William Dillingham, *A Sermon at the Funeral of the Lady Elizabeth Alston*, 41.

14 BL, Harleian MSS 227, f. 11 and 379, f. 65.

15 *Hutchinson Memoirs*, 11, 208.

16 BL, Portland MSS, BL Loan 29/202, ff. 195–6.

17 Timothy Woodroffe, *A Religious Treatise upon Simeon's Song*, epistle dedicatory. Sir James Harrington, *A Holy Oyl*, 127. G.E.C. (ed.), *Complete Baronetage*, i, 53.

18 *Hutchinson Memoirs*, 11.

19 G.E.C. (ed.), *Complete Baronetage*, i, 1, 28, 44.

20 BL, Harleian MSS 384, f. 21 and 386, f. 191, and Cotton Charter, xvi, 13, f. 15. G.E.C. (ed.), *Complete Baronetage*, ii, 103.

21 BL, Harleian MSS 7033, f. 247.

22 PRO, Wills, PROB 11/179/49 and 145/29.

23 N. E. McClure (ed.), *The Letters of John Chamberlain*, i, 138.

24 Thomas Wotton, *The English Baronetage*, ii, 153. PRO, Chancery, Entry Books of Decrees and Orders, C.33/clxxix/f.38.

25 W. H. Coates, (ed.), *The Journal of Sir Simonds D'Ewes*, 6. BL, Harleian MSS, 98, f. 20.

26 John Aubrey, *The Natural History and Antiquities of the County of Surrey*, iii, 310–11. Guildford Muniment Room: Loseley MSS, LM1654, f. 93.

27 PRO, Wills, PROB 11/123/9.

28 J. J. Muskett, *Suffolk Manorial Families*, i, 283.

29 *Suffolk's Tears*, epistle dedicatory addressed to Lady Jane Barnardiston by Samuel Fairclough the younger. PRO, Wills, PROB 11/232/376.

30 Richard Baxter, *The Autobiography of Richard Baxter* (ed. J. M. L. Thomas), 82–3.

31 Robert Harris, *Samuel's Funerall*, dedication to the godly reader. John Hinckley, *A Sermon Preached at the Funerals of that Worthy Personage George Purefoy the Elder*, 35.

32 This work appeared in 1633 in a volume entitled *Three Treatises*.

33 John Barlow, *The True Guide to Glory*, 48.

34 John Clarke, *Holy Incense for the Censers of the Saints*, epistle dedicatory.

35 Richard Stock, *A Stock of Divine Knowledge*, epistle dedicatory. H. I. Longden, *Northamptonshire and Rutland Clergy from 1500*, iii, 283.

36 BL, Egerton MSS 2644, ff. 203, 240; 2645, ff. 142–3, 224, 281; 2646, ff. 104, 163–4; 2650, ff. 274, 333. *Essex Archaeological Society Transactions*, new series, ii, 33. R. A. Marchant, *The Puritans and the Church Courts in the Diocese of York 1560–1642*, 96–102.

37 A. G. Matthews, *Calamy Revised*, 412.

38 PRO, Institution Books, Series A, ii, f. 6. BL, Additional MSS 35,331, f. 64.

39 BL, Egerton MSS 2643, ff. 1, 3 and 2650, f. 318.

40 William Trevethick, *A Sermon Preached at the Funeral of the Honourable Colonel Robert Rolle of Heanton Sachville in the County of Devon*, epistle dedicatory. Samuel Clark, *The Lives of Thirty-Two English Divines*, 173.

41 Bolton, *op. cit.*, 176–7.

42 Sir William Waller, *Divine Meditations*, 137–40, 143, 144.

43 *Gentleman's Magazine*, new series, xxxvi, 373.

44 BL, Harleian MSS 3364, f. 9. *C.S.P.Dom.*, *1619–23*, 514–15.

45 Sir James Harrington, *Horae Consecratae*, 356.

46 PRO, Chancery Proceedings, C.8/89/160.

47 J. R. Tanner (ed.), *Constitutional Documents of the Reign of James I 1603–1625*, 56.

48 Sir William Waller, *Divine Meditations*, 131–2.

49 BL, Harleian MSS 646, f. 47 and Additional MSS 33,147, ff. 6, 16, 37. Sir Simonds D'Ewes, *The Diary of Sir Simonds D'Ewes* (ed. Elizabeth Bourcier), 81.

50 *C.S.P.Dom., 1636–7*, 223. BL, Egerton MSS 2716, f. 245.

51 William Perkins, *The Workes*, ii, 163–4.

52 William Trevethick, *A Sermon preached at the Funeral of the Honourable Colonel Robert Rolle of Heanton Sachville in the County of Devon*, epistle dedicatory. William Martyn, *Youth's Instruction*, 92–3.

53 Bartholomew Parsons, *A Sermon Preached at the Funerall of Sir Francis Pile Baronet*, 36.

54 BL, Harleian MSS 646, ff. 52, 105.

55 BL, Additional MSS 37,343, f. 144. *Essex Archaeological Society Transactions*, new series, xii, 214.

56 A. Young, *Chronicles of the First Planters of the Colony of Massachusetts Bay, 1623–1636*, 522–6.

57 BL, Portland MSS, BL Loan 29/124.

58 Robert Bolton, *Mr Bolton's Last and Learned Worke of The Foure Last Things*, biographical account, no pagination, and *A Discourse about the State of True Happinesse*, 73–4.

59 Sir James Harrington, *Horae Consecratae*, 345–7, 368, 371.

60 Thomas May, *The History of the Parliament of England*, 16. Sir Edward Peyton, *The Divine Catastrophe of the Kingly Family of the House of Stuarts*, 47.

61 *Essex Archaeological Society Transactions*, new series, xii, 214. J. A. Manning (ed.), *Memoirs of Sir Benjamin Rudyerd*, 30. William Earl of Pembroke, *Poems*, 46.

62 See below, 171.

63 *Library*, fourth series, xviii, 440. BL, Portland MSS, BL Loan 29/202, between ff. 230 and 231.

64 William Perkins, *The Workes*, ii, 163. For a general account see P. A. Scholes, *The Puritans and Music*.

65 *Chetham Society*, xxxv, 185, 187, 191, 225 and xli, 302, 305. A. B. Grosart (ed.), *The Letter-Book of Sir John Eliot*, 127.

68 *Essex Archaeological Society Transactions*, new series, xii, 210, 211, 214, 217.

67 Norfolk Record Office: Kimberley MSS, Box 14, 159. PRO, Wills, PROB 11/278/354.

68 BL, Additional MSS 53,726, ff. 8, 9, 16, 45.

69 William Martyn, *Youth's Instruction*, 95–6.

70 Edmund Rudyerd, *The Thunderbolt of God's Wrath*, epistle dedicatory and 74–6.

71 *Camden Society*, xli, 15. BL, Harleian MSS 646, f. 105. Harbottle Grimston, *A Christian New-Year's Gift*, 105.
72 BL, Harleian MSS 193, *The Whole Booke of Psalmes* collected into English metre by Thomas Sternhold, John Hopkins and others. This was published in 1628.

Chapter 8 Godliness Under Threat

1 See Paul A. Welsby, *George Abbot the Unwanted Archbishop*, 119, 121, 136–7.
2 BL, Harleian MSS 646, f. 61.
3 Clarendon, i, 119. Peter Heylyn, *History of the Presbyterians*, 383–4. Dr Williams's Library: Morrice MSS, G, 639.
4 R. A. Marchant, *The Puritans and the Church Courts in the Diocese of York 1560–1642*, 29, 166 and *The Church under the Law*, 132.
5 Benjamin Brook, *The Lives of the Puritans*, ii, 292. BL, Additional MSS 4460, f. 4. Arthur Onslow, *The Life of Dr George Abbot, Lord Archbishop of Canterbury*, 151. John Hacket, *Scrinia Reserata*, 43. Rushworth, i, 420–1.
6 Thomas Fuller, *The Church-History of Britain*, xi, 144.
7 Thomas Birch (ed.), *The Court and Times of James I*, ii, 319–20. Sir Simonds D'Ewes, *The Diary of Sir Simonds D'Ewes* (ed. Elizabeth Bourcier), 181–2.
8 J. R. Tanner (ed.), *Constitutional Documents of the Reign of James I 1603–1625*, 80–2. William Pemble, *Vindiciae Gratiae*, epistle dedicatory.
9 *Surtees Society*, lii, 22.
10 *Camden Society*, xli, 84. *C.J.*, i, 804. For a discussion of the significance of the growth of Arminianism see Nicholas Tyacke, 'Puritanism, Arminianism and Counter-Revolution' in *Origins of the English Civil War* (ed. Conrad Russell), 119–43.
11 Bodleian: Tanner MSS 72, f. 61.
12 *C.J.*, i, 817. Sir Edward Peyton, *The Divine Catastrophe of the Kingly Family of the House of Stuarts*, 3.
13 *C.J.*, i, 845. Rushworth, i, 209–12.
14 Thomas Fuller, *The Church-History of Britain*, xi, 109, 131.
15 Rushworth, i, 412–13.
16 *Camden Society*, xli, 93.
17 Thomas Birch (ed.), *The Court and Times of Charles the First*, i, 105.
18 Sir Edward Peyton, *The Divine Catastrophe of the Kingly Family of the House of Stuarts*, 42–3, 60, 117. BL, Harleian MSS 3364, ff. 9, 11, 15, 25, 32.
19 *Hutchinson Memoirs*, 42, 46.
20 Sir Simonds D'Ewes, *The Diary of Sir Simonds D'Ewes* (ed. Elizabeth Bourcier), 76, 147. BL, Harleian MSS 383, f. 57.

21 BL, Additional MSS 53,726, f. 32.

22 Thomas Birch (ed.), *The Court and Times of Charles the First*, i, 161–2, 165, 177, 188, 190, 243, 249. *Acts of the Privy Council, 1627*, 345, 347. PRO, Wills, PROB 11/154/70. Essex County Record Office: Hatfield Broad Oak MSS, D/DBa/F43.

23 Seth Wood, *The Saint's Enterance into Peace and Rest by Death*, 22.

24 *A Remonstrance of the True State of the Kingdom*, 10. (BL, Thomason Tracts, E. 181(2)).

25 Rushworth, i, 431–3.

26 BL, Harleian MSS 383, ff. 55–6 and 646, f. 118; and Portland MSS, BL Loan 29/27.

27 *C.J.*, i, 873. Dr Williams's Library: Morrice MSS, G, f. 793.

28 BL, Harleian MSS 384, f. 188. Rushworth, i, 620–2.

29 *C.J.*, i, 922. BL, Harleian MSS 646, f. 118.

30 W. Notestein and F. H. Relf (ed.), *Commons Debates for 1629*, 18–19, 116. *C.J.*, i, 922–3. S. R. Gardiner (ed.), *The Constitutional Documents of the Puritan Revolution, 1625–1660*, 78–82.

31 BL, Egerton MSS 2645, ff. 13, 21.

32 BL, Harleian MSS 646, f. 118.

33 William Prynne, *Canterburies Doome*, 164–5.

34 Prynne, *op. cit.*, 252, 267, 287. BL, Additional MSS 35,331, f. 36.

35 Bodleian: Tanner MSS 71, ff. 68, 109. BL, Harleian MSS 646, f. 162.

36 S. R. Gardiner (ed.), *The Constitutional Documents of the Puritan Revolution, 1625–1660*, 138.

37 See, for example, John Harrington's record of a sermon in BL, Egerton MSS 2711, f. 6.

38 A. G. Watson, *The Library of Sir Simonds D'Ewes*, 120, 165, 166, 185. *Library*, fourth series, xviii, 434, 437, 442. PRO, S.P.Dom., Charles I, S.P.16/ccclxxxvii/79.

39 PRO, Wills, PROB 11/179/49.

40 William Prynne, *Canterburies Doome*, 368–70, 383.

41 BL, Additional MSS 35,331, f. 45. *V.C.H., Essex*, ii, 51–3.

42 John Rogers, *The Doctrine of Faith*, epistle dedicatory.

43 BL, Egerton MSS 2645, ff. 75, 77. Bodleian: Tanner MSS 68, ff. 30, 49.

44 A. Young, *Chronicles of the First Planters of the Colony of Massachusetts Bay, 1623–1636*, 522–6. PRO, Institution Books, Series A, i, f. 45 and S.P.Dom., Charles I, S.P.16/ccxxxix/53 and cccli/100. *V.C.H., Essex*, ii, 52. Essex County Record Office: Hatfield Broad Oak MSS, D/DBa/F5/1 and 2.

45 William Prynne, *Canterburies Doome*, 374, 376. BL, Harleian MSS 384, f. 189. Lambeth Palace Library: Register Laud, i, ff. 289–90.

46 Thomas May, *The History of the Parliament of England*, 39.

47 R. A. Marchant, *The Church under the Law*, 131 and *The Puritans and the Church Courts in the Diocese of York 1560–1642*, 185–6.

48 PRO, S.P.Dom., Charles I, S.P.16/cclxxiv/12. *C.S.P.Dom., 1634–5*, 250.

49 PRO, S.P.Dom., Charles I, S.P.16/dxxxv/26. John Nichols, *The History and Antiquities of the County of Leicester*, ii, pt i, 123, 125–6.

50 *C.S.P.Dom., 1634–5*, 51, 110, 117, 121. PRO, S.P.Dom., Charles I, S.P.16/cclxi/55,56.

51 BL, Additional MSS 36,776, ff. 72, 73. PRO, Institution Books, Series A, iii, f. 45 and S.P.Dom., Charles I, S.P.16/cclxxiv/12 and ccclxxxii/68. *Bedfordshire Notes and Queries*, ii, 313, 314 and iii, 7. *C.S.P.Dom., 1637–8*, 550. *C.S.P.Dom., 1641–3*, 31. W. A. Shaw, *A History of the English Church, 1640–1660*, ii, 298. *C.J.*, ii, 282. Thomas Fuller, *The Church-History of Britain*, x, 49–50. At this time Haynes was commonly spelt 'Hawnes'.

52 Canon 71. Statutes 21 Henry VIII, cap. xiii; 25 Henry VIII, cap. xvi; and 33 Henry VIII, cap. xxviii.

53 Thomas Gataker, *Discours Apologetical*, 46–7.

54 William Laud, *The Works*, v, 308. Lambeth Palace Library: Register Laud, i, 217. BL, Additional MSS 4275, f. 166.

55 William Prynne, *Canterburies Doome*, 383.

56 Lambeth Palace Library: Register Laud, i, f. 255.

57 PRO, S.P.Dom., Charles I, S.P.16/cccxlv/85. Lambeth Palace Library: MS 943, f. 295.

58 Lambeth Palace Library: MS 943, f. 293. See above, 111–12.

59 *Camden Society*, lxxiv, 185. PRO, S.P.Dom., Charles I, S.P.16/dxxxv/26.

60 BL, Egerton MSS 2646, f. 104; 2648, f. 84; and 2650, f. 333. PRO, Institution Books, Series A, i, f. 45. R. A. Marchant, *The Puritans and the Church Courts in the Diocese of York 1560–1642*, 100.

61 PRO, S.P.Dom., Charles I, S.P.16/cccli/100 and Wills, PROB 11/256/389. Benjamin Brook, *The Lives of the Puritans*, iii, 419–22 and 477–82. T. W. Davids, *Annals of Evangelical Nonconformity in the County of Essex*, 167–8. Harold Smith, *The Ecclesiastical History of Essex under the Long Parliament and Commonwealth*, 27.

62 *Life and Death of Mr Henry Jessey*, 4–7. *Massachusetts Historical Society Collections*, fourth series, vi, 459. Marchant, *op. cit.*, 123.

63 Thomas Cawton the younger, *The Life and Death of that Holy and Reverend Man of God Mr Thomas Cawton*, 14–16.

64 PRO, S.P.Dom., Charles I, S.P.16/cdxxxiv/ff.78,79,222. Richard Bernard, *Iosuah's Resolution for the Well Ordering of his Household*, epistle dedicatory.

Chapter 9   Godly Patronage

1 Canon 36.

2 BL, Egerton MSS 784, f. 90. PRO, Institution Books, Series A, ii, f. 74.

3 For donative cures see Patrick Collinson, *The Elizabethan Puritan Movement*, 339–41.

4 John Hart, *Trodden Down Strength, by the God of Strength*, 117–18. Camden Society, new series, vi, 71.

5 Lambeth Palace Library: MS 943, ff. 333–5. *C.S.P.Dom., 1631–3*, 383–4. Dr Williams's Library: Morrice MSS, J, no pagination.

6 BL, Egerton MSS 2645, ff. 269, 271. PRO, S.P.Dom., Charles I, S.P.16/cccxlv/85.

7 Clarendon, i, 128.

8 Joseph Hall, *The Works*, i, autobiographical account, xxxv. Cf. Thomas Edwards, *Gangraena*, 95–6.

9 Thomas May, *The History of the Parliament of England*, 55. *Life and Death of Mr Henry Jessey*, 5. See also Clive Holmes, *The Eastern Association in the Civil War*, 17–19, 34.

10 *Suffolk in the XVIIth Century. The Breviary of Suffolk by Robert Reyce, 1618*, 21, 59.

11 Clarendon, i, 137. BL, Harleian MSS 646, f. 171. See also Harleian MSS 7001, f. 139.

12 Lambeth Palace Library: Register Laud, i, f. 255.

13 *Massachusetts Historical Society Collections*, fourth series, vi, 411. BL, Harleian MSS 646, f. 171 and Thomason Tracts, E. 199(2).

14 BL, Harleian MSS 379, f. 58.

15 BL, Additional MSS 15,520, f. 154. PRO, Institution Books, Series A, iii, ff. 158, 238, 239, 240. Bodleian: Tanner MSS 178, ff. 81, 82.

16 Calamy, *Account*, 477–8. John Brinsley, *The Glorie of the Latter Temple Greater Then of the Former* and *The Preacher's Charge and People's Duty*, epistle dedicatory.

17 BL, Portland MSS, BL Loan 29/172, f. 42. *C.S.P.Dom., 1640–1*, 520–1. PRO, Institution Books, Series A, iii, ff. 158, 240.

18 Bodleian: Tanner MSS 68, ff. 88, 96, 98, 99. *C.S.P.Dom., 1635–6*, 530–1.

19 Bodleian: Tanner MSS 68, f. 216 and 314, f. 183. PRO, Institution Books, Series A, iii, f. 247.

20 PRO, Institution Books, Series A, iii, ff. 227, 228. *Lincoln Record Society*, xxiii, 352. Anthony Wood, *Fasti Oxonienses*, i, 363. BL, Harleian MSS 646, f. 73.

21 Samuel Clark, *The Lives of Sundry Eminent Persons*, pt i, 160–3, 173 and pt ii, 113. Calamy, *Account*, 635–40. Dr Williams's Library: Morrice MSS, J, no pagination. PRO, Institution Books, Series A, iii, f. 227.

22 Clark, *op. cit.*, pt i, 157, 163–5, 170. PRO, Wills, PROB 11/232/376.
23 Bodleian: Tanner MSS 68, f. 200; 178, f. 61; 220, ff. 52–3; 314, ff. 120, 122, 189. PRO, Institution Books, Series A, iii, f. 228. *Al. Cant.*, iii, 290. *Suffolk's Tears*, 46. BL, Harleian MSS 384, f. 27. *C.J.*, ii, 73.
24 D. E. Smith, *Assington Through the Centuries*, 6. Benjamin Brook, *The Lives of the Puritans*, iii, 238–41. PRO, S.P.Dom., Charles I, S.P.16/ccxciii/128 and Institution Books, Series A, iii, f. 251. Lambeth Palace Library: Register Laud, i, f. 137. A. G. Matthews, *Calamy Revised*, 505. Bodleian: Tanner MSS 68, f. 200 and 314, ff. 120, 122, 137, 191. *Al. Cant.*, ii, 275; iii, 479; iv, 319.
25 S. B. Babbage, *Puritanism and Richard Bancroft*, 206–8. W. Notestein, F. H. Relf and H. Simpson (eds), *Commons Debates, 1621*, ii, 368, 370; iii, 260, 265; iv, 346–7; v, 167; vii, 606–8.
26 Dr Williams's Library: Morrice MSS, I, 373(14).
27 Samuel Clark, *The Lives of Thirty-Two English Divines*, 170–1. Robert Bolton, *Mr Bolton's Last and Learned Worke of The Foure Last Things*, biographical account by Edward Bagshawe, no pagination.
28 PRO, Court of Wards, Feodaries' Surveys, Wards 5/30 and Decrees, Wards 9/xcviii, f. 70. H. I. Longden, *Northamptonshire and Rutland Clergy*, xv, 111. *Al. Cant.*, iii, 359.
29 PRO, Institution Books, Series A, iii, f. 17. Longden, *op. cit.*, vii, 19. Anthony Tuckney, *Death Disarmed*, 51, 58. Lambeth Palace Library: Commonwealth Surveys, COMM XIIa/20,15.
30 PRO,S.P.Dom.,Charles I,S.P.16/cccviii/52 and S.P.16/cdlxvi/24.
31 PRO,Chancery Proceedings,C.10/175/118.
32 Samuel Clark, *The Lives of Thirty-Two English Divines*, 170. John Dod and Robert Cleaver, *A Plaine and Familiar Exposition of the Fifteenth, Sixteenth and Seventeenth Chapters of the Proverbs of Salomon*, epistle dedicatory.
33 Lambeth Palace Library: Commonwealth Surveys, COMM XIIa/20,31.
34 Benjamin Brook, *The Lives of the Puritans*, iii, 2. *C.S.P.Dom., 1611–18*, 92, 254.
35 Longden, *op. cit.*, xv, 149.
36 *C.S.P.Dom., 1634–5*, 601.
37 John Walker, *Sufferings of the Clergy*, pt i, 91.
38 PRO, S.P.Dom., Charles I, S.P.16/ccxciii/128.
39 Longden, *op. cit.*, xiii, 15 and xv, 168–9. PRO, S.P.Dom., Charles I, S.P.16/cccviii/52. Dr Williams's Library: Morrice MSS, I, 373(14).
40 Dr Williams's Library: Morrice MSS, I, 373(14).
41 Samuel Clark, *The Lives of Thirty-Two English Divines*, 171.
42 PRO,S.P.Dom.,Charles I,S.P.16/ccxciii/128 and S.P.16/cccviii/52.
43 John Dod, *A Plaine and Familiar Exposition on the Lord's Prayer*, epistle dedicatory.

44 PRO, Institution Books, Series A, iii, f. 44. Longden, *op. cit.*, xv, 85. *Camden Miscellany*, third series, xi, 55. Barbara Shapiro, *John Wilkins, 1614–1672*, 14, 16–17, 20.

45 Calamy, *Account*, 2, 120–1, 746. J. W. Ryland, *Records of Wroxall Abbey and Manor*, intro., lviii-lxi, lxiv-lxv, 190, and *The Parish Registers of Wroxall*, 7, 8. William Laud, *The Works*, v, 356–7. William Cooke, *A Learned and Full Answer to a Treatise Intituled, The Vanity of Childish Baptisme*, epistle dedicatory by the editor, Francis Woodcock.

46 J. W. F. Hill, *Tudor and Stuart Lincoln*, 112, 116.

47 *Lincoln Record Society*, xxiii, intro., civ, 230, 233, 304, 310, 320, 329, 330, 335, 340, 352, 356, 357, 363.

48 PRO, Institution Books, Series A, iii, ff. 136, 139. Benjamin Brook, *The Lives of the Puritans*, iii, 60–2. *Al. Cant.*, i, 43, 44. W. M. Palmer, *Episcopal Visitation Returns for Cambridgeshire*, 31. Bodleian: Tanner MSS 68, ff. 49, 50, 173 and 314, f. 122.

49 Dr Williams's Library: Morrice MSS, I, 697(6), (8), (10), (12), (14). Seth Wood, *The Saint's Enterance into Peace and Rest by Death*, 17–20. PRO, Chancery, Inquisitions *Post Mortem*, James I, C.142/cccxciv/73. *Lincoln Record Society*, xxiii, intro., cxv, 301, 319, 363, 365–8.

50 PRO, Institution Books, Series A, iii, ff. 109, 113. Seth Wood, *op. cit.*, 20–1. Calamy, *Account*, 440. Hill, *op. cit.*, 121.

51 Thomas Froysell, *The Beloved Disciple*, 99–101.

52 BL, Lansdowne MSS 721, ff. 90, 91, 93–5, 107, 108, 112, 113, 115, 130. Thomas Pierson, *Excellent Encouragements against Afflictions*, preface by Edmund Calamy. *HMC, Fourteenth Report*, Appendix, pt ii, 6–7, 25.

53 BL, Portland MSS, BL Loan 29/27 and 172, ff. 67, 69. Longden, *op. cit.*, iv, 239.

54 BL, Portland MSS, BL Loan 29/172, ff. 77, 79.

55 *Shropshire Archaeological and Natural History Society Transactions*, third series, v. 359. BL, Lansdowne MSS 721, f. 146. Calamy, *Account*, 540.

56 i.e. the Act of Uniformity, 1559.

57 BL, Portland MSS, BL Loan 29/119.

58 BL, Portland MSS, BL Loan 29/172, f. 87. R. A. Marchant, *The Puritans and the Church Courts in the Diocese of York 1560–1642*, 264, 285–8, 298. *Shropshire Archaeological and Natural History Society Transactions*, third series, v 359.

59 BL, Portland MSS, BL Loan 29/123.

60 For Richard Symonds see above, 78.

61 *C.S.P.Dom.*, *1637–8*, 249. BL, Portland MSS, BL Loan 29/172, ff. 216, 308, 309.

62 *HMC, Fourteenth Report*, Appendix, pt ii, 73.

63 See Frances Rose-Troup, *John White the Patriarch of Dorchester*.

64 BL, Egerton MSS 784, f. 110 and Additional MSS 35,331, f. 64. PRO,

Institution Books, Series A, ii, ff. 12, 45 and S.P.Dom., Charles I, S.P.16/cdvi/97. *C.S.P.Dom., 1633–4*, 581. *C.S.P.Dom., 1635*, 435, 459, 500. Dorset County Record Office: P54/REI, parish register of Frampton, no pagination.

65 PRO, Institution Books, Series A, ii, ff. 14, 17, 22. W. D. Christie (ed.), *Memoirs, Letters and Speeches of Anthony Ashley Cooper, First Earl of Shaftesbury*, 28–9.

66 Calamy, *Account*, 281–2. Lambeth Palace Library: Commonwealth Surveys, COMM XIIa/5, ff. 399–400. Dorset County Record Office: Lane MSS, D60/T103,3. *C.S.P.Dom., 1634–5*, 182. BL, Egerton MSS 784, f. 105.

67 BL, Egerton MSS 784, f. 107 and Lansdowne MSS 459, f. 27. Calamy, *Account*, 146.

68 Anthony Wood, *Athenae Oxonienses*, iii, 404–5.

69 Frances Rose-Troup, *John White the Patriarch of Dorchester*, 61–3, 454. John Hutchins, *The History and Antiquities of the County of Dorset*, iii, 507, 514. PRO, Institution Books, Series A, ii, f. 17. *Lincoln Record Society*, xxiii, 366.

70 See above, 172.

71 PRO, Institution Books, Series A, ii, f. 98 and v, Hampshire, 16. BL, Egerton MSS 2645, ff. 112, 196, 219, 339 and Additional MSS 35,331, f. 72. Anthony Wood, *op. cit.*, iii, 151, J. Peile (ed.) *Biographical Register of Christ's College, 1505–1905*, i, 270. *DNB* (Daniel Dike, Jeremiah Dike and his son Daniel).

Chapter 10   Despair and Hope

1 Clarendon, i, 93.

2 PRO, S.P.Dom., Charles I, S.P.16/cclxxiii/13. John Stoughton, *The Heavenly Conversation and the Naturall Man's Condition*, 88.

3 J. T. Rutt (ed.), *Diary of Thomas Burton*, iii, 89–90.

4 *C.S.P.Dom., 1631–3*, 445–6. *C.S.P.Dom., 1634–5*, 494, 532. *C.S.P.Dom., 1635*, 192, 199, 215, 221, 604. *C.S.P.Dom., 1641–3*, 547. William Laud, *The Works*, iv, 184.

5 *C.S.P.Dom., 1634–5*, 52, 125. *C.S.P.Dom., 1635–6*, 108, 112, 118, 126. *C.S.P.Dom., 1639–40*, 213, 275. *C.S.P.Dom., 1640*, 380, 383, 385, 392, 405, 409, 414, 416, 419, 420, 424, 429. *C.S.P.Dom., 1640–1*, 383, 384, 389, 392, 395. *C.S.P.Dom., Addenda, 1625–1649*, 512. W. Notestein (ed.), *The Journal of Sir Simonds D'Ewes*, 11–12. For Sir Richard Strode and Sir Henry Rosewell see above, 161, 167–8.

6 William Prynne, *Canterburies Doome*, 524–6. Sir Anthony Hungerford, *The Advise of a Sonne Professing the Religion Established in the Present Church of England to his Deare Mother a Roman Catholike*.

7 BL, Portland MSS, BL Loan 29/27, 122, 124. Thomas Froysell, *The Beloved Disciple*, 105.

8 Sir Simonds D'Ewes, *The Primitive Practise for Preserving Truth*, 1.

9 BL, Harleian MSS 646, f. 167.

10 *C.S.P.Dom., 1635–6*, 288–9, 348–9, 361, 395. *C.S.P.Dom., 1636–7*, 118, 155, 197, 231, 391.

11 *C.S.P.Dom., 1635*, 377–8. Frances Rose-Troup, *John White the Patriarch of Dorchester*, 297. PRO, Chancery, Crown Office Docquet Books, C.231/v/ 217.

12 *Massachusetts Historical Society Collections*, fourth series, vi, 546, 552, 561.

13 BL, Portland MSS, BL Loan 29/27 and Harleian MSS 646, f. 161.

14 BL, Thomason Tracts, E.200(9).

15 BL, Portland MSS, BL Loan 29/172, f. 105.

16 Thomas Froysell, *The Beloved Disciple*, 102, 107. BL, Portland MSS, BL Loan 29/79.

17 *HMC, Fourteenth Report*, Appendix, pt ii, 25.

18 *C.S.P.Dom., 1635–6*, 385.

19 *C.S.P.Dom., 1631–3*, 528–9.

20 Thomas Froysell, *The Beloved Disciple*, 105–6.

21 *C.S.P.Dom., 1641–3*, 549–50. William Laud, *The Works*, iv, 171.

22 Lambeth Palace Library: Register Laud, i, f. 215 and MS 943, f. 295. *C.S.P.Dom., 1639–40*, 386–7. *C.S.P.Dom., 1640*, 398. Anthony S. Fletcher, *A County Community in Peace and War: Sussex 1600–1660*, 93, 241.

23 Bedfordshire County Record Office: St John of Bletsoe MSS, DDJ 1361. *C.S.P.Dom., 1639*, 442.

24 *Complete Prose Works of John Milton*, i, 585.

25 *Massachusetts Historical Society Collections*, fourth series, vi, 546. *Al. Cant.*, i, 403; ii, 403; iv, 333, 360–1, 429.

26 BL, Portland MSS, BL Loan 29/119.

27 Robert E. Moody (ed.), *The Saltonstall Papers, 1607–1815*, i, 10–11, 128–9.

28 William Knowler (ed.), *The Earl of Strafforde's Letters and Dispatches*, i, 463. George Sikes, *The Life and Death of Sir Henry Vane*, 8.

29 *Massachusetts Historical Society Collections*, fourth series, vi, 43, 364. A. P. Newton, *The Colonising Activities of the English Puritans*, 177–80, 185.

30 *Massachusetts Historical Society Collections*, fourth series, vii, 163–9. J. T. Cliffe, *The Yorkshire Gentry from the Reformation to the Civil War*, 306–8.

31 BL, Harleian MSS 385, f. 92; 388, ff. 186, 191; 646, f. 172.

32 For a detailed account of the Providence Island Company see A. P. Newton, *The Colonising Activities of the English Puritans*.

33 PRO, Colonial Entry Books, Bahamas, C.O.124/ii/ff. 1, 2, 4, 7, 38, 141. Essex County Record Office: Hatfield Broad Oak MSS, D/DBa/02/1, 5, 6, 10, 23, 25.

34 BL, Harleian MSS 287, f. 265 and 386, ff. 156, 157. Newton, *op. cit.*, 244–6.

35 BL, Harleian MSS 593, f. 139.

36 R. A. Marchant, *The Puritans and the Church Courts in the Diocese of York 1560–1642*, 100.

37 *C.S.P., Colonial Series: America and the West Indies, 1574–1660*, 262–4. See above, 136.

38 BL, Additional MSS 37,343, f. 160.

39 BL, Additional MSS 48,016, f. 11. See Bryan W. Ball, *A Great Expectation. Eschatological Thought in English Protestantism to 1660*. Paul Christianson, *Reformers and Babylon: English Apocalyptic Visions from the Reformation to the Eve of the Civil War*, and Katharine R. Firth, *The Apocalyptic Tradition in Reformation Britain 1530–1645*.

40 BL, Portland MSS, BL Loan 29/202 (between ff. 230 and 231). B. S. Capp, *The Fifth Monarchy Men*, 29–30, 49. John F. Wilson, *The Pulpit in Parliament*, 211–12. *The English Revolution. I. Fast Sermons to Parliament*, xii, 7–46 (Gower's sermon was entitled 'Things Now-a-doing').

41 J. Peile (ed.), *Biographical Register of Christ's College*, i, 212. Capp, *op. cit.*, 30. Joseph Mede, *The Works*, biographical account, II, XI, and 581.

42 Robert Parker, *The Mystery of the Vialls Opened*, 14.

43 See, for example, the epistle dedicatory addressed to Sir Anthony and his wife by Thomas Cawton the younger in *The Life and Death of that Reverend Man of God Mr Thomas Cawton*.

44 Calamy, *Continuation*, ii, 787. *Al. Cant.*, iv, 169. Capp, *op. cit.*, 264.

45 John Tillinghurst, *Mr Tillinghast's Eight Last Sermons*, preface by Christopher Feake. O. Manning and W. Bray, *History and Antiquities of Surrey*, ii, 238. Benjamin Brook, *The Lives of the Puritans*, iii, 308–11. Capp, *op. cit.*, 52, 176–7, 179, 248–9. Sir Samuel Owfield presented Edward Shove to the living of Elsham in 1630 and Samuel Oates in 1641 (PRO, Institution Books, Series A, iii, f. 97).

46 Thomas Goodwin, *The Works*, ii, 190. John Archer, *The Personall Reign of Christ upon Earth*, 47, 53–5. Wilson, *op. cit.*, 224. Capp, *op. cit.*, 30–1, 79, 240. Ball, *op. cit.*, 87, 119, 165.

47 Sir Henry Vane, *Two Treatises*, 53, 69, 71, 75, 76, 78, 82. For further evidence of his millenarian views see also *The Retired Man's Meditations* and *A Pilgrimage into the Land of Promise*.

48 Sir James Harrington, *Noah's Dove*, 2–3 and *A Holy Oyl*, 243–4.

49 BL, Egerton MSS 2711, f. 24.

50 *Camden Society*, lviii, 29, 41. John Napier, *A Plaine Discovery of the Whole Revelation of St John*, 11. *HMC, Fourteenth Report*, Appendix, pt ii, 57.

51 *Library*, fourth series, xviii, 444.

52 A. G. Watson, *The Library of Sir Simonds D'Ewes*, 166, 197. Ball, *op. cit.*, 58, 59, 74, 80, 83, 117. Thomas Fuller, *The Church-History of Britain*, x,

49–50. BL, Lansdowne MSS 721, ff. 90–1 and Harleian MSS 374, ff. 69–71.

53 Thomas Goodwin, *A Fair Prospect*, epistle dedicatory.

54 Sir Edward Peyton, *The Divine Catastrophe of the Kingly Family of the House of Stuarts*, 6–7, 125.

55 Rushworth, iii, 910–15.

56 PRO, Chancery Crown Office Docket Books, C.231/v/215, 219, 222, 223, 229, 237, 251, 255, 275, 352.

57 *Ibid*, 193, 213, 217, 237, 255, 266, 311, 319, 349, 356, 360, 373. PRO, S.P.Dom., Charles I, S.P.16/cdv. Cf. T. G. Barnes, *Somerset 1625–1640*, 303–6.

58 PRO, Chancery, Petty Bag Office, Sheriffs' Rolls, C.227/595/22 and S.P.Dom., Charles I, S.P.16/cdxxxii/33, 34.

59 BL, Harleian MSS 379, ff. 60, 61 and 386, f. 156.

Chapter 11   Doing God's Work

1 *C.S.P.Dom., 1639–40*, 580–3.

2 John Nalson, *An Impartial Collection of the Great Affairs of State*, i, 279–80.

3 *Massachusetts Historical Society Collections*, fourth series, vi, 548.

4 BL, Portland MSS, BL Loan 29/74 and 172, between ff. 252 and 253, and 254.

5 BL, Portland MSS, BL Loan 29/172, ff. 251–2.

6 See, for example, *Camden Fourth Series*, xix, *Proceedings of the Short Parliament of 1640*.

7 *Ibid.*, 237.

8 *Massachusetts Historical Society Collections*, fourth series, vi, 565.

9 BL, Harleian MSS 7657, f. 216. PRO, S.P.Dom., Charles I, S.P.16/cdlix/21.

10 BL, Harleian MSS 98, ff. 150–1 and Additional MSS 25,277, ff. 21–48.

11 PRO, S.P.Dom., Charles I, S.P.16/cdlvii/28 and cdlix/55.

12 BL, Harleian MSS 382, f. 88.

13 Thomas Fuller, *The Church-History of Britain*, xi, 169–70. BL, Additional MSS 35,331, f. 77 and Harleian MSS 164, f. 217.

14 BL, Harleian MSS 384, f. 66. Thomas Brightman, *The Workes*, 611. See also the comment made by John Pym to Edward Hyde as recorded in Clarendon, i, 222. St Matthew, ch. 3, v. 10 may have been the scriptural source for such language: 'And now also the axe is laid unto the root of the trees: therefore every tree which bringeth not forth good fruit is hewn down and cast into the fire.'

15 Northamptonshire Record Office: Dryden MSS, D(CA) 906, f. 2. BL, Harleian MSS 384, f. 90 and Portland MSS, BL Loan 29/173, ff. 92–3.

16 *The Spie*, no. 14, 110 (BL, Thomason Tracts, E.44(18)).

17 BL, Portland MSS, BL Loan 29/119; 172, ff. 309, 346; 173, f. 315.

18 Richard Baxter, *The Autobiography of Richard Baxter* (ed. J. M. L. Thomas), 22.

19 Bodleian: Tanner MSS 220, ff. 54–6 and 145 (case of Robert Peck whose patron was Sir Thomas Wodehouse). *C.S.P.Dom.*, *1640*, 385, 392, 409, 414, 419, 424, 429. *C.S.P.Dom.*, *1640–1*, 384, 389, 392, 395. For Sir Nathaniel Barnardiston see above, 177.

20 W. Notestein (ed.), *The Journal of Sir Simonds D'Ewes*, 6, 63, 64. Bodleian: Tanner MSS 321, f. 4. BL, Lansdowne MSS 493, ff. 93–6, 132–4. Clarendon, ii, 469. Dagon was the god of the Philistines.

21 John Nalson, *An Impartial Collection of the Great Affairs of State*, i, 523. BL, Lansdowne MSS 493, f. 135. Notestein, *op. cit.*, 65.

22 See above, 207.

23 Richard Bernard, *The Ready Way to Good Works*, epistle dedicatory. *The Seaven Golden Candlestickes* had been published in 1621. His main work in this field was *A Key of Knowledge for the Opening of the Secret Mysteries of St John's Mysticall Revelation* (1617).

24 Notestein, *op. cit.*, 138. BL, Harleian MSS 379, f. 77; Harleian MSS 646, ff. 44, 46, 61; and Additional MSS 37,343, f. 10. *Chetham Society*, i, 81–2. For Thomas Morton see also above, 147, 171.

25 Notestein, *op. cit.*, 139–40.

26 BL, Lansdowne MSS 493, ff. 136–7.

27 *C.J.*, ii, 54.

28 *C.J.*, ii, 52. Notestein, *op. cit.*, 169. BL, Additional MSS 37,343, ff. 11–12. H. R. Trevor-Roper, *Archbishop Laud*, 421.

29 *HMC, Fifteenth Report*, Appendix, pt vii, 64.

30 Notestein, *op. cit.*, 249–50, 258.

31 BL, Harleian MSS 164, f. 219.

32 *Surrey Archaeological Collections*, ii, 212–19. BL, Harleian MSS 382, ff. 14, 90, 106, 108 and 386, f. 191. O. Manning, *History of the County of Surrey*, i, 646–7.

33 *HMC, Fourteenth Report*, Appendix, pt ii, 72. Notestein, *op. cit.*, 277. BL, Portland MSS, BL Loan 29/119 and 120.

34 John Nalson, *An Impartial Collection of the Great Affairs of State*, i, 523. Clarendon, i, 272, 323. Notestein, *op. cit.*, 283. William M. Lamont, *Godly Rule. Politics and Religion, 1603–1660*, 95.

35 *C.J.*, ii, 287. BL, Harleian MSS 385, f. 107 and 646, f. 153. E. A. Ebblewhite (ed.), *The Parish Registers of Great Hampden*, 174. Notestein, *op. cit.*, 277. William Haller, *Liberty and Reformation in the Puritan Revolution*, 17, 35.

36 *Camden Society*, lviii, 111.

37 Notestein, *op. cit.*, 249, 282, 283, 375. See also W. A. Shaw, *A History*

of the English Church, 1640–1660, i, 19, 21, 22, 26, 43 and Anthony S. Fletcher, *The Outbreak of the English Civil War*, 92–7, 107–9.

38 Notestein, *op. cit.*, 375. *C.J.*, ii, 89. R. N. Worth (ed.), *The Buller Papers*, 31, 33. Nalson, *op. cit.*, i, 795. *Camden Society*, lviii, 113–14.

39 BL, Portland MSS, BL Loan 29/81. Notestein, *op. cit.*, 334–8. Rushworth, iv, 183–4, 187. A draft of Usher's proposals was printed without his authority in 1641 and again in 1642. In 1656 a definitive version was published with the title *The Reduction of Episcopacie unto the Form of Synodical Government Received in the Ancient Church*.

40 *C.J.*, ii, 25, 81. *Camden Society*, xxxi, 4–14.

41 Shaw, *op. cit.*, i, 78. A. M. Everitt, *The Community of Kent and the Great Rebellion 1640–60*, 88. *C.J.*, ii, 159.

42 BL, Harleian MSS 164, ff. 211–14, 216 and 379, f. 88; Egerton MSS 2651, f. 104; and Thomason Tracts, E.198(20), 3–4. Shaw, *op. cit.*, i, 81–2.

43 *Camden Society*, xxxi, 94. W. H. Coates (ed.), *The Journal of Sir Simonds D'Ewes*, 151. Clarendon, i, 309.

44 Richard Baxter, *Penitent Confession*, 30. *DNB* (Thomas Morton). Morton became tutor to Sir Christopher's son Henry who subsequently contributed a preface to a treatise of his entitled *The Episcopacy of the Church of England* which was published in 1670.

45 Sir Clements R. Markham, *Admiral Robert Fairfax*, 144.

46 BL, Thomason Tracts, E.198(8).

47 Clarendon, iii, 62.

48 Sir Henry Vane, *Two Treatises*, 53, 75. Thomas Fuller, *The Church-History of Britain*, xvii, 50. *A Revelation of Mr Brightman's Revelation* (BL, Thomason Tracts, E.164(11)). Richard Bernard, *A Key of Knowledge for the Opening of the Secret Mysteries of St John's Mysticall Revelation* and *A Short View of the Prelaticall Church of England* (BL, Thomason Tracts, E.206(2)). See above, 206–10.

49 BL, Harleian MSS 164, f. 219 and Thomason Tracts, E.198(40). Coates, *op. cit.*, 51.

50 BL, Portland MSS, BL Loan 29/173, f. 116. *HMC, Fourteenth Report*, Appendix, pt ii, 77.

51 BL, Harleian MSS 163, f. 337.

52 Clarendon, iii, 221. See also Violet A. Rowe, *Sir Henry Vane the Younger*, 200.

53 Richard Baxter, *Penitent Confession*, 30. Patrick Collinson, *The Elizabethan Puritan Movement*, 141–5, 149, 353–4, 397–8, 441.

54 Thomas Froysell, *The Beloved Disciple*, 109.

55 *Camden Society*, lviii, 140.

56 S. R. Gardiner, *History of England, 1603–1642*, ix, 407.

57 *C.J.*, ii, 84.

58 *C.J.*, ii, 279, 283.
59 BL, Portland MSS, BL Loan 29/173, f. 165. John Tombes, *The Leaven of Pharisaicall Wil-Worship*, 7, 13. See also *Hutchinson Memoirs*, 54.
60 BL, Harleian MSS 386, f. 197.
61 BL, Thomason Tracts, E.131(24).
62 See, for example, BL, Harleian MSS 164, ff. 279, 280.
63 BL, Thomason Tracts, E.199(26). See Robert Ashton, *The English Civil War*, 154–6.

Postscript

1 *HMC, Fourteenth Report*, Appendix ix, 476, 483. John Walker, *Sufferings of the Clergy*, pt i, 91. Derbyshire Record Office: Chandos-Pole-Gell MSS, Box 41/31. Josiah Ricraft, *A Survey of England's Champions*, 79. *Cheshire's Successe*, 25 March 1643. For a hostile view of Sir John Gell see *Hutchinson Memoirs*, 67–8.

BIBLIOGRAPHY

Primary Sources

I MANUSCRIPT

British Library

ADDITIONAL MSS, in particular

4274, 4460	Thoresby MSS
5831	Collections of William Cole
6167	Surrey collections of Richard Symmes
8846	Commonwealth surveys of Dorset livings
10,114	Memorandum book of John Harrington
14,030	Yelverton MSS
15,520	Suffolk church notes, Commonwealth period
18,777	Parliamentary journal of Walter Yonge
19,077, 19,080, 19,081, 19,098, 19,103, 19,116	Suffolk collections of David Elisha Davy
24,476	Hunter MSS
24,860	Papers of Richard Major
25,277	Political and miscellaneous papers
27,400	Gawdy MSS
28,008	Oxinden MSS
29,599	Carew MSS

33,137, 33,145, 33,147, 33,154	Pelham MSS
35,331	Diary of Walter Yonge
36,776	Benefices in England and Wales, 1622
37,343	Autobiography of Bulstrode Whitelocke
40,135	Holme Hall MSS
46,369, 46,381	Harrington MSS
48,016, 48,109	Yelverton MSS
53,726	Autobiography of Bulstrode Whitelocke
53,728	Sermons of Bulstrode Whitelocke

COTTON CHARTERS

xvi, 13	D'Ewes MSS

EGERTON MSS

784	Diary of William Whiteway
2643, 2644, 2645, 2646, 2648, 2650, 2651	Barrington correspondence
2711	Commonplace book of John Harrington
2716	Gawdy MSS

HARGRAVE MSS

107	Catalogue of Yelverton Library

HARLEIAN MSS

97, 98, 163, 164, 165, 193, 227, 280, 287, 339, 365, 373, 374, 376, 378, 379, 382, 383, 384, 385, 386, 387, 388, 486, 593, 646, 3987, 7657, 7659, 7660	D'Ewes MSS
389, 390	Letters of Joseph Mede
965, 991	Notebooks of Richard Symonds
1598	Gurdon and Winthrop papers
2217	Parliamentary papers
3364	'A Discours of Court and Courtiers' by Sir Edward Peyton
3783	Correspondence of William Sandcroft
6861	Samuel Somast's account of Devonshire families

7001	Collection of letters, 1633–4
7033	Papers primarily relating to Cambridge University
7038	Papers relating to Cambridge University
7162	Speeches in the Short and Long Parliaments
7517	Life of Thomas Pierson

HARLEY CHARTERS

57, H.43 and 44	D'Ewes MSS

LANSDOWNE MSS

459	Commonwealth surveys of church livings
493	Speeches in the Long Parliament
721	Life of Thomas Pierson
724	Sir Richard Ingoldsby, essay on the ancient philosophers
887, 888	Collections of John Warburton for Bedfordshire
1025	Collections of White Kennet for the Diocese of Peterborough

PORTLAND MSS

BL Loan 29/27, 73, 74, 78, 79, 81, 83, 84, 119, 120, 121, 122, 123, 124, 172, 173, 202	Harley MSS

SLOANE MSS

271	Northamptonshire Puritanism

Public Record Office

CHANCERY
Proceedings, Series I (C.2), Series II (C.3) and Six Clerks' Series (C.5–10)
Depositions (C.22)
Entry Books of Decrees and Orders (C.33)
Close Rolls (C.54)
Commonwealth Church Surveys (C.94)
Inquisitions *Post Mortem* (C.142)
Petty Bag Office, Miscellaneous Rolls (C.212) and Sheriffs' Rolls (C.227)
Crown Office, Docquet Books (C.231)

COURT OF WARDS
Feodaries' Surveys (Wards 5)
Miscellaneous Books (Wards 9)

EXCHEQUER
Parliamentary Surveys (E.317)
Land Revenue, Miscellaneous Books (L.R.2)

INSTITUTION BOOKS
Series A, 1556–1660

LORD CHAMBERLAIN'S OFFICE
Entry Books of Recognizances (L.C.4)

SIGNET OFFICE
Docquet Books

STAR CHAMBER
Proceedings, James I and Charles I (Star Chamber 8)

STATE PAPER OFFICE
State Papers Domestic Series, James I (S.P.14), Charles I (S.P.16), Committee for Compounding (S.P.23), Commonwealth Exchequer Papers (S.P.28)
State Papers Colonial Series, Colonial Entry Books: Bahamas (C.O. 124).

WILLS
Wills proved in the Prerogative Court of Canterbury (PROB 11)

Dr Williams's Library, London
Morrice MSS

Greater London County Record Office
Northwick Collection

House of Lords Library
House of Lords MSS

Lambeth Palace Library
Commonwealth Surveys of Livings
MS 943
Register Laud

Bedfordshire County Record Office
St John of Bletsoe MSS

Bodleian Library, Oxford
Carte MSS
Tanner MSS
MS Top. Beds., d.4.

Borthwick Institute of Historical Research (University of York)
Wills in the York Registry

Derbyshire Record Office
Burdett of Foremark MSS
Chandos-Pole-Gell MSS
Gresley of Drakelow MSS

Devon County Record Office
Drake of Buckland Abbey MSS
Orphans' Court Wills

Dorset County Record Office
Browne of Frampton MSS
MSS deposited by Mrs E. Cockburn
MSS deposited by Mrs J. M. Lane
MSS deposited by Mr G. D. Roper
Parish registers

Essex County Record Office
Hatfield Broad Oak MSS

Guildford Muniment Room
Loseley MSS
Onslow MSS

Hampshire Record Office
Daly MSS
Jervoise of Herriard Park MSS

Hull University Library
Wickham-Boynton MSS

Humberside County Record Office
Bethell of Rise MSS
Harford of Holme MSS

Leicestershire Record Office
Papers of Lord Hazlerigg of Noseley

Lincolnshire Archives Office
Cor. B/3

Norfolk Record Office
Kimberley MSS

Northamptonshire Record Office
Dryden (Canons Ashby) MSS
Isham Correspondence

North Yorkshire Record Office
Darley MSS

Sheffield Central Library
Crewe MSS

Somerset Record Office
Harrington of Kelston MSS (documents deposited by Messrs Corbould, Rigby & Co.)

Yorkshire Archaeological Society Library
MD 59/19

II PRINTED

A Certificate from Northamptonshire (1641).
Acts of the Privy Council
ADAMS, Thomas, *The White Devile* (1613).
AINSWORTH, Samuel, *A Sermon Preached at the Funerall of that Religious Gentle-woman Mrs Dorothy Hanbury* (1645).
ARCHER, John, *The Personall Reign of Christ upon Earth* (1642).
ASHE, Simeon, *Gray Hayres Crowned with Grace* (1655).
ASHLEY COOPER, Anthony, Earl of Shaftesbury, *Memoirs, Letters and Speeches of Anthony Ashley Cooper, First Earl of Shaftesbury*, ed. W. D. Christie (1859).
A True Picture of the Much Honoured and Reverend Mr John King (1680).
ATTERSOLL, William, *Three Treatises* (1633).
AUBREY, John, *The Natural History and Antiquities of the County of Surrey*, 5 vols (1719).

AUBREY, John, *Aubrey's Brief Lives*, ed. Oliver Lawson Dick (1972).

BAMFORD, Francis (ed.), *A Royalist's Notebook* (1936).

BAMPFIELD, Francis, *A Name, an After-one* (1681).

BARLOW, John, *The Good Man's Priviledge* (1618).

BARLOW, John, *The True Guide to Glory* (1619).

BAXTER, Richard, *The Saints Everlasting Rest* (1659).

BAXTER, Richard, *Penitent Confession* (1691).

BAXTER, Richard, *Reliquiae Baxterianae*, ed. Matthew Sylvester (1696).

BAXTER, Richard, *The Autobiography of Richard Baxter*, ed. J. M. L. Thomas (1931).

BERNARD, Richard, *A Key of Knowledge for the Opening of the Secret Mysteries of St John's Mysticall Revelation* (1617).

BERNARD, Richard, *The Seaven Golden Candlestickes* (1621).

BERNARD, Richard, *Looke Beyond Luther* (1623).

BERNARD, Richard, *Iosuah's Resolution for the Well Ordering of his Household* (1629).

BERNARD, Richard, *The Ready Way to Good Works* (1635).

BERNARD, Richard, *A Short View of the Prelaticall Church of England* (BL, Thomason Tracts, E.206(2)) (1641).

Bibliotheca Gloucestrensis (1823).

BIRCH, Thomas (ed.), *The Court and Times of James I*, 2 vols (1848).

BIRCH, Thomas (ed.), *The Court and Times of Charles I*, 2 vols (1848).

BOLTON, Robert, *Mr Bolton's Last and Learned Worke of The Foure Last Things* (1632).

BOLTON, Robert, *A Three-fold Treatise* (1634).

BOLTON, Robert, *A Short and Private Discourse between Mr Bolton and one M.S. Concerning Usury* (1637).

BOLTON, Robert, *A Discourse about the State of True Happinesse* (1638).

BOLTON, Robert, *The Workes* (1641).

BOWND, Nicholas, *The Doctrine of the Sabbath Plainely Layde Forth* (1595).

BRADSHAW, William, *English Puritanisme* (1605).

BRAMSTON, Sir John, *Autobiography*, ed. Lord Braybrooke, *Camden Society*, xxxii (1845).

BRERETON, Sir William, *Travels in Holland, United Provinces, England, Scotland and Ireland*, ed. Edward Hawkins, *Chetham Society*, i (1844).

BRIGHTMAN, Thomas, *Apocalypsis Apocalypseos* (1609).

BRIGHTMAN, Thomas, *The Revelation of St. John* (1644).

BRIGHTMAN, Thomas, *The Workes of that Famous, Reverend and Learned Divine, Mr Thomas Brightman* (1644).

BRINSLEY, John, the elder, *Ludus Literarius or the Grammar School* (1612).

BRINSLEY, John, the younger, *The Glorie of the Latter Temple Greater then of the Former* (1631).

BRINSLEY, John, the younger, *The Preacher's Charge and People's Duty* (1631).

BRINSLEY, John, the younger, *The Saints' Solemne Covenant with their God* (1644).

BROUGHTON, Hugh, *A Revelation of the Holy Apocalyps* (1610).

BURNET, Gilbert, *History of his Own Time*, 6 vols (1833).

BURTON, Thomas, *Diary of Thomas Burton*, ed. J. T. Rutt, 4 vols (1828),

BUTLER, Samuel, *The Posthumous Works of Mr Samuel Butler*, 2 vols (1715).

BYFIELD, Nicholas, *The Rule of Faith* (1626).

CALAMY, Edmund, *The Happinesse of Those who Sleep in Jesus* (1662).

CALAMY, Edmund (grandson of the above), *An Account of the Ministers, Lecturers, Masters and Fellows of Colleges and Schoolmasters who were Ejected or Silenced after the Restoration in 1660*, vol. ii of a 2-vol. work (1713).

CALAMY, Edmund (grandson of the above), *A Continuation of the Account of the Ministers, Lecturers, Masters and Fellows of Colleges and Schoolmasters who were Ejected and Silenced after the Restoration in 1660*, 2 vols (1727).

CALAMY, Edmund (grandson of the above), *The Nonconformist's Memorial*, ed. Samuel Palmer, 2 vols (1775).

Calendar of State Papers, Colonial Series: America and the West Indies.

Calendar of State Papers, Domestic.

Calendar of the Proceedings of the Committee for the Advance of Money.

CAPEL, Richard, *Tentations* (1658).

CASE, Thomas, *The Vanity of Vaine-Glory* (1655).

CAWTON, Thomas, the younger, *The Life and Death of that Holy and Reverend Man of God Mr Thomas Cawton* (1662).

CHAMBERLAIN, John, *The Letters of John Chamberlain*, ed. N. E. McClure, 2 vols (1939).

Cheshire's Successe (1643).

CLARK, Samuel, *A Collection of the Lives of Ten Eminent Divines* (1662).

CLARK, Samuel, *The Marrow of Ecclesiastical History* (1675).

CLARK, Samuel, *The Lives of Thirty-Two English Divines* (1677).

CLARK, Samuel, *The Lives of Sundry Eminent Persons* (1683).

CLARKE, John, *Holy Incense for the Censers of the Saints* (1634).

CLEAVER, Robert, *A Declaration of the Christian Sabbath* (1625).

COLLINGES, John, *Par Nobile. Two Treatises* (1669).

Commons Journals.

CONANT, John, the younger, *The Life of the Reverend and Venerable John Conant, D.D.* (1823).

COOKE, William, *A Learned and Full Answer to a Treatise Intituled, The Vanity of Childish Baptisme*, ed. Francis Woodcock (1644).

COOPER, Thomas, *The Worldling's Adventure* (1619).

COPE, Esther S. and COATES, W. H., *Proceedings of the Short Parliament of 1640*, Camden Fourth Series, xix (1977).

COSIN, John, *The Correspondence of John Cosin, D.D.*, ed. G. Ornsby, *Surtees Society*, lii (1869).

COTTON, John, *The Way of Congregational Churches Cleared* (1648).

DENT, Arthur, *The Ruine of Rome or an Exposition upon the Whole Revelation* (1628).

D'EWES, Sir Simonds, *The Primitive Practise for Preserving Truth* (1645).

D'EWES, Sir Simonds, *The Journal of Sir Simonds D'Ewes. From the Beginning of the Long Parliament to the Trial of the Earl of Strafford*, ed. W. Notestein (1923).

D'EWES, Sir Simonds, *The Journal of Sir Simonds D'Ewes. From the First Recess of the Long Parliament to the Withdrawal of King Charles from London*, ed. W. H. Coates (1942).

D'EWES, Sir Simonds, *The Diary of Sir Simonds D'Ewes (1622–1624)*, ed. Elizabeth Bourcier (n.d.).

DILLINGHAM, William, *A Sermon at the Funeral of the Lady Elizabeth Alston, wife of Sir Thomas Alston, Knight and Baronet, 10 September 1677* (1678).

DOD, John, *A Plaine and Familiar Exposition on the Lord's Prayer* (1635).

DOD, John, and CLEAVER, Robert, *A Plaine and Familiar Exposition of the Fifteenth, Sixteenth and Seventeenth Chapters of the Proverbs of Salomon* (1609).

DOD, John, and CLEAVER, Robert, *Three Godlie and Fruitful Sermons* (1610).

DOD, John, and CLEAVER, Robert, *A Plaine and Familiar Exposition of the Ten Commandements* (1622).

DOWNAME, John, *The Plea of the Poore* (1616).

DOWNAME, John, *Guide to Godliness* (1622).

DYKE, Jeremiah, *Good Conscience* (1624).

EARLE, John, *Micro-cosmographie* (1650).

EBBLEWHITE, E. A. (ed.), *The Parish Registers of Great Hampden, co. Bucks from 1557 to 1812* (1888).

EDWARDS, Thomas, *Gangraena* (1646).

ELIOT, Sir John, *The Letter-book of Sir John Eliot (1625–1632)*, ed. A. B. Grosart, vol. ii of a 2-vol. work (1882).

EVELYN, John, *The Diary and Correspondence of John Evelyn*, ed. William Bray, (n.d.).

FAIRCLOUGH, Samuel, *The Saint's Worthinesse and the World's Worthlesnesse* (1653).

FARMER, Richard, *A Sermon Preached at Paul's Crosse* (1629).

FENTON, Roger, *A Treatise of Usurie* (1611).

FIRTH, Sir Charles and RAIT, R. S. (ed.), *The Acts and Ordinances of the Interregnum, 1642–1660*, 3 vols (1911).

FOSTER, C. W. (ed.), *The State of the Church in the Reigns of Elizabeth and James I, Lincoln Record Society*, xxiii (1926).

FREWEN, John, *Certaine Sermons upon the 2, 3, 4, 5, 6, 7 and 8 Verses of the Eleventh Chapter of St Paule his Epistle to the Romanes* (1612).

FROYSELL, Thomas, *The Beloved Disciple* (1658).

FRY, E. A. (ed.), *The Dorset Protestation Returns* (1912).

FULLER, Thomas, *The Church-History of Britain*, together with *The History of the University of Cambridge since the Conquest* (1655).

FULLER, Thomas, *The Worthies of England*, ed. J. Freeman (1952).

GARDINER, Dorothy (ed.), *The Oxinden Letters, 1607–1642* (1933).

GARDINER, S. R. (ed.), *Debates of the House of Commons in 1625, Camden Society*, new series, vi (1873).

GARDINER, S. R. (ed.), *The Constitutional Documents of the Puritan Revolution, 1625–1660* (1906).

GATAKER, Thomas, *The Spirituall Watch* (1619).

GATAKER, Thomas, *God's Parley with Princes* (1620).

GATAKER, Thomas, *Marriage Duties Briefely Couched Togither* (1620).

GATAKER, Thomas, *True Contentment in the Gaine of Godlines* (1620).

GATAKER, Thomas, *A Good Wife God's Gift, and A Wife Indeed* (1624).

GATAKER, Thomas, *Abraham's Decease* (1627).

GATAKER, Thomas, *Two Sermons: Tending to Direction for Christian Cariage* (1633).

GATAKER, Thomas, *Certaine Sermons First Preached and After Published at Severall Times* (1637).

GATAKER, Thomas, *Discours Apologetical* (1654).

GOODWIN, Thomas, *The Works of Thomas Goodwin, D.D.*, 5 vols (1681–1704).

GOODWIN, Thomas (minister of South Weald, Essex), *A Fair Prospect* (1658).

GOUGE, William, *Of Domesticall Duties* (1622).

GRANGER, Thomas, *The Tree of Good and Evill* (1616).

GRIMSTON, Harbottle, *A Christian New-Year's Gift* (1644).

HACKET, John, *Scrinia Reserata* (1693).

HALL, Joseph, *Contemplations upon the Principall Passages of the Holie Storie*, 8 vols (1612–26).

HALL, Joseph, *The Works of Joseph Hall, D.D.*, 12 vols (1837).

HARLEY, Lady Brilliana, *Letters of the Lady Brilliana Harley*, ed. T. T. Lewis, *Camden Society*, lviii (1854).

HARRINGTON, Sir James, *Noah's Dove* (1645).

HARRINGTON, Sir James, *A Holy Oyl, and a Sweet Perfume* (1669).

HARRINGTON, Sir James, *Horae Consecratae* (1682).

HARRIS, Robert, *Samuel's Funerall* (1618).

HART, John, *The Burning Bush Not Consumed* (1616).

HART, John, *Trodden Down Strength, by the God of Strength, or Mrs Drake Revived* (1647).

HERBERT, William, Earl of Pembroke, *Poems* (1660).

HEYLYN, Peter, *Cyprianus Anglicus* (1668).

HEYLYN, Peter, *Aërius Redivivus, or the History of the Presbyterians* (1672).

HICKES, Gaspar, *The Life and Death of David* (1645).

HIERON, Samuel, *Three Sermons* (1607).

HIERON, Samuel, *A Helpe unto Devotion* (1608).

HIERON, Samuel, *The Bridegroome* (1613).

HIERON, Samuel, *All the Sermons of Samuel Hieron* (1614).

HIERON, Samuel, *The Spirituall Fishing* (1616).

HINCKLEY, John, *A Sermon Preached at the Funerals of that Worthy Personage George Purefoy the Elder of Wadley in Berkshire, Esquire* (1661).

HISTORICAL MANUSCRIPTS COMMISSION:
Fourth Report (*Emmanuel College MSS and House of Lords MSS*).
Sixth Report (*House of Lords MSS*).
Seventh Report (*Lowndes MSS*).
Twelfth Report (*Coke MSS*).
Thirteenth and Fourteenth Reports (*Duke of Portland MSS*).
Fifteenth Report (*Somerset MSS*).
Duke of Buccleuch MSS.
Hatfield MSS (*Salisbury* (*Cecil*) *MSS*).
Marquis of Lothian MSS (*Blickling Hall*).
Duke of Portland MSS.
Earl of Verulam MSS.
House of Lords MSS, new series, xi.

HOBBES, Thomas, *Behemoth or The Long Parliament*, ed. Ferdinand Tonnies (1889).

HUMPHREY, Laurence, *The Nobles* (1563).

HUNGERFORD, Sir Anthony, *The Advise of a Sonne Professing the Religion Established in the Present Church of England to his Deare Mother a Roman Catholike* (1639).

HUTCHINSON, Lucy, *On the Principles of the Christian Religion* (1817).

HUTCHINSON, Lucy, *Memoirs of the Life of Colonel Hutchinson*, ed. James Sutherland (1973).

HYDE, Edward, Earl of Clarendon, *The History of the Rebellion and Civil Wars in England ... by Edward, Earl of Clarendon*, ed. W. D. Macray, 6 vols (1888).

JOSSELIN, Ralph, *The Diary of Ralph Josselin, 1616–1683*, ed. A. Macfarlane (1976).

KING, Benjamin, *The Marriage of the Lambe* (1640).

KNAPPEN, M. M. (ed.), *Two Elizabethan Puritan Diaries* (1933).

LAUD, William, *The Works of William Laud*, 7 vols (1847–60).

LEY, John, *A Patterne of Pietie* (1640).

Life and Death of Mr Henry Jessey (1671).

LLOYD, David, *Memoirs* (1668).

Luctus Posthumus (1612).

LUDLOW, Edmund, *The Memoirs of Edmund Ludlow*, ed. Sir Charles Firth, 2 vols (1894).

LUDLOW, Edmund, *A Voyce from the Watch Tower*, ed. A. B. Worden, *Camden Fourth Series*, xxi (1978).

LUKE, Sir Samuel, *The Letter Books 1644–45 of Sir Samuel Luke*, ed. H. G. Tibbutt (1963).

MANNINGHAM, John, *Diary of John Manningham*, ed. J. Bruce and W. Tite, *Camden Society*, xcix (1868).

MARTYN, William, *Youth's Instruction* (1612).

MAY, Thomas, *The History of the Parliament of England* (1812).

MAYER, John, *The English Catechisme* (1621).

MAYER, John, *A Commentarie upon the Foure Evangelists and the Acts of the Apostles* (1631).

MAYER, John, *A Commentary upon the Whole Old Testament*, 2 vols (1647).

MAYO, C. H. (ed.), *The Minute Books of the Dorset Standing Committee* (1902).

MEADS, D. M. (ed.), *The Diary of Lady Margaret Hoby 1599–1605* (1900).

MEDE, Joseph, *The Works of the Pious and Profoundly Learned Joseph Mede, B.D.* (1672).

MILTON, John, *Complete Prose Works of John Milton*, 6 vols (1953–73).

MOODY, Robert E. (ed.), *The Saltonstall Papers, 1607–1815*, vol. i, *Massachusetts Historical Society Collections*, lxxx (1972).

MORE, Sir George, *A Demonstration of God in his Workes* (1597).

MORTON, Thomas, *The Episcopacy of the Church of England* (1670).

NALSON, John, *An Impartial Collection of the Great Affairs of State*, 2 vols (1682–3).

NAPIER, John, *A Plaine Discovery of the Whole Revelation of St John* (5th edition, 1645).

NEWCOMEN, Matthew, *A Sermon Preached at the Funerals of . . . Mr Samuel Collins* (1658).

NICCOLS, Richard, *The Cuckow* (1607).

NICHOLS, J.'G. and BRUCE, J. (ed.), *Wills from Doctors' Commons, Camden Society*, lxxxiii (1863).

NORTON, Luke, *Elegies on the Death of that Worthy and Accomplish't Gentleman Colonel John Hampden Esquire* (1643).

NOTESTEIN, W., RELF, F. H. and SIMPSON, H. (ed.), *Commons Debates, 1621*, 7 vols (1935).

NOTESTEIN, W. and RELF, F. H. (ed.), *Commons Debates for 1629* (1921).

OGLANDER, Sir John, *The Oglander Memoirs*, ed. W. H. Long (1888).

OTES, Samuel, *An Explanation of the Generall Epistle of Saint Jude* (1633).

PARK, Thomas (ed.), *Nugae Antiquae* (1804).

PARKER, Henry, *A Discourse Concerning Puritans* (1641).

PARKER, Robert, *The Mystery of the Vialls Opened* (1651).

PARKHURST, Nathaniel, *The Faithful and Diligent Christian Described and Exemplified* (1684).

PARSONS, Bartholomew, *Dorcas* (1631).

PARSONS, Bartholomew, *A Sermon Preached at the Funerall of Sir Francis Pile Baronet* (1636).

PARSONS, Bartholomew, *Tithes Vindicated to the Presbyters of the Gospel* (1637).

PAYBODY, Thomas, *A Just Apologie for the Gesture of Kneeling in the Act of Receiving the Lord's Supper* (1629).

PECK, Francis (ed.), *Desiderata Curiosa*, 2 vols (1779).

PEEL, Albert (ed.), *The Seconde Parte of a Register*, 2 vols (1915).

PEMBLE, William, *Vindiciae Gratiae. A Plea for Grace* (1627).

PENINGTON, Mary, *A Brief Account of My Exercises in My Childhood* (1848).

PERKINS, William, *A Christian and Plaine Treatise of the Manner and Order of Predestination and of the Largenes of God's Grace* (1606).

PERKINS, William, *The Workes*, 3 vols (1608, 1609).

PEYTON, Sir Edward, *A Discourse Concerning the Fitnesse of the Posture Necessary to be Used in Taking the Bread and Wine at the Sacrament* (1642).

PEYTON, Sir Edward, *The High-way to Peace* (1647).

PEYTON, Sir Edward, *The Divine Catastrophe of the Kingly Family of the House of Stuarts* (1652).

PHILLIPS, Edward, *Certaine Godly and Learned Sermons* (1605).

PIERSON, Thomas, *Excellent Encouragements against Afflictions* (1647).

PRESTON, John, *The Golden Scepter Held Forth to the Humble* (1638).

PRESTON, John, *Grace to the Humble* (1639).

PRESTON, John, *An Abridgement of Dr Preston's Works* (1648).

PRIDEAUX, John, *The Doctrine of the Sabbath* (1634).

PRINCE, John, *The Worthies of Devon* (1701).

PRYNNE, William, *Canterburies Doome* (1644).

RAINBOWE, Edward, *Labour Forbidden and Commanded* (1635).

RANDALL, John, *Twenty Nine Lectures of the Church* (1631).

REYCE, Robert, *Suffolk in the XVIIth Century. The Breviary of Suffolk by Robert Reyce, 1618* (1902).

REYNOLDS, John, *Th' overthrowe of Stage-Playes* (1599).

RICRAFT, Josiah, *A Survey of England's Champions* (1647).

ROGERS, Daniel, *Treatise of the Two Sacraments of the Gospell: Baptisme and the Supper of the Lord* (1635).

ROGERS, Ezekiel, *The Chief Grounds of Christian Religion, Set Down by Way of Catechizing* (1648).

ROGERS, John, *The Doctrine of Faith* (1629).

ROGERS, Richard, *Seven Treatises* (1603).

ROUS, John, *Diary of John Rous*, ed. Mary Anne Everett Green, *Camden Society*, lxvi (1856).

RUDYERD, Edmund, *The Thunderbolt of God's Wrath* (1618).

RUSHWORTH, John, *Historical Collections of Private Passages of State, Weighty Matters in Law, Remarkable Proceedings in Five Parliaments*, 8 vols (1721).

RYLAND, J. W. (ed.), *The Parish Registers of Wroxall* (1903).

SAMPSON, William, *Virtus Post Funera Vivit* (1636).

SCLATER, William, the elder, *The Sick Soul's Salve* (1612).

SCUDDER, Henry, *A Key of Heaven: The Lord's Prayer Opened and so Applied* (1620).

SCUDDER, Henry, *The Christian's Daily Walk in Holy Securitie and Peace* (1627).

SHUTE, Christopher, *Ars piè Moriendi: or the True Accomptant* (1658).

SIBBES, Richard, *A Fountaine Sealed* (1637).

SIBBES, Richard, *The Bride's Longing for her Bride-Groomes Second Comming* (1638).

SIKES, George, *The Life and Death of Sir Henry Vane, knight* (1662).

SPELMAN, Sir Henry, *The English Works of Sir Henry Spelman, Knight* (1727).

SPICER, John, *The Sale of Salt, or The Seasoning of Soules* (1611).

SPRINGETT, Lady Mary, memoirs, *Gentleman's Magazine*, new series, xxxvi (1851).

STILLINGFLEET, Edward, *Origines Sacrae* (1662).

STOCK, Richard, *A Stock of Divine Knowledge*, ed. James Cranford (1641).

STOUGHTON, John, *The Heavenly Conversation and the Naturall Man's Condition* (1640).

Suffolk's Tears (1653).

SYMMER, Archibald, *Rest for the Weary* (1624).

SYMONDS, Richard, *Diary of the Marches of the Royal Army During the Great Civil War*, ed. C. E. Long, *Camden Society*, lxxiv (1859).

TANNER, J. R. (ed.), *Constitutional Documents of the Reign of James I 1603–1625* (1961).

TAYLOR, Thomas, *The Progresse of Saints to Full Holinesse* (1630).

The County of Suffolke Divided into Fourteene Precincts for Classicall Presbyteries (1647).

The English Revolution. I. Fast Sermons to Parliament, 34 vols (1970–1).

The House of Mourning (1640).

Thomason Tracts (British Library) (the more important works are listed individually).

TILLINGHURST, John, *Mr Tillinghast's Eight Last Sermons* (1659).

TOMBES, John, *Fermentum Pharisaeorum, or The Leaven of Pharisaicall Wil-Worship* (1643).

TOZER, Henry, *Directions for a Godly Life* (1671, 8th edn).

TREVELYAN, Sir Walter C. and TREVELYAN, Sir Charles E. (ed.), *Trevelyan Papers*, pt iii, *Camden Society*, cv (1872).

TREVETHICK, William, *A Sermon Preached at the Funeral of the Honourable Colonel Robert Rolle of Heanton Sachville in the County of Devon Esquire* (1661).

TUCKNEY, Anthony, *Death Disarmed* (1654).

USHER, James, *The Reduction of Episcopacie unto the Form of Synodical Government Received in the Ancient Church* (1656).

VANE, Sir Henry, the younger, *The Retired Man's Meditations* (1655).

VANE, Sir Henry, the younger, *Two Treatises* (1662).

VANE, Sir Henry, the younger, *A Pilgrimage into the Land of Promise* (1664).

Verney Papers, Camden Society, xxxi (1844).

VICARS, John, *England's Worthies* (1647).

Vindiciae Veritatis (1654).

WALKER, John, *Sufferings of the Clergy* (1714).

WALLER, Sir William, *Divine Meditations upon Several Occasions, with a Dayly Directory* (1680).

WALLER, Sir William, *Recollections* (in *The Poetry of Anna Matilda*, 1788).

WALLER, Sir William, *Vindication of the Character and Conduct of Sir William Waller* (1793).

WARD, Samuel, *The Wonders of the Load-Stone* (1640).

WELLES, John, *The Soules Progresse to the Celestiall Canaan* (1639).

WENTWORTH, Thomas, Earl of Strafford, *The Earl of Strafforde's Letters and Dispatches*, ed. W. Knowler, 2 vols (1739).

WESTERNE, Thomas, *The Flaming Bush* (1624).

WHITELOCKE, Bulstrode, *Memorials of the English Affairs*, 4 vols (1853).

WILFORD, John, *Memorials and Characters, Together with the Lives of Divers Eminent and Worthy Persons* (1741).

WILKINS, John, *Ecclesiastes* (1646).

WING, John, *The Saint's Advantage* (1624).

WINTHROP, John, *Winthrop Correspondence, Massachusetts Historical Society Collections*, fourth series, vi (1863).

WOOD, Anthony, *The History and Antiquities of the Colleges and Halls in the University of Oxford*, ed. John Gutch, 2 vols (1786, 1790).

WOOD, Anthony, *Athenae Oxonienses* (together with *Fasti Oxonienses*), ed. Philip Bliss, 4 vols (1815).

WOOD, Seth, *The Saint's Enterance into Peace and Rest by Death* (1651).

WOODROFFE, Timothy, *A Religious Treatise upon Simeon's Song* (1659).

WORTH, R. N. (ed.), *The Buller Papers* (1895).

WROTH, Sir Thomas, *The Abortive of an Idle Houre or A Centurie of Epigrams, and a Motto upon the Creede* (1620).

WROTH, Sir Thomas, *The Destruction of Troy or the Acts of Aeneas* (1620).

YONGE, Walter, *The Diary of Walter Yonge, Esq.*, ed. George Roberts, *Camden Society* xli (1848).

YOUNG, A., *Chronicles of the First Planters of the Colony of Massachusetts Bay, 1623–1636* (1846).

Secondary Sources

I BOOKS

ADAIR, John, *Roundhead General. A Military Biography of Sir William Waller* (1969).

ADAMSON, J. H. and FOLLAND, H. F., *Sir Harry Vane. His Life and Times 1613–1662* (1974).

Admissions to the College of St John the Evangelist in the University of Cambridge, 4 pts (1882–1931).

ANDRIETTE, Eugene, A., *Devon and Exeter in the Civil War* (1971).

ASHTON, Robert, *The English Civil War* (1978).

ATKYNS, Sir Robert, *The Ancient and Present State of Glocestershire* (1712).

AYLMER, G. E., *The King's Servants: The Civil Service of Charles I, 1625–1642* (1961).

BABBAGE, S. B., *Puritanism and Richard Bancroft* (1962).

BAKER, George, *The History and Antiquities of the County of Northampton*, 2 vols (1822, 1841).

BALL, Bryan W., *A Great Expectation. Eschatological Thought in English Protestantism to 1660* (1975).

BARNARD, E. A. B., *The Rouses of Rous Lench, Worcestershire* (1921).

BARNES, T. G., *Somerset, 1625–1640: a County's Government during the 'Personal Rule'* (1961).

BAYLEY, A. R., *The Great Civil War in Dorset 1642–1660* (1910).

BEHRENS, Lilian Boys, *Under Thirty-Seven Kings* (1926).

Biographical List of Boys at King Edward VI Free Grammar School, Bury St Edmunds, From 1550 to 1900 (1908).

BLOMEFIELD, Francis, *An Essay towards a Topographical History of the County of Norfolk*, 11 vols (1805–10).

BOASE, C. W. (ed.), *Register of the Rectors, Fellows and Other Members on the Foundation of Exeter College, Oxford, Oxford Historical Society*, xxvii (1894).

Brasenose College Quatercentenary Monographs, vol. ii, pt i, *Oxford Historical Society*, liii (1909).

BRIDGES, John, *The History and Antiquities of Northamptonshire*, 2 vols (1762, 1791).

BROOK, Benjamin, *The Lives of the Puritans*, 3 vols (1813).

BROWNE, John, *History of Congregationalism and Memorials of the Churches in Norfolk and Suffolk* (1877).

BRUNTON, D. and PENNINGTON, D. H., *Members of the Long Parliament* (1954).

CAMPLING, Arthur, *The History of the Family of Drury* (n.d.).

CAPP, B. S., *The Fifth Monarchy Men* (1972).

CHAUNCY, Sir Henry, *The Historical Antiquities of Hertfordshire*, 2 vols (1826).

CHRISTIANSON, Paul, *Reformers and Babylon: English Apocalyptic Visions from the Reformation to the Eve of the Civil War* (1978).

CLIFFE, J. T., *The Yorkshire Gentry from the Reformation to the Civil War* (1969).

CLUTTERBUCK, R., *The History and Antiquities of the County of Hertford*, 3 vols (1815–27).

COATE, Mary, *Cornwall in the Great Civil War* (1963).

COKE, Dorothea, *The Last Elizabethan: Sir John Coke, 1563–1644* (1937).

COLLIER, C. V., *An Account of the Boynton Family* (1914).

COLLINSON, Patrick, *The Elizabethan Puritan Movement* (1967).

CURTIS, M. H., *Oxford and Cambridge in Transition 1558–1642* (1959).

CUST, Lady Elizabeth, *Records of the Cust Family. Series II. The Brownlows of Belton, 1550–1779* (1909).

DALTON, Charles, *History of the Wrays of Glentworth, 1523–1852*, 2 vols (1880).

DAVIDS, T. W., *Annals of Evangelical Nonconformity in the County of Essex* (1863).

Dictionary of National Biography.

DORE, R. N., *The Civil Wars in Cheshire* (1966).

DUGMORE, C. W. and DUGGAN, C. (ed.), *Studies in Church History*, vol. i (1964).

DURRANT, C. S., *A Link between Flemish Mystics and English Martyrs* (1925).

ELIOTT-DRAKE, Lady, *The Family and Heirs of Sir Francis Drake*, 2 vols (1911).

EVELYN, Helen, *The History of the Evelyn Family* (1915).

EVERITT, Alan M., *Suffolk and the Great Rebellion, 1640–1660, Suffolk Records Society*, iii (1960).

EVERITT, Alan M., *The Community of Kent and the Great Rebellion, 1640–1660* (1966).

Fawsley Park, Northamptonshire. Catalogue of the Library (1914).

FINCH, Mary E., *The Wealth of Five Northamptonshire Families 1540–1640, Northamptonshire Record Society*, xix (1956).

FIRTH, Katharine R., *The Apocalyptic Tradition in Reformation Britain 1530–1645* (1979).

FLETCHER, Anthony S., *A County Community in Peace and War: Sussex 1600–1660* (1975).

FLETCHER, Anthony S., *The Outbreak of the English Civil War* (1981).

FOSTER, J. (ed.), *Alumni Oxonienses: the Members of the University of Oxford, 1500–1714*, 4 vols (1892).

GARDINER, R. B. (ed.), *The Registers of Wadham College*, pt i (1889).

GARDINER, S. R., *History of England from the Accession of James I to the Outbreak of the Civil War, 1603–1642*, 10 vols (1896–1901).

GARDINER, S. R., *History of the Great Civil War, 1642–1649*, 4 vols (1901).

G.E.C. (ed.), *Complete Baronetage*, 6 vols (1900–9).

GEORGE, Charles H. and GEORGE, Katherine, *The Protestant Mind of the English Reformation 1570–1640* (1961).

GLOVER, Stephen and NOBLE, Thomas, *The History of the County of Derby* (1829).

GREEN, V. H. H., *Religion at Oxford and Cambridge* (1964).

GRENVILLE, George, Lord Nugent, *Some Memorials of John Hampden* 2 vols (1832).

HALLER, William, *The Rise of Puritanism* (1938).

HALLER, William, *Liberty and Reformation in the Puritan Revolution* (1955).

HALLER, William, *Foxe's Book of Martyrs and the Elect Nation* (1963).

HALLEY, Robert, *Lancashire: its Puritanism and Nonconformity* (1872).

HARCOURT, E. W. (ed.), *The Harcourt Papers*, 14 vols (1880–1905).

HARRISON, A. W., *Arminianism* (1937).

HASTED, Edward, *The History and Topographical Survey of the County of Kent*, 12 vols (1797–1801).

HEXTER, J. H., *The Reign of King Pym* (1968).

HILL, Christopher, *Economic Problems of the Church* (1956).

HILL, Christopher, *Puritanism and Revolution* (1958).

HILL, Christopher, *Society and Puritanism in Pre-Revolutionary England* (1964).

HILL, Christopher, *Intellectual Origins of the English Revolution* (1965).

HILL, J. W. F., *Tudor and Stuart Lincoln* (1956).

HOARE, Sir Richard Colt, *Hungerfordiana* (1823).

HOLMES, Clive, *The Eastern Association in the Civil War* (1974).

HUTCHINS, John, *The History and Antiquities of the County of Dorset*, 4 vols (1861–73).

IRBY, P. A., *The Irbys of Lincolnshire and the Irebys of Cumberland*, 2 vols (1938).

ISHAM, Sir Gyles, *Easton Mauduit and the Parish Church of SS. Peter and Paul, Northamptonshire Record Society* (1974).

JORDAN, W. K., *Philanthropy in England 1480–1660* (1959).

JORDAN, W. K., *The Charities of Rural England 1480–1660* (1961).

KEARNEY, Hugh F., *Scholars and Gentlemen. Universities and Society in Pre-Industrial Britian, 1500–1700* (1970).

KEELER, M. F., *The Long Parliament, 1640–1641. A Biographical Study of its Members. American Philosophical Society* (1954).

KENNET, White, *A Register and Chronicle Ecclesiastical and Civil* (1728).

KETTON-CREMER, R. W., *Norfolk in the Civil War* (1969).

KNAPPEN, M. M., *Tudor Puritanism* (1965).

LAMONT, William M., *Godly Rule. Politics and Religion, 1603–1660* (1969).

LEGARD, Sir James D., *The Legards of Anlaby and Ganton* (1926).

LIPSCOMB, George, *The History and Antiquities of the County of Buckingham*, 4 vols (1847–51).

LOCKE, A. Audrey, *The Hanbury Family*, 2 vols (1916).

LONGDEN, H. I., *Northamptonshire and Rutland Clergy from 1500*, 15 vols (1938–43).

LYSONS, Daniel, *The Environs of London*, 2 vols (1810).

MACRAY, W. D. (ed.), *A Register of the Members of St Mary Magdalen College, Oxford*, new series, 8 vols (1894–1915).

MALLET, Sir Charles, *A History of the University of Oxford*, 3 vols (1924, 1927).

MANNING, Brian (ed.), *Politics, Religion and the English Civil War* (1973).

MANNING, J. A., *Memoirs of Sir Benjamin Rudyerd, Knight* (1841).

MANNING, O. and BRAY, W., *The History and Antiquities of the County of Surrey*, 3 vols (1804–14).

MARCHANT, R. A., *The Puritans and the Church Courts in the Diocese of York 1560–1642* (1960).

MARCHANT, R. A., *The Church under the Law* (1969).

MARKHAM, Sir Clements R., *Admiral Robert Fairfax* (1895).

MATTHEWS, A. G., *Calamy Revised* (1934).

MESSITER, M. (ed.), *Repton School Register 1557–1910* (1910).

MILLAR, Oliver, *The Age of Charles I: Painting in England 1620–1649* (1972).

MOLLER, F. S. (ed.), *Alumni Felstedienses* (1931).

MONTAGU, William Drogo, Duke of Manchester, *Court and Society from Elizabeth to Anne*, 2 vols (1864).

MORETON, C. Oscar, *History of Waddesdon and Over Winchendon* (1929).

MORGAN, I., *Prince Charles's Puritan Chaplain* (1957).

MORRILL, J. S., *Cheshire 1630–1660* (1974).

MULLINGER, J. B., *St John's College* (1901).

MUSKETT, J. J., *Suffolk Manorial Families*, 3 vols (1900–10).

NEAL, Daniel, *The History of the Puritans*, 5 vols (1822).

NEALE, Sir John, *Elizabeth I and her Parliaments 1559–1581* (1953).

NEW, John F. H., *Anglican and Puritan* (1964).

NEWCOURT, Richard, *Repertorium*, 2 vols (1710).

NEWTON, A. P., *The Colonising Activities of the English Puritans* (1914).

NICHOLS, John, *The History and Antiquities of the County of Leicester*, 4 vols (1795–1811).

NUGENT, Lord, *Some Memorials of John Hampden*, 2 vols (1832).

ONSLOW, Arthur, *The Life of Dr George Abbot, Lord Archbishop of Canterbury* (1777).

OMEROD, George, *The History of the County Palatine and County of Chester*, 3 vols (1875–82).

PALMER, W. M., *Episcopal Visitation Returns for Cambridgeshire* (1930).

PEILE, J. (ed.), *Biographical Register of Christ's College, 1505–1905*, 2 vols (1910).

POLWHELE, Richard, *The History of Devonshire*, 3 vols (1793–1806).

PORTER, H. C., *Reformation and Reaction in Tudor Cambridge* (1958).

RICHARDSON, R. C., *Puritanism in North-West England* (1972).

ROSE-TROUP, Frances, *John White the Patriarch of Dorchester* (1930).

ROWE, Violet A., *Sir Henry Vane the Younger* (1970).

RUSSELL, Conrad (ed.), *The Origins of the English Civil War* (1973).

RUSSELL-BARKER, G. F. and STENNING, A. H., *The Records of Old Westminsters*, 2 vols (1928).

RYLAND, J. W., *Records of Wroxall Abbey and Manor* (1903).

SARGANT, W. L., *The Book of Oakham School* (1928).

SCHOLES, P. A., *The Puritans and Music* (1934).

SCOTT, J. R., *Memorials of the Family of Scott, of Scot's Hall, in the County of Kent* (1876).

SCOTT-GILES, C. W., *Sidney Sussex College* (1951).

SEAVER, Paul S., *The Puritan Lectureships. The Politics of Religious Dissent 1560–1662* (1970).

SHAPIRO, Barbara, *John Wilkins, 1614–1672* (1969).

SHAW, W. A., *A History of the English Church, 1640–1660*, 2 vols (1900).

SHAW, W. A., *The Knights of England*, 2 vols (1906).

SHEILS, W. J. (ed.), *The Puritans in the Diocese of Peterborough 1558–1610*, Northamptonshire Record Society, xxx (1979).

SMITH, D. E., *Assington through the Centuries* (1974).

SMITH, Harold, *The Ecclesiastical History of Essex under the Long Parliament and Commonwealth* (n.d.).

SOMERVILLE, Sir Robert, *History of the Duchy of Lancaster*, 2 vols (1953, 1970).

SOMERVILLE, Sir Robert, *Office-Holders in the Duchy and County Palatine of Lancaster from 1603* (1972).

SPALDING, Ruth, *The Improbable Puritan. A Life of Bulstrode Whitelocke, 1605–1675* (1975).

STONE, Lawrence, *The Crisis of the Aristocracy, 1558–1641* (1965).

STONE, Lawrence, *The Causes of the English Revolution 1529–1642* (1972).

STONE, Lawrence, *The Family, Sex and Marriage in England 1500–1800* (1977).

STONE, Lawrence (ed.), *The University in Society*, 2 vols (1975).

TOLMIE, Murray, *The Triumph of the Saints. The Separate Churches of London 1616–1649* (1977).

TREVOR-ROPER, H. R., *Archbishop Laud 1573–1645* (1962).

UNDERDOWN, David, *Pride's Purge* (1971).

UNDERDOWN, David, *Somerset in the Civil War and Interregnum* (1973).

URWICK, William, *Nonconformity in Hertfordshire* (1884).

VENN, J. and J. A. (ed.), *Alumni Cantabrigienses. A Biographical List of all*

Known Students, Graduates and Holders of Office at the University of Cambridge, from the Earliest Times to 1751. 4 vols (1922–7).

Victoria County History: various counties.

VULLIAMY, C. E., *The Onslow Family 1528–1874* (1953).

WALKER, T. A. (ed.), *Admissions to Peterhouse* (1912).

WALZER, Michael, *The Revolution of the Saints* (1966).

WATERS, R. E. C., *Genealogical Memoirs of the Extinct Family of Chicheley*, 2 vols (1878).

WATSON, A. G., *The Library of Sir Simonds D'Ewes* (1966).

WEAVER, F. W. (ed.), *Somerset Incumbents* (1889).

WELSBY, Paul A., *George Abbot the Unwanted Archbishop 1562–1633* (1962).

WILLCOX, W. B., *Gloucestershire: a Study in Local Government 1590–1640* (1940).

WILLIAMS, Franklin, B., junior, *Index of Dedications and Commendatory Verses in English Books Before 1641. The Bibliographical Society* (1962).

WILSON, John F., *The Pulpit in Parliament: Puritanism during the English Civil Wars, 1640–1648* (1969).

WOOD, Alfred C., *Nottinghamshire in the Civil War* (1937).

WOTTON, Thomas, *The English Baronetage*, 4 vols (1741).

WRIGHT, Thomas, *History and Topography of the County of Essex*, 2 vols (1831, 1835).

YULE, George, *The Independents in the English Civil War* (1958).

ZAGORIN, Perez, *The Court and the Country* (1969).

ZIFF, Larzer, *The Career of John Cotton. Puritanism and the American Experience* (1962).

II ARTICLES

BLAAUW, W. H., 'Passages of the Civil War in Sussex, from 1642 to 1660', *Sussex Archaeological Collections*, v (1852).

BOHANNON, Mary Elizabeth, 'A London Bookseller's Bill, 1635–1639', *Library*, fourth series, xviii (1938).

COKAYNE, G. E., 'Skinners' Company: Apprenticeships', *Miscellanea Genealogica et Heraldica*, third series, i (1896).

CURTIS, M. H., 'The Alienated Intellectuals of Early Stuart England', *Past and Present*, no. 23 (1962).

DEELEY, A. P. and SKILLINGTON, S. H., 'An Old Hazlerigg Deed', *Leicestershire Archaeological Society Transactions*, xvii (1932–3).

EVANS, J., 'The Vicar of Godalming and his Parishioners in 1640', *Surrey Archaeological Collections*, ii (1864).

FARNHAM, G. F. and HAMILTON THOMPSON, A., 'The Manor of Noseley', *Leicestershire Archaeological Society Transactions*, xii (1921–2).

FARNHAM, G. F. and HERBERT, A., 'Fenny Drayton and the Purefey Monuments', *Leicestershire Archaeological Society Transactions*, xvii (1932–3).

FLETCHER, Anthony S., 'Petitioning and the Outbreak of the Civil War in Derbyshire', *Derbyshire Archaeological Journal*, xciii (1973).

FOSTER, Stephen, 'The Presbyterian Independents Exorcized', *Past and Present*, no. 44 (1969).

GALPIN, F. W., 'The Household Expenses of Sir Thomas Barrington', *Essex Archaeological Society Transactions*, new series, xii (1913).

GEORGE, Charles H., 'Puritanism as History and Historiography', *Past and Present*, no. 41 (1968).

GREEN, I., 'Career Prospects and Clerical Conformity in the Early Stuart Church,' *Past and Present*, no. 90 (1981).

HARLAND, John (ed.), 'The House and Farm Accounts of the Shuttle-worths', *Chetham Society*, xxxv (1856) and xli (1856).

HILL, J. H. 'Noseley', *Leicestershire Archaeological Society Transactions*, ii (1870).

KETTON-CREMER, R. W., 'The Rhyming Wodehouses', *Norfolk Archaeology*, xxxiii (1965).

KIDSON, Ruth M., 'The Gentry of Staffordshire, 1662–3', *Collections for a History of Staffordshire, Staffordshire Record Society*, fourth series, ii (1958).

LAMONT, William M., 'Puritanism as History and Historiography, Some Further Thoughts', *Past and Present*, no. 44 (1969).

LANDOR, W. N., 'Staffordshire Incumbents and Parochial Records (1530–1680)', *Collections for a History of Staffordshire, William Salt Archaeological Society* (1916).

LOWNDES, G. A., 'The History of the Barrington Family', *Essex Archaeological Society Transactions*, new series, ii (1884).

ANON., 'Clergy List for Bedfordshire Archdeaconry, 1605', *Bedfordshire Notes and Queries*, ii (1889) and iii (1893).

ANON., 'Institutions of Shropshire Incumbents', *Transactions of the Shropshire Archaeological and Natural History Society*, third series, v (1905).

ANON., 'Lincolnshire Families, Temp. Charles II', *Herald and Genealogist*, ii (1865).

ANON., 'The Shardloes Muniments', pt iii, *Records of Buckinghamshire*, xiv (1942).

INDEX

Bampfield, Francis, 4, 109
Bampfield, John, 92, 109, 223
Bampfield, Sir John, 222, 223, 229
Banbury, Oxon., 5
Bancroft, Richard, Archbishop of
  Canterbury, 6, 98, 146, 147, 169
Banger, Bernard, 190
Barlow, John, 15, 24–5, 104, 134
Barmston, Yorks, 166
Barnardiston, Suffolk, 175, 176
Barnardiston, family of, 68, 133
Barnardiston, Lady Anne, 64, 130, 177
Barnardiston, Arthur, 108
Barnardiston, Giles, 79
Barnardiston, Lady Jane, 133, 216
Barnardiston, Sir Nathaniel, 2, 11, 12,
  16, 31, 34, 39, 42, 45, 46, 57–8, 61,
  64, 69, 73–5, 79, 101, 106, 108, 113,
  120, 121, 133, 175–7, 196, 200, 215,
  216, 218, 219; children of, 39, 69,
  73–5, 177
Barnardiston, Nathaniel, 108
Barnardiston, Pelatiah, 108
Barnardiston, Samuel, 57, 108
Barnardiston, Sir Thomas (d. 1610), 12,
  175
Barnardiston, Sir Thomas (d. 1619), 12
Barnardiston, Sir Thomas (d. 1669),
  101
Barnardiston, William, 108
Barnes, Robert, 86
Barrington, family of, 21, 44, 68, 71, 79,
  135, 159
Barrington, Sir Francis, 11, 38, 42, 48,
  57, 59, 112, 124, 130, 153, 159
Barrington, Gobert, 26
Barrington, Lady Joan, 15, 21–2, 44,
  61, 66, 135–8, 156, 159, 171, 191
Barrington, Sir John, 55, 78, 117, 235
Barrington, Lady Judith, 8, 25–6, 55,
  65–6, 107, 117, 211
Barrington, Lucy, 144
Barrington, Oliver, 78
Barrington, Sir Thomas, 2, 11, 25, 26,
  65–6, 78, 107, 117, 120–1, 124, 136,
  141, 143, 144, 149, 152, 156, 158, 159,
  165, 171, 204, 205, 210, 214–16, 222,
  226, 228–30
Barrington, Lady Winifred, 131
Barrow, Maurice, 81, 113, 118
Bath, 14
Baxter, Richard, 9–10, 36, 133, 219,
  229, 232
Bayley, Thomas, 85, 86

Baylie, Richard, 84
Beale, William, 84, 100
Beard, Nicholas, 159
Bedell, William, 93
Bedfordshire, 68, 74, 94, 97, 160, 161,
  171, 210, 226
Bennet, Robert, Bishop of Hereford,
  186
Berkshire, 15, 60, 86, 127
Bernard, Richard, 30–1, 105, 109, 119,
  123, 221, 230, 231
Beverley Free School, 80
Bishops Stortford, Herts., 165
Blackburne, Mr (tailor), 55
Blandford School, 80
Blickling, Norfolk, 9
Blinman, Richard, 78
Blyton, Lincs., 184
Bocking, Essex, 178
Bolton, Robert, 10, 11, 25, 36, 37, 39,
  66, 92, 100, 103, 111–13, 115, 126,
  127, 138, 142, 179
Boston, Lincs., 94; Grammar School, 80
Boston, Massachusetts, 203
Bourchier, family of, 68; Sir John, 11
Bourchier, Sir John, 11
Bowles, Oliver, 97; Samuel, 93, 97
Bownd, Nicholas, 40, 91
Bowyer, Sir William, 59
Boynton, family of, 166
Boynton, Sir Francis, 68
Boynton, Sir Matthew, 68, 74, 140, 166,
  202–3, 208
Boys, Sir Edward, 66
Boys, Judith, 66
Bradshaw, William, 7, 24, 88, 97
Bradwell, Suffolk, 174
Braintree, Essex, 78, 204
Brampton Bryan, Herefordshire, 28, 33,
  57, 77, 89, 185, 186, 189, 201, 209,
  226; Castle, 77, 78, 187, 189, 198
Bramston, Sir John, 81, 107
Brent, Sir Nathaniel, 81, 159–61, 178,
  181–3, 190
Brereton, Sir William, 92, 195, 212,
  220–2, 226, 236
Brice, William, 188
Bridgwater, Somerset, 105
Brightman, Thomas, 162, 186, 205, 206,
  208, 210–11, 218, 230–1
Brinsley, John, 72
Brinsley, John (son of above), 121,
  174–5
Bristol, Bishop of, 190

Scotland, 205, 206, 210, 212, 219, 231
Scott, Sir Thomas, 8
Scudder, Henry, 36, 44, 46, 120
Seaton, John, 80
Sedgwick, Richard, 34
Servants, 32–4, 49, 55, 70, 73, 106, 122, 124, 125, 135, 162, 203, 205
Shakespeare, William, 143
Shaw, John, 99
Sheffield, 188; Grammar School, 80; parish church, 188
Shepard, Thomas, 142, 158, 159
Shepherd, Thomas, 41–2
Sherfield, Henry, 118
Ship money, 107, 195, 196, 205, 211, 212, 216, 219
Shirley, Walsingham, 162
Shrewsbury, 33, 78, 187
Shropshire, 13, 187
Shrubland Hall, Suffolk, 159
Shute, Christopher, 76
Shuttleworth, Richard, 143
Sibbes, Richard, 19, 22, 25, 36–8, 40–1, 50, 73, 79, 100–1, 103, 108–9, 120, 158
Sibthorpe, Robert, 196
Silchester, Hants., 86
Silk Willoughby, Lincs., 80, 185
Simony, 114
Skinners Company, 108
Sleigh, Gervase, 66
Sleigh, Gervase (son of above), 99
Sleigh, Sir Samuel, 66, 99
Slingsby, Sir Henry (d. 1634), 66
Slingsby, Sir Henry (1602–58), 66
Smith, Lady Judith, 65
Smith, Sir Richard, 118
Smyth, John, 107
Snow, Robert, 91
Soame, Sir Stephen, 121
Soame, Sir William, 121
Somerleyton, Suffolk, 174–5
Somerset, 14, 61, 63, 170, 190, 196, 212
Spain, King of, 209
Spelman, Sir Henry, 113
Spicer, Christopher, 182, 183
Spring, Sir William (c.1589–1638), 45, 96, 154, 159–60, 196
Spring, Sir William (1613–54), 96–7
Springett, Herbert, 115
Springett, Herbert (son of above), 102
Springett, Katherine, 70, 192, 122–3
Springett, Lady Mary, 4, 27–8, 70, 102, 139

Springett, Sir William, 4, 27–8, 70, 102, 115, 122, 139; children of, 70
Sprint, John, 40
Spurstowe, William, 101, 226
Staffordshire, 145, 183
Stainby, Lincs., 161
Stanley, Thomas, 216
Star Chamber, 194, 217
Steane, Northants., 25, 43
Stephens, Nathaniel, of Eastington, Glos., 87, 148–9, 211, 214
Stephens, Anne, of Little Sodbury, Glos., 41
Stephens, Edward, of Little Sodbury, Glos., 41
Stock, Richard, 135
Stoneham, Benjamin, 207
Stoughton, John, 93, 136–7, 187–8, 190, 193–6, 206; wife of, 193
Stretton, Dorset, 190
Strickland, John, 170
Strickland, Sir William, of Boynton, Yorks., 12, 54
Strickland, William, of Boynton, Yorks., 12
Strode, family of, 58
Strode, Anne, 49
Strode, John, 140
Strode, Lady Mary, 15, 26, 35, 38–9, 59, 134
Strode, Sir Richard, 49, 161, 194, 196
Strode, Sir William, 15, 38, 58–9, 140, 161
Strode, William, 49
Strong, William, 101
Stuart, James, Duke of Lennox, 151
Stubbes, Henry, 214
Stuteville, Sir Martin, 5
Styles, Matthias, 91
Sudbury, Suffolk, 218
Suffolk, 12, 34, 68, 77, 79, 81, 94, 97, 111, 113, 118, 121, 130, 132, 133, 140, 159, 165, 172, 174, 175, 178, 196, 212, 215, 223, 226
Suffolk, Earl of, see Howard, Theophilus
Surrey, 94, 140, 170, 217, 224, 234, 236
Sussex, 79, 94, 111, 134
Sutton, Beds., 74, 97
Sweden, 197
Symonds, Richard, 78, 189
Symondsbury, Dorset, 136

Tallents, Francis, 35
Tate, Zouch, 107, 232; children of, 107

Taylor, Thomas, 44
Thatcher, Peter, 187
Thornborough, John, Bishop of
  Worcester, 171, 183
Thorncombe, Devon, parish church,
  167
Thornhagh, Sir Francis, 94
Titchmarsh, Northants., 95, 179, 180
Tiverton, Devon, 41
Toller, Thomas, 188, 189
Tombes, John, 87, 88, 206, 223, 234
Towers, John, Bishop of Peterborough,
  200
Tozer, Henry, 91
Tracy, Sir Paul, 214
Traske, John, 161
Treasurer, Lord, *see* Weston, Sir
  Richard
Trenchard, family of, 190
Trenchard, Sir Thomas, 190–1
Tuckney, Anthony, 93
Tuke, Hugh, 36, 80, 185
Tuke, Thomas, 36
Turner, Jerome, 191
Tutchin, Robert, 190–1
Twickenham, Middx., 38

Upper Clatford, Hants., 191
Uppingham School, 80
Usher, James, Archbishop of Armagh,
  189, 227
Usury, 60, 61, 111, 114–17
Uttoxeter, Staffs., 59
Uxbridge, Middx., 166

Valentine, Henry, 77, 99
Vane, Sir Henry, 16
Vane, Sir Henry, the younger, 2, 16,
  39, 62, 201–2, 208, 228–30, 232
Vere, Lady Mary, 163
Villiers, George, Duke of Buckingham,
  148–50, 156

Wadeson, James, 80, 98
Walker, Thomas, 178
Wallace, John, 80
Waller, Lady Anne (Finch), 55, 64
Waller, Lady Anne (Harcourt), 21, 26,
  33, 64, 70
Waller, Lady Jane, 64
Waller, Sir William, 2, 10, 27, 33–4, 39,
  51–3, 62, 64, 66, 105, 111, 126, 139,
  140, 204, 229; children of, 70
Wanstead, Essex, 94

Ward, Nathaniel, 95, 201
Ward, Samuel, Master of Sidney
  Sussex, Cambridge, 93, 97–8, 149,
  157
Ward, Samuel, of Ipswich, 103
Wards, Court of, 170, 171
Warwick, Earl of, *see* Rich, Robert
Warwickshire, 183
Waveney, River, 174
Weld, Thomas, 201
Wentworth, Peter, 12
Wentworth, Thomas, Earl of Strafford,
  201
Wentworth of Somerleyton, Suffolk, Sir
  John, 121, 174–5
Westminster, *see* London and
  Westminster
Westminster Assembly of Divines, 101,
  184
Westminster School, 16–17, 98
Weston, Sir Richard, Earl of Portland,
  107
Wethersfield, Essex, 158
Wharton, Philip, Lord Wharton, 68
Whitaker, Jeremy, 80
Whitaker, William, 93, 99
Whitchurch, Shropshire, 187
White, John, 170, 189–91
White, Thomas, 136, 165
Whitelocke, Bulstrode, 5, 21, 39, 40,
  107, 109–10, 112, 124, 141, 144, 152,
  193, 205–6, 221, 223; children of, 107
Whitelocke, Lady Elizabeth, 5
Whitelocke, Frances, 107
Whitelocke, Sir James, 109
Wickes, Robert, 175
Wigmore, Herefordshire, 185
Wilkins, John, 183
Wilkinson, Henry (1610–75), 87, 88
Wilkinson, Henry (1616–90), 88
Wilkinson, John, 87, 88
Williams, John, Bishop of Lincoln, 147,
  171, 184, 185, 221
Williams, Roger, 137–8, 165
Williamson, Robert, 179
Williamson, Robert (son of above), 179
Willoughby, Elizabeth, 65
Willoughby, Sir Henry, 65
Wilson, John, 201
Wilson, Thomas, 197–8
Wiltshire, 113, 114
Winch, Sir Humphrey, 131
Winch, Onslow, 94, 117
Winchelsea, Earl of, *see* Finch, Thomas